Harvard Political Studies

A Brief History of the Constitution and Government of Massachusetts. By *Louis Adams Frothingham.*

The Political Works of James I. Edited by *Charles Howard McIlwain.*

Politica Methodice Digesta of Johannes Althusius. Edited by *Carl Joachim Friedrich.*

Municipal Charters. By *Nathan Matthews.*

A Bibliography of Municipal Government. By *William Bennett Munro.*

Town Government in Massachusetts, 1630–1930. By *John F. Sly.*

Interstate Transmission of Electric Power. By *Hugh Langdon Elsbree.*

American Interpretations of Natural Law. By *Benjamin Fletcher Wright, Jr.*

Sanctions and Treaty Enforcement. By *Payson Sibley Wild, Jr.*

Foreign Relations in British Labour Politics. By *William Percy Maddox.*

Administration of the Civil Service in Massachusetts. By *George C. S. Benson.*

International Socialism and the World War. By *Merle Fainsod.*

The President's Control of the Tariff. By *John Day Larkin.*

Federal Commissioners. By *E. Pendleton Herring.*

Government Proprietary Corporations in the English-Speaking Countries. By *John Thurston.*

The Physiocratic Doctrine of Judicial Control. By *Mario Einaudi.*

The Failure of Constitutional Emergency Powers under the German Republic. By *Frederick Mundell Watkins.*

The Treasury and Monetary Policy, 1933–1938. By *C. Griffith Johnson, Jr.*

The Art and Technique of Administration in German Ministries. By *Arnold Brecht and Comstock Glaser.*

The Political Life of the American Medical Association. By *Oliver Garceau.*

Nazi Conquest through German Culture. By *Ralph F. Bischoff.*

The Regulation of Railroad Abandonments. By *Charles R. Cherington.*

The City of Reason. By *Samuel H. Beer.*

Presidential Agency: The Office of War Mobilization and Reconversion. By *Herman Miles Somers.*

Philosophical Foundations of English Socialism. By *Adam B. Ulam.*

The Labor Problem in the Public Service. By *Morton Robert Godine.*

Muddy Waters: The Army Engineers and the Nation's Rivers. By *Arthur Maass.*

American Conservatism in the Age of Enterprise. By *Robert Green McCloskey.*

National Minorities: An International Problem. By *Inis L. Claude, Jr.*

The Politics of Distribution. By *Joseph Cornwall Palamountain, Jr.*

The Politics of German Codetermination. By *Herbert J. Spiro.*

The English Health Service. By *Harry Eckstein.*

The President's Cabinet: An Analysis from Wilson to Eisenhower. By *Richard F. Fenno, Jr.*

THE PRESIDENT'S CABINET

Harvard Political Studies
Published Under the Direction of the
Department of Government in
Harvard University

THE PRESIDENT'S CABINET

AN ANALYSIS IN THE PERIOD
FROM WILSON TO EISENHOWER

Richard F. Fenno, Jr.
University of Rochester

Harvard University Press
Cambridge, Massachusetts
1959

Quotations from the following copyrighted works are reprinted by permission of the publishers. From *Woodrow Wilson, Life and Letters* by Ray Stannard Baker, copyright 1927, 1939 by Doubleday & Co., Inc. From *Woodrow Wilson as I Know Him* by Joseph Tumulty, copyright 1921 by Doubleday & Co., Inc. From *The Secret Diary of Harold L. Ickes: The First Thousand Days*, Copyright © 1953 by Simon and Schuster, Inc. From *The Secret Diary of Harold L. Ickes: The Inside Struggle*, Copyright © 1954 by Simon and Schuster, Inc. From *The Secret Diary of Harold L. Ickes: The Lowering Clouds*, Copyright © 1954 by Simon and Schuster, Inc. From *Inside the Democratic Party* by Jack Redding, Copyright 1958 by The Bobbs-Merrill Company, Inc.

© Copyright 1959 by the President and Fellows of Harvard College

Distributed in Great Britain by Oxford University Press · London

Library of Congress Catalog Card Number 59-9272

Printed in the United States of America

TO NANCY

PREFACE

The purpose of this book is to help fill a void in the literature on American government by undertaking a political analysis of the President's Cabinet. Since the network of relationships which affects the Cabinet include the President, the executive branch of the government, the Congress, political parties, and pressure groups, a study of the Cabinet becomes in its broadest sense a study of American politics in general. The treatment is analytical, emphasizing functions and relationships rather than historical development. Most of the illustrative material is drawn from the Cabinet experiences in a concrete historical period — generally, the 20th century, but specifically in the period from Wilson to the present. The Cabinet is examined on three analytical levels: (1) *the Cabinet as a distinct institution* — its origins, its growth, its personnel, the Cabinet meeting, its strengths and weaknesses as an advisory, decision-making and coordinating body; (2) *the close President-Cabinet relationship* — the nature, dimensions, and types of presidential influence, the ways in which various Presidents have selected and used their Cabinets, the limitations under which Presidents function in their Cabinet relations; (3) *the patterns of influence between the President-Cabinet nexus on the one hand, and the larger political system on the other* — the interplay of factors which constitutes the process of Cabinet appointment, the influences which govern the behavior (in Cabinet meeting and out) of individual Cabinet members, the impact of clientele, partisan, legislative and departmental influences on the President-Cabinet member relationship.

Since no full length political analysis of the Cabinet has ever been written, this book is designed to provide some evidence and some understanding which will inform future observations on a much neglected, though very familiar American political institution. Hopefully, readers will find the study revealing not only of the single institution but also of the broader context in which it functions — the American system of government.

RICHARD F. FENNO, JR.

Rochester, New York
November, 1958

ACKNOWLEDGMENTS

Many people have been of assistance to me in the preparation of this book. I should like to take this opportunity to acknowledge my debt to them, without implicating them in any way in its deficiencies.

In the earliest stages, Paul Appleby commented helpfully on my general outline; and Dr. Geoffrey May provided much valuable advice in his painstaking reading of first draft materials. At a later date parts of the manuscript were read by my colleagues Earl Latham and Robert Rosenzweig of Amherst College, and by Seymour Scher of the University of Rochester — all of whom furnished helpful suggestions, substantive and stylistic. My debt to William Y. Elliott of Harvard University arises from the fact that he has been, from start to finish, a constant source of encouragement and assistance. I owe a great deal, finally, to my wife, without whose unfailing encouragement and help this book would probably not have been written.

I am heavily indebted to numerous people who have shared their first hand experience to help me to better understand my subject—especially as it pertains to the Eisenhower period. Among these are Maxwell Rabb, former Secretary to the Cabinet, Bradley H. Patterson, Jr., Assistant to the Secretary to the Cabinet, Elmer F. Bennett, Solicitor of the Department of the Interior, Roger W. Jones, Assistant Director of the Bureau of the Budget, William W. Parsons, Assistant Secretary of the Treasury, and Ralph W. E. Reid, Assistant Director of the Bureau of the Budget.

For financial assistance, I should like to thank the Lucius Root Eastman Fund of Amherst College, the Committee on Grants-in-Aid of the University of Rochester, and, most especially, the Department of Government and its Committee on Publications, of Harvard University.

CONTENTS

Introduction 3

Chapter One · The Cabinet in Perspective 9
- ORIGINS AND RELATIONSHIPS 9
- PATTERNS OF DEPARTMENTAL DEVELOPMENT 20
- DIMENSIONS AND TYPES OF PRESIDENTIAL INFLUENCE 29

Chapter Two · The Appointment Process 51
- THE PRESIDENT'S INFLUENCE 54
- THE INCENTIVES AND DRAWBACKS OF CABINET OFFICE 59
- THE CONDITIONS OF THE TIME 62
- THE CABINET NORM 63
- THE CRITERIA OF AVAILABILITY AND BALANCE 67
  - a. *The Components of Availability* 68
  - b. *The Components of Balance* 77
- PRESIDENT, CABINET APPOINTMENT, AND POLITICAL PROCESS 81

Chapter Three · The Cabinet Meeting: I 88
- THE POTENTIAL FUNCTIONS OF THE MEETING 88
- THE FORM OF THE MEETING — INSTITUTIONAL BAREBONES 92
- THE FORM OF THE MEETING — SOME PROBLEMS 98
- THE PRESIDENT AND THE CABINET MEETING 113

Chapter Four · The Cabinet Meeting: II 131
- THE CABINET MEMBER AND THE CABINET MEETING 131
- THE CABINET MEETING AND INTERDEPARTMENTAL COORDINATION 141
- THE CABINET MEETING: CONCLUSION 154

Chapter Five · The Cabinet and Politics: I   157

PRESIDENT, CABINET, AND PUBLIC PRESTIGE   159
    a. *The President as Chief Representative*   159
    b. *Cabinet and Prestige: Possibilities and Limitations*   160
    c. *Andrew Mellon and Cordell Hull: Case Studies*   171

PRESIDENT, CABINET, AND PARTY   178
    a. *The President as Party Chief and Chief Legislator*   178
    b. *Cabinet and Party: Possibilities and Limitations*   180
    c. *Harry Daugherty and William Jennings Bryan: Case Studies*   187

Chapter Six · The Cabinet and Politics: II   196

PRESIDENT, CABINET, AND CONGRESS   196
    a. *The Cabinet Member in the Legislative-Executive Context*   196
    b. *Cabinet and Congress: Possibilities and Limitations*   199
        1. The Cabinet member and the liaison function   200
        2. The Cabinet member and legislative control   203

PRESIDENT, CABINET, AND DEPARTMENTAL ADMINISTRATION   216
    a. *The President as Chief Executive*   216
    b. *Cabinet and Departmental Administration: Possibilities and Limitations*   218

JESSE JONES: A CASE STUDY   234

THE CABINET AND POLITICS: SOME CONCLUSIONS   247

Chapter Seven · The Cabinet and Reform   250

IMPROVING EXECUTIVE-LEGISLATIVE RELATIONS   251

IMPROVING THE ORGANIZATION OF THE PRESIDENCY   263

Notes   273

Index   313

THE PRESIDENT'S CABINET

Introduction

THE President's Cabinet is a distinct, discrete, and describable political institution. To the casual observer of American government, it is probably one of the most familiar. Yet, in the words of one distinguished political scientist, "A critical volume on the Cabinet is something badly needed."[1] In the years just prior to World War I, two direct, full-length institutional histories were written,[2] but political analyses of the Cabinet have remained fragmentary and tangential. Out of the large body of related studies, however, have come some observations and judgments on the Cabinet which are well known to the student of American government. There is, for instance, an attitude of skepticism about the Cabinet's importance. One conclusion drawn from wartime experience was that "The Cabinet as an institution, if indeed it may be called that, continued its dismal course. . . ."[3] More recently, it has been described as "at best a relic of a simpler past."[4]

On the other hand, there is a substantial literature of reformist optimism in which one finds prescriptions for "vitalizing" or "revitalizing" or making "fuller use of" or "augmented use of" or "restoring to its original significance" the President's Cabinet.[5] In the third place, there is a widespread opinion that the present Cabinet under President Eisenhower has belied the skepticism of the past if it has not, indeed, fulfilled the optimism as to the future.[6]

The focus of this study, unlike previous ones, is directly and primarily on the Cabinet, on the group and on its members. It is mainly an attempt at understanding the operation of the Cabinet in the American political system; only secondarily is it aimed at substantiating or modifying existing ideas. The period on which it draws for illustrative material is that from Woodrow Wilson's first term to the present. Hopefully, however, its general observations will have a less circumscribed applicability.

"To understand an institution," it has been written, "one is certainly aided by knowing its development and the circumstances of its development, but a knowledge of its history cannot tell us how it functions in social life. To know how it has come to be what it is, and to know how it works are two different things."[7] While acknowledging a debt to the original researches of the historians of the Cabinet, it is necessary to move beyond their rather restrictive boundaries in order to understand the institution. The tendency of the historical approach was to perceive of the Cabinet largely in terms of its relatively permanent, internal, organizational characteristics and to neglect, accordingly, both the variable human elements and the external relationships involved. As an institution, the Cabinet should be conceived of in dynamic terms, as a network of interpersonal relations, as a matter of human action.

For definitional purposes, an institution exists "when a group of people . . . meet together in isolation often enough, regularly enough, and long enough each time to do something intensely enough and emotionally enough so that as a separate entity, the group builds up its own set of rules, its own internal equilibrium, and its own structure."[8] In these terms, the Cabinet appears as a human group. Its internal relations are seen realistically as matters of degree. For purposes of analysis, it can be abstracted from the total political system, yet there is a recognition that only to some variable degree can it exist "in isolation" or "as a separate entity." On this basis, one can study an institution not exclusively "as an institution," but as part of a continuous interaction and a constantly changing set of relationships among individuals, groups, and other institutions.

The Cabinet's institutional credentials are fairly simple. Its core personnel constitute an identifiable group, holding positions in the government which are created and defined by statute. As a matter of custom they meet together with a relatively high degree of frequency and for a considerable length of time. They have developed over a period an observable set of rules with respect to procedure and with respect to the relations of the group to certain other groups. Their interaction as individuals and, thus, the activity of the group tend to follow a recognizable pattern. At times the group exhibits a tendency to maintain its identity by resisting forces pressing upon it from the outside. The very thought of its abolition would constitute an unpardonable offense to public expectations and public sensitivities. Though its institutional characteristics are by no means fixed and final, the constituent elements do demonstrate a degree of interdependence and cohesiveness at any given time. Thus there is a tendency to stability as well as a receptivity to change. In all of these ways the Cabinet attains a degree of institutionalization which clearly sets it off, for example, from such an entity as a "kitchen cabinet."

As an institution, however, the Cabinet is (to twist Emerson) the lengthened shadow of another institution — the Presidency. The Cabinet is a secondary political institution, understandable only in terms of a primary one. It lives in a state of institutional dependency to promote the effective exercise of the President's authority and to help implement his ultimate responsibilities. The Cabinet is his instrument, to use as he sees fit. Its attachment to him and its consequent reliance upon him prevent the Cabinet from developing a high degree of autonomous institutional strength. While it is more institutionalized (but less intimate) than a "kitchen cabinet," it is less institutionalized (but more intimate) than, say, the Bureau of the Budget.

The Cabinet partakes of a degree of institutionality and of intimacy taken together, and the mutually contradictory tendencies involved contain a vital clue to its institutional problems. The more institutionalized it becomes, the more autonomy and the less intimacy it will tend to develop. The more intimacy it develops, the more will it tend to lose its institutionality. In this sense, the Cabinet can neither live without the President nor with him. At any rate, the essential point is that, though the Cabinet is a distinct institution, its relation to the Chief Executive is the condition and the measure of its existence.

But we cannot stop here. Through the President, if in no other way, the Cabinet will feel the impact of other influences, for his actions with respect to the Cabinet will usually be taken with regard to the larger context in which he functions. Above and beyond the President's intermediary influence, however, the Cabinet members themselves are inextricably involved in the activities of the legislature, the bureaucracy, the political parties, and the political interest groups. The Cabinet, and especially its individual members, participates in a great multiplicity of external relationships which are not in the first instance matters of its internal characteristics nor of its presidential tie. They so heavily condition Cabinet behavior that ultimately the Cabinet must be understood as part of what might be called the entire governmental process.

In sum, a study of the Cabinet must proceed on three distinct levels of analysis, running from the particular to the general. We begin by examining the Cabinet as a discrete institution, but the limitations of this approach become quickly apparent. Thus, on a second level, we are led to focus on the binary President-Cabinet relationship. But the Cabinet and the President are so susceptible to external influences that their relation makes sense only in terms of its interactions with forces external to it — within the total governmental process. This provides us with a third level of analysis. The points of interlock and overlap between one analytical level and another define, furthermore, the areas of tension most central to this study. In view of the extent to which our analysis reflects a great complex of interrelations, generalizations about the Cabinet become generalizations about American politics. This being true, the only satisfactory framework for the study is one which not only makes a unity out of the three levels of analysis but which encompasses most of American political life. Despite its vagueness, therefore, our ultimate orienting idea must be the American political system itself.

"The fundamental meaning of system," writes David Easton, "is that interrelated parts tend to cohere."[9] With respect to this study, system implies that the Cabinet exists as part of an interacting whole whose separate parts hang together to the extent that change in one part affects every other part. Once one grasps the fact that the Cabinet can be discussed only in terms of the constant interaction of diverse elements, the concept of system provides a broad framework within which one can examine the nature of the interactions. The reactive forces involved cannot be quantitatively weighed or measured, but a cabinet, like any other institution which has persisted through time, tends to stabilize its activity within predictable limits. Certain fairly constant relations can be isolated and examined, together with the forces making for change. The idea of system provides us with an analytic overview of the Cabinet which neglects none of the important forces affecting it and which, by understanding them, enables us to understand the institution we are studying. Since the most particular, that is, the Cabinet, and the most general, that is, the American political system, each provides us with ways of looking at the other, this book should be read as an attempt to understand both.

CHAPTER ONE

The Cabinet in Perspective

ORIGINS AND RELATIONSHIPS

CABINET is modern terminology for an ancient institution. A "cabinet" originates in the universal need on the part of any single Chief Executive to consult with others and draw upon the advice of others in exercising his political power. It persists as an aid to intelligent and informed decision-making. "It is already the practice of kings," writes Aristotle in the *Politics*, "to make themselves many eyes and ears and hands and feet. For they make colleagues of those who are friends of themselves and of their governments." [1] Wherever a Chief Executive has a group of advisers identifiable by both a degree of intimacy and a degree of institutionalization, then the idea of a cabinet or a cabinet-like institution is present.

Etymologically, "cabinet" derives from the designation "Cabinet Council," first given to an inner circle of the King's advisers in England in 1622.[2] When the term "cabinet" was adopted in the United States it was intended to connote no more than an intimate and institutionalized advisory body to the Chief Executive. Insofar as the English Cabinet Council fits this description, the two cabinets could, at that time, bear comparison without violating the idea which the Americans had in mind. But the American Cabinet "was in no sense a conscious imitation of any organization in existence at the epoch of its creation." [3] The American Cabinet was not a copied product. Its terminological affinity with the English institution should not be stretched to connote other similarities except in the most general and, indeed, universal sense.

Scattered anthropological findings suggest that there is an element of universality in the advisory function which the Cabinet performs and in the existence of the Chief Executive-Cabinet relationship. On the one hand, we find that "the chieftainship has been a key position, existing almost universally in primitive societies." [4] On the other hand, "The one universal instrument of government is the council. No tribe or nation does without it. No man can govern alone, nor is he permitted to. Monarchy, if taken literally, is a misnomer. Every king or chief operates within the network of his advisers and cronies." [5] And when anthropologists chart their path of inquiry into this relationship, their ideas have a familiar ring. In the words of a Royal Institute study guide, "Chiefs are usually assisted by councils. It must be shown how they perform their double role of agents of the chief and spokesmen of the community and how far and by what means they may control the chief executive." [6]

A study of cabinet-like institutions and of chief executive-advisory group activity in uncomplicated political systems suggests the universality of some broader relationships which provide insight into the more complex American context. For example, a comparative examination of primitive systems would place possible chief executive-cabinet relationships along a continuum ranging from a powerful executive-superfluous cabinet setup at one extreme to an impotent executive-collectively responsible cabinet setup at the other.[7] This helps point up for us the basic nature of the formal and/or informal power-responsibility relationship for the study of any "cabinet." In these terms, we can see that during the eighteenth century the English King-Cabinet power-responsibility relationship was in the process of shifting from one end of the continuum to the other. The advisory Cabinet was on its way to becoming the English executive. At the time of the Constitutional Convention, then, the thrust of the English system was radically different from our own. We see the single executive losing popular support, the steady increase in the administrative power of his advisers, and the close relationship of the advisers to the Parliament. Though we adopted British terminology at a time when the actual operation of the two institutions seemed similar, almost everything that happened after the birth of the English Cabinet propelled it in the opposite direction from its American namesake.

By 1787, the roots of the American Cabinet were already sunk deep in American practice. Most of the colonial governments provided for a Council or Assistants to consult with the Governor, though they were selected in a variety of ways. There is, however, no evidence that these advisers held administrative posts;[8] the idea of permitting administrative officers to double as executive counselors was grounded in another pre-federal experience in administrative organization. Four executive offices were created in 1781 to help administer problem areas made obvious by the war — a Secretary of Foreign Affairs, a Superintendent of Finance, a Secretary of War, and a Secretary of Marine. The idea of a single department head was an advance over the earlier use of an impermanent and inefficient series of committees and boards and, if anything, it reflects a French and not an English influence.[9] More likely, however, this was a natural organizational response to conditions, both in terms of subject matter and administrative experience.

In any case, by 1789 the two main ingredients for a cabinet were in existence, and they represented a residue of prior experience in self-government. Executive advisers and single-headed administrative departments were both familiar to the men who met to frame a new article of government.[10] There was no doubt in their minds that the executive would need advice and that there would be executive departments. The only remaining step was the transformation of these raw materials into a recognizable product.

The task was not accomplished by a direct effort at the Constitutional Convention, but rather as the offshoot of two other master decisions taken there. The first involved the creation of a strong, independent Chief Executive. The second was the structural decision which resulted in the separation of powers with checks and balances.

From the very first, the question of an advisory council was linked as a strictly secondary matter to the primary problem of the new Chief Executive. Some of those who opposed the idea of a powerful executive argued for constitutional provisions requiring the President to consult some form of council in specifically defined areas. George Mason sought to require consultation with respect to appointments.[11] Roger Sherman felt that an advisory council might somehow help to limit the arbitrariness of a single executive, though it is not clear whether or not he intended consultation to be compulsory.[12] Charles Pinckney, the first person in the Convention to offer a plan for an advisory council,[13] maintained that any such advisory relationship would have to be a voluntary one. Otherwise, he said, "Give him [the President] an able council and it will thwart him; a weak one, and he will shelter himself under their sanction." [14] His advice was eventually followed.

In spite of sporadic references to the need for a general advisory council, no action was taken until late in the proceedings. On August 20th Gouverneur Morris introduced a proposal for a Council of State composed of the Chief Justice and five heads of executive departments: foreign affairs, commerce and finance, domestic affairs, war, and marine. The President, he said, "may from time to time submit any matter to the discussion of the Council of State and he may require written opinions of any one or more of the members. But he shall in all cases exercise his own judgment and either conform to such opinions or not as he may think proper." [15] Worked over by the Committee of Detail, this plan was amended to include the President of the Senate and Speaker of the House on the "privy council." Included again was the President's right to consult "respecting the execution of his office. . . . But their advice shall not conclude him nor affect his responsibility for the measures which he shall adopt." [16]

Along with other "sundry resolutions etc." this proposition was sent to the Committee of Eleven from which emerged the final constitutional provision, bearing only the faintest resemblance to Morris's original elaborate plan. "He may require the opinion in writing, of the principal officers in each of the executive departments, upon any subject relating to the duties of their respective offices." From what we can discern, it seems that this committee feared that a President might avoid responsibility if a council were formalized. As Alexander Hamilton said, "A council to a magistrate, who is himself responsible for what he does, are generally nothing better than a clog upon his good intentions, are often the instruments and accomplices of his bad, and are almost always a cloak to conceal his faults." [17] Having made their crucial decision to provide for "unity" and "energy" in the executive, the framers felt that a formalized council might tend to create plural responsibility and lack of vigor.

The constitutional decision in favor of a strong and independent single executive set the basic contours of the President-Cabinet power-responsibility relationship, because its corollary was the failure to institutionalize any advisory group within the executive branch. Thus the formal power-responsibility complex was fixed at the start somewhere between the center of the spectrum and the extreme of complete individual authority. If this relationship was at all related to what existed in Great Britain, it was related to what existed there in the seventeenth century, not the nineteenth. The President was given ultimate formal authority and responsibility in the executive branch of the government. The department head was given no authority over the President, nor was there any mutual responsibility between the two; least of all was there any notion of the collective responsibility of his advisers. The fact was established that any advisory organ he used (provided it was not in another branch of the government, i.e., the Senate) would exist merely to implement his primary responsibility.

The second master decision for the Cabinet was the adoption of the separation of powers, plus the checks and balances idea. This was an attempt so to structure the national government internally as to give each of the three branches the motives and the means for checking each other. "Ambition," said Madison, "must be made to counteract ambition." [18] The Chief Executive-Cabinet nexus is, therefore, subjected to the continuous tugs and pulls set in motion by a deliberate attempt to encourage intramural conflict. The Cabinet in the first instance partakes of the President's role in the official trinity of powers, but individually and jointly they are affected by the interplay of external forces.

The major effect of the separation of powers as it operated in the earliest years was to help create the Cabinet, by rendering the department heads the most likely advisers to the President. Since the Constitution had mentioned both "Executive Departments" and "the Heads of Departments," it was assumed that the first Congress would establish them. Three departments (State, War, and Treasury), each with a Secretary at its head, and an Attorney General without a department, were created in 1789.[19] In spite of the fact that nothing was said in the earliest congressional debates about the possibility of these officials' forming a Cabinet Council (a term first used in the American context by Charles Pinckney in 1787), few could have been surprised at the event. It is the clear intent of Article Two, Section Two, of the Constitution that "the opinion, in writing, of the principal officer in each of the executive departments" would be an important source of advice for the President. Moreover, he obviously needed help. At the conclusion of the debates Washington wrote: "The impossibility that one man should be able to perform all the great business of the state I take to have been the reason for instituting the great departments, and appointing officers therein to assist the supreme magistrate in discharging the duties of his trust." [20]

The separation of powers also promoted the coalescence of the separate advisers into a group. Of great importance in this respect was the desire of the framers that "each department . . . should be so constituted that the members of each should have as little agency as possible in the appointment of the members of the others." [21] Although the President appoints his department heads "by and with the advice and consent of the Senate," the first statutes clearly established the principle that they would hold office only at his pleasure.[22] As a matter of courtesy the Senate has from the very outset (in all cases but two) consented to confirm his choice. Following the debates on the matter in 1784, his removal power in respect to these positions was not and has not since been challenged.[23] Whereas under the Confederation the department heads owed their appointment to Congress and were intimate with it, they were now attached by appointment, and removal power, to the newly established executive.

During the first months of the young government's existence, as each of the three branches became increasingly conscious of its own corporate interest, each tended to draw boundaries around its own prerogatives. In the famous affair over an Indian treaty, Washington was rebuffed in his attempt to establish intimate working relations with the Senate and to use it as a consultative body. Moreover, the Constitution expressly forbids legislators to hold any positions simultaneously in the executive branch, which weakened the opportunity to use individual congressmen. The Supreme Court, anxious like the Senate to protect its bailiwick, choked off another avenue of advice by refusing to render advisory opinions. When departmental Secretaries tried to come before the House of Representatives to talk about their problems and policies, that body twice refused to allow it.[24] This interaction not only tended to interdict advisory relationships between the President and the other branches, but it also helped to develop the bonds between the President and the heads of the executive departments. Restricted in his use of the Senate, he had to rely on his executive subordinates; shut off from Supreme

Court advice, he sought the legal counsel of his Attorney General; and since the department heads could not gain formal access to Congress, they would be apt to develop more easily some community of interest with the President.

Not every effect of the separation of powers operated, however, to strengthen the President-Cabinet nexus. Theories stressing legislative control and the department heads' responsibility to the legislature were common from the outset. James Hart, in his study of the early presidency, stresses the "divergence of views which emerged in the first session (of Congress)" with regard to "the place of the department heads in the system, in terms of who should possess, in relation to these officers, the powers of administrative direction and removal." [25] Insofar as individual Secretaries were dependent upon Congress for money, personnel, and other resources with which to operate their departments, the strengthening of legislative relationships, at the expense perhaps of presidential ties, could become a pre-condition of survival. For just such practical purposes, Secretary of the Treasury Hamilton took advantage of statutory provisions peculiar to the Treasury Department[26] to exploit the ambiguities in responsibility. In Jefferson's words, "He endeavored to place himself subject to the House when the executive should propose what he did not like, and subject to the executive when the House should propose anything disagreeable." [27] Hamilton's pattern of behavior is a familiar one. It is an early indication that, though the power-responsibility relationship between the President and his Cabinet is unambiguous, the relationship between the President and the individual Cabinet member may, in the context of the separation of powers, be considerably less clear.

Constitutional provisions like the independent single executive and the separation of powers help to create a fundamental framework of relationships to which the Cabinet and its members react and adjust. But what the structural arrangements do not by themselves indicate is that characteristic of the Cabinet which, as we shall see, renders it so especially defenseless in the face of external influences emanating from the Congress, from the separate departments, or from the social constituencies which they serve. *The Cabinet's institutional existence rests upon a completely customary basis.* The story of the Cabinet's birth illustrates this condition as clearly as anything.

From the outset of his administration, Washington sought every conceivable kind of advice in informal conversation and in writing from his three Secretaries and other officials, especially the Attorney General, the Vice-President, and the Chief Justice.[28] Gradually, he began to differentiate between the first four (three of whom were his intimate friends) and the last two, until calling the four into consultation had become settled practice. The first recorded meeting of any of these advisers took place in 1791 at the President's suggestion but in his absence. Present were the three Secretaries and the Vice-President but not the Attorney General.[29] According to Jefferson's record, this is the first and only meeting attended by the Vice-President. Soon the Attorney General was considered a member of the group, though not in pursuance of any policy other than convenience and expediency. The appearance of legal issues (such as the chartering of the Bank) and the Attorney General's admittedly broad talents, but to an equal extent Washington's close personal friendship with Mr. Randolph, combined toward this end.[30] Several records of meetings of these four in 1792 exist.

In the following year, the frequency of Cabinet meetings varied in direct proportion to the gravity of the issue at hand.[31] During the crisis of the spring of 1793, Jefferson noted that they met "almost every day." [32] The persistence of the habit probably brought the group to the attention of the interested public — at least to the eyes of discerning officials like James Madison, who in 1793 was apparently the first to apply the term "cabinet" to the group.[33] About five years later the word began to be heard in congressional debates, and by the end of Jefferson's administrations "cabinet" was a commonly understood name referring to the body of five (the Navy Department was added in 1798) presidential advisers.

The casualness with which the Cabinet evolved is testimony enough to its customary nature, but Washington settled other practices and relationships as well — especially the exposure of the Cabinet to party influence. The breach within his original Cabinet, due to differences of principle, was dramatized by the resignation of Thomas Jefferson in 1793. Not only does this mark the start of a two-party system, but it also settled the partisan nature of the Cabinet. Two years later the President affirmed: "I shall not, while I have the honor to administer the government bring a man into an office of consequence knowingly, whose political tenets are adverse to the measures which the general government are pursuing; for this, in my opinion, would be a sort of political suicide."[34] In every Cabinet since, the party affiliation of its members has been entirely or overwhelmingly the same as that of the President.

Some practices which were established by Washington during this early period were later cast aside, thereby giving us another indication of the same basic mutability of the Cabinet. One of these was Washington's practice of deciding questions by a vote at the Cabinet meeting and announcing the decision on the spot. Of Washington's early meetings Jefferson says: "In these discussions, Hamilton and myself were daily pitted in the cabinet like two cocks. We were then but four in number, and according to the majority, which of course was three to one, the President decided."[35] Of his own Cabinet Jefferson said the method was one ". . . in the gravest cases of calling them together, discussing the question maturely and finally taking the vote, on which the President counts himself but as one. So that in all important cases the executive is in fact a directory."[36] In spite of the discontinuance of such a method,[37] it served a valuable purpose in the formative stages — that of crystallizing a new idea by formalizing a procedure. Voting in the meeting helped to establish the importance of the meeting itself. Once Washington's basic concept had become accepted, procedural details could be easily altered.

The American Cabinet was in 1793 and is today an extralegal creation, functioning in the interstices of the law, surviving in accordance with tradition, and institutionalized by usage alone.[38] Its characteristics fluctuate with the dictates of time and circumstance, accident and personality. Whereas the institutions most closely related to it draw their sanction from the Constitution, the Cabinet must rely wholly upon custom. Within the American system this places the Cabinet at a distinct disadvantage. To use Max Weber's analysis, institutional authority tends to be legitimized in America by legal-rational rather than by customary means — as, for instance, it is in primitive societies.[39] Especially is this true of the Constitution, revered in America as the embodiment of our ideals, as a higher law. "The American people [writes Denis Brogan] after more than a century and a half of experience is as much convinced as ever that, within the framework of the Constitution and in no other way lies political salvation for them. This may be a foolish doctrine but it is the doctrine, the living political faith of the American people."[40] The arrangements which the Constitution explicitly sanctions are highly visible. They are fixed and bound by the majesty of the fundamental law. And they are inordinately durable.

Custom may, of course, provide as solid a basis for an institution as written law. But the point is that the American political system is less characterized by reliance on the sanctions of custom than many others and more characterized by an adherence to legalistic-rationalistic sanctions. In attempting to develop institutional strength, therefore, the Cabinet is deprived of one very important resource. It must continually confront the limitations inherent in its lack of legalized group prerogatives. The simple fact that the President is not required by law to form a Cabinet or to keep one helps to explain its dependence upon him. Most textbooks on American government take pains to cite the Cabinet as an example of the force of custom in our political system. But they frequently neglect the crucial point that this customary foundation is a basic source of weakness for the Cabinet in action.[41]

PATTERNS OF DEPARTMENTAL DEVELOPMENT

The Cabinet is a schizophrenic body. Its personnel can be divided into members of the Cabinet and men of Cabinet rank. The members of the Cabinet are selected at the President's behest; Cabinet rank, however, is accorded by a variety of legislative sanctions involving salaries, titles, and position with respect to presidential succession. The first group always contains the second but the reverse is not true. The Attorney General is a case in point. Every Attorney General since 1789 has been reckoned a member of the President's Cabinet, yet it was not until 1853 that his salary was equalized with those of the Secretaries. In 1870 a Department of Justice was created to put the Attorney General, so it said, "on precisely the same footing as the other heads of departments." [42] By 1886, the prestigial trappings of Cabinet office were made complete with the acknowledgment, retroactive to 1789, of his position with respect to presidential succession.[43] He could then be correctly considered as having graduated from one category of confidants to another — to be a man of Cabinet rank as well as a member of the Cabinet.

A recent case paralleling that of the Attorney General involved the elevation of the Federal Security Agency to Cabinet status as the Department of Health, Education and Welfare. The Administrator of this agency had from time to time since 1939 sat in the Cabinet, especially under Presidents Roosevelt and Eisenhower. The following exchange between Budget Director Joseph Dodge and some members of the House Committee on Government Operations, during consideration of the legislation required, illustrates the effect of the change and, incidentally, something of the confusion surrounding this problem.

MR. DODGE: "I do not believe that the mere creation of this as a Department makes Mrs. Hobby a member of the cabinet. She has been made a member of the cabinet. I do not understand that there is any law which specifies who the members of the cabinet shall be, that they consist of any group of advisers the President may wish to select and use for that purpose. Mrs. Hobby was invited to do that when she became Administrator and that has not changed . . ."

THE CHAIRMAN (Mr. Hoffman): "Doesn't Section 1 of Title 5 define what is and what is not the department?"

MR. DODGE: "Yes, I am sure it does, but I don't think. . . ."

THE CHAIRMAN: "The only way to bring this in is by the first sentence there, 'Creation of a Department Secretary.' There is hereby established an 'executive department.' The word 'executive' is the only way that brings this one in. Does that automatically make her a member of the cabinet?"

MR. DODGE: "I don't know that it does, Mr. Hoffman. I haven't yet had anyone point out to me any statute or anything else which defines the membership of the cabinet. This does make a department, an executive department, but she already is a member of the cabinet. . . ."

THE CHAIRMAN: "I thought she came in as a sort of invited guest. Maybe I am mistaken."

MR. DODGE: "I am sorry. I am there, too, and I'm. . . ."

THE CHAIRMAN: "You wouldn't be there if you were not the head of the executive department; would you?"

MR. JUDD: "He isn't the head."

MR. DODGE: "I am not the head of the executive department."

. . . . .

MR. JUDD: "The fact is, though, that when the FSA is given department status, she is on a par as far as salary, rank and so forth, and in every sense equal in prerogatives with cabinet status. Whoever is the head of this Agency is therefore given more prestige and more standing, and is on an equal basis. Is that correct?"

MR. DODGE: "That is correct. It puts her post on a par with the other major executive departments of the government." [44]

The evolution of the Cabinet from the Department of State and three others to the recent Department of Health, Education and Welfare can be understood only within a socio-economic context. Its growth has been a faithful record of the growth of the nation. It reflects our westward expansion, our industrialization, the burdens of world responsibility, the concern for social justice. Each of these great transformations in American life has opened up new problem areas for government. New areas of concern have meant new administrative burdens and organizational complexities, and with each change the public (or publics) which is interested in and affected by government action has grown. One typical response to change has been the creation of executive departments to meet administrative or social need. Since 1789, when the first three departments were set up, there have been nine separate responses of this nature. They have been scattered over 164 years of history, called forth for a variety of reasons under a variety of circumstances to meet different requirements. There are both similarities and differences in this development, and both illuminate the continuing problems of the Cabinet.

The prebirth period of these different organizations reveals a common pattern. There was, in most cases, early recognition of a new problem area by a few interested individuals or groups, coupled with marked reluctance on the part of the national legislature to recognize change or to acknowledge a real need. Thus the Navy Department was "forced into being — extracted from a Congress that contained both hostile and inert elements — by a few leaders" after nearly ten years of presidential agitation.[45] Between President Harding's initial recommendation in 1923 and the creation of a department thirty years later, five separate reorganization studies advocated the departmental consolidation of the government's health, education, and welfare programs, and two specific presidential proposals to this effect were rejected by Congress.[46] From the initial formal proposal, by interest group or public official, to final legislative enactment, the waiting period was thirty-seven years for Interior[47] and Agriculture,[48] thirty-nine years for Commerce,[49] forty years for Justice,[50] and forty-five years for Labor.[51]

Most of the departments began as lesser organizations and rose in the administrative hierarchy, as their duties expanded (Post Office would be an exception here) or as their constituency grew. Thus, for example, there was a General Post Office, a Commissioner of Agriculture, a Bureau and then a Commissioner of

Labor, an Attorney General's Office, and a Federal Security Agency, each of which later became a department. Considered together, the development of the ten departments reflects, in common, a great deal of the change to big and to bigger government. They are a representative cross section of an administrative revolution — lagging behind, but nonetheless reflecting the social, political, and economic change in the community at large.

On any but the most general level, however, one is struck not by the similarities but by the important differences which characterize the member units. One is struck, in other words, by those factors present in the early development of the executive departments which should lead us to differentiate among units of the Cabinet rather than lump them indiscriminately into a preordained institutional homogeneity.

The complex of forces which precipitated the formation of each executive department was different in nearly every case. Sometimes congressional receptivity to change was produced by some especially compelling set of circumstances — strained foreign relations in the case of Navy, problems of post-Civil War legal administration in the case of Justice,[52] wartime experience in the case of Defense.[53] (Thus, it was predictable that Sputnik and related events would precipitate a cry for a new department concerned with scientific and outer space problems.) Yet Navy was carved out of an existing department (War), Justice grew out of the Attorney General's Office, and Defense consolidated two old, established departments. The first Secretary of Health, Education and Welfare was helped toward Cabinet rank by the President, who invited her to sit with the Cabinet while she still did not have Cabinet status. He also made an unprecedented appearance before the American Medical Association to conciliate that previously implacable group on the question of the new department.[54] With respect to the elevation of the Postmaster General, "Undoubtedly the deciding factor was the need for another Cabinet position with which to reward the ambitious head of the General Post Office for his services in the presidential campaign."[55] Three other members of the Cabinet were pushed into the inner circle from below — by the pressures of farmers, businessmen, and workers, exerted through such organizations as the U. S. Agricultural Society or the American Federation of Labor.[56] The Interior Department was created without the marked assistance of the President and without organized group support — assuming, that is, that neither Indians, nor inventors, nor pensioners, nor census takers, nor users nor buyers of the public lands constituted organized, political interest groups.

In examining the constituent units of the chief's council in primitive society, one is struck by the ways in which the power of private groups (in this case, kinship, geographical, and religious groups) is converted into publicly effective power through their participation in the advisory institution.[57] Among the units of the President's Cabinet, the degree and kind of support they can muster from private groups in the country is illuminated by the conditions of their establishment. Agriculture, Commerce, and Labor were created in part by a specialized clientele, and the close relationships established then have been strengthened since. These departments have, from the beginning, been subjected to lines of influence which often pull them away from the President. Their position is quite different, for example, from the Secretary of State who came into being without any group support at a time when his international function was being minimized and when his position had many characteristics of an impotent "Home Office." He was, and has been ever since, greatly dependent upon the President. The Attorney General, who got his start with the Cabinet due partly to the President's personal friendship, has ever since been both a personal legal adviser to the President and chief legal officer of the government as well. The birth processes of the Defense Department and the Health, Education and Welfare Department show a magnitude of group support somewhere in between State and Agriculture. Each of the former includes within itself powerful groups. These groups may provide a basis of support when the prerogatives of the department are under attack from the outside. But they may also generate internal conflict, affecting in turn the over-all activities of their agency or its effectiveness in the Cabinet. Scars inflicted at the time of birth may help account for the attitudes toward each other of the Army, Navy, and Air Force in the one case and of the conservative doctors and liberal social security administrators in the other.

In primitive systems, advisers who represent social constituencies (i.e., family, clan, tribe, secret society) perform a representative or a political function in the chief's "cabinet." [58] Similarly, the representatives of powerful socio-economic groups are equipped to do the same in the American Cabinet. The Secretaries of Agriculture or Labor or Commerce can tell the Chief Executive how a given decision is likely to affect key groups. They can inform him as to the likely response of their constituencies in terms of their willingness or unwillingness to "go along." In short, the President could use these individuals, and the others who have important constituencies of one sort or another, as a political sounding board to keep him responsive to the attitudes of various social groups and to make it easier for him to perform his own mediatory or integrative function.

Among those Cabinet members who do not so obviously represent social constituencies, there is the alternative role of expert to be performed. The Secretary of State and the Attorney General are examples. In primitive councils, the advisers of special talent are most often the elder, the warrior, or the orator.[59] The specialization and bureaucratization of modern society almost inexorably add managerial aspects to the notion of expert in the Cabinet, replacing the wise elder with a man of administrative ability, which means, of course, that administrative talent will be expected of most members. But a distinction between the political and the expert functions in the Cabinet can be seen from the perspective of the development of the departments.

No single administrative rationale was at work on all of the departments at the times of their creation. Three were descended directly from the experience under the Articles of Confederation. They tended to be well integrated in administrative organization. Others, like Interior, were created to provide an administrative home for orphan agencies. Interior, Health, Education and Welfare, and Defense are much like holding companies for agencies that had established an independent existence elsewhere and have retained this attitude in their new department. Among the clientele departments, some are tightly integrated (Commerce) and some very loosely integrated (Labor). The attitude of the medical profession in 1953 dictated a particular kind of organizational structure for one department; the attitude of the Navy in 1947 and 1949 helps to account for the allocation of authority in the Defense Department. At the time that the Labor Department was formed, on the other hand, labor leaders were unable to spell out in any definitive way just what they considered its proper functions to be. This uncertainty has returned to plague them over and over again in the frequent partitioning of that department. The creation of the Post Office Department represented the politicization of the most businesslike organization in the government, and the Department's involvement in top level decision-making is minimal.

In all these ways, then, and in many others as well, the particular conditions which existed at the time of birth have left the constituent units of the Cabinet with distinguishing birthmarks — marks which have affected their lives ever since. The total governmental process impinges upon and envelops an institution from its very beginnings. It is these differences among the executive departments which best reflect an early exposure to the multiplex influences of the American political system. Constantly and continuously we will find these forces shaping the behavior and the attitudes of the departmental Secretaries inside and outside of the Cabinet.

A less tangible, but equally crucial element in accounting for departmental differences is this: just as the growth of the Cabinet parallels and records the expansion of the nation, so too does the

Cabinet reflect the atomistic and uncoordinated nature of that expansion. Just as the presence of Turner's "free land" encouraged a reckless, unplanned exploitation of natural resources, and just as the frontiers encouraged unrestrained competition in industry, so did the existence of administrative frontiers promote similar characteristics in governmental organization. Administrative growth was rapid, uncontrolled, and topsy-like. Organizations did not wait patiently to find their place within an established pattern nor were they at all conscious of an over-all structure. They literally fell all over themselves trying to get into the Cabinet and, as we have seen, for different reasons. Typically, labor leaders did not have any detailed idea of what a Labor Department should do;[60] they just wanted to secure a spot close to the President's ear, and the Cabinet qualified. To secure "labor's voice in the Cabinet," they needed a department. Similarly, the supporters of the Agriculture Department could not spell out its functions.[61] The Interior Department's functions were literally undefinable. The Health, Education and Welfare Department, the result of an administrative reorganization following a proliferation of minor agencies, bears many similarities to Interior — an indication that the administrative frontier, at least, is far from closed. Also, organizations of tremendous importance have sprung up and exist beyond the borders of the Cabinet. In the undigested, *ad hoc,* and oftentimes frenzied protestations of the opposition, too, one can sense the speed and the scope of the transformation and the impossibility of trying to understand it as an ordered, controllable pattern. It was a growth process wholly without internal logic or structure.

It was in this "frontier-like" atmosphere that the several Secretaries came to the Cabinet table. They were independent and self-reliant. There were divergencies in their ideas, interests, and functions. Each one was ambitious for himself. Each one was interested in promoting and expanding his own domain without concern for the others. To twist David Riesman somewhat, a Cabinet member was more apt to be "inner directed" than "outer directed" in his association with other department heads. Neither the theory nor the practice of coordination presented itself as a pressing problem. The ideas of integration and of interrelatedness did not exercise the members greatly. The idea of the public interest, an underdeveloped area which lay beyond the administrative frontier, was neglected. Living alone was so rich and rewarding that living together hardly seemed to be a problem at all. It was difficult, in this context, to establish a common frame of reference for the Cabinet members. There were few influences in this unpatterned process which were especially conducive to a spirit of cooperation, or to a feeling of mutual responsibility for public policy.

The events and circumstances surrounding the establishment of the constituent departments did not provide any great incentive for working hard at coordination early in the game. One can only speculate that, had such considerations been present, a mold of tradition and custom might have been formed around cooperative effort at the beginning, a mold which might have built into the Cabinet something more solid — that intangible quality, teamwork. An attitude of cooperation is an index not only to the morale but to the effectiveness of any working organization, but there was little in the process of Cabinet growth to create the idea of teamwork or to fix it with the preservative of custom. Customs and traditions promotive of cohesiveness and unity could not draw nourishment from the climate in which Cabinet expansion took place.

The establishment and development of the executive departments reflect the pluralism of the American political system. In so doing, they introduce us to one of the focal points of this study, the interplay, within the total governmental process, of forces making for diversity and those making for unity in Cabinet activity. Forces affecting the constitution of its basic units will predictably impinge upon the Cabinet in action. In this case, inter-departmental differences make for difficulty in promoting unity. Recognition of this fact, however, brings us to inquire into the presence of countervailing influences, of forces making for unity in Cabinet action — and hence, to the greatest of these, the President.

DIMENSIONS AND TYPES OF PRESIDENTIAL INFLUENCE

It is a first lesson of this study that the Cabinet is dependent on the President. It is a first lesson of history that no two Presidents will behave exactly alike. We can expect to find, therefore, that the President's importance to the Cabinet will be manifested in as many different ways as there are Presidents. Short run variations in actual Cabinet behavior are, in fact, traceable more to the influence of the President than to any other single factor — and traceable ultimately to the differences in temperament, ability, desire, experience, and habit which distinguish one presidential personality from another. The impact of presidential behavior runs, however, within some broad institutional limits which need to be located before an examination of dimensions and types of influence is undertaken.

In the first place, the structure of the American Executive fixes a lower limit to Cabinet activity. The President's power to use or not to use it is complete and final. The Cabinet is his to use when and if he wishes, and he cannot be forced into either alternative. He has the power of life or death over it at this point. He is a policeman with sole and unlimited control over the traffic signals. Without the green light which only he can flash, and for reasons largely of his own choosing, the Cabinet cannot even begin to function; whatever it does, it is always subject to his desire to change the signal from green to red. Here is the point at which the rock-bottom dependence involved in the power-responsibility relationship becomes most strikingly obvious. It is the point at which the time-honored anecdote about Lincoln's decision which was taken contrary to the unanimous vote of his Cabinet ("seven noes, one aye — the ayes have it") is applicable.

In this formal sense, Jonathan Daniels' statement is accurate, that "No institution is more a body of one man's men than the American President's Cabinet." [62]

In the second place, the nature of the presidential function sets certain upper limits to Cabinet activity, limits which varying presidential attitudes cannot alter. The President can render the Cabinet useless, but he cannot mold it to any use he may desire. That is to say, there are real limits to the kind and the extent of assistance he can get from the Cabinet. A widespread tendency exists, however, to assume otherwise. Thus it is a commonly accepted platitude of Cabinet commentary that "An able Cabinet will go far to make up for the deficiencies of a weak President." [63] This expression of what might be labeled "the compensatory Cabinet theory" carries with it no implication of upper limits to Cabinet usefulness. In the light of at least two cases during the period under study, it is a theory which stands in need of some revision.

Warren Harding repeatedly expressed the idea that his Cabinet was comprised of the "best minds." Implicit in this concept was a self-awareness of his own personal inadequacies. He felt that he could compensate for them by surrounding himself with men who possessed the talent and the experience which he lacked. One reviewer put the compensatory Cabinet theory succinctly in this fashion: "He could not be a Mellon, but he got Mellon; he could not be a Hughes, but he got Hughes; he could not be a Hoover, but he got Hoover; he could not be a Hays, but he got Hays." [64] This comment fails to consider the total picture.

In the very act of constituting the Cabinet, Harding began to display weaknesses of inconsistency and lack of direction. He not only "got" Hughes, Hoover, and Mellon, but he also made the less happy appointments of Daugherty, Denby, and Fall. Harding's compensatory Cabinet was an extremely heterogeneous one. Furthermore, the "best minds" concept required that someone integrate the diverse contributions of the group: firm principles and clear policy direction were required of the President. Warren Harding could furnish neither. The lack of a consistently thought-out program, the dearth of general constructive principles on which to base action, the personal qualities which produced poor appointments — all of these were Harding's own weaknesses. They were fatal, and no Cabinet could compensate for them. Under these circumstances, the "best minds" idea was in its consummation a dream-wish, a mythical conception of a superstructure which well qualified builders might construct on a perilously shaky foundation. A President who aspires to be only the simple sum of his Cabinet advisers will be hardly anything at all.

The pre-presidential experience of Herbert Hoover was of a type that eminently fitted him for some of the tasks of the Presidency, but which did not equip him for others. His jobs in engineering, in the Food Administration, and in the Department of Commerce required organizational talent, the ability to plan and direct large enterprises. He came to the Presidency, therefore, prepared and trained to organize and administer the governmental business as he had done in lesser areas. He brought with him well digested plans for construction and development. No one in the nation was more abundantly endowed with the necessary qualifications, but the fields in which he had labored before differed from those of his new office. His previous activities had not been exposed to constant public scrutiny and political debate. His success had not depended upon his own participation in the give and take, the pressures, and the conflicts that characterize the democratic process. He had not been required to sell his basic purposes or his program to Congress, or to his party, or to the public at large to the degree which became necessary in the Presidency. In these respects, his experience and his temperament did not equip him for survival in the new environment — especially so considering the magnitude and the novelty of the problems which arose to upset all his preconceived plans.

Commentaries on Hoover as President confirm his difficulties in providing democratic leadership. "This job," he said, "is nothing but a twenty ring circus — with a whole lot of bad actors." [65] And the President, he felt, should not descend to the role of ringmaster. "This is not a showman's job. I will not step out of character." [66] With this attitude, he was bound to be less effective in working where there was a conflict of wills, in persuading Congress and party, or in guiding public opinion in the midst of controversy. On these grounds, a uniform complaint arose from his Cabinet members, from his party leaders in Congress, from political commentators of all convictions, from newspapermen, and from private citizens — phrased differently, but always with the same dominant theme. William Allen White summed it up: "President Hoover is a great executive, a splendid desk man. But he cannot dramatize his leadership. A democracy cannot follow a leader unless he is dramatized. A man to be a hero must not content himself with heroic virtues and anonymous actions. He must talk and explain as he acts — drama." [67]

There is no evidence at all that Hoover, like Harding, recognized a personal shortcoming and attempted to offset it in selecting his Cabinet. There is some evidence to support the proposition, true in Harding's case, that the President's personal deficiencies are as likely as not to be mirrored in the composition of his Cabinet. The uniform tenor of commentary on the Hoover Cabinet stressed its homogeneity and its undramatic quality — "a solid and impregnable and [journalistically speaking] dismally unsensational Gibralter," "solidity and dependableness," "serenity and tranquillity, and stability and loyalty and reliability," "co-operators rather than individualists," "no solo performers," "little of the spectacular," "averageness," "efficient and machine-like," "solid and substantial internal harmony." [68] When Hoover selected men of political experience for the Cabinet, he failed to rise above his own source. The two "politicians" whom he chose were uninspiring and workmanlike, ordinary individuals without any popular appeal. They were "pinnacles of composure" rather than men of distinction.[69] They were singularly unqualified to save the President from the effects of his awkwardness in public political relations. Most important, they could not have done so under any circumstances.

The Harding and the Hoover experiences serve equally well to support the following conclusion: there are certain fundamental qualities and abilities which the President and he alone must possess and for which no Cabinet can compensate. He is, after all, more than the leader of the Cabinet. He is the leader of the nation. If he lacks the basic equipment to fill this primary role, the Cabinet can be of only patchwork assistance. Indeed, Presidents may not be able to rise above their own inadequacies in the act of Cabinet selection. As Harding's case shows, the Chief Executive must give a steady purpose and a direction to his administration, choosing wisely from among competing policies where he himself has none. As Hoover's difficulties demonstrate, the President must dramatize issues, lead and persuade his party, guide and shape public opinion. These requirements form the essence of successful democratic leadership. Conversely, they establish some irreversible limits to Cabinet usefulness. The implications of the compensatory Cabinet theory must be held strictly within the boundaries set by the necessities of presidential leadership.

The President's influence on Cabinet activity is circumscribed by lower and upper limits, both of which spring not from personality factors but from the basic nature of the presidential function. As an independent executive, he has absolute power over the use of his advisory group, and it represents an institutional impossibility to expect the Cabinet to pull itself up by its own bootstraps. The President's leadership function also sets irreversible limits to what the Cabinet can do to help him; the Cabinet cannot act as a surrogate for him where the quintessence of leadership is involved. Within this broadly limiting framework lies the permissive realm of actual Cabinet performance. It is here that the President's personal influence comes into play and manifests itself in the varieties of Cabinet activity.

The precise relationship between presidential personality and Cabinet activity is impossible to gauge, especially given the memoir, manuscript, public, and secondary materials available for this study. The diffused, refractory, and uneven nature of the sources make an elusive subject even more slippery. One can, however, indicate what seem to be the relevant areas of presidential behavior and suggest their likely effect on the Cabinet.

At a most general level, it is probable that particular presidential interpretations of the Presidency will affect the activity of the Cabinet. Theodore Roosevelt's ideas about the necessity for vigorous presidential leadership led to a certain reluctance to consult with his Cabinet before taking important action. As he put it, "A council of war never fights, and in a crisis the duty of a leader is to lead and not to take refuge behind the generally timid wisdom of a multitude of counsellors." [70] Woodrow Wilson developed a theory of strong executive leadership, according to which the President divined the popular will and then led the other organs of government. From his twin-pronged faith in public opinion and in his own ability to plumb its depths, he developed a "teacher-tribune" conception of presidential leadership. Whenever he assumed this role, he was markedly unreceptive to words of reconsideration, compromise, or, indeed, advice of any kind.[71] During the struggle over the League of Nations, for instance, he turned a deaf ear not only to the protestations of the Senate, but also to the pleas of his own Cabinet. Several of these individuals urged a more conciliatory course, but to no avail.[72]

Warren Harding, on the other hand, explicitly attacked the broad Wilsonian concept of leadership, which Harding labelled "personal government, individual, dictatorial, autocratic or what not." [73] During his campaign speeches he claimed that he would introduce "plural leadership" into the administration, and that he would substitute government by men of the "best abilities" for "one man government." [74] He repeatedly said that his own view of the job placed emphasis upon building a Cabinet comprised of the "best minds" in the nation. In his acceptance speech, he lost no time in declaring: "Our vision includes more than a Chief Executive; we believe in a Cabinet of the highest capacity, equal to the responsibilities which our system contemplates." [75] Referring to this recurrent theme, one observer summarized: "Mr. Harding gave signs during the campaign of believing that almost any Republican of good standing would do well enough as President, but that the Cabinet was the place for men of great mental force." [76]

One kind of interpretation looks toward a full realization of the potentialities of the Presidency for leadership; the other deliberately underplays these possibilities. Historically, an emphasis on the Cabinet is frequently associated with a set of attitudes and beliefs which minimizes strong executive leadership. Individuals of this persuasion are apt to accent "the men around me," "the best minds," or "the team," to the relative detraction of the presidential office. President Eisenhower, whose cautious attitude toward the powers of the Presidency in a system of "coordinate" powers falls somewhat nearer that of Harding than that of Wilson, has placed a heavy emphasis on "the team" and on "the Cabinet" as opposed to "my Cabinet." [77] Historical reactions to "excessive" presidential activity have been paralleled in many cases by assertions of devotion to the Cabinet. The Whig theory of the Presidency may have as a corollary a Whig theory of the Cabinet — a relationship which did, in fact, hold for the Whigs,[78] and is strikingly evident in such sequences as the Wilson-Harding one. The likelihood is that Wilson and Presidents whose attitudes approximate his will tend to rely on the Cabinet less than Harding and those whose attitudes approximate his.

The generic function of the President's Cabinet is to advise the President. To say that every President takes advice is true but meaningless, for within the limits of such a truism there remains ample room for variety in application. The Cabinet has no one stereotyped and immutable role to play in presidential decision-making, and the President's own desire for, receptivity to, and use of advice is a key variable in determining that role for any particular Cabinet.

A gross distinction between Presidents who require a great deal of advice and those with a greater intellectual self-sufficiency might be useful. Thus we have Harding's constant self-depreciation, as revealed graphically in this outburst to a friend.

John, I can't make a damn thing out of this tax problem. I listen to one side and they seem right, and then God! I talk to the other side and they seem just as right, and there I am where I started. I know somewhere there is a book that would give me the truth, but hell, I couldn't read the book. I know somewhere there is an economist who knows the truth, but I don't know where to find him and haven't the sense to know him and trust him when I did find him. God, what a job.[79]

Harding's attitude might be contrasted with that of Wilson and Hoover, the two men during the period who were frequently accused of not taking (nor, indeed, wanting) much advice.[80] The extreme indictment will not stand up in either case, but the preference of the two men for intellectual self-sufficiency was marked. Such a preference might lead to less Cabinet activity than, say, the Harding position.

In a slightly different vein, we might contrast Harry Truman's receptivity to advice given "whether he liked it or not" with Herbert Hoover's sometime sensitivity to adverse criticism. Truman wrote: "I made it a point always to listen to Cabinet officers at length and with care, especially when their points of view differed from mine. . . . I would ask the Cabinet to share their counsel with me, even encouraging disagreement and argument to sharpen up the different points of view." [81] Hoover, on the other hand, evinced only the mildest enthusiasm for the single Cabinet member who did differ vigorously with him, Henry Stimson.[82] There is no evidence that any of his Cabinet advisers advised him to alter his direction or his pace or presented him with counter proposals during the economic crisis, and perhaps this willingness to follow stemmed from a reluctance to criticize.[83]

Presidents may be more amenable to some kinds of advice than to others. As between what we have called "expert" and "political" advice, Wilson and Franklin Roosevelt accommodated the first much more readily than the second. Where specialized advice of a military, economic, administrative, or narrowly partisan nature was concerned, Wilson utilized experts,[84] yet in the delicate synchronization of diplomatic maneuvering with domestic public opinion preceding World War I, he acted alone and over the protests of many of his advisers. Likewise, too, in the matter of political timing in pushing his legislative program, he made the major decisions himself and in the face of advice to the contrary.[85] Similarly, Roosevelt deferred to such groups as the Chiefs of Staff and the "Brain Trust,"[86] but when a decision involved the subtleties of public political relations, he relied mostly on his own abilities and instincts. The efforts of Henry Stimson and Harold Ickes to prod Roosevelt to more decisive action in 1941 and 1942, in the face of what they considered to be the President's exasperating deliberateness at this time, provides an excellent example. Ickes' agitated concern over Roosevelt's handling of the 1936 presidential campaign is another.[87] Depending on what kind of advice a Cabinet is best equipped to furnish, differences in attitudes such as these may have consequences for Cabinet activity.

Probably the most important of all factors relating to advice is that complex of presidential attitudes and habits which goes to make up his distinctive pattern of decision-making.

Herbert Hoover's decision-making procedure was characterized by the extent to which he dominated it through a personal involvement at all levels. His secretary writes that "He had to originate every last recovery program put forward by his administration."[88] Hoover "had to" not because others were incapable of doing so, but because this was the method which best suited his ability and temperament. In all of his prior executive experience he had stressed the necessity of tight one man control over an organization.[89] It was, for instance, almost a conditioned response to the onset of a new problem for Hoover to call a conference of specially qualified experts. But he did not call it until after he had first formulated a set of proposals, laying out the line of approach he desired.

"Whatever the plan or program, he always prepared it to the last detail prior to holding the conference at which he was to project it." [90] The group discussion was designed not to initiate, but to explore ramifications and consequences, to bring about a meeting of the minds, and to enlist voluntary cooperation — all based on Hoover's original propositions. The tempo of decision-making as well as the substance of policy was controlled by him. On the way to a decision, he planned and organized his moves with a constitutional deliberateness which impatient advisers could not alter. He wanted, above all, to know exactly where he was going before he rendered a decision. The gradual reduction of alternatives was a slow process, accompanied by long hours of intellectual application to the problem. His decision on the moratorium on war debts is a case in point.[91] It is difficult to imagine Hoover going before his advisory body with the unadorned question: "What shall I do?" If they did hash over a proposal, it was likely to be strictly his own, and more than likely to have been rolled over in his own mind for a long time previously.[92]

Woodrow Wilson, like Hoover, had a distinctive method of decision-making, intellectually structured and carried through with enough consistency to provide an important clue to his Cabinet relations. In the earliest stages, before he had made up his mind and settled on a course of action, he was receptive to advice, even though, as Colonel House said, "it mostly comes gratuitously and not by his asking." [93] He was anxious to listen to all sides of an argument, to obtain a complete picture of each issue, and to make certain that he lacked no pertinent facts or information. His attitude and behavior in the controversy over plans for the army in 1916 is a case in which he had no preconceived ideas. Here, he was open-minded to the point of being indiscriminating about the alternatives.[94] Once he had availed himself of the necessary preliminary information and arguments, he reached his decisions by himself, after lengthy, painstaking, and solitary deliberation. He did not make up his mind in the presence of conflicting voices, and very often characterized his own procedure as that of a man with a "one track mind." [95]

Once Wilson had thought a problem through to a decision, his attitude hardened almost to intransigeance. William McAdoo, Secretary of the Treasury, and Colonel House put it succinctly: "He listens quite patiently, and makes up his mind and then stays put." [96] Franklin Lane concurred, that "Once he has reached a conclusion, that conclusion becomes a part of his nature. He is inflexible." [97] Given this pattern, Wilson's Cabinet could at best be effective as an advisory body only at that stage in the decision-making process where Wilson felt he needed to delineate and document a problem requiring his decision. Between this point and his announcement of a decision his advisers were not likely to be involved. This does not mean that Wilson would be averse to submitting some of his final conclusions to their discussion, but it does indicate that when he did do so his mind usually would be well fixed. At this point, he would be testing out their reactions or seeking their reassurances, but not inviting debate.

Franklin Roosevelt's decision-making procedure was quite different from Hoover's or Wilson's. His personal involvement was regular only in its irregularity, and predictable only in its unpredictability. This is because his decision-making habits were essentially experimental, grounded in his own subtle sense of timing. His advisers could and did complain alternately about his slowness in making up his mind and his "weakness for snap decisions." [98] He would make exploratory decisions, sometimes in the form of trial balloons, which he did not consider final and irrevocable. He would make a quick tentative decision and then change direction, as in the case of the Morgenthau plan. Or, he would pursue a course of watchful delay as in the third term and the cross-channel invasion decisions.[99]

Roosevelt frequently delayed in making difficult decisions because he disliked argument and hoped that differences of opinion could be compromised. Indeed, he commonly reached decisions by simply withdrawing to "hold the ring" while the disputants debated to some outcome.[100] He would step in himself, listening to advice and deciding, only if there were no other recourse. Yet, "He would take a suggestion from anyone, anywhere." [101] All of these decision-making methods tended toward one result — keeping his advisers off-balance, unable to forecast or rationalize their own advisory role, and uncertain as to whether he was or was not taking their advice.

Calvin Coolidge's decision-making procedure was, by contrast with Roosevelt's, conducted in the most explicit conformity with the canons of regularity. It was neither impulsive nor imaginative, but "calculated, direct, safe, and sure." [102] It was studied in its avoidance of executive initiative and in its eager deference to the Cabinet.[103] Coolidge's strategy of control over decision-making was to "sit down and keep still" in the face of problems rather than to confront them, to "remain silent until an issue is reduced to its lowest terms, until it boils down to something like a moral issue." "If you see ten troubles coming down the road," he philosophized, "you can be sure that nine will run into the ditch before they reach you and you have to battle with only one." [104] He followed this prescription in two of his biggest decisions as an administrator, the Boston police strike and the firing of Harry Daugherty. He followed it with respect to his public policy decisions on the farm problem.[105] Indeed, as his most sympathetic biographer says: "The one important occasion when Coolidge did not keep his mouth shut . . . proved to be the most unfortunate blunder he ever made." [106] Coolidge consciously prescribed extensive Cabinet participation in decision-making, and he stated flatly that "I rarely failed to accept their recommendations." [107] But his calculated inactivity and his general reluctance to set in motion the machinery of decision-making indicates that the members would probably be given relatively few opportunities to exercise influence.

Probably the best example of a decision-making procedure with extensive, built-in Cabinet reliance is that of President Eisenhower. He is, unlike Roosevelt, not addicted to "snap or unconsidered decisions." [108] His tempo of decision-making is slow and deliberate, sometimes painfully so. His "compelling desire to have his decisions turn out right" [109] dictates not only the pace of the process but also his receptivity to the advice of others. "Before reaching his conclusions," said one of his Cabinet-level officials, "he wants to be sure that he has considered the views of all those who properly have something to contribute." [110] His use (unlike Hoover) of representative study committees to lay the foundation for his programs is evidence of this fundamental desire. The study group device is evidence too of another personal characteristic, his preference for having the groundwork thoroughly laid and the issues boiled down before he finally confronts them.[111]

As he nears the point of final decision, there is still much room for advisory activity. This is mostly because Eisenhower, unlike Wilson, "likes to reach his conclusions by talking out his thoughts rather than brooding." [112] "He likes to take in by ear all that he can." [113] This means that he will pass problems around for discussion among his advisers, listen carefully to their debates, and use them as a sounding board for his own ideas. He is apt, in other words, to do his thinking in the presence of others, in a group meeting. Most important of all, he frequently if not usually makes his final decision on the spot. When he is ready to act, he wants to make certain that his decision is clear, understood by all and concurred in by all, conditions which are best secured in a meeting rather than afterward. On-the-spot decision-making is easy for him since, as he has said, "I have trained myself as soon as a matter is finished and a decision is made to put it out of my mind and to go on with the next subject." [114] Eisenhower's procedure is not characterized by tight personal control over it.

It is a generalization worth considering, perhaps, that other things being equal, a President who exercises a tight control at many points in the decision-making sequence will tend to rely on his Cabinet less than one whose intervention in the process is more limited.

A President's administrative habits and attitudes are related to, but distinguishable from, those regarding decision-making procedures, and they are equally crucial in their effect on the Cabinet in action. Especially is this true of the techniques and extent of delegation. Should the President employ a haphazard, nonhierarchical, or highly personalized method of delegation, his Cabinet subordinates may be accorded no special emphasis. If he delegates regularly through the chain of command, a greater Cabinet reliance may be indicated. Similarly with the extent of delegation: in those areas where he is reluctant to delegate, the participation and the value of the member or members involved may be diminished in the policy-making process. Delegation which proceeds, however, to the point of abdication is equally likely to impair Cabinet usefulness, by depriving the President of any control over it.[115]

Calvin Coolidge's administrative behavior followed, in every respect, the tenets of orthodoxy. His philosophy concerning delegation was formalistic and simple. He was especially lavish in the field of foreign affairs. "The only way to succeed when there is a job to be done," he said, "is to look around and find the best man to do it and then let him do it." [116] To those sent on foreign missions he gave a virtual *carte blanche*.[117] He placed the task of directing and coordinating our foreign policy almost wholly in the laps of Secretaries Hughes and Kellogg. The all-important matter of timing, for instance, in the Kellogg-Briand negotiations he left entirely to the discretion of Kellogg.[118] Nor would Coolidge weaken or subvert the formal hierarchy of responsibility and authority. Psychologically, he found it necessary to keep his friend Frank Stearns around him as a kind of buffer-companion-confessor, yet he would not work through him or consult him in any way. During a conversation about Colonel House, the President made clear the strict limitations of his friend's role. " 'Mr. Stearns, an unofficial adviser to a President is not a good thing and is not provided for in our form of government.' Stearns replied, 'Did I ever try to advise you?' 'No,' was the reply, 'but I thought I had better tell you.' " [119] "I have never relied on any person to be my unofficial adviser. . . ." Coolidge said, "My counsellors have been those provided by the Constitution and the law." [120]

Harry Truman, too, attached special importance to the Chief Executive's ability "to delegate responsibility and then back up those he trusts." And he underscores, in his writings, the inherent connection between his techniques of delegation and his claim to have "revived the Cabinet system." [121] He looked upon his Cabinet as "a board of directors appointed by the President to help him carry out the policies of the government," or, alternatively, as "the principal medium through which the President controls his administration." [122] Truman learned through experience, however, that he could not delegate too much without losing control of his own job. Having begun by delegating copiously to his Secretary of State, he finally wrote to Secretary Byrnes:

I have been considering some of our difficulties. As you know, I would like to pursue a policy of delegating authority to the members of the Cabinet in their various fields and then back them up in the results. But in doing that and in carrying out that policy, I do not intend to turn over the complete authority of the President, nor to forego the President's prerogative to make the final decision.[123]

He followed this practice with Secretaries of State Marshall and Acheson, freely delegating authority (as in Marshall's China mission),[124] and interfering only occasionally (albeit sometimes impulsively, as with the proposed trip to Moscow by the Chief Justice), but retaining throughout "his own basic power of decision and direction."

It has been said that "the Eisenhower and Truman administrations . . . are a good deal alike . . . in their patterns for the delegation of authority." [125] In the case of President Eisenhower the germinal influence is, again, his military habituation to the chain of command. "He imported from the army a form of the staff system in which all functions and responsibilities flow in a more or less fixed order and sequence from the President on down." [126] As a general rule, it may be suggested, those presidents like Coolidge, Truman, and Eisenhower, who have most frequently expressed their resolution to delegate, who have been hyperconscious of this particular administrative virtue, and for whom it forms an integral part of their administrative philosophy, can be expected to delegate in large measure through their Cabinet members. This, in turn, will facilitate (should they wish) useful, informed, and informative Cabinet discussions. This does not mean that these men were, in fact, equally reliant upon the Cabinet. For instance, the contrast between Coolidge's admitted penchant for "avoiding the big problems" and Truman's unflinching attitude in the face of the big foreign policy decisions of 1945–1952 probably indicates that Truman was less "Cabinet-reliant" than Coolidge. Such differences are hard to calculate. But it is useful to contrast the attitude of the three Presidents listed above with, for example, that of Woodrow Wilson in the field of foreign affairs, to isolate one kind of influence on the Cabinet in action. On the evidence, Wilson wanted to be, and was, his own Secretary of State. His relationship with Robert Lansing was a product of this desire; it neutralized Lansing's Cabinet performance and helped to remove the Cabinet from the center of activity in this area.[127]

Franklin Roosevelt's approach to delegation was noteworthy both for its technique and for its extent. He "was a great believer in alternatives. He rarely got himself sewed tight to a program from which there was no turning back." He sought always to preserve his discretionary "freedom of action." [128] He accomplished this by delegating responsibility and authority in small, vague, and sometimes conflicting fragments, to a point where only he could contribute consistency and direction. "Nothing whatever counted in the entire administration," said Henry Wallace, "except what went on inside FDR's head." [129] The result was an essentially unpatterned technique of administration. It resulted in fuzzy lines of responsibility, no clear chain of command, overlapping jurisdictions, a great deal of personal squabbling, and a lack of precision and regularity. It was, in short, a "fantastically complex administrative mechanism," so labelled by Henry Stimson who protested vigorously over its sometime sterilizing effect on Cabinet officers.[130]

In the field of foreign affairs, for example, Roosevelt confided to a friend that he felt it was necessary to be his own Secretaries of State, War, and Navy.[131] He did this by personal intervention and by delegating tasks to his own personal representatives and to others outside the direct chain of command. No Secretary of State with a different temperament and who was not as mild-mannered and patient as Cordell Hull could have suffered as much circumvention of his proper authority as Roosevelt's personal leadership in foreign affairs involved. First Raymond Moley and later Sumner Welles, as subordinates of Hull, were given direct lines of access to the White House. Each of them embarrassed and undercut Hull on numerous occasions — the most famous denouements coming at the London Economic Conference of 1933 and the Rio Conference of 1942. Furthermore, Roosevelt sent personal envoys on foreign missions (Hopkins, Harriman, Wallace, Hurley, Donovan, Davies) who consequently reported to him and not to the State Department. Some of our ambassadors, like William Bullitt, were encouraged to report directly to FDR rather than via State Department channels.[132] Hull was not taken to any of the meetings of the Big Three (in sharp contrast to Truman and Byrnes). The President handed over State Department functions to other departments, as when he authorized Henry Morgenthau to initiate conversations leading to the recognition of Russia.[133] The entire procedure irritated

Hull, who complained feelingly in his *Memoirs,* but he was able to console himself somewhat naively with the thought that things were not really as bad as they seemed.[134] Yet they clearly affected Hull's ability to contribute usefully to Cabinet discussions.

In domestic affairs, too, the technique was similar though the extent of delegation was greater. "He is bypassing me right and left," complained the Secretary of the Interior, whose grievance was shared especially by the Secretary of the Treasury.[135] When Roosevelt did delegate, it was common for him to do so in a trial and error way, dividing responsibility yet not basing his delegation on any preliminary job analysis. He might set up a two-headed program like work relief with Hopkins and Ickes, or institute two-headed agencies like the National Defense Advisory Commission. He set up other agencies in which there was no concentrated responsibility, like the War Production Board. He conceived of the CCC program and then delegated the details wholesale to a committee representing three separate departments. This method of delegation left jurisdictional boundaries to be mapped out by conquest or agreement. It promoted much "stimulating" inter-departmental conflict which could and did eventually land in his own lap.[136]

Neither Roosevelt nor Wilson harbored Coolidge's scruples against unofficial advisers, which helps to explain why Harry Hopkins and Colonel House performed so many important administrative functions. Both men remained outside of the formal hierarchy. Colonel House was offered a Cabinet position but declined.[137] Hopkins was made Secretary of Commerce for a while but, significantly, this coincided with the period when he was being built up as an independent figure, and when his influence with the President was least important. Each man served the President informally as buffer, communication line, sounding board, coordinator, listening post, and mouthpiece abroad.[138] Their activities affected the Hoover Commission's prescribed "clear line of command" and the Cabinet members' formal position as "chief assistants" or "chief lieutenants" of the Chief Executive.[139] In short, Hopkins and House performed some functions and provided some types of assistance that might be associated *a priori* with the Cabinet. Thus, to some degree, a President's working habits with respect to unofficial advisers do affect his Cabinet activity.

A final aspect of administrative behavior which has relevance to Cabinet activity concerns the exercise of the removal power. Here, as in the other areas discussed, the institutional prescriptions are broad, the expected patterns of behavior are few, and the opportunity for the exercise of personal presidential influence is correspondingly great. In the controlling Supreme Court decision of *Meyers v. United States*, the unimpeded legality as well as the administrative imperatives of the removal power were established by Chief Justice Taft, speaking as he was from both judicial and executive experience.[140] For a variety of reasons, however, Presidents have exercised this authority with extreme moderation. Where discretion does operate, the ultimate determination most often centers upon the nexus of loyalty, both personal and programmatic, which binds the two individuals involved. A decision to remove or not to remove will depend upon the limits of toleration which the participants place upon this relationship.

Franklin Roosevelt, for example, tolerated a greater amount of personal and programmatic "non-loyalty" than any of the other Presidents studied. When Harry Woodring was Secretary of War, he and his Assistant Secretary "were at swords' points all the time" [141] over policy decisions. Woodring was basically isolationist, while Louis Johnson, in company with the President, believed in pushing an armament program. As a result, Roosevelt instructed others to treat Johnson as if he were Secretary of War, bypassing Woodring.[142] War Department functions were allocated to the State and Treasury Departments for accomplishment.[143] Other Cabinet members (Ickes, Morgenthau, and Farley at least) were fully aware of the anomalous situation, called it "a public scandal . . . bringing no credit to the Administration,"[144] and recommended removal. Some put the argument squarely in terms of loyalty.[145] Roosevelt, however, would not fire his recalcitrant Cabinet official. He forestalled resignations and was almost unable to remove several other members who were totally ineffective or in whom he had no confidence; yet removal might have promoted cohesiveness, smoothed out working relationships, and it almost certainly would have lifted the morale of his Cabinet. By keeping the group intact he left it as a chain with several weak links.[146] Behavior such as this would seem to be some measure of a President's disregard for the Cabinet as a working team.

Calvin Coolidge's attitude was governed by a narrow and inflexible sense of propriety. When Harding died Coolidge proclaimed that it was "a sound rule" and "the duty" of the successor "to maintain the counsellors and policies of the deceased President."[147] Acting on the basis of this principle, he repeatedly declined to ask for the resignation of Harry Daugherty — in spite of the fact that Daugherty's presence was seriously damaging the prestige of his administration. He finally removed Daugherty when the situation had become absolutely intolerable, but he based his request for resignation purely on the grounds of legality.[148] Of the entire Harding Cabinet, only Daugherty was ever requested to leave, and none of those who resigned did so in protest. Coolidge's formalistic deference to a preceding President's Cabinet, with the indifference to personal allegiance inherent in such an attitude, does not demonstrate a very complete grasp of that group's potentialities as a flexible instrument of the President.

Harry Truman's reaction to his inherited advisers was strikingly different. He understood, as Coolidge had not, the essential principle that "every President must have a Cabinet of his own choosing" and that "when there is a change in administration, there are bound to be some changes in the Cabinet."[149] In six months time, six Cabinet positions had changed hands, whereas Coolidge did not reach that figure for five years. Discounting the differences in external conditions, it is clear that Coolidge and Truman did not place the same emphasis on personal loyalty. Truman's biographer notes his habitual use of the aphorism "politics is not a one-way street" to punctuate the idea of loyalty as the superlative human virtue. Its importance had probably been impressed upon him during his long apprenticeship in the political ranks.[150] He required a close loyalty, and he reciprocated in full measure when any of his subordinates (like Dean Acheson) were under fire from the outside.[151]

Whenever he generalized about the nature of his office, Truman stressed the idea of loyalty to his decisions.

I never allowed myself to forget that the final responsibility was mine. . . . I expected Cabinet officers to be frank and candid in expressing their opinions to me. At the same time I insisted that they keep me informed of the major activities of their departments in order to make certain that they supported the policy once I had made a decision. If a Cabinet member could not support the policy I had laid down, I tried to work out an understanding with him. But I could not permit, any more than any President can, such differences of opinion to be aired in public by a dissenting member of the Cabinet.[152]

It was within this context that he viewed the "resignations" of Secretaries Byrnes, Ickes, and Wallace. In none of these cases was removal related to the ability of the member involved. All turned on the question of loyalty, personal and programmatic seamlessly joined. An index to the strict construction which Truman placed on loyalty is the fact that whereas Harold Ickes' two resignations proffered to Roosevelt were quickly rejected, a similar "gesture" to Truman was summarily accepted.[153] Probably Truman's behavior indicates a more serious attention to his Cabinet as a developer of, in his words, "teamwork wisdom."

Presidential interpretations of the Presidency, receptivity to advice, kinds of advice accommodated, decision-making procedures, habits of delegation, use of the removal power — all these represent relevant areas in which the personal impact of the President on Cabinet activity may be examined. In no particular situation is there a one-to-one relationship beween presidential attitude and Cabinet behavior.

No attempt has been made here to predict which types of presidents will utilize their Cabinets most and how. For the person who wishes to develop such a calculus there are, perhaps, some clues in this section. For the more casual observer, there are some suggested areas into which he might probe in trying to explain the behavior of any given Cabinet at a given time. Ultimately, however, the students' task is not this simple. The President-Cabinet nexus is subject to the impingement of other forces. The presidential personality cannot be "the answer" to Cabinet activity because the President is only one relevant factor among many. His influence on the Cabinet is always crucial, but it is always being shaped, counter-balanced, and transformed by other influences in the American political system.

CHAPTER TWO

The Appointment Process

THE natural history of every Cabinet begins with its selection by the President-elect. At this time, more than at any other point in its life cycle, the Cabinet draws widespread attention and comment. The presidential decisions leading to the composition of a new "official family" are taken during the peak period of public interest which attends the national election campaign. As executive decisions go, they are preeminently concrete and visible. Among the earliest of presidential moves, they are treated as symbolic acts of considerable significance. Out of the quadrennial avalanche of commentary, there usually emerge two distinct attitudes which the bulk of interested Americans take toward Cabinet-making — attitudes which reflect the public's normal expectations about the over-all President-Cabinet relationship and about the potentialities of the Cabinet in action.

One view of Cabinet appointment stresses the President-oriented character of the event. On the implicit assumption that the Cabinet is of great importance to the President and that he exercises a tight control over its selection, the appointment decisions are treated as matters of the greatest moment. Weighty judgments are based on the outcome. The President-oriented view was stated this way by Professor Samuel Lindsay:

No single act of the President transcends in importance the appointment of his Cabinet. The country forms its judgment of his underlying purposes and theories of government, it takes his measure and draws more conclusions from this single act than it does from his platform, his campaign pledges, his inaugural address or his first message to Congress. It represents in a vivid way the President's concept of the essential, vital and controlling organization of the executive government.[1]

In one form or another, this view is certain to make its appearance at every selection period. During the pre-inaugural Cabinet-prediction sweepstakes, the attitude frequently reveals itself in the form of a corollary that since the Cabinet is so important to the President, one can surely predict its membership by drawing up a list of the most prominent men in American public life — from which list the President will, logically, choose.

The second approach to Cabinet appointment which enjoys considerable popularity is rather more process-oriented than President-oriented. Stated in extreme form, the view is that the whole selection process is a lottery-like business, with little rhyme and less reason. Widely shared is the general suspicion that the methods and the results of the decisions on Cabinet appointment are not logical or rational. As far as the President is concerned the tendency is to be sympathetic, on the assumption that there is really very little he can do about it. It is the whole haphazard, amorphous process which is to blame. Mr. Dooley's skeptical comment, made after William McKinley's election, is apposite.

> If 'twas one of the customs of this great republic of ours, for to appoint the most competent men for the places, he'd have a mighty small lot for to pick from. But, seein' as only them is eligible that are unfit he has the devils own time selectin'. . . . It may be hard for Mack, bein' new at the business, to select the right man for the wrong place. But I'm sure that he'll be advised by his friends, and from the lists of candidates I've seen he'll have no trouble in findin' timber.[2]

Devotees of the Dooley position can be counted upon to react with wry jokes about the number of splinters turned up during the search. More seriously, however, their viewpoint is reflected in the number of criticisms which assume that there is an objectively "right man" for each Cabinet position — and since this obviously "right man" was not selected, the selection process is faulty.

THE APPOINTMENT PROCESS 53

To the extent that there are elements of importance and of illogic in Cabinet appointment, the Dooley and the Lindsay viewpoints both have validity. It is the major aim of this chapter, however, to demonstrate the limits within which these views are applicable. With respect to the President-oriented approach, it becomes necessary not only to see him as the central figure in Cabinet recruitment, but also to understand the interplay of other factors which narrow down his area of discretion and make it impossible for him to exercise a tight control over selection. Concerning the process-oriented attitude, the problem is one of knowing what that process consists of. The appointment process has an explicable logic to it, within the framework of the American political system, that will be missed if judgment be rendered on the basis of a single criterion or a particular example. To anticipate a conclusion, a valid attitude toward Cabinet-making ought neither to expect too much of the President nor to view the process as political illogic. And, having taken this attitude, one ought to expect the Cabinet in action to be responsive to presidential influences and to non-presidential influences, both of which are registered in the selection of its members.

Cabinet appointment must be looked upon as a many-sided process, involving the interaction in time of several component variables. These variables have consistently affected selection since the Cabinet's beginnings. Random, unconnected observations about different Cabinets and examples of particular appointments must be forsaken for examination of uniformities and patterns. Key factors affecting Cabinet recruitment must be isolated and identified, and their interaction discussed in terms of an overall process of appointment. Five basic variables are involved. They are the presidential influence, the incentives and drawbacks of Cabinet office, the conditions of the time, the Cabinet norm, and the criteria of availability and balance. To a greater or lesser degree, these five factors are operative in the formation of every Cabinet.

THE PRESIDENT'S INFLUENCE

The President-elect or the President is obviously the central figure in the appointment process. His constitutionally grounded power of appointment formed one of the early bonds between him and his departmental advisers. Though the power is subject to the "advice and consent of the Senate," in practice that is hardly a limitation at all upon the ultimacy of the presidential decision. The Senate ordinarily extends him the courtesy of approving his selections. Its attitude is based on the recognition of the intimacy of this "official family." Only once during the period being investigated did the Senate refuse to approve a Cabinet nomination. Though the case is the rank exception and not the rule, it is nonetheless instructive.

Calvin Coolidge appointed a Michigan attorney, Charles Warren, to the post of Attorney General in 1927. One episode in Warren's background, his close association with the American Sugar Refining Company, or "The Sugar Trust," made the appointment especially odious to the progressive members of the President's own party. For them and for the Democrats, Warren was a stick with which to beat the President. Warren was alleged to be an unfit person to administer the anti-trust laws. The rhetoric of the struggle was in terms of the obligation of Senators to act according to their consciences and the constitution, as opposed to the President's right to have his own Cabinet.[3]

The orthodox theory of appointment was invoked by the Coolidge supporters: "We ought to leave the President a free choice and hold him responsible for the faithful execution of the laws. . . . I think the President is responsible for his Cabinet in a way in which he is not responsible for the other general officers of the government."[4] Opponents admitted that "it has been the practice to confirm without question the nominations by the President of the members of his Cabinet," but they claimed that this was an exceptional case.[5] In order to find firmer ground on which to stand, the opposition frequently raised the point that the Cabinet was only customary and that, whereas the Senate might not have any responsibility toward that group, it did have a clear responsibility where a federal line department was concerned. "The Attorney General," said Senator Robinson, "is an adviser of the President, but his more important and far-reaching duties have relation to every department and agent of the government and the public at large."[6] Warren was defeated on a tie vote 40–40. Coolidge resubmitted the nomination, and it was again rejected — this time 46–39. Coolidge's action was taken in an unfavorable set of circumstances to be sure, but the episode may have other lessons as well. A candidate for Attorney General cannot be a man who might be suspected of being "a special pleader for special interests" of any sort.[7] More generally, the Warren story points up the omnipresence of checks and balances, and of countervailing power. Although the President does operate in the appointment process with a free hand, he does so at the sufferance of the United States Senate.

If formal restrictions are ordinarily not worth reckoning with in presidential influence, other less institutionalized elements are. Most generally, as we have indicated, the presidential influence is affected by the impingement of the other variables upon it, but this is a matter of multi-factor analysis which must be postponed until the end of the discussion. More immediately, it is the President's personality, as it finds expression in particular attitudes toward the appointment process, which is a key variable in any ultimate calculation. Among the many desirable qualifications for Cabinet office, which ones will be most highly valued by a given President? What methods does he use in appointing people? Is he especially liable to be influenced by others in making his selections? With what kind of people does he usually surround himself? What uses is he likely to foresee for his Cabinet?

Woodrow Wilson was the only President to develop a coherent theory about the role of the Cabinet in our political system. In his early years, after the appearance of *Congressional Government* (1885), he felt that the great need was for "harmonious, consistent, responsible party government . . . and we can get it only by connecting the President as closely as may be with his party in Congress. The natural connecting link is the cabinet." [8] He felt that this kind of government could only be accomplished by making the Cabinet "The President's responsible party council," and by appointing to it "representative party men who have accredited themselves for such functions by long and honorable public service." [9]

In later years, impressed by the potentialities of the presidency for political leadership, Wilson's theory of the Cabinet changed. By the time he himself was put to the acid test, he described the Cabinet as "an executive, not a political body," for which the President should seek "men of the best legal and business gifts." Furthermore, he would rely on their advice because they were "representative citizens . . . and not because they are supposed to have had any intimate contact with politics or to have made a profession of public affairs." [10] This is a remarkable about-face in Wilson's own thinking. He constructed his Cabinet ideal first primarily in political terms and then in primarily administrative terms. In picking his own advisory group, he pursued his conception of the Cabinet members as executives handling the administration of the government.

Actually, Wilson's prime consideration in evaluating Cabinet choices was not a theory but a matter of personal temperament — a desire to have as his advisers people loyal to him personally. He told Robert Lansing that he had been appointed Secretary of State because "their minds ran together." [11] Wilson removed Lansing later, however, in favor of Bainbridge Colby, "someone whose mind will more willingly go along with mine." [12] To him this phrase meant more than a general sympathy of views. It meant a willingness to follow without deviation or dispute once the President had determined the course. Thus, when questioned about Colby's instability of opinion, Wilson replied: "At any rate, he is loyal." [13] Wilson's tendency to translate sincere official differences into personal feuds is of a piece with this hypersensitivity to loyalty.

Herbert Hoover, like Wilson, paid scant heed to party considerations. According to one of his secretaries, he "selected his key men with relatively little thought of politics." [14] (The results, as we saw earlier, reflect this.) He was interested primarily in the two elements of integrity and administrative ability. The Harding administration had rendered him especially sensitive to the first. This, added to his own experience and range of interests, led him naturally to focus more on executive ability and "the housekeeping of government" than any other factor. Hoover looked upon the government as "the greatest business on earth" and sought his Cabinet accordingly.[15] Warren Harding, on the other hand, was by temperament, by instinct, and by experience a regular party man; his appointments were heavily conditioned by the party environment. In his acceptance speech he assured his supporters, "I believe in party sponsorship in government. I believe in party government as distinguished from personal government. . . ." [16] In choosing his Cabinet, he leaned for advice on his partisan-minded associate Harry Daugherty, a man who considered that "civil service is a hindrance to the government," [17] and whose guiding principle of political action was, "I just play ball with the fellows on my team." [18]

Although all Presidents realize that the final voice in Cabinet selection is theirs, some do not carry this responsibility too weightily. It is a fixed certainty in the life of the President-elect that he will be deluged by advice from self-appointed Cabinet makers. Some, however, will be more influenced by outside suggestions than others.

Wilson's keen dislike, and indeed his incomplete comprehension, of patronage caused him to draw back from the job of appointing people. He did not play the game with acumen or relish. The task of gathering, sifting, and evaluating the mass of information fell by default to men who did — Joseph Tumulty and Colonel House. No one reached the initial Cabinet without the approval of the latter.[19] In view of this, House's wonderment at the whole procedure is significant. "The thing that impresses me is the casual way in which the President-elect is making up his Cabinet. I can see no end of trouble for him in the future unless he proceeds with more care."[20] Wilson's first offer for the Secretaryship of War was tendered to a Quaker.[21] He had never met his Secretary of the Interior until Franklin Lane introduced himself at the routine handshaking festivities following the inauguration.[22]

In marked contrast to Wilson's behavior was Franklin Roosevelt's more solitary approach to appointments. Meeting with his close political associates, he said that ". . . the members of my Cabinet will be members of my family — my official family. I don't want anybody naming a single one of them. . . ."[23] He understood the problem as Wilson did not. His choices were personal to a degree that the preceding Democratic president's had not been. Neither Raymond Moley nor James Farley exerted any influence, nor were they critically involved in the process. Both discussed it with Roosevelt and both conveyed messages to prospective candidates, but neither was invited to advise. They were told what the composition of the Cabinet was going to be.[24] Louis Howe had perhaps more influence (which is not saying much), but at least one of his favorite suggestions was turned down and one of whom he disapproved was appointed.[25] Interestingly enough, the fact that Roosevelt took an extraordinary personal interest in his Cabinet did not make it any less exempt from the overall unmethodical quality which worried Colonel House. Moley writes: "There was always casualness . . . there was neither a well-defined purpose nor underlying principle in the selection."[26]

The degree of personal interest which the President takes is a relevant factor but obviously not a controlling one in Cabinet-making. This is true, in turn, because the President is only partially responsible for the kind of Cabinet he gets.

THE INCENTIVES AND DRAWBACKS OF CABINET OFFICE

One very evident factor which limits the President's freedom of action is the push and pull of the incentives and, especially, the drawbacks involved in accepting a Cabinet post. The drawbacks are frequently so great that the President simply cannot get the men he wants. Four of Hoover's first choices promptly refused.[27] He indicated that the two compelling reasons were the "smearing and irresponsible attack" which accompanies public office, and the comparatively low salary. The former reason apparently motivated three of these men, at a time when the Republican progressives were particularly pugnacious. The acrimonious dispute over Charles Warren's confirmation was an experience within recent memory. Though Senate confirmation is rarely a hurdle in itself, it may be an unpleasant experience for the uninitiated. Apprehension on both scores caused Wilson to surrender one of his earliest personal choices and an obviously strong one — Louis D. Brandeis.[28]

Reluctance to accept financial sacrifices has kept many men from leaving private life. Some who later accepted hesitated for this reason. Some have left early because of it. Some have stayed till the end and left penniless. This condition militates against certain groups of people, and in favor of men of private means.[29]

Another substantial drawback is a feeling that there is relatively little opportunity to accomplish anything in the Cabinet. One man, a member of the ICC, expressed the sentiment admirably:

> I am doing just as big work and as satisfactory work as any member of the Cabinet. The work that a Cabinet officer chiefly does is to sign his name to letters or papers that other people write. There is very little constructive work to be done in any Cabinet office. . . . The glamour of intimate association with the President — the honor that comes from such a position — appeals to me. . . . Yet the position that I occupy is of so much usefulness that I do not want to change it.[30]

Jesse Jones, while head of the RFC, twice declined to accept Cabinet office for similar reasons. He accepted only when the job he was doing was incorporated into the Cabinet post.[31] Regarding the Secretaryship of Commerce, Herbert Hoover said: "If I take the post it will be only because I believe that Senator Harding will stand behind me in making a real Department of Commerce. . . . Unless this is done, I am not warranted in shifting my responsibility for relief work." [32]

Sometimes the prestige of Cabinet office is sufficient to allay other doubts, but even here there is a law of diminishing prestige within the Cabinet which makes some offices less desirable than others. This follows roughly the order of their establishment, which fixes the official hierarchical status. For instance, once Wilson agreed to invite Bryan, it would have been an insult had he been offered anything less than the "premiership" of the Cabinet, the office of Secretary of State. When feelers were sent to Henry Stimson regarding the prospects of his taking the Justice or State Department, he said he was interested only in the latter.[33] Cordell Hull took this same job after weighing in the balance the contribution to "international economic peace" he could make there as compared to the Senate.[34] Given this standard he could have accepted no other position. Some men are given a choice of seats as an inducement, but others are shunted from one portfolio to another, as Cabinet-making proceeds, with little discrimination.

A combination of elements — prestige, opportunity to do a constructive job, and others — operate to keep men in Congress from accepting Cabinet office. Senator Reed voiced a common congressional sentiment when he said of Senator Fall's departure from the Senate: "Fall astounded his associates . . . By stepping from his high place in the Senate to the subordinate position of the Secretary of the Interior. The job he took is filled with the drudgery of details and in no respect compares with the dignity and importance of the office of a Senator." [35] More than this, there is a high rate of rotation and not much stability to Cabinet office. Once out of the Senate or House it may be hard to return. Since 1920, only one Cabinet member (Clinton Anderson) has come from Congress and returned to it. Indeed, he is the only man to go from the Cabinet to Congress during the last twenty-five years. The Cabinet is more often than not the end of a public career, a condition in which symptom and cause become wrapped up in a vicious circle. Even if a man should return to the Congress, the seniority rule will rob him of key committee posts although his service in the executive branch may have equipped him with extraordinary experience. This has happened to several men — to Carter Glass in the period studied. When Franklin Roosevelt eyed the Senate for possibilities, some were eliminated because he felt he needed them where they were, and at least four others who were asked declined.[36] In view of the patent desirability of having some men with the legislative outlook in the Cabinet, the drawbacks create a serious problem.

Quite apart from the loss of particular individuals, the effect of repeated refusals may be to make the eventual choice a haphazard one. If Cabinet posts remain unfilled as inauguration day approaches, less controllable forces are introduced, giving the appointment process its closest approximation to Mr. Dooley's grab bag image. When Roosevelt failed to get his first choice as Secretary of the Interior, he hastily appointed a man whom he had met only a few hours before, because "I liked the cut of his jib." Harold Ickes admitted that it was a "miracle." "Accident, I certainly was." [37]

When Woodrow Wilson's first choice for Secretary of War refused, the President called his Secretary Joseph Tumulty to ask for a suggestion.

I told him [writes Tumulty] that I was anxious to see a New Jersey man occupy a place at his cabinet table and we discussed the various possibilities over the phone, but without reaching any definite conclusion. I informed the President that I would suggest the name of someone within a few hours. I then went to the library in my home in New Jersey and looking over the Lawyers' Diary I ran across the name of Lindley Garrison, who at the time was Vice-Chancellor of the State of New Jersey. Mr. Garrison was a resident of my home town and although I had only met him casually and had tried a few cases before him, he had made a deep impression on me as a high type of equity.[38]

Garrison was invited and accepted. In neither of the two cases here was the President able to act with forethought or on the basis of any compiled information. Roosevelt had no way of foreseeing the lucky success that he was to have with his "grab," nor could Wilson expect the unlucky incompatibility which he had with his.

THE CONDITIONS OF THE TIME

A third relevant factor in the appointment process is the external conditions of the time, or the climate of opinion of the period. The conditions of the time may dictate that certain Cabinet positions are going to be the most important and most publicly prominent, leading, in turn, either to a more intensive search to fill the place properly or to indifference toward it. Depending on the circumstances, reluctant men might be induced to assume office. No one, for instance, could look forward to accomplishing constructive tasks in the Labor Department under Harding or the Commerce Department under Roosevelt. On the other hand, whoever accepted the Treasury under Wilson or Agriculture under Roosevelt was certain to have large opportunities. In time of international crisis the President may want to assume a different relation to his Secretary of State than otherwise, and this might affect his choice. If one political party has been without power for a long period, it is limited as to the number of nationally recognized individuals it can call to office. This may affect the "big men" rating of a Cabinet, as it did in 1912, and to a somewhat lesser extent in 1952.

The expectations and the mood of the public enter the picture, too. Do they want a period of retrenchment and "normalcy," or one of "bold experimentation"? Or, more accurately, what will the public allow to be done without excessive complaint? The attachment in the public mind of the Hoover administration to big business, and to the depression, placed real limits on the composition of the first Roosevelt Cabinet. FDR was studious in his avoidance of anything remotely connected with such firms as J. P. Morgan.[39] By contrast, "the times" of 1932 simply would not have permitted Roosevelt to appoint the kind of Cabinet which was selected twenty years later by Dwight Eisenhower — a Cabinet dominated by businessmen, industrialists, and corporation lawyers, five of whom were millionaires.[40]

By 1952, the public was not unreceptive to a "business cabinet." It was not unreceptive to the virtues of this kind of Cabinet — thrift, frugality, economy, efficiency — nor to its aims to reduce spending, eliminate deficits, control inflation, and lower taxes. During his campaign General Eisenhower pledged to bring the "best business brains" to Washington,[41] and he did. The Secretary of the Interior, Douglas McKay, characterized the administration as "an administration representative of business and industry."[42] Henry Ford 2nd wrote, "In the eyes of people everywhere, the new administration will be regarded as a representative of business thinking and responsibility."[43] For his Secretary of Defense, the President-elect eagerly chose Charles E. Wilson, President of General Motors and the highest paid corporation executive in the United States. "Who would you rather have in charge of that," President Eisenhower asked later, "some fellow that never did anything or a successful businessman? I got the head of the biggest company I could find. . . ."[44] Under other conditions, this approach would not have been warmly received, as Mr. Wilson himself implied in his confirmation hearings. "The people," he said, "are not afraid of businessmen like me *right now*."[45]

THE CABINET NORM

In evaluating new Cabinet personnel, praise and criticism are usually meted out by measuring the actual group against a Cabinet norm — against a notion of what the personnel requirements of a Cabinet ought to be. Whereas the incentives and drawbacks of Cabinet office and the condition of the times exercise a permissive or negative effect on Cabinet selection, the Cabinet norm imparts a more positive direction. Though shadowy in formulation, the frequent articulation of an ideal testifies to its existence and to the ethical supervision which it exercises over participant and observer alike.

The norm has two components. First, Cabinet members as individuals should possess certain ideal qualities in order to do their particular jobs well. This involves an idea of a Cabinet of individuals equipped with political and/or administrative talents for their specific jobs. As Theodore Roosevelt put it, "For a Cabinet place, the man should if possible be eminently fit for the administrative work of his department, but also if possible a party leader of weight."[46] Secondly, the Cabinet should be able to work together to achieve teamwork. This aspect of the norm refers to the ability and the willingness (assuming a meaningful opportunity) of the Cabinet as a group to produce a co-operative organizational product. The ideal Cabinet, then, is made up of men who are eminently fitted to perform special tasks, yet these individuals must cohere as a unit if the name Cabinet is to have more than honorific significance.

An explication reveals what most commentators do not take time to worry about, that instead of one internally consistent norm, there is a norm with two major components. The components are not necessarily compatible and, in fact, often are not. The *Christian Science Monitor*'s lead story on the Eisenhower Cabinet was headlined: "IKE'S CABINET CHOICES MARK TEAM OF SHREWD STAUNCH INDIVIDUALISTS."[47] The crucial question as to the effect of "shrewd staunch individualists" on the "team" was not raised and probably not considered. Three days later, the same paper printed a page one feature article entitled, "Quality and Balance in Ike's Cabinet Choices."[48] There followed a discussion of individual "quality," without any further mention of team "balance." The clear implication is either that the team aspect does not matter or that qualified individuals, i.e., "the right men for the jobs," will *ipso facto* make a good team. Treatment of the Cabinet norm in this confusingly superficial way blurs a distinction which would provide a more sensitive evaluative device, and provide a clue to one of the real problem areas of the Cabinet in action.

Comments on the group aspect of the Cabinet norm are no less shallow. Observers often feel obliged to pass judgment on the possibilities of teamplay. "A Cabinet must be judged first of all . . . from the point of view of its promise as a *tout ensemble* or a team." [49] Such commentaries usually close by assuring the public that no problems are involved. "My judgment, therefore, is that the Cabinet will function well, that it contains all the necessary parts to make it a homogeneous whole. . . ." [50] Typically, this kind of statement is accompanied by extravagant schemes detailing the "contributions" of each member to the "perfectly balanced whole." A little duty or "peculiarly significant role" can be allocated to the most inconspicuous or little known member, leaving the reader with a "can't miss" feeling about "the team." These pictures of perfection are more amusing than accurate, but their frequency attests to the presence of that part of the ideal devoted to the Cabinet as a working organization.

The Cabinet norm is always in the consciousness of those who are involved in the appointment process. This is especially true of the President, as the following referencees to it demonstrate.

WILSON: "I wish to find the very best men for my cabinet regardless of consequences. I do not forget the party as an instrument of government, and I do not wish to do violence to it. But I must have the best men in the nation." [51]

HARDING: "Three things are to be considered in the selection of a Cabinet. First, there is the man's qualification for public service. This is the most important consideration of all. Second, there is the attitude of the public concerning men under consideration. Third, there is the political consideration. As to that — well, this is going to be a Republican Cabinet you may count on that, and you may be sure it will be a Cabinet of which the whole country may be proud. You can put that in black type and a box." [52]

HOOVER: "I had to choose ten men who represented different parts of the country, who were men of public esteem, and who had proved by their success as administrators that they could conduct a great department in the greatest business on earth." [53]

Newspapermen traveling with the Eisenhower campaign train in 1952 noted that he invariably made one promise to his listeners — a promise related to the Cabinet norm. A typical statement of what observers labelled "the pledge" was: "I pledge to you that [for] every single man and woman brought to Washington to serve in the Executive Departments . . . the single qualification will be merit, dedication, loyalty." [54]

With respect to the group aspect, too, every President professes a desire to obtain a congenial, cooperative Cabinet. President Eisenhower's emphasis on "the team" is highly publicized and may be revealing, but it is not unique.

Warren Harding looked for men who would "associate with each other in effective teamwork . . . fit together, work together, and respect each other's work." [55] Franklin Roosevelt would say to Miss Perkins, when she suggested Cabinet possibilities, "I just don't think I want him around. I don't feel easy about him. I think there would be trouble over that man." [56] When Ickes was appointed the President-elect said to him, "Mr. Ickes, you and I have been speaking the same language for the past twenty years and we have the same outlook." [57] Both of these remarks reflect Roosevelt's search for congeniality, for agreeable personal working relations.

The limitations upon the Cabinet norm as the primary source of positive direction for the selection process are severe. It is by no means a self-executing proposition. Even granting the possibility of internal consistency, once interpretation and articulation begin there is little likelihood that any two people will agree on its substance. Such formulations as "the best man for the job" and "the best possible Cabinet team" possess an abstractness and an infinity which make them practically useless as standards. Since agreement on more specific terms would be hard to get, they are allowed to persist, and they permit almost any selection method and sanction almost any result. The Cabinet norm is easily compromised, refined, modified, or forgotten when the impact of the other variables is felt upon it.

THE CRITERIA OF AVAILABILITY AND BALANCE

A final factor in the appointment process is composed of the criteria of availability and balance. These criteria, when broken down into their component elements, constitute the most narrow, and hence the most controlling, guide lines for Cabinet selection. But considered in terms of the relation between availability and balance, or the interaction among their component elements, or the impact of the other four factors on availability and balance, this fifth variable is not a very rigidly controlling one.

A prospective Cabinet member, like a preconvention presidential hopeful, must be "available." He must possess certain qualifications which interested persons attach to the position; he must not have, in his personal background, characteristics which might automatically disqualify him as a choice. Availability has both positive and negative implications: a Secretary of Agriculture must come from the West, but a westerner without a direct association with farming is automatically ineligible. Taken together, the positive and negative aspects enable a person to qualify as a potential Cabinet member. "Availability" is, then, simply an entrance requirement which gets a person to the starting line in the race for one or more particular jobs. It narrows down the field of prospective appointees as a whole and it limits the possibilities for each particular Cabinet post. Thus, availability operates to restrict the channels of access to the positions of power which the secretaryships represent.

Since the Cabinet, unlike the Chief Executive, is plural, the analogy of "availability" is insufficient. It must be coupled with a pluralistic consideration in the case of the Cabinet, i.e., "balance." Whereas availability pertains only to the qualifications of the particular individual, balance is a group attribute. Balance refers to the extent to which the pluralism and diversity of American society are reflected by a similar pluralism within the Cabinet. The Secretary of Agriculture may have to be a westerner, but an entire Cabinet of westerners would violate the dictates of balance. Indeed, it is imperative that all the Cabinet members do not possess the same qualifications. In a dream world, perhaps, every candidate would possess a full complement of all the virtues and talents in suitable quantities. Since they do not, there is usually an attempt to sprinkle ingredients of each in concocting the Cabinet dish, thus achieving balance. The precise composition of the balanced Cabinet is in each case affected by other factors as well. The Eisenhower Cabinet achieved balance within a far different set of circumstances than that of Roosevelt. Availability operates within the limits prescribed by balance; both exist, in part, as a function of the other factors involved in the appointment process.

a. The Components of Availability

Availability can be considered in five general categories: party, personal loyalty, geography, socio-economic factors, and specialized talents.

Typically, the entire Cabinet is of the same political party as the President. This is one convention settled in Washington's time and honored in the observance ever since. The few exceptions serve only to prove the rule. Many deviations from this norm are more apparent than real, involving men whose ideas and sympathies obviously do not coincide with their partisan labels. William Mitchell in the Hoover Cabinet[58] and Harold Ickes and Henry Wallace in the succeeding ones were clearly in the process of changing their party affiliations. The appointments of Henry Stimson and Frank Knox, Republicans, to the Cabinet in 1940 were of a slightly different order. They did not change their partisan affiliations, and Stimson has described their status: "a Republican doing non-partisan work for a Democratic President because it related to international affairs, in which I agreed and sympathized with his policies."[59] The appointments had the advantage of giving a coalition tinge to the Cabinet at a time and in a field where broad support from the nation was desirable. Martin Durkin's selection as a partisan Democrat in the Eisenhower Cabinet, and in a field where he was not in basic sympathy with the ideas of the rest of the administration, was the clearest recent violation of the party criterion. His early resignation is ample testimony to the difficulty of achieving bipartisanship or supra-partisanship at the Cabinet level.

Once members of the opposition party have been eliminated from the range of possible selectees, availability in terms of party can be given positive application. Cabinet office may be a political reward, as was Roosevelt's gift of the Secretaryship of Commerce to former Vice-President Henry Wallace.[60] More often, it requires that some important service has been rendered in the party organization. The Postmaster Generalship was created originally to provide a place for a party manager at the highest levels of government, and the tradition has been continued. The Postmaster General is nearly always a person who has held a high level post in the party — most frequently, Chairman of the National Committee. Will Hays in the Harding Cabinet, James Farley and Frank Walker in the Roosevelt Cabinet, Robert Hannegan in the Truman Cabinet, and Arthur Summerfield in the Eisenhower Cabinet were all chairmen of their party's National Committee when they were appointed as Postmaster General. Hays, Farley, and Walker held the two offices concurrently.[61]

The job as head of a businesslike service organization whose policy decisions are not particularly crucial is the easiest in the Cabinet. The Postmaster General has time to devote to the handling of party patronage, and most of them do this in addition to handling their administrative duties. They are in the Cabinet as members of the party organization and will continue to concern themselves with its problems. They are in a position to advise the President on matters of party management. Their presence in the advisory group attests to the inevitable impingement of organized partisanship upon Cabinet decision-making. Even when he has not been national chairman of the party, the Postmaster General is likely to be selected for his political background. Woodrow Wilson wanted "at least one thoroughgoing politician" for his Cabinet and he found him in Congressman Albert Burleson, whom he made Postmaster General.[62] The same description would apply to Postmasters General Harry New in the Harding Cabinet, who was a former Senator, Hubert Work in the Coolidge Cabinet, who later became Chairman of the Republican National Committee, and Walter Brown in the Hoover Cabinet, who was a former Congressman. Of all the men in the period, only career official Jesse Donaldson in the Truman Cabinet disrupts the regular pattern.

If a party politician lands in the Cabinet at some other post, it is likely to be that of Attorney General. This was true of Harry Daugherty, Harding's campaign manager; Senator Homer Cummings, who was also a former Democratic National Chairman, in the Roosevelt Cabinet; J. Howard McGrath, Democratic National Chairman, in the Truman Cabinet; and Herbert Brownell, top official in three Republican campaigns, in the Eisenhower Cabinet. The extra qualification that the Attorney General be a lawyer is usually not a great barrier if the President chooses to make such an appointment, since the great majority of top level party leaders are lawyers by profession.

There can be no doubt but what a campaign donation is a contribution to availability as well. A crass money *quid pro quo* is probably never the case; in all of the outstanding instances of members who donated large sums of money to the party, there are additional reasons for their appointment too.[63] It is safe to say that, however true it might be of lesser offices, no man can buy his way into the President's Cabinet.

Every President searches for Cabinet members who will be personally loyal — in the abstract. Yet they do not place a uniform construction upon it in the appointment process. For some, personal loyalty is intertwined with party loyalty. Thus, for Franklin Roosevelt preconvention support was a criterion of availability. Nine out of the ten whom he appointed had been "for Roosevelt before Chicago." On the other hand, Wilson had only four men who fell into this category, Eisenhower four, Hoover two, and Harding one.[64] For Wilson, personal loyalty was gauged by the readiness of an individual to follow his lead without undue questioning. Extreme personal loyalty can be identified at the point where it least requires official sanction — intimate friendship. Harry Daugherty is the only outstanding example of a friend to whom the president owed a great deal. However, Ray Lyman Wilbur was a close personal associate of Hoover, Henry Morgenthau and Harry Hopkins were to Roosevelt, and John Snyder was to Harry Truman. Wilson offered Colonel House his choice of Cabinet seats but he declined, leaving Wilson with no really intimate personal friends and several members whom he did not even know.[65] Eisenhower's situation, in this respect, was very much the same.

President James Monroe formulated the geographical criterion long ago when he said that his Cabinet "should be taken from the four sections of the Union, the East, the Middle, the South and the West. . . . Each part of the Union would be gratified by it, and the knowledge of local details and means which would be thereby brought into the Cabinet would be useful."[66] If an executive department has its functions and its clientele concentrated in a distinct area of the country, interested people in that area expect that a Cabinet member will represent their interests. "I can go scarcely anywhere in the West without coming into contact with my own jurisdiction as Secretary of the Interior," wrote Harold Ickes. "Everywhere there are parks, reclamation projects or public lands, or Indians or what not."[67] Thus, residence in the area becomes an essential qualification. As Senator Edwin Johnson of Colorado expressed it, "Out in the West we have felt, ever since the Department of the Interior was created, that the office should be filled by a Western man . . . , a man who understands at firsthand the problems of the West." [68] This view has been honored since 1912, with the exception of an in-term appointee from Virginia who served at the end of the Wilson administration for less than a year. The same sectional qualification pertains for the Secretary of Agriculture, since the heart of America's farmland is in the West. Since 1912, every man in that position has come from the West with the exception of one in-term appointee from West Virginia who served only a few months.[69] Iowa leads as the state which has produced the most Secretaries of Agriculture — three out of eleven since 1912. California and Illinois have furnished the most Secretaries of the Interior — four out of eleven since 1912. Sectional interests are loosely defined, and the sectional requirements of availability are satisfied in these two cases if a man resides somewhere in the West — Middle or Far.

Actually the geographic criterion is usually intertwined with socio-economic factors.[70] A form of economic geography prevails in the selection of two other department heads. The Secretary of Commerce and the Secretary of Labor normally come from industrialized states. Only Hoover's Secretary of Labor and Roosevelt's Secretaries of Commerce provide deviations from the pattern. This irregularity is perhaps one index of the indifference with which each of these Presidents regarded the office involved.

A socio-economic rationale is built into three of the executive departments in a way that the sectional rationale is not. The Departments of Agriculture, Commerce, and Labor have as their clientele the three largest segments of our economy — farmers, businessmen, and workers. Each one of these groups is concerned with the development of the organization which serves it. Distinct groups in the population thus become protagonists in supporting the interests of a particular department.[71] They are organized to an extent that purely sectional groupings are not. They pursue their overall goals, i.e., the promotion and protection of their interests, by working through any channels of access to those who make public policy. Since they do have a direct and continuing interest in the decisions which are made by the department head, he represents one point of access, and the groups involved try to influence those Cabinet selections. In the appointment process, their efforts are directed at refining the criteria of availability so as to bring them within a desired frame of reference.

The Farm Bureau Federation, the National Grange, and the National Farmers' Union engage in an active effort to help write the specifications for the Secretary of Agriculture. They feel that a model Secretary of Agriculture, one best suited to represent the farmer constituency, will have in his background some actual farm experience. Thus, Harding and Cox each promised farm audiences, during the campaign of 1920, that he would appoint a "dirt farmer" as Secretary of Agriculture.[72] Usually, the farm organizations become more involved than this. Before he appointed his Secretary of Agriculture, Calvin Coolidge solicited suggestions from the Farm Bureau, Grange, Farmers' Union, and the American Livestock Association.[73] Some such form of communication, formal or informal, solicited or not, between the Cabinet makers and the organized group interests precedes most appointments to these offices. Yet it should be realized that group interest is not always tantamount to influence. A few years after Coolidge had exhibited such deference, Herbert Hoover selected a Secretary of Agriculture who had never lived on a farm, and selected him without deferring to the desires of the farm groups.[74]

Organized labor has sought to exercise its influence in the appointment of "labor's voice in the cabinet," the position it helped bring into existence. In fact, according to the orthodox "Union theory" of the Department, "the crucial fact . . . is the attitude of the Secretary."[75] Early in the history of the Department of Labor, a tradition seemed to be established whereby its Secretary was a union man. This was true of the first two, William B.

Wilson and James J. Davis, though the latter was a wealthy man who had kept up his early membership in the Amalgamated Iron and Steel Workers Union. Wilson, a former official of the United Mine Workers, was clearly an AFL choice. When he was a congressman, the AFL had intervened actively to promote his selection as Chairman of the House Labor Committee, a position he held for a term before becoming the first Secretary of Labor.[76] While on the committee, he had been "the man most active in securing the passage of the organic act" setting up the Labor Department.[77] In 1928, Herbert Hoover's choice for the job was his campaign labor adviser, William N. Doak, vice-president of the Railway Trainmen's Union. His selection ran into the bitter opposition of William Green, president of the AFL. Green suggested John L. Lewis, or at least someone from the AFL which, he said, "is regarded as the labor movement." Hoover demurred to the veto power of the AFL and asked Secretary Davis to remain in the new Cabinet. Davis, writes Hoover, was "good at keeping labor quiet."[78] When Davis resigned later to run for the Senate, Doak was appointed.[79] Thus an AFL tradition was broken but the criterion of availability regarding union membership remained.

In 1932, the AFL and William Green supported the head of the International Teamsters' Union, Dan Tobin, for the Roosevelt Cabinet. But the President-elect, arguing that unorganized as well as organized labor should be represented, appointed a woman, Frances Perkins, the New York State Industrial Commissioner. Her selection was opposed by most of organized labor.[80] In 1940, Wendell Willkie tried to appeal to the unions by making a campaign promise that "I will appoint a Secretary of Labor directly from the ranks of organized labor."[81] By this time, the split in the labor movement had complicated the problem, and the next two Secretaries were chosen from outside labor's ranks. After that, a union member did not serve until Martin Durkin, president of the International Union of Plumbers and Pipe Fitters (AFL), was appointed to the Eisenhower Cabinet. His service was short-lived and a union member has not been appointed since. With the exception of Miss Perkins, organized labor has not been unfavorably disposed toward any of the non-union appointees, even though they were not consulted — as in the case of Secretary Schwellenbach.[82] Perhaps one explanation of the more recent use of the criterion of union membership is related to the condition of the parties. Republican presidents are moved to appoint a union member as a method of wooing a hostile labor movement; Democratic presidents, whose party policies have been more favorable to organized labor, do not feel impelled to make gestures involving the Secretaryship of Labor. In any case, organized labor does exercise and will continue to exercise a surveillance over the appointment of the Secretary, thus helping to influence availability.

A final category of availability is that of special individual capabilities. It can be divided into political and administrative capabilities — not a distinct, but an analytically useful division. The political talent most necessary in a Cabinet member is the ability to get along in a public environment, where persuasion and compromise are the methods and the conflict of interested groups provides the setting. Especially is this so with respect to congressional relations, on which the survival of the Cabinet member literally depends. Prior experience in this area can be of great value to the individual himself and to the President as well. The administrative talent, or the executive talent, is equally important in a Cabinet member. Each department is a huge organization, requiring managerial ability at the top. Previous experience of a specialized nature, i.e., in diplomacy for the Secretary of State, in banking for the Secretary of the Treasury, may be assessed as a part of this talent. The idea of executive ability, perhaps including specialized experience, bulks largest of all in the Cabinet norm. This is the yardstick used by most people when they praise an appointee as "best man for the job."

William Jennings Bryan was chosen for the Wilson Cabinet because of a superior political talent. Three times the Democratic candidate for President, he had a greater claim to appointment on the basis of party service than any other Democrat. He was not a friend of Wilson's, although he had swung the tide toward him at Baltimore. Wilson, on the other hand, was not one to be persuaded by the nature or extent of prior party service, and his readiness to appoint "all irregular party men" was of great concern to Colonel House. Furthermore, Wilson did not believe Bryan was fitted for the Secretaryship in question. What convinced him was Bryan's party influence with relation to the projected legislative program. Bryan, he realized, would be more helpful and less damaging inside the official family than out. Or, in the rationalization of Mr. Dooley, "I'd rather have him close to me bosom than on me back." [83] Since it represented a conscious concession to partisan expediency, Wilson did not make the appointment with confidence. He was so hesitant and worried about this departure from his standards that he repeatedly called Colonel House to inquire if he "still held" to his advice that Bryan be appointed.[84]

"You know," Warren Harding once said, "before I was elected President, I thought the chief pleasure of it would be to give honors and offices to old friends — I thought that was the one big personal satisfaction a President would get. But you know, you can't do that when you're President of the United States; you have to get the best man." [85] If Wilson, whose predilection was for administrators, ended up appointing an eminently available party politician like Bryan, it is not surprising that Harding, who was predisposed toward party politicians, should appoint a man recognized for his great executive ability.

In Harding's case, the man was Herbert Hoover, wartime Relief Director and Food Administrator. Harding did not know Hoover well and he sent Daugherty to scout reports on Hoover's standing, which proved to be low with the organization men of the Senate. Harding wrote back to his messenger that while he did not wish to quarrel with the Senators, it was his judgment that ultimately counted.

I do hold him in the very highest esteem and think his appointment would appeal to the cordial approval of the country. The more I consider him the more do I think well of him. . . . Of course, I shall do nothing in the matter until I have an opportunity to see you again and get such information as you have to offer. . . . I think it is fair to say, however, that the opposition of a number of men mentioned in your letter does not very deeply impress me.[86]

To Senators Penrose and Knox, who proposed Mellon but were blocking Hoover, Harding put the proposition, "Hoover and Mellon or no Mellon!" Thus a man of exceptional executive capability was appointed. Measured against Bryan and Hoover, most Cabinet members are men of mediocre talents when they are chosen, and the effort to paint them otherwise is a part of the mythology of public commentary.

b. *The Components of Balance*

Availability operates within the limits prescribed by balance. Availability is an individual matter; balance is a composite or group matter. A balanced Cabinet is one in which a diversity of interests and talents are represented. The areas of importance are much the same as we have discussed — party, geography, socioeconomic factors, and special capabilities — but here the Cabinet is surveyed as a whole for the way in which it meets the test of top-level representation for as many relevant interests as possible.

Contrary to common understanding, balance is not the same as teamwork. Balance is strictly a drawing-board concept; teamwork refers to the Cabinet in action. The two ideas are related, since a Cabinet team cannot be fashioned out of men with the same virtues and vices any more than a football team can be composed of eleven quarterbacks or eleven centers. The idea of balance will make teamwork possible, but its achievement by no means guarantees the realization of teamwork. A search for balance may yield a pacifist politician Bryan and a militarist administrator Garrison, a personal friend Hopkins and a stranger Ickes, an aggressive McAdoo and a modest Baker, an expert farmer Harry Wallace and an expert engineer Hoover, a conservative

Jones and a liberal Henry Wallace, a business leader Weeks and a labor leader Durkin. Each of these well-balanced Cabinet twosomes engaged in a substantial amount of personal feuding and/or policy disagreement. They failed to achieve a result in terms of teamwork commensurate with their promise in terms of balance.

Some Presidents have utilized the appointment process as a means of ameliorating the intra-party factionalism which poses a constant threat to its unity and its energy. They attempt to knit the party together by selecting representatives of the various factions, thus arranging a party coalition in the Cabinet to reflect the party coalition outside the Cabinet. A Cabinet balanced in terms of party may mean increased support for the President's legislative program. Warren Harding offered posts to both of the men he defeated for the nomination,[87] but neither Wilson nor Roosevelt did. Roosevelt was pointedly allergic to his pre-Chicago opponents.[88] Both men, however, made appointments which pleased other factions of their party, selections like Cordell Hull, a personal supporter of Roosevelt's. Coolidge, plagued by the progressive wing of his party, did not try to placate them or harness their energies by a Cabinet appointment.[89] Hoover, confronted with the same difficulty, made one halfhearted attempt to do this.[90] Eisenhower sought the advice of his defeated rival, appointed at least one of Senator Taft's choices, and selected others favorable to him.[91] Probably the most one can say now is that the President's own views on party politics, and the emphasis he places on personal rather than party attachment, will be controlling.

The purpose of a geographically balanced Cabinet is to give a form of representation to all of the important sections of the country. The administration does not gain any more friends by picking a man from Illinois than it loses by not honoring a candidate from Missouri, but whichever the choice, interested people in the Midwest are satisfied that they have a representative at the Cabinet level to bespeak their interests. And Cabinet members recognize and service their sectional constituencies, regardless of their department. Thus Secretary of War George Dern, from Utah, frequently discussed the problems of the beet sugar industry in the Roosevelt Cabinet meetings — problems of the West and not of the War Department.[92]

The more important a state is politically, the more apt it is to secure Cabinet representation. No Cabinet is without a member from New York. Illinois, Ohio, and Pennsylvania rank close behind. The President's home state will ordinarily have at least one, but should not have too many. Aside from this, most Cabinets have a representative from New England and one from the Far West. When they do not, it is made a matter for comment, as when Governor Dewey in his 1944 campaign called the attention of the West Coast to the fact they lacked representation in the Roosevelt Cabinet.[93] Truman moved to correct this in one of his first appointments — Lewis Schwellenbach from Washington. The Secretaryships of Agriculture and Interior assure the West of two representatives, but this is never all that they receive. In fact, when as few as three (Roosevelt's Cabinet) members are from the West, the Cabinet is considered quite unorthodox. Most Democratic Cabinets will have at least one member from the South. Wilson and Roosevelt each had three in their original Cabinets, and Harry Truman appointed three when the opportunity presented itself.[94] The Republicans, without electoral support from the South, have neglected it in their Cabinets. Harding and Coolidge appointed none; Hoover's original Cabinet contained none, though he later selected one (William Doak of Virginia); Eisenhower recognized the South for its electoral backing with the appointment of Mrs. Hobby of Texas. Thus, geographical balance is intertwined with political considerations.

Since the combination of administrative and political talent in any one individual is rare indeed, the President compensates for it by seeking a balanced group. In every Cabinet, above and beyond the former party official who handles patronage, there will be an individual who has had congressional experience.

Wilson had four former members of Congress, three of them from the most recent membership of the House of Representatives. Harding selected two former Congressmen and two Senators, one of whom was in office at the time. The Coolidge Cabinet always contained at least one man with congressional experience, though not one of Coolidge's own appointees was of such a category. Herbert Hoover's original group contained two former Congressmen, but not a single person from the most recent legislature. Roosevelt took two members of his Cabinet from the Senate and another was a former Senator. Out of Truman's first six appointments, two were former Representatives, one was a Representative, and one was a former Senator. The Eisenhower Cabinet was the only one in the twentieth century without a single member who had been elected to Congress. (Two of its members had served small bits as appointees in the Senate.) It was criticized sharply on this score — a lack of balance. Alfred M. Landon said that this lack of balance was the administration's "only real weakness." The Cabinet, he said, was "unpleasantly reminiscent" of the Hoover Cabinet — long on executive ability, but short on "political savvy." [95]

By selecting some individuals for their political and others for their executive capabilities, the President automatically achieves a kind of occupational balance. If he heeds the views of organized interest groups, he will appoint to three of the Secretaryships men experienced in and partial to the fields of agriculture, business, and labor. There is at least one lawyer in the Cabinet and usually more. In all of these ways, then, the Cabinet will probably achieve socio-economic balance without a concentrated effort to produce it. If a Cabinet threatens, however, to be excessively weighted toward one socio-economic group, the President will attempt to remedy it.

An instructive example of one such attempt was Eisenhower's selection of Martin Durkin as Secretary of Labor. With the exception of Durkin, the Cabinet which he selected was dominated by socially and economically conservative men. All spoke for or were in close sympathy with the business-industry-manufacturing point of view. Most of them were wealthy men. They were all Republicans and all Protestants. Observers agreed that they were men "whose business and economic background promise a coherent, relatively homogeneous outlook on the conservative side." [96] From a purely socio-economic standpoint this was not a particularly well balanced group. Durkin's credentials presented the sharpest kind of contrast. He was president of the AFL Plumbers and Pipe Fitters Union, a life-long union man whose views on labor legislation were widely divergent from the rest of the Cabinet. Politically, he was an ardent Democrat. His religious affiliation was Roman Catholic. So at variance was this choice with every orthodox expectation that it was labeled "an incredible appointment" by the leading member of the President's party in Congress. One cannot know, but the evidence is certainly great that the Durkin selection was an attempt to widen the socio-economic base of the Cabinet. In terms of economic background, social philosophy, political affiliation, and religious belief, Mr. Durkin was all the balance that the Eisenhower Cabinet had. This quixotic attempt at one man balance was simply too much for any individual to bear. Durkin was a "plumber in a group of millionaire businessmen," "the poor relation at the Cabinet table," "a square peg in a round hole." "He felt frustrated from the start in everything he tried." [97] The experiment ended in his resignation, perhaps demonstrating that the notion of balance has its own outer limits.

PRESIDENT, CABINET APPOINTMENT, AND POLITICAL PROCESS

A discussion of the component variables in the appointment process reveals a diverse and complicated interaction of forces, no one of which can be said to dictate the result. In this light, any attitude which begins by assuming tight presidential control and ends by basing serious judgments about him on the outcome is unrealistic. His voice is the most positive one in the process, but it speaks in a limited and contingent manner. His margin of discretion is cut on all sides by the impingement of the other four factors. Although it is formally correct to hold him responsible for his Cabinet, it is wrong to imagine that he exercises a free and unfettered choice. Even when he articulates a consistent norm, he is not likely to get a Cabinet which completely fulfills it. There is no guarantee that the "best man for the job" in the President's eyes will get the position. Even less is there any assurance that nicely blended personal relationships will result.[98] And if either of these norms are fulfilled to the observer's satisfaction, that result may bear no relation to the dominance of the presidential influence in the process.

Given the intricacies of availability and balance, Cabinet-making often bears a striking resemblance to the game of musical chairs. The President sits at the piano, with the power to stop and start the music. But the keyboard on which he plays does not give him a very refined control over who it is that is eliminated and who it is that remains in the chair when the game is over. His "official family" is certainly official, but in view of the complex appointment process, one ought to strike a more inquisitive attitude toward its familial attributes.

Presidential influence over Cabinet selection reaches its maximum in choosing replacements for the original group. In-term appointments are made in slightly altered circumstances. Popular curiosity is lower and the various interested publics exercise less of a surveillance over the choice. The original Cabinet is, and to this extent Professor Lindsay is correct, a symbolic show window for an incoming President, and he must expect the critical scrutiny of all those interested in sizing up the administration. The idea of balance, involving the representation of diverse interests, is of major importance in this political assessment. The in-term appointment, made when the Cabinet is a going concern, is more insulated from the pressure of these external political factors. The President receives less unsolicited advice when he is filling a position for the second or third time. His own circle of eligible acquaintances may be larger. The exigencies of legislation may not appear as compelling as they did at the beginning of his term. He is more experienced and may know more precisely what tasks are paramount in certain Cabinet posts. For all of these reasons, an in-term appointment is likely to be a more personal choice than the original one.

In-term appointments tend to be dominated by two components of availability — close personal acquaintance and public administrative experience. Conversely, they are less likely to be made on the basis of legislative or partisan experience or to be influenced by men of this background. The second time around, both Roosevelt and Truman appointed intimate personal friends to the Secretaryship of the Treasury.[99] Wilson knew many of his replacements much better and for a longer period of time than he had known their original counterparts.[100] Eisenhower was well acquainted with seven out of his first eight in-term appointees. Three of these seven had served at the undersecretary level in his administration, one had been a member of the White House Staff, one had been Director of the Office of Defense Mobilization, and one had been Chairman of the Atomic Energy Commission.[101] Two of Hoover's four in-term appointees were promoted from lower-level departmental positions.[102] After twelve years and fifteen in-term selections, the Roosevelt Cabinet was without a single man of congressional experience. Reacting to this situation, Truman's first appointments show a greater sensitivity to problems of legislative relations than his subsequent ones.[103] Coolidge made (or tried to make, in the case of Warren) several replacements without consulting the customary party people.[104]

The special properties of the in-term appointment result in a somewhat more controllable presidential choice, accenting personal friendship and administrative capacity. Yet each one of the other factors continues to operate and continues to hold his influence within bounds. Many replacements spring, indeed, from the very lack of presidential control, as when a Cabinet member whom he wishes to retain cannot be dissuaded from resigning. The fact that his circle of public administrative acquaintances increases may operate to decrease his elbow room as far as considering men of other qualifications is concerned. There is still no great probability that the President will get what he wants or, as we shall see, that a person chosen with certain criteria in mind will come up to expectations. The Chief Executive's operating freedom in appointing a Lansing, a Woodring, or a Jones was relatively substantial, but relations of personal confidence were not enhanced thereby. It is impossible to put the distinction in terms of a statistic, especially because so many in-term appointments are simply stop-gap affairs and thus incommensurable with an original selection. In general, however, the difference is one of degree and not of kind. It marks, perhaps, the restrictiveness of even the outermost limits of presidential influence. The circumstances surrounding the in-term appointment make of it a distinguishable case, but they do not free the President from the necessity of exercising his appointment power within a multidimensional context of limitations.

If the shortcomings of the President-oriented attitude toward Cabinet-making are revealed by the very fact of complexity, the weaknesses of the Dooley-like, process-oriented skepticism are made evident by the nature of that complexity: the forces that interact in comprising the appointment process are the basic forces of the American political system. What smaller frame of reference can possibly apply when the relevant factors are those of presidential personality, public mood, partisan politics, group interests, geographic dispersion, socio-economic diversity, organizational structure, public prestige, and political ideals? The appointment process is what it is because of the larger realities of American politics. Its logic is the logic of the total system. It is unrealistic to criticize the methods or results of Cabinet recruitment from any one isolated perspective. For this reason, the objectively right man for any Cabinet position is a political mirage. There are doubtless in each case many men equally "right" for a given Cabinet job. Criticisms of the appointment process ought to be focused primarily on the political system of whose logic it partakes. Anything less is an example of misplaced and, hence, misspent energy.

There is another characteristic of American politics which is relevant to the "right man" problem. It also helps to explain the difficulties of predicting Cabinet selection on the basis of a preconceived list of important men. In America there is simply no recognized reservoir of public men from which Cabinet leaders are drawn. This fact helps to explain the invariably low batting averages of speculators in the public press (witness the pre-inaugural pages of the *New York Times*) and the conspicuous ignorance even of men in public life in commenting on new appointees. "I cannot comment on Stone's appointment [Harlan Stone as Attorney General] because I never heard of him before," said Senator Burton Wheeler in 1924.[105]

Moreover, when the becoming outbursts of modesty and swooning are discounted, many Cabinet appointees have exhibited genuine astonishment at their own selection. Cordell Hull was "thunderstruck" and Robert Lansing was "surprised." Harold Ickes, although he had actively sought a position, was "taken by surprise" and commented that "it wouldn't happen again in a millennium."[106] Ezra Benson and Douglas McKay were "surprised" at their selection, and most of the remainder of the Eisenhower Cabinet expressed the feeling that they had been "drafted" against their inclinations and prophecy.[107] Even after he had been Secretary of Commerce for more than a year, Robert Lamont still had no idea why he was chosen for the job. "I guess I more or less fitted into the Cabinet pattern the President was making," was the best he could answer.[108] Edwin Denby was unable to restrain himself: "The invitation took me off my feet. I was overwhelmed. Am I glad to get the job? You bet I am!"[109] The fact that we do not have a small body of leaders from which the Cabinet is chosen simply reflects the fact that in this country we do not have many distinctly public men. If we did, they would be the most likely source. Only the

Secretary of State is normally a man of particular national prominence. With this single exception (and perhaps that of the Postmaster General), nothing is so dead in the morning as last night's Cabinet prediction. Cabinet members, as a rule, make a reputation in private life which carries them to their public position, and they ordinarily return to private life after their governmental interlude. This set of facts helps to place both the "right man" and the "prominent man" views of Cabinet-making in proper perspective.

It is doubtful whether a very precise calculus of Cabinet appointment can be drawn up. The interaction and the interdetermination of the component variables are characterized by a pervasive uncertainty. In addition, the problems of commensurability seem insuperable. Perhaps the best that can be said in terms of an overall pattern is that certain variables are always involved and that they interact in such a way as to preclude any one of them from controlling the others. It is beyond the power of any one of the factors to transform the nature of the appointment process, and unless changes in the total governmental process supervene, no change in this patterned uncertainty is likely.

Some attempt has been made to discover a patterning in terms of the personal backgrounds and social characteristics of Cabinet members. They are found to be not literally representative of all segments of the population, and these findings are used to buttress conclusions about their elitist character.[110] It is, perhaps, worth recognizing that whatever other factors may enter into the appointment process, those which would guarantee an accurate Cabinet reflection of the census statistics do not. But the setting up of this statistical norm seems even more oversimplified, and further removed from the realities of the appointment process, than the ordinary rule-of-thumb standards by which Cabinet-making is judged. To be sure, some aspects of Cabinet selection can be quantified, but the problem remains as to whether anything meaningful is being measured. In any case, the bias of this study is to urge a more qualitative appreciation of the multidimensional recruitment process and of the Cabinet as but one institution in a cohering interdependent system. From this standpoint, what seems worthy of mention is the extent to which the Cabinet reflects the plural elements of American society and thus represents a comparatively wide sharing of power by those elements.

The process of Cabinet selection is a sub-process, related at every point to the American political system as a whole, and revealing something of the reactive nature of the Cabinet as an institution. The process finds its underlying consistency in the fundamental pluralism of American politics. Until such time as the basic contours of the system change, Cabinet appointment will continue to frustrate those who seek a neatly rational scheme of selection to which they can apply equally well-structured systems of prediction and of judgment. Ultimately, the significance of Cabinet selection lies not in the facts of the process, but in its effect on the Cabinet in action. In this sense, one ought, finally, to consider the appointment process as revealing a set of expectations about Cabinet performance. It is a kind of prediction about the forces and counter-forces which will affect day-to-day President-Cabinet-Cabinet member relations. It is to these relations that we now turn.

CHAPTER THREE

The Cabinet Meeting: I

"CABINET" is a group concept. It refers to what several people can do by way of assisting a chief executive when they function as a group rather than as individuals. It refers to a group working together to serve some end which could not be served so adequately by the same persons working separately. This being true, an essential precondition to the Cabinet's existence is the existence of a corporate framework within which a group can operate. This framework is provided by the Cabinet meeting. Since a Cabinet which never met is a contradiction in terms, the Cabinet meeting becomes the heart of any discussion of the Cabinet as an institution. Indeed, the term and the institution originated in the presence of precisely these ingredients, i.e., several persons whose group identity and group activity were established by the fact of their frequent meetings with President Washington.

THE POTENTIAL FUNCTIONS OF THE MEETING

The setting of this chapter is the Cabinet meeting; the subject matter is group activity. At the outset it is helpful to indicate the functions which might be performed for the Chief Executive in the context of a group meeting — some categories of potential Cabinet usefulness. They will provide us with standards or guideposts to help us in evaluating or interpreting actual performance. Keeping in mind the special properties of the Cabinet as a group of highest level, interdepartmental advisers to the President, it could hypothetically serve three distinguishable functions. If any or all of them are fulfilled to a significant degree, the Cabinet cannot be passed off as an unimportant institution.

As *presidential adviser*, the Cabinet is a group of men who can help the President to make his decisions by placing their information, their experience, and their judgment at his disposal. They may provide the Chief Executive with expert advice — with specialized information and a technical judgment on the subject matter at hand. Or, they may furnish political advice, apprising the President of opinions, likely reactions, and areas of support among the people who will be affected by the decision. Some Cabinet members are experts in particular areas and all of them can draw upon the expertise of the departments which they head. Some of them are representatives of large public constituencies, equipped to discuss the responsiveness of their groups to proposed public policies. What the President would receive in any meeting would be a blend of the two, with a tendency, probably, for the political elements to dominate. Viewed in the abstract, an interchange, competitive or harmonious, among such people would bring many perspectives to a focus during the making of a presidential decision.

If the Cabinet fulfilled its advisory function at all, the President would be provided with a sounding board for his partially developed ideas, superior in range of attitude and key of reaction to anything he could achieve by approaching them singly. By listening to the diversity of knowledge and opinion, he could clarify and weigh the possible consequences of his decision in terms of public opinion and group support, tapping more than one line of political intelligence. In a negative sense, the President's area of ignorance would be narrowed by his acquiring information and opinion he did not have, thus preventing him from making avoidable mistakes. In a more positive sense, the group might help him to identify possible alternatives of action or to mold an approach to a problem, or it might foresee future problems and make plans for their solution. Group discussion may help the President through competition as well as through acquiescence; indeed, some competition of ideas is of great value. But the final purpose of the discussion must be to fulfill the Cabinet's role as adviser to the President, with all the willingness to implement his responsibility which that role implies. The diversity of advice which stems from segmented areas of knowledge and interest can be put to the service of the President usefully only so long as it is not offered willfully to oppose or subvert that government-wide outlook which is the prerequisite of presidential leadership.

The twentieth-century President faces the problem of managing a complex bureaucracy, and especially the problem of *coordination.* Agreement and unity must be had by relating the activities of many co-equal agencies one to the other. A relatively new dimension to this problem is the tremendous number of programs and policies which cut across departmental lines, and hence the increasingly heavy burden of interdepartmental business which must be supervised and directed by the President. On the face of it, a Cabinet meeting would seem to be an ideal forum in which to discuss and settle interdepartmental problems.

In modest proportions, the Cabinet might be a clearing house of information, providing a channel whereby department heads could exchange information which they otherwise might not obtain. If the process were presided over by the President, he could set the stage for such an interchange by informing the Secretaries of the most pressing problems. Both the goals and the emerging dilemmas of established programs could be clarified. Clearance could be obtained for new policies and plans that touched several departments. At its best, the discussion of interdepartmental business might result in the settling of programmatic or jurisdictional conflicts. Agreement might be secured short of the President by a group discussion at which the President sat as moderator rather than as judge. Even if this did not succeed, a thorough airing of interdepartmental matters would have laid bare the areas of program conflict. If presidential action were needed, it could be taken on the spot and the whole group would know what it was and could take action in accordance with it. If the Cabinet served either the clearing house or the reduction of friction function it would facilitate the President's task of interdepartmental coordination.

The success of any organized effort rests on the maintenance of the intra-group channels of communication. The Cabinet meeting is just such a channel of communication and contact — department head to department head, President to department head, department head to President — a fact which is assumed in any discussion of the Cabinet's coordinating role. But more basic perhaps than the communication of programmatic details in the search for unity of program is the communication of a climate of cooperation in the search for unity of purpose. It is intangible, perhaps, but it is essential to the tangible success of any corporate enterprise. We have called it *administrative coherence*. It refers not especially to the fact of a unified effort but to the spirit that promotes it, to the atmosphere in which cooperation can take root and grow. If the departmental Secretaries pull in unison with the President and with each other, they will be reflecting something less tangible — a group-mindedness which is the essence of coherence.

The very fact of a periodic Cabinet meeting can assist mightily in producing coherence by infusing a degree of group identification which would not otherwise be secured. Even if the group does not advise or coordinate, its members can listen to each other and to the President, gaining some sense of where they are going and a renewed *esprit* with which to tackle their respective tasks. Beyond these minimum aspects of coherence, the Cabinet meeting offers a positive opportunity for the members to assist the President in defining and formulating the essential purposes and goals of their administration. In either case, the unity associated with coherence is participant unity. The Cabinet member who joins in the deliberations or discussions of the group is more apt to feel a part of the organization, to share its purposes on all levels, and hence to be more willing to support the decisions which emerge from it. These lines of agreement in attitude and action are the basis of administrative success. They depend ultimately upon the President, but could be nourished more immediately and with prospects of great reward by the effective use of a device like the Cabinet meeting.

THE FORM OF THE MEETING — INSTITUTIONAL BAREBONES

Whatever function the Cabinet fulfills, its activity will proceed within the boundaries set by the form of the meeting. Since this form is wholly the product of custom and tradition, it retains a fundamental plasticity. Nonetheless, it has acquired enough continuity and regularity in terms of *periodicity, personnel,* and *procedure* to give substance to the Cabinet as an institution.

Since George Washington's time, Cabinet meetings have been convened at the President's discretion. Yet tradition, at least since Polk, prescribes that they be held periodically and at regularly stated intervals, rather than at the President's whim and urge.[1] Abraham Lincoln in 1860 and Woodrow Wilson over fifty years later wanted to hold meetings only when they desired, and both retreated from this position.[2] The customary practice has been to hold meetings on Tuesday and Friday. Each of the Presidents began his administration by adhering to this pattern but admittedly some, and probably all, found it necessary to accommodate tradition to practicality. Wilson and Roosevelt, during their emergency periods, dropped the Friday and the Tuesday sessions respectively.[3] They retained the periodicity, but simply lengthened the interval. Neither Harding nor Coolidge adhered consistently to the established pattern.[4] Truman held Cabinet meetings "at least once a week (on Monday) and sometimes twice a week."[5] Eisenhower holds one regular weekly conference on Friday. Surely all Presidents must have canceled meetings on occasion. At any rate, we can safely conclude that established practice rests somewhere between what tradition permits and practicality requires.

The reasons for interrupting or extending the conventional

regularity of the Cabinet meeting have generally been the same. Presidents have simply felt that they could accomplish more under the prevailing circumstances by dispensing with it. Wilson, by far the most irregular of modern Presidents in convening meetings, was apt to let relatively long periods elapse, preferring to hold individual conferences.[6] Harding, too, substituted individual meetings for Cabinet discussion.[7] Coolidge often compromised by holding a formal meeting for a few minutes and then having discussions with the members individually.[8] During wartime, Wilson and Roosevelt frequently filled their appointed Cabinet day with meetings of a group whose activities were more directly related to the prosecution of the war. The situation is, therefore, flexible enough that the President may, on occasion, replace the Cabinet meeting with an *ad hoc* meeting more beneficial to himself and to others.

Evidence of the basically flexible nature of the Cabinet meeting can be found, too, in the way in which its personnel fluctuates around the hard core of departmental Secretaries. When the layman considers the Cabinet, he thinks only of those men with a legally equalized status as heads of departments, receiving identical salaries, and formally differentiated only by the familiar State-to-Health, Education and Welfare hierarchy within the group. But attendance at Cabinet meetings was never, during the period under investigation, restricted exclusively to these people. Nor, indeed, has it ever been since Vice-President Adams and Attorney General Randolph were included in the Washington group.[9]

The Vice-President sat in the Cabinets of Harding, Hoover, Roosevelt, Truman, and Eisenhower. Thomas Marshall did not sit in Wilson's Cabinet, but he did preside over a few of its sessions while Wilson was in Paris. While no "unofficial" person sat regularly in the Wilson Cabinet, agency heads were called in from time to time when the subject matter was pertinent.[10] By Roosevelt's third term, a whole galaxy of agency heads and wartime administrators attended meetings, swelling the total to near twenty. These included representatives of the Federal Security Agency, Federal Works Agency, Federal Loan Agency, National Housing Agency, and Office of War Mobilization, and individuals like Harry Hopkins. President Truman invited a half-dozen individuals of non-Cabinet rank to his meetings: Chairman of the National Security Resources Board, Mutual Security Administrator, Director of the Office of Defense Mobilization, Assistant to the President, and the President's private secretary. President Eisenhower's Cabinet meetings are customarily attended by the Budget Director, the Director of the Office of Defense Mobilization, the Permanent Representative to the United Nations, the Special Assistant to the President for National Security Affairs, the Assistant to the President, the Special Assistant to the President for Disarmament, the Chairman of the Civil Service Commission, and the Secretary to the Cabinet. Subordinates of the department heads have customarily filled in during the absence of their superiors. The pattern is well established, and the number of people beyond the "official family" who attend meetings has been steadily increasing. It would be an extremely safe guess that, under the present system, the men of Cabinet rank will continue to be joined by others in the Cabinet meeting.

Since its earliest meetings with George Washington, the essence of the Cabinet's procedures has been their informality. Yet, long usage has cast them in a generally accepted mold. To some degree, procedural informality is a fixed corollary to the power-responsibility relationship. Since the Cabinet has no collective responsibility, formal votes are not taken and recorded, nor are collective decisions made. Some Presidents in the past reportedly operated by taking a vote and abiding by the majority. None has done so in the last hundred years, and it is hard to believe that any President would abdicate his responsibility by allowing himself to be outvoted on any but the most trivial issues.

No formal records of the discussions are kept, and no set of Cabinet minutes exists for any administration prior to Eisenhower's. Some Presidents (Truman, for example) have requested a private secretary to sit in and to take down fragmentary notes for the President's personal use, but in no sense was this person a recording secretary of the group. Most Presidents have observed these informal yet traditional practices in order to protect themselves from formal commitments which might undermine their ultimate responsibility.

Resting less firmly on the logic of presidential responsibility, a traditional method of transacting Cabinet business has developed. The key fact about it is the lack of an agenda prepared and circulated prior to the meeting. Since this condition does not hold for the Eisenhower Cabinet, it deserves special mention later; but until the present one, all Presidents have conducted meetings in the same way.

The President, of course, presides over the meeting. If he has some problem that he desires to lay before the Cabinet, if he wants to make a report, or if he simply wishes to comment on some current situation, he will ordinarily open the meeting in this fashion. Any concern that is on his mind, therefore, will be the first order of business. Depending on the nature of the President's remarks, an interchange of ideas or information may or may not follow. All other business is initiated by the time-honored custom of proceeding around the table from the Secretary of State to the Secretary lowest on the ladder of prestige (now, exclusive of other agencies, the Secretary of Health, Education and Welfare), giving each in turn an opportunity to make any reports or other comments he may desire or to raise some matter which invites group discussion. It was Wilson's practice to begin his sessions alternately with the Secretary of State and the Secretary of Labor so that there would be an equal chance for the Secretaries to lay their business before the Cabinet.[11] Through this procedure, the President is provided with a channel through which to request the assistance of his official family, to make his views known to them, or to announce his decisions. There is a similar opportunity for each member to raise any or all issues which are the legitimate business of the group.

If proof be needed of the basic flexibility of Cabinet procedures, it can be found in President Eisenhower's easy departure from traditional practice. The centerpiece of his innovation is the creation of a Secretary to the Cabinet, an official charged with the task of preparing and circulating an agenda on which meetings are based. He also has the job of following up decisions that are made in Cabinet meetings, a phase of his activity which does not concern us now but which does help define his position as the manager-in-chief of Cabinet activity. The Cabinet Secretary attends all meetings of the group where he takes not Cabinet minutes but "extensive notes" on the proceedings — more extensive than in any previous administration.

The function of the Cabinet agenda is twofold: to provide a procedure that will ensure extensive consideration of every item before it arises in the meeting, and to acquaint each member with the items to be discussed so that he may prepare himself. Items are placed on the agenda by the President (or for him by one of his top level aides — for six years this man was Presidential Assistant Sherman Adams), by the department head, or by either at the request of the Cabinet Secretary himself. The Secretary, until May 1958 Maxwell Rabb and now Robert K. Gray,* acts not as a passive intermediary but as an active trouble shooter, seeking out problems that seem to require Cabinet attention and "suggesting" to the participants involved that they place the item before the group via the agenda. Once a matter is scheduled for Cabinet attention it may be some time before it is dealt with, especially where a department head is advocating Cabinet action. In this case, much time will be spent working

* The description of the operation of the Eisenhower Cabinet in Chapters Three and Four is based on the period of Rabb's Secretaryship. The basic procedures were developed and regularized during his tenure of office, and the assumption is made here that the Cabinet Secretariat functions similarly under Mr. Gray, formerly a Special Assistant to the President working on patronage matters.

up a presentation for the Cabinet and consulting with interested departments. During the process, the Cabinet Secretary plays a role of surveillance — checking the methods of presentation, "cutting the script," listening, perhaps, to a trial run, making certain that all departments and the White House staff have a copy of the proposed agenda item.

On the Monday preceding the Friday Cabinet meeting, the Secretary discusses the proposed agenda with the Assistant to the President, which may result in changes. On Wednesday or Thursday, these two officials may go over the entire agenda with the President, with an eye to time and priority. If a new item arises out of these later conversations, it is circulated to the participants. Each member brings with him to Friday's Cabinet meeting a large Cabinet notebook containing the agenda for the session — not only a list of items, but a one-page brief on each one and various Cabinet documents (usually four to six pages each, but sometimes as long as fifty pages) containing pertinent information on other matters. The Eisenhower system for pre-conference planning, culminating in an agenda, represents a greater degree of institutionalization than has heretofore characterized the Cabinet meeting or the Cabinet as an institution.[12]

We stated in the Introduction that an institution exists "when a group of people . . . meet together in isolation often enough, regularly enough, and long enough each time to do something together intensely enough and emotionally enough so that as a separate entity the group builds up its own set of rules, its own internal equilibrium and its own structure." Tested by these standards, the Cabinet qualifies as an institution. The group of people involved "as a separate entity" is clear enough in terms of its personnel, and they do meet together "often enough, regularly enough, and long enough each time to do something together. . . ." The group has built up its own set of procedural rules. It has an internal equilibrium to this extent at least: it can maintain itself against any attempts to tamper with it drastically. Its personnel cannot be sharply reduced. The fact that the

President cannot abolish it is evidence of its institutional structure. However, a description of these structural minima leaves the important questions about them — questions of degree, of desirability, and of performance — still unanswered.

THE FORM OF THE MEETING — SOME PROBLEMS

The form of the meeting raises, in each of its aspects — when, who, and how — the problem of the accommodation of a fundamental flexibility to an encrusted tradition. These problems, in turn, coalesce into the larger problem of the effect of institutionalization on the performance of the Cabinet's three potential functions.

Consider the problem of periodicity. In terms of the potentialities of the Cabinet, both flexibility and tradition possess reason and unreason. On behalf of regularity, it can be said that it is essential to the life of any institution that the people involved meet "regularly enough" to acquire a group self-awareness. If the group is to be utilized effectively, there must be frequent intragroup communication and contact. Regular meetings are an essential for administrative coherence. If meetings are not held regularly, they are apt not to be held at all, and *ad hoc* meetings sap the cohesiveness of the group by decreasing its internal interaction relative to the other contacts of its members.

On the other hand, if one wishes to make optimum use of the Cabinet, one may find regularity a mixed blessing. Many Presidents have felt that their time could be spent more profitably in less regularized ways. Members, too, have shared this belief. Harold Ickes wrote that "in general it would have been just as good, if instead of regular meetings the President had called special meetings on occasion when he wanted us to express our views on questions as to which he wanted advice."[13] If the President or the members do not think a meeting worthwhile, the periodicity prescribed by tradition may result in formal conferences without substance — a high level group engaged in "busy work." Such a result would certainly not exemplify the optimum use of a Cabinet meeting, and it might defeat the very end of coherence by deflating the importance of the group in the minds of its members. Thus, two of Roosevelt's members agreed "that Cabinet meetings are such a waste of time," and "that members of the Cabinet should be used for real counsel and advice on important questions." [14] The tradition surrounding the regularity of Cabinet meetings cuts two ways at once. Their success depends on their being held regularly, yet the President must preserve a discretionary power in this respect as a necessary safeguard against Cabinet dry rot.

Viewed from the standpoint of personnel, the flexibility of the Cabinet meeting is essential in enabling it to keep pace with external change. It has allowed the President to react to tremendous innovations in the political system as a whole by making the Cabinet, potentially at least, more adequate to its tasks. The government's responsibilities and its machinery in peace, war, and cold war have mushroomed far beyond the purview of the traditional departments. No group which did not contain the Budget Director, the Director of the Office of Defense Mobilization, or (earlier) the Mutual Security Director could hope to perform the function of interdepartmental coordination. Without the flexible base of the Cabinet and the presidential discretion over personnel, the usefulness of the Cabinet could hardly have been preserved. As in the case of periodicity, however, the accommodation of informality and formality creates problems.

While the expansibility of the Cabinet may be cited as proof of the value of a customary institution, it fails to indicate the extent to which this expansibility is superintended by a rigid tradition. This tradition prescribes that the expansibility be *irreversible*. As a limitation, it now stands as firmly on the legs of custom as it would on the pages of the statute books. Men of Cabinet rank cannot be excluded from the meeting, even though the rationale behind their omission may be as compelling as that which lies behind the inclusion of others. The Postmaster General may be as useless in an interchange of opinion on the coordination of foreign policy as the Delegate to the United Nations is essential. Postmaster General Farley has been described, for example, as not interested unless political matters were under discussion in meetings, and as confessing little knowledge of economics or international affairs.[15] There may be little wisdom in thrashing out certain issues before members who are so fundamentally opposed to the basic approach of the administration as to be of no help whatsoever — Cordell Hull on domestic policy, for example.[16] Furthermore, the continued introduction of new members without compensating reductions may subject the Cabinet to acute institutional indigestion and render it unwieldy as a vehicle for group thinking. In matters such as these, elements of prestige are engrafted on tradition to prevent change. But, along with the possible loss in prestige goes a possible loss in administrative coherence, unless some equally regular system were substituted for the present one. The fact is, however, that in terms of its core personnel the Cabinet meeting has institutionalized the "one-way stretch." And one cannot resist the thought that the form of the meeting may need more streamlining than this permits. The Cabinet has been more successful in meeting the charge that it is too small than it has been in meeting the complaint that it is too large — as the presence of the National Security Council will attest. One can conclude that in meeting the problems of change the existing degree of flexibility in personnel has preserved the Cabinet's potential usefulness and has, at the same time, rendered it more difficult to use.

In the case of the procedure of the Cabinet meeting, the traditional form (not the present one) retains an almost boundless flexibility. No possible Cabinet function is enjoined by the method, and no high-level question is beyond the Cabinet's scope. There is ample opportunity for initiation of activity to come from all sides. The traditional procedure is, therefore, a neutral one which does not automatically foreclose on the performance of any of the three functions mentioned earlier. But the reverse side of the coin is this, that while the procedure is flexible enough to accommodate any function and while tradition precludes none, the method itself neither indicates nor guarantees that a single one of the wide-ranging possibilities will be realized. While there is no need to search for iron-clad guarantees, the lack of any positive stimulant has its dark side. For all that the procedure counts, the Cabinet's success might be an accident and its failure might be uselessness. Flexibility, whether it is supported or undermined by custom, generates problems of its own.

A survey of memoir material brings a rich yield of evidence of what may happen when meetings are conducted according to established practice. Josephus Daniels records a Cabinet meeting of October 2, 1917, a synopsis of which runs something like this. The Cabinet was ostensibly discussing Germany's failure to prosecute the war more vigorously — admittedly a nebulous and hardly suitable topic for the group. As they started, Attorney General Gregory mentioned a rumor he had heard. This reminded Wilson of a story which he proceeded to tell. Then the subject shifted to draft exemptions. Wilson read a letter from a complaining woman. Then the discussion was brought back to the original topic. Wilson told another anecdote and the meeting adjourned shortly thereafter. The Wilson Cabinet, Daniels said, discussed everything, big and little, and his book is an impressive chronicle of the "little" things as well as the big — the debate over the merits of the "p" in "comptroller," the ludicrous preoccupation with a weird assortment of rumors before the war.[17]

In scarcely less perilous times, October 10, 1941, the same meandering method produced this sequence in a Roosevelt Cabinet meeting. The President began by expressing his concern that so many young men were being rejected for military service for physical reasons. The members chimed in to discuss, among other things, bad teeth and venereal disease, whereupon the matter was dropped. As the around-the-table routine began, it was reported that stolen jewelry was being sent from Italy to the United States. When it was suggested that this was being accomplished by diplomatic pouch, a facetious discussion ensued concerning the proprieties involved. The subject of "the nourishability of food in England" was then raised, because some members had heard that "in many parts of England the people look hungry." This ill-grounded discussion of English hunger led somewhat more nationalistically to the problem of buying Icelandic fish for the U.S.A. From here, the focus of attention lurched to "the radio situation in Nevada," where a station had been awarded to a close friend of a Senator. The meeting was brought to a close with two reports, one on the British oil situation and the other on the British labor situation. There was apparently no discussion on these items.[18]

This type of meeting is not atypical under the traditional procedure; while the relationship is by no means one of cause and effect, it is certain that this procedural form aggravates whatever other difficulties are present. The discussion is unplanned, unfocused, and uneven. There is no doubt but what crucial questions come before the group, but they may pop up without forewarning or in a form that is not comprehensible to all, resulting in an immature exchange. For example, the Roosevelt group discussed most of the important topics of the day, but the point is that problems frequently came upon them like a flash flood, which either submerged them beyond their depth or struck the surface without being absorbed at all. Neither Roosevelt (because he cared not to) nor the members (because they could not) focused the problems for more effective discussion. Usually the President made a comment and the members asked ill-considered, superficial questions or talked along off the tops of their heads.[19]

A problem which pops up in the course of circling the table will be handled in much the same way. As far as the members are concerned, the prospect of submitting some vital question to a rambling discussion is not inviting, and they may raise trivial issues instead when faced with the conventional request as to whether they "have anything to say today." From all the information available, it seems fair to say that the great majority of Cabinet meetings under the traditional procedure have consisted of an opening disquisition or comment by the President and some discussion of it, followed by a series of unrelated, straightforward, non-controversial reports or comments by the individual members.[20] Presidential decisions might or might not be made, depending on the individual involved.

In creating a Cabinet Secretary and an agenda, President Eisenhower took dead aim on some of the less satisfactory procedural features of the Cabinet meeting. By the use of staff work before and after the meeting, he sought to eliminate the trivial, aimless, and unpremeditated nature of the discussions.[21] For nearly a year, preparation for Cabinet meetings consisted of random attempts by various White House aides such as Gabriel Hauge, General Paul T. Carroll, or Sherman Adams to "whip up" an agenda, sometimes by calling around on Thursday night to find items for the next morning. The result of this attempt to graft new functions onto traditional procedures was that, as one person put it, "we wouldn't have anything," culminating presumably in unsatisfactory Cabinet sessions.

On the basis of a study done at the request of the President in the summer of 1953, steps were taken toward systematizing procedures involving the Cabinet. Maxwell Rabb, an Assistant to the President in civil rights matters, was also designated to be Co-ordinator of Cabinet Affairs on a one-year trial basis. Beginning in November, a more serious, though still informal, attempt was made to prepare for and report on Cabinet meetings. While this setup produced some striking successes, in terms of its goals, much room for improvement remained. The Cabinet agenda was still described as a place "for items which are half ripe or hastily gathered just in order to have a full basket on Friday mornings." Both the successes and the shortcomings of this arrangement led to a presidential request for a restudy in the summer of 1954. President and Cabinet were urged in this study to "keep on the same road and finish the creation of a system, so long familiar to the President in his previous experience." It recommended, and the President accepted, the establishment of what is now the Cabinet Secretariat — and in practically its present form.

The fundamentals of the new system were presented to the Cabinet in August, 1954, substantially as they had been presented to the President and his staff earlier, and Eisenhower's unequivocal position that "this thing's got to stick" was made crystal clear to the members. In September (and specifically with the Cabinet meeting of October 19), Cabinet Secretary Rabb and his single career assistant, Bradley H. Patterson, Jr., began functioning as the first formal Cabinet Secretariat in history. It is obviously too early to pass judgment on this system. Some revealing clues do make some tentative comments possible, however. In general, the clues indicate the presence of new improvements and the persistence of old difficulties — even though the improvements and the difficulties sometimes manifest themselves in forms unforeseen by those who established the system. They indicate, also, that neither the new nor the old features are wholly explainable in terms of Cabinet procedure. To carry this point further, the Eisenhower experience indicates that there are rather narrow limits within which purely procedural changes are likely to affect total Cabinet performance.

The Eisenhower Cabinet's performance is most impressively different when it is used as a high-level forum in which one member presents, analyzes, and defends his department's overall program or one of its policies. The characteristics of this type of presentation are that it is painstakingly prepared, that it is the focus for a large portion of a Cabinet session, and that the discussion results in a general Cabinet consensus and, almost always, in a presidential decision. It is used almost exclusively for domestic matters.

The first policy-presentation type of Cabinet meeting involved a presentation by Mrs. Hobby of her Department's 1954 program for social security expansion. It represented, in October of 1953, the first noteworthy success of the Co-ordinator for Cabinet Affairs, and as such it became a turning point on the road to the present Secretariat. Following Mrs. Hobby's explanation of the program, the meeting was taken up with a wide-ranging discussion on social security — on certain substantive features of her proposed bill, on alternative bills which were originating in the Congress, on the attitude which the administration should strike toward these bills, and, when Cabinet preference for Mrs. Hobby's bill was established, on the administration strategy for pushing its own bill. After a summary statement by Mrs. Hobby, the President made a final statement indicating his acquiescence in the proposed program, and the meeting adjourned.[22]

Lacking the cordial personal relationship which existed between Mrs. Hobby and Rabb, and her willingness to do him a favor by giving his procedure a try, the experiment would have been infinitely harder to get off the ground. As it was, the "electrifying" impact of the one and one-half hour performance (given after three "trial runs" under Rabb's supervision) helped convince other members that similar meetings could be useful to them, individually as well as collectively. As a result of captured confidences and reduced reluctance, the policy-presentation type of meeting has come to constitute the major proportion of those agenda items which require Cabinet action of some sort (as opposed to purely informational items or reports).

To give another example, in the summer of 1955 Secretary Rabb read a magazine article about the overcrowded condition of our national parks and saw in the problem a possible item for a Cabinet presentation. The Interior Department, which had already begun a ten-year, "Mission 66" program for expanding park facilities, agreed. In November, Rabb and Patterson went to Interior, heard the program outlined, and then began to work with the people in that department in order to sharpen up their Cabinet presentation. They helped, for example, by insisting that the program explanation be accompanied by realistic price tags, checked through the Budget Bureau. Two months, three dry runs, and a "dress rehearsal" later, Secretary McKay and four assistants presented "Mission 66" to the Cabinet. In addition to the use of charts and diagrams, the Cabinet room was darkened for movies during the presentation. The program, as it became understood by all, won their immediate support, so much so that the President, who had just sent an election year budget to Congress, agreed on the spot to approve a supplemental budget request and to send a supporting letter to Congress.

The policy-presentation type of meeting can and has served each of the three possible Cabinet uses. From the standpoint of advice, the President has the opportunity to benefit from a succinct, documented, and planned statement of policy, and to educate himself as to its dimensions — both essential if he is going to embody the proposal in a legislative message. There may also be a dividend of advice on matters of strategy and timing in implementation, even if, as is the case with Eisenhower, he may not wish to commit himself on the spot in such matters. Insofar as Cabinet understanding and Cabinet support can be had for a fairly concrete program, the function of administrative coherence is also served. Interdepartmental communication of this sort can heighten the sense of participant unity within the group.

As for coordination, the meeting is directed at the achievement of legislative clearance, a result which is made more likely when the President, after hearing disagreements, makes a decision. Hopefully, too, the interdepartmental consultation encouraged by the preparation for the meeting will reduce friction and promote cooperation in future activities involving the program. But it needs to be noted that typically this type of meeting is *not* a sharply controversial one. Indeed, one might even say that if the subject were expected to incite controversy it would not have been brought to the group, for the Eisenhower Cabinet members are no different than their predecessors in their natural reluctance to throw serious, interdepartmental conflicts into the meeting or to subject themselves to sharp cross-examination. In most cases, policy presentations are made for programs on which the other participants have not formed a firm position one way or the other. The result is usually to inform, to smooth off any ragged edges of doubt which may exist, and to gain fairly clear group backing for a program. If this can be accomplished all at once in a central, top-level forum, rather than piecemeal through an infinite number of smaller conferences, it is very much to the advantage of the department head to avail himself of the meeting. For relatively noncontroversial programs prior to their submission to the legislature, the policy-presentation meeting serves the functions of clearance and coordination.

The full dress presentation of a policy or program in the Cabinet meeting doubtless represents a considerable innovation in form and technique. It seems, however, most suitable for periods of special legislative urgency — the early years of an administration, the period before a State of the Union Message, or during the formulation of a key policy like the farm program of 1956.[23] Thus, as compared with the legislative program for 1954, the preparation of the 1955 program was characterized by "somewhat less wide-ranging Cabinet consultation." [24] The same thing occurred in 1957, when the legislative program was very similar to that of the previous year. It is, most probably, the policy-presentation type of meeting that one observer had in mind when he wrote that, "The system, with its bag and baggage of position papers and agendas, is best suited for the long range objectives of an administration. . . . It cannot readily keep abreast of the sudden and swift surges of daily events. . . ." [25]

Furthermore, agenda items of the type we have discussed do not constitute even a majority of the sum total. More than one-third of all the agenda items have been simply informational ones, reports of the traditional type; nearly half of those items to be considered for Cabinet action could not be called full-scale policy presentations. A Cabinet member may put some very vague idea on the agenda and be reluctant to work it up beforehand with the aid of the Secretariat. The President may initiate a piece of business for reasons of his own which may not become clear until the meeting itself. Sometimes the most critical and urgent matters arise so suddenly and so sporadically that they have to be rushed to the agenda without any opportunity for painstaking preparation. They may even be mentioned by the President for the first time at the meeting itself. Meetings dominated by informational items or items not pre-planned will not show the characteristics of the policy-presentation type.

If the evidence of Robert Donovan's book (much of it compiled before the full-fledged Secretariat went into operation) is reliable, traditional difficulties are still found in a large number of Eisenhower meetings. He reports that the Korean situation arose five times in the Cabinet meeting. Once a discussion of it was precipitated unannounced as an offshoot of a discussion of consumer credit controls. A second time, the Secretary of State reviewed the situation; the third time, only the President spoke. Twice more, the Secretary of State reported to the Cabinet about what was going on, and the last time, the President was not even in attendance.[26] When important events intervened, like the execution of Beria, the Cabinet occupied its time speculating in all directions about the consequences. Sometimes the President's opening remarks would pertain to something quite unexpected by the members. Though it was not on the agenda, he opened one meeting by reading a prepared statement replete with facts and figures on fiscal policy. It took the Cabinet completely by surprise, but they spent most of the meeting talking about it anyway.[27]

From all that can be gathered here and elsewhere, Cabinet discussions are still attended with varying degrees of interest and participation by the members. Some still complain that the agenda (which averages about five items per session), and hence the business of the meeting, is trivial or technical instead of being devoted to high-level policy matters. Less than a fistful of the Eisenhower-chaired meetings in five years could be called sharply controversial ones. Though they are presented with an agenda, many Cabinet members do not do their homework to any great extent. Some may ask to be briefed by their department on as few as one or two Cabinet items a year. Some may give the agenda a cursory glance on Wednesday or Thursday and not see it again until Friday morning. Others may come with a great deal of information available to them, but which they have not had time to read. This variety of attitudes is a familiar staple of every Cabinet. It may, in this Cabinet as in others, lead to unpremeditated, if not aimless, discussions. There are, it seems, some inherent difficulties which lie beyond the pale of procedural reform.

If there is evidence in a great many Eisenhower meetings of traditional difficulties, there is also evidence in these same meetings that one of the potential functions — administrative coherence — is being particularly well served. The Cabinet has been kept abreast of current problems, and on key issues where no decision has been necessary the process of communication has gone forward in the meeting. This is true of Cabinet discussions during the recession of 1954 and with respect to the Bricker Amendment, where the presidential attitude was not shaped but was communicated in the meeting, and this in spite of the desultory nature of discussion.[28] President Eisenhower does acquaint and even educate the members with his perspective on particular matters, by indicating quite clearly his own opinion and, in general, by stressing the fact that he is "President of all the people." The atmosphere and the President's attitude have all made the Cabinet meeting a vehicle for developing a common purpose and for obtaining administration solidarity. It is in this area that the Eisenhower Cabinet has achieved its most outstanding success — in having a sense of participant unity and acting as a "team." The words and actions of the group during the President's heart attack (in contrast, for example, to Cabinet response during Wilson's illness) are testimony to the presence of a relatively high degree of coherence, the highest, perhaps, of all the Cabinets studied.[29]

Assuming that the policy-presentation type of meeting and the high degree of administrative coherence represent successes under the new Eisenhower procedures, the question arises as to whether one should assign more credit to the procedure or to Eisenhower. One can say that the Cabinet Secretary and the agenda have resulted in less trivia and a clearer direction in the policy-presentation type of meeting. The Secretariat devotes a tremendous amount of time and energy to the conception, preparation, and staging of these performances. But this type of meeting is a perfectly logical outcome of Eisenhower's peculiar habits with respect to delegation and decision-making. It is made possible by his basic willingness to delegate so much policy-making authority to his department heads and to wait until it is quite fully worked out before listening to it. It is made necessary by his instinctive antipathy toward policies thrown at him without prior thought or interdepartmental consultation. Beyond this, it reflects his penchant for routinized procedures, his desire to educate himself through a focused discussion, and his willingness to make decisions in the meeting. Where these initial inclinations are not present, a President might not find the new procedures very congenial. It is impossible to imagine a President with the attitudes and habits of Franklin Roosevelt operating within the Cabinet Secretary-agenda framework.

With respect to administrative coherence, there is no doubt but what the introduction of more formal procedures conveys the idea to the members that the President takes the Cabinet seriously. Yet one could argue that here, too, the procedure is effective only as a reflection of a particular presidential influence — in this case, one which places a distinctive stress on cooperative team play. Observers in close contact with the system see its "really extraordinary" achievement as an increase in "cohesiveness." They note that the intangible sense of unity has paid off in tangible acts of interdepartmental cooperation and a decline in back-biting.[30] Yet it is interesting to note that this result *was not even expected,* and has come as a surprise dividend to those who set up the Secretariat in order to put Cabinet meetings "on a more businesslike basis." Harmony exists at the Cabinet table in large part because that is what the President wants and expects, and because the members know that. It should be noted, also, that the outstanding example of friction within the Cabinet (Durkin and Weeks) was eliminated not by the Secretariat but by the resignation of the one-man balancer, Secretary Durkin. Though the new procedure has surely helped, the presidential influence and the relative homogeneity of personnel may provide even more basic explanations for the administrative coherence of the Eisenhower Cabinet.

To whatever extent the new method of transacting business in the Cabinet reflects Eisenhower's particular working habits, there is a good possibility that future Presidents will not wish to follow it. Aside from this there arises, as in the areas of periodicity and personnel, an inquiry concerning the possible harmful effects of institutionalization. The problem which comes most readily to mind is that an emphasis on institutionalized procedures, while it yields benefits in terms of efficiency and teamwork, may sacrifice something by way of spontaneity and creativity. Serious attention to procedure may produce harmony, but it is apt to stifle the conflict of viewpoints. It was Calvin Coolidge, with his unsurpassed devotion to procedural regularity, who boasted that "there never ought to be and never were differences of opinion in my Cabinet."[31] Of course such differences existed,[32] but he suppressed them in his eagerness for harmony in the meeting — a course which he justified with a painfully literal interpretation of proper procedure. "As their duties were not to advise each other, but to advise the President, *they could not disagree among themselves.*"[33] Increased institutionalization may serve only to lessen the likelihood of stimulation through disagreement, of the type which Truman and Roosevelt valued so highly. Truman valued his Cabinet meeting precisely because it was a battleground of ideas, and though some of his Cabinet members urged that an agenda and Secretary be created, he preferred to improve Cabinet performance in informal ways, as by inaugurating a regular Cabinet luncheon prior to meetings.[34]

In the case of the Eisenhower Cabinet, the question is by no means settled as to whether various points of view and conflicting policy positions are given an adequate presentation at the Cabinet level — a more serious problem when the President relies so heavily on the group. When a departmental action paper comes before the Cabinet, how are the policy alternatives presented? It is in the nature of the system that the efforts of the Secretariat will be devoted to helping the department involved present *its* point of view as effectively as possible, and not to insuring a presidential hearing for alternative ones. A policy presentation replete with movies, slides, charts, and graphs may simply overwhelm or disarm its potential critics. Or, might not the prolonged passing around of policy papers, while promoting premeditated discussion, result in a somewhat watered down compromise proposal which produces only perfunctory discussion in the Cabinet? Might not some crucial disagreements be buried by the procedure, or at least so blunted by it that the President never sees the sharp clash of issues?

It is valuable to have the Cabinet rally round a well-staged policy proposal and pledge support to it, but there is a more creative and educational (for the President) function which might not be as well served. The institutional interest of the Secretariat is, after all, to produce relevant agenda items and to have well-planned meetings and not necessarily to create the conditions for effective presidential decision-making. In those *ad hoc* discussions of the group which cannot be brought within the full scope of the new procedure, President Eisenhower *has* been subjected to a range of clashing viewpoints. In the Cabinet's emergency session on the advisability of the natural gas bill veto, he received conflicting opinions and used the Cabinet as a sounding board to sharpen his own predispositions about the alternatives and their consequences. But is he as well served in policy-presentation type meetings dominated by the new procedure?

The questions raised are not matters of anyone's conscious desires. President Eisenhower wants to hear all sides of a question, and the Secretariat is fully aware of the problem of insulating him. In Cabinet affairs, however, as well as in other matters, the road to poor public policy may be paved with the best intentions; the end as well as the means must be kept fully in mind.

It is impossible to say whether the Eisenhower reforms represent a prelude or an interlude. The people involved in it are convinced that they are building something indispensable which, with public recognition, is here to stay. Yet, another President might scrap the entire apparatus; or he might retain it as an ornamental shell.

The Eisenhower experience does reinforce a conclusion about the more ultimate problem of accommodation between plasticity and rigidity in the form of the meeting. In the areas of periodicity, personnel, and procedure alike, *neither increased nor decreased institutionalization is an absolute good* to be pursued like the Holy Grail. This does not mean that greater institutionalization, like the Eisenhower reforms, is not valuable. It may well be. But potential disadvantages lie in this direction as well as in the other, and the point is that steps in either direction will be at best ameliorative. They cannot guarantee anything. This should come as no surprise to anyone who understands that the essential strengths and the essential weaknesses of the Cabinet do not spring from within the institution but from without.

THE PRESIDENT AND THE CABINET MEETING

The reason for the preservation of a basic flexibility in the form of the Cabinet meeting is to enable each President to use it in ways that are congenial to him. It is a safe assertion that no two have used it in exactly the same way; it is equally safe to say that there are some similarities in President-Cabinet relations. Using a gross distinction between Presidents inclined to use the Cabinet and those disinclined to do so, we can investigate presidential differences and similarities. By observing certain forms of behavior in each category, we can make some generalizations about the importance of the Cabinet meeting itself.

Warren Harding was as reliant on the advice of others as a President could be. He selected as his "one great attribute" the fact that "All along, in my life, I have preached conference, counsel, exchange of opinions, and the meeting of many minds." [35] His method was an offshoot of his temperamental desire to maintain cordial personal relations with everyone and to irritate no one. He would simply compromise and conciliate until agreement had been achieved. As he described it: "Now if I had a program that I wanted to have adopted by a town meeting, I should go to the three or four most influential men in my community. I should talk it out with them. *I should make concessions to them until I had got them to agree with me.* It's the same in the nation. . . . I should always go first to the two or three leading men." [36]

He conceived of his Cabinet as the "leading men," and whenever he was able to secure agreement by this self-contradictory technique, he would cite the agreement as a justification for his actions. What is most revealing, however, is not the extent to which a man with all of Harding's predispositions relied on the Cabinet, but the extent to which in spite of his predispositions he deviated from normal expectations. In seeking to explain these deviations, we can uncover some important limitations on Cabinet effectiveness.

Like every Cabinet, though perhaps more so than some, Harding's was a heterogeneous one, from which he naturally received heterogeneous advice. One biographer writes that "there were red hot discussions in the Cabinet [because] . . . each member had to face the intensity of diverging opinion." [37] Though Harding's attempt to manage his "best-minds" Cabinet with sweet reasonableness was particularly inept, the dilemma he faced is a normal one. A President who wants to rely on his Cabinet and who finds it offering divergent advice — let alone divergent personalities, talents, loyalties, sympathies, and interests — is presented with difficulties. He cannot persist in relying on the group by letting its members battle to a consensus and then accepting it. No President in the period behaved this way and no President is ever likely to do so. Every President, a Harding as well as a Wilson, knows that he has the ultimate decision-making power, and he will not behave as if our system sanctioned collective responsibility.

Harding's solution to his dilemma — how to use a Cabinet which gave him divergent advice — was to seek, from within the "best minds," one or two "bestest" minds, and to rely heavily upon them. During much of his administration, Harding placed a disproportionately heavy trust in Attorney General Daugherty. A special private telephone, the only one of its kind in the White House, connected their offices. "Ordinarily," says Mark Sullivan, "Harding called Daugherty from five to twenty times a day." [38] In facing one of his most serious domestic problems, the Railroad Strike of 1922, Harding leaned immediately upon his Attorney General. For Daugherty, the strike was "a threat against civilization," "a conspiracy to overturn the government itself," a "civil war" demanding the most suppressive measures at the government's command. He favored a vigorous and severe court injunction. Calling this plan "an inspiration," Harding gave Daugherty *carte blanche* and promised to back him up "with all the power at my command." If we can believe Daugherty's own account, Harding listened and acquiesced eagerly while his adviser unfolded his proposal. But more than this, Harding explicitly and deliberately promised not to say anything about it to anyone, "*inside the Cabinet* or outside."

The news of the injunction was broken to the remainder of the

Cabinet in the newspapers on the morning of a scheduled Cabinet meeting. Herbert Hoover, who considered the injunction to be "an obvious transgression of the most rudimentary rights of man," and Hughes, who felt that it was "outrageous in law as well as morals," discussed their outrage and their surprise while walking to the meeting. Hoover, mindful of the economic consequences for his own Commerce Department, decided to raise the issue with assurances of Hughes' support. At the meeting there were strong protests against Daugherty's action by at least four men, and there is no evidence of any support for the Attorney General.

Albert Fall censured Harding's initial failure to consult the Cabinet; he said, "The Attorney General has laid this Cabinet, Mr. President, open to criticism. The public is going to think you and the Cabinet have sanctioned his acts." Fall says he even threatened to resign. Theodore Roosevelt, Jr., substituting for Secretary of the Navy Edwin Denby, protested the injunction at some length, which "greatly amused" Daugherty. Herbert Hoover relates that, "I expressed myself fully and called upon Hughes to verify the legal points of my protest. He did it vigorously." The weight of their opinion, however, was apparently not humorous either to Daugherty or to Harding. Hoover continues:

> Daugherty was obviously flabbergasted, and when Harding turned upon him demanding explanation of this illegal action, could only mumble that the objectionable passages were approved by the lawyers as being within the constitutional rights of the government. Harding very abruptly instructed him to withdraw those sections of the injunction at once — Daugherty dropped the whole action as quickly as possible.[39]

As a matter of general, high-level policy which came under the legitimate jurisdiction of at least half the Cabinet, the Railroad Strike was tailor-made for Cabinet discussion. Yet, Harding preferred to lean upon a single adviser instead; when the subject was finally forced into the Cabinet meeting, the actions there showed what Harding lost by circumventing the group. Had the question been aired in conference before, rather than after, the decision, Harding would have been made aware of the alternatives of action and the differences of opinion, and would at least have made an informed decision. Even if he could not have obtained agreement, he would have assuaged the feelings of those members who felt they were being subverted and would have maintained greater administrative coherence within his official family. As it was, he made an uninformed decision; he was not aware of the views of his other top advisers; he hostaged himself completely to one man; he incurred the resentment of some of his Cabinet; and he was ultimately forced to backtrack on a decision which was in the process of being executed.

The case of the Railroad Strike is a virtual catalogue of the potential dangers in this sort of Cabinet circumvention by a man who needs to rely on his advisers. It also demonstrates what positive gains are to be had by working through the Cabinet meeting. But the fact that Harding deliberately chose to forego the gains and brave the liabilities indicates that there are probably strong objective reasons for doing so. No President can ever be expected to sign what amounts to an exclusive consultation contract with any predetermined group, let alone one as diverse as the Cabinet. Harding's response to the lesson of the Railroad Strike was not to place his trust henceforth in the Cabinet meeting, but to turn increasingly away from Daugherty to rely on a different "inner cabinet," composed of Secretaries Hughes, Mellon, and Hoover.[40]

Calvin Coolidge was another President strongly predisposed to use his Cabinet but who nonetheless discriminated within the group, relying extensively on a few and ignoring others. Secretaries Hughes and Mellon dominated his administration. "Hughes acted as a sort of premier, being consulted on all the important issues relating to the welfare of the country. The two men got along admirably together."[41] Mellon's disproportionate influence was indelibly stamped on the Coolidge economy measures: the bonus veto, the veto of the postal salary increase, and the tax reductions.[42] On the other hand, Coolidge was fundamentally at odds with his Secretary of Agriculture and established no kind of rapport with him.[43] The influence of Hoover, which had waxed strong in the later part of Harding's tenure, waned under Coolidge. Although he characteristically allowed Hoover to run the Commerce Department "according to his own ideas,"[44] Coolidge was not very receptive to Hoover's advice on extra-departmental matters. Many of Hoover's projects cost money, which was sufficient grounds for a deaf ear. The President complained to another Cabinet member, "That man [Hoover] has offered me unsolicited advice for six years, all of it bad."[45]

The similarities in the Harding and Coolidge patterns of behavior suggest that the differentiation among Cabinet members is inevitable. When it happens, it will cut into the potentialities of the Cabinet meeting. The President will not look upon the members of the group equally and may be unwilling to treat them as equals. The Cabinet may be his official family, but there is a crucial distinction between his blood relatives, kissing cousins, and black sheep. It is simply not a valid assumption that in a Cabinet meeting all views will be weighted equally by the President.

President Eisenhower once said, "In Cabinet meetings I always wait for George Humphrey to speak. I sit back and listen to the others talk while he doesn't say anything. But I know that when he speaks he will say just what I am thinking."[46] This condition confirms the absurdity of taking a vote in the Cabinet meeting with each vote counting as one, when the President obviously does not look at it that way. More than this, it casts real doubt on the effectiveness of the whole Cabinet as a decision-making body.

The formation by the President, from the subtle materials of personality, abilities, and confidence, of an inner core of advisers is by no means restricted to those Presidents like Harding and Coolidge who seem originally predisposed to use the Cabinet. These Presidents have been cited in order to put the case for inevitability in its most convincing form. What *is* likely to distinguish one group of Presidents from the other is that while the first group turns to an "inner cabinet," the second is apt to utilize a "kitchen cabinet." The difference between the two is that the "kitchen cabinet" is composed of non-Cabinet officials, while the "inner cabinet" is taken from the Cabinet membership. The first real "kitchen cabinet" served Andrew Jackson, who was as notorious as any President for ignoring his official Cabinet advisers. Wilson and Roosevelt moved freely beyond the borders of the Cabinet to lean disproportionately upon unofficial advisers. Hoover, in his extensive reliance on Secretary of the Treasury Ogden Mills, followed more closely the "inner-cabinet" pattern.[47]

Where they go and how they get their non-Cabinet-meeting advice is a matter of personal habits and attitudes and will vary among Presidents, but the essential point is that the President will want to remain perfectly free to do so. No President will hostage himself to the Cabinet as a collectivity. Thus we are driven again to acknowledge the dependence of the Cabinet on the Chief Executive, and to the conclusion that *the limitations of the Cabinet meeting mark the frontiers of presidential leadership.*

If the performance of two Cabinet-reliant Presidents like Harding and Coolidge reveals a limitation on the Cabinet meeting, then the performance of two self-reliant Presidents like Wilson and Roosevelt sheds light on the most likely successes of the meeting. The rationale behind Wilson's use of his Cabinet was an intellectual one, reflected in a well-structured and modulated decision-making process which discouraged any interference between the information-gathering and decision-making points. The rationale behind Roosevelt's Cabinet relations was an administrative one, reflected in his habits of tapping diverse sources of advice, delegating in a disorderly manner, and retaining all final coordinating authority in his own hands. Neither man used his official family to any great extent, but on the other hand, each of them found some occasional value in Cabinet meetings.

Woodrow Wilson viewed his Cabinet members as departmental administrators. Pursuant to this view, which involved a high degree of delegation in domestic affairs, Wilson himself initiated only foreign-policy matters in the Cabinet.[48] This attitude, plus the reluctance of his department heads to raise their own problems in that forum, effectively eliminated large areas of domestic policy from the attention of the group. A further result was that the coordinating possibilities of the group were vitiated. Wilson himself admitted on occasion that he had completely lost track of what his department heads were doing.[49] In the area of foreign policy, Wilson was temperamentally compelled to lead. He did not delegate as copiously, did not follow his Secretaries of State, and broke with two of them. Robert Lansing seldom spoke in the Cabinet meeting, even on such vital problems as the propriety of declaring war. With this official neutralized, the profitability of collegial discussions of foreign affairs was radically diminished.[50]

Wilson's technique in Cabinet relations is graphically illustrated by his behavior during the events leading up to the declaration of war. When the *Lusitania* was sunk on May 7, 1915 he prepared the United States' reply in seclusion and without consulting his Cabinet jointly or individually. "He could obtain from its members nothing new except their emotional reactions to the appalling catastrophe — which were precisely what he wanted to avoid."[51] One member called the President to press his views and was told to submit a memorandum.[52] Four days later, at the routine meeting, Wilson read the draft to the Cabinet, which hardly discussed its contents at all but busied itself speculating on possible consequences.[53] After reversing himself on Bryan's privately suggested "postscript" (the only recorded suggestion by a member, and it done, significantly enough, in private), the note was sent "practically as drafted by the President."[54]

Upon receiving the German reply on May thirty-first, Wilson drafted a second letter, "working entirely alone." It was completed that day and presented to the regular Cabinet meeting on the following day. There was, once again, almost no comment on the Wilson draft, conversation running with apparently more heat than light to the general situation and especially to attitudes toward Great Britain.[55] When the Cabinet met next, on June fourth, the note had not yet been sent to Germany and Wilson's action in the matter was still hanging fire. Of this meeting Houston writes, "The President spent several minutes looking up something, and a confused and somewhat tiresome discussion followed. It tried the President's patience and tired him perceptibly. It did not help him. The meeting did not last long."[56] Wilson admitted the next day that he could extract from the discussion no clear idea of what the Cabinet view had been.

On June ninth, the group met again. There was a discussion of the general situation, punctuated by Bryan's late arrival after he had announced his resignation. Houston made some suggestions in which the President was noticeably interested. Wilson touched up his original draft of the note and dispatched it later the same day. It is amply evident that during these delicate negotiations the Cabinet was of little concrete assistance, except for the eleventh-hour suggestions of emphasis by Secretary Houston at the June ninth meeting. The only evident result of the President-Cabinet interaction was the one which underlined Wilson's own primacy — the disclosure of differences which led to the resignation of the Secretary of State.[57]

During the interval of neutrality that followed, half of Wilson's Cabinet was urging upon him more aggressive steps than he, mindful of both domestic public opinion and his own innate desire for peace, was willing to take. There is no doubt but what Wilson broached many important subjects to the Cabinet during the period prior to the actual declaration of war, but his method of approach was similar to the Lusitania episode. For instance, when he decided to request the warring nations to state their aims in December of 1916, he read his note to the Cabinet and invited discussion, but said that "I will send this note or nothing."[58] Cabinet protests against sending it were of no avail, and it went forward as written.

On January 31, 1917, Wilson learned that the Germans were about to resume unrestricted submarine warfare. He did not consult with his Cabinet until their regular meeting, February second. Baker says that this hiatus was characteristic because "he usually delayed such action until he was nearing a decision himself." [59] He invited discussion as to the next move. During the response, Wilson revealed impatience at the impulsive reactions of the group, observing that these did not help him at all and asking for concrete suggestions.[60] Although he had apparently come to the meeting convinced of the necessity for a diplomatic break, and although the Cabinet members agreed, he typically gave no indication of his decision to the group.[61]

During the month of February, as the world situation grew more tense, the President held his course in the face of increasingly vocal opposition from some of the Cabinet. His reluctance to request armed neutrality caused the nearest thing to a Cabinet crisis of Wilson's Presidency. Lane wrote, "We have had to push and push and push to get him to take any forward step. . . . The President wants to be alone and unbothered. He probably would not call Cabinet meetings if Congress adjourned." [62] In Cabinet meetings, McAdoo was insistent, and he "nettled" Wilson with his "emphatic manner and language." Lansing and Redfield were of the same general opinion. Houston urged quick action and spoke of resigning.[63] The most animated discussions of the entire eight years were held at this time, and the hair-trigger attitude of some members resulted not infrequently in emotional excursions into rumors and wild suppositions.[64] All of this was of no appreciable aid to the President, who was passionately seeking every alternative to war.

When Wilson finally made the decision to go before Congress to advocate the arming of merchant ships, he did so himself, fixed in his determination to act by the Zimmerman note which he did not divulge to the Cabinet. Throughout March the Cabinet simply waited to see "what our policy will be as to Germany." [65] Certainly they did not make this policy. After an agonizing debate with himself for ten days in near seclusion, Wilson met his Cabinet on March twentieth. He put two questions to the group, which clearly indicated the direction in which his mind was already moving: Should he convene Congress early? If so, what should he say? The Cabinet was uniformly convinced of the advisability of a quick special session devoted to a declaration of war. Wilson, though his intention must have been quite clear, gave no indication of a final decision.[66]

The next morning he called for Congress two weeks ahead of schedule, a result which Colonel House felt could be attributed largely to the unanimous opinion of his Cabinet. If this is so, it is the closest thing to direct and recorded Cabinet influence during his term of office.[67] At any rate, Wilson went to work on a war message but did not reveal any of its contents to the Cabinet (not even to the Secretary of State) at the Cabinet meetings in the interim.[68] When he did finally turn to talk about the message, it was the night before it was to be delivered, and he went not to the Cabinet but to an old newspaper friend.[69]

During the war, Cabinet meetings were brief but were complemented by separate meetings between the Secretaries and the President.[70] For those members most vitally concerned with the prosecution of the war, individual meetings were frequent, but some of the others felt distinctly on the outside. In March, 1918, Secretary of the Interior Lane complained, "Nothing talked of at Cabinet that would interest a nation, a family, or a child. No talk of the war. No talk of Russia or Japan. Talk by McAdoo about some bills in Congress, by the President about giving the veterans of the Spanish American War leave with pay to attend their annual encampment. And he treated this seriously, as if it were a matter of first importance."[71] For weeks in the fall of that year, he said, the Cabinet spent its time "largely in telling stories."[72]

Cabinet desuetude continued well into the period of peace negotiations, but on October 22, 1918, and again at the next week's meeting Wilson discussed the armistice negotiations with the group. These are the first conferences that Houston mentions in nearly a year and a half, and Lane wrote enthusiastically, "Again we talked like a Cabinet." The President requested and received reactions to Germany's latest note and suggestions as to a third note from the United States. Two drafts of this note had already been written, however, and Wilson did not accept any of the subsequent Cabinet advice which would have changed its general import.[73] After the meeting, Wilson wrote another draft and presented it the next day to his War Cabinet. He asked for suggestions, rejected the only one offered by this group, and "not one word of it was changed."[74] On such a vital question as the acceptance of Germany's armistice terms it was fitting that the leading figures of the administration should have an opportunity to express an opinion, but this opportunity came only after Wilson had practically decided on his position.

Wilson was not dependent on his Cabinet group in any sense. He was often interested in hearing their opinions and in gaining a general sense of the meeting, but just as often, it appears, he avoided this by taking action and presenting the group with a *fait accompli*. He did not stifle the variety of opinion which frequently existed within the group, but neither did he follow those who were inclined to disagree with him, nor hesitate because the Cabinet was split. He asked for advice and comment, but most often he did this when his own mind was made up, or nearly so. What he wanted and received by way of opinions were reactions to, and not the bases for, his policy. He wanted to obtain the sense of the meeting, not as a positive guide or as the answer to a problem, but as a sounding board against which to project his own ideas. When a President uses the Cabinet in this way there is always an appearance of disorder — perhaps of pointlessness. At times it seems as if Wilson could anticipate the members' habitual responses, or as though the discussion was so emotional that there was little point to the meeting at all. Yet a President may wish, simply as a matter of information, to get the reactions of these men and of the constituencies they represent. This purpose can be accomplished in a very intermittent, haphazard way, and while it may not reflect the optimum use of the Cabinet, it may be very helpful.

The other main value of Cabinet "participation" in foreign policy was that of communication and coherence. The President could and did marshal their support for his position, thus providing unity and a common perspective within the administration. Although Wilson was not inclined to announce a decision in the meeting, the conclave did help the members. It gave them an opportunity to find out some little bit of what the President was thinking, of what his larger purposes were. The very fact of a meeting, the very fact of discussion, no matter how low its quality, has value for both the members and the President. Neither one would accept the alternative of no meeting at all.

General estimates of the worth of Roosevelt's Cabinet meetings do not vary much. None of the members who has written about it claimed an important advisory role for the group; some of them spoke quite feelingly to the contrary. As early as 1935, Harold Ickes wrote what he had been thinking "for a long time":

> The cold fact is that on important matters we are seldom called upon for advice. We never discuss exhaustively any policy of government or question of political strategy. The President makes all of his own decisions and so far at least as the Cabinet is concerned, without taking counsel with a group of advisers, . . . it is fair to say that the Cabinet is not a general council upon whose advice the President relies, or the opinions of which, on important matters, he calls for. Our Cabinet meetings are pleasant affairs, but we only skim the surface of routine affairs.[75]

Jesse Jones recalled that "Matters of high government policy were seldom discussed at Cabinet meetings. . . . There was not a great deal of discussion."[76] In his diary, Henry Stimson recorded a "typical" evaluation of a Cabinet meeting as "The same old two and sixpence, no earthly good."[77] Secretaries Perkins and Forrestal, as well as Vice-President Truman, concurred in this general opinion.[78]

In both foreign and domestic matters Roosevelt's disregard of his Cabinet was similar. In 1937, for instance, he convened the

Cabinet "hastily at eleven o'clock one morning" to reveal to them for the first time his "court-packing" bill. The bill itself was already on its way to Congress. The Attorney General was the only Cabinet member who had any knowledge of it. From time to time the problem of the Supreme Court had popped up in Cabinet meeting and the President may have received reactions, but he did not seek their advice on a specific program. He did not consult them on his 1937 State of the Union message which criticized the Court. "As far as the Cabinet [was] concerned we were confronted with a *fait accompli*." "Even if our advice had been sought, it would have been ineffective." They were "totally unprepared," and "there was relatively little comment on it." [79]

When Germany invaded Poland, Roosevelt called the Cabinet together. They talked at length about what it would mean to the United States, and Roosevelt told them of what he planned to do.[80] He convened the Cabinet to read his War Address to them and rejected the pleas of Hull that he change it.[81] The same *de facto* formula was used with regard to the Panay incident and to the diplomatic recognition of Russia.[82] Cordell Hull records that "The President's Cabinet filled, in general, a very minor role in the formulation of foreign policy. I did not find as much discussion of foreign relations at Cabinet meetings as might be supposed except in certain instances where a given question was very acute and was being highly publicized. . . . No decisions on foreign policy were taken by the Cabinet." [83]

There were notable exceptions to ordinary practice in both foreign and domestic areas. One foreign policy meeting did make quite a marked impression on at least Hull, Stimson, and Miss Perkins. This meeting occurred on November 7, 1941 at a time when negotiations with the Japanese were becoming increasingly strained and nearing the breaking point. Roosevelt, after relating the Lincoln story, turned the meeting over to Hull who described the current state of affairs, the dangers, and the possible consequences. The President then canvassed each Cabinet member for his opinion on the gravity of the situation. Each was asked, in turn, to assess the probable public reaction should a shooting war with Japan develop. The Cabinet was unanimous both as to the degree of the danger and as to their conviction that the American people would support military action in such a case. They further concurred that it was desirable to educate the public for any eventuality. Hull said this was the closest that the Cabinet ever came to a vote. Stimson felt "it was one of the best Cabinet meetings we ever had," and Miss Perkins agreed.[84]

A Cabinet meeting devoted to domestic affairs, held in November, 1937, provides another illustration of Rooseveltian Cabinet usage. In the course of going around the table, Roosevelt heard similarly gloomy reports of the business situation and of declining employment from several members, including Morgenthau and Perkins. When they had finished, Roosevelt remarked that while he was glad to receive these reports, "I am sick and tired of being told by the Cabinet, by Henry [Morgenthau], and by everybody else for the past two weeks what's the matter with the country and nobody suggests what I should do." After some hesitation, Morgenthau opined that Roosevelt, above all, ought to reassure business. With some impatience the President exclaimed that this would just mean turning on "the old record," which he had done "again and again." The Secretary of the Treasury asserted that it was precisely the reading of the record on taxes, budget balancing, and the health of capitalism that business wanted to hear. He said that this should be done "for the fifteenth time if necessary." At this point, James Farley stepped in to support Morgenthau, urging Roosevelt to make "a quieting statement." The Vice-President agreed.

Roosevelt replied that there were "altogether too many statements being issued now and too much talking," much of which was uncoordinated and contradictory. The Department of Agriculture, he remarked, had been saying that national income was falling, while at the same time the Commerce Department reported that it was rising. Henry Wallace and Miss Perkins rushed to the defense of Agriculture's figures, whereupon Roosevelt "glared" at the Secretary of Commerce, in whom he had little confidence, and cut him off before he could explain his side of the picture.

Most of the Cabinet, with the exception of Undersecretary of State Welles, then joined in a discussion of housing, railroads, and the utilities situation. Roosevelt agreed to "read the record again." He concluded the meeting with a statement, part of which read, "It's easy enough to criticize but it's another thing to help. I want all of you — everyone — when offering criticisms to make suggestions which are constructive. I am fully conscious of the situation which exists. I have been studying it for a long, long time. . . ." Postmaster General Farley felt that this was "one of the best (if not the best) Cabinet meetings we ever had," and he reports that the President agreed with him. Harold Ickes wrote that "We were in session for almost two and a half hours, and it was more like what I had always supposed a Cabinet meeting should be than any that I have attended. . . . I have never seen him so eager for counsel from his Cabinet."[85]

The meetings of November, 1941, and November, 1937, had similar values. In the first place, both discussions focused on likely public reactions to policy. Where he had specifically asked for an appraisal of public opinion (in 1941), it was probably assuring to him, if not revealing, to receive such a single-minded interpretation. Where the subject of public opinion was pressed upon him (in 1937), it is probable that the discussion apprised him of the attitude of constituencies in the country with which he was not in very close contact. In the one instance his position was confirmed by Cabinet discussion; in the other, he was moved to take a step that he had not thought necessary. In reflecting public opinion, or the opinion of the publics they represent, Cabinet members are again performing a sounding-board function. But as in the case of Wilson, it was performed by giving reactions off the top of the head. Roosevelt's complaint about the lack of constructive suggestions in 1937 parallels Wilson's sometime attitude about the purely emotional quality of discussion.

The second accomplishment of the two meetings was improved administrative coherence. In both cases there was widespread participation by members in discussing a subject which was fairly well delineated and which affected all of them. Participation of this sort increases Cabinet *esprit* and increases the chances of unified Cabinet support for the President. In one case, Cabinet agreement was reassuring to Roosevelt in the face of possible danger; in the other, he sought a unified and harmonious administrative approach to the public. In both cases, the function of President-to-member and member-to-President communication was well served. To be sure, the discussions were impromptu — dropped into the laps of the members by the President in 1941 and elicited from the tenor of the random remarks of the members in 1937 — but some degree of administrative coherence can be promoted in the meeting even though the circumstances are fortuitous.

Administrative coherence is an intangible condition. Since it is created by the mere fact of communication, it cannot be measured in terms of the tangibles of efficiency. The most discursive discussion can be of considerable value if the Cabinet members can catch something of the President's attitude toward problems and be stimulated by his example. A reading of the Ickes diaries leads to the conclusion that the most continuous value which the Roosevelt Cabinet meetings served was to give the members an idea of the direction in which the President was moving or the emphasis which he placed on certain matters. The diaries are studded with entries about Cabinet meetings which report that "the President is considering . . ." "the President's feeling is . . ." or "the President is wondering about. . . ." There was no coming to grips with specific issues and debating them to a decision, but from out of all the discontinuity came a valuable sense of the President's thinking. Frequently there was a similar meeting of the minds among the members, which was vague ("the feeling seemed to be") but none the less important.

Beyond this was (and is) another intangible dividend in terms of organization morale. In spite of his remarks about the "vacuity" of meetings, Ickes wrote, "You go in [to Cabinet meetings] tired and discouraged and out of sorts and the President puts new life in you. You come out feeling like a fighting cock." [86] Miss Perkins wrote that "It wasn't so much what he said as the spirit he conveyed." [87] Cabinet members may, as one member of the Eisenhower group has said, "look forward to Cabinet meetings as a source of inspiration," [88] a value which bears no necessary relation to some of the limitations we have encountered.

The Wilson and Roosevelt experiences lead to the conclusion that the uses most easily and naturally served by the Cabinet meeting are those of the political sounding board and administrative coherence. This conclusion is certainly confirmed by the experience of the Truman Cabinet, even though Truman consulted more seriously with them.[89] The performance of these two functions does not carry with it any possible restrictions of presidential predominance. Each function can be performed with only a minimum of institutionalization, but they do need that minimum. Only through participation in some recognized group which meets regularly and observes certain procedures can administrative coherence be achieved. This does not mean that one might not improve the performance of these functions by change or that some Presidents may not be more effective than others. It does mean that even under Presidents where it seems least important and most ineffective, the Cabinet meeting performs some valuable functions, functions which might not be performed as successfully by any other advisory group.

CHAPTER FOUR

The Cabinet Meeting: II

THE CABINET MEMBER AND THE CABINET MEETING

IT is evident from the investigation of institutional form and presidential behavior that forces beyond the Chief Executive-Cabinet nexus condition Cabinet-meeting activity. The most significant of these are the centrifugal forces which come into play through the actions of individual Cabinet members. These forces will be examined in detail in succeeding chapters. Suffice it to say now that the members have a participant's-eye view of the meeting, with a non-presidential, non-Cabinet logic quite its own. It is a logic the compelling assumptions of which are rooted in the pluralism of the American political system. The pattern of development for the several departments was one of great diversity in purpose, structure, and clientele. The atmosphere of their growth encouraged a free-wheeling independence among the Cabinet's constituent units. Each Cabinet member, moreover, is the product of an appointment process characterized by the inter-determination of many variables — a process designed to build diversity into the Cabinet.

The objectively pluralistic conditions of departmental growth and of Cabinet appointment nourish their own subjective counterparts. Each Cabinet member has his own particularistic, departmental *raison d'être*. His attitude tends, likewise, to be particularistic and departmental. He develops much less of a group feeling than an individualistic one, and he more readily identifies with his department than with the Cabinet. His lack of group identification is aggravated, furthermore, by all the personal differences — temperamental and philosophical — which give rise to interpersonal friction within the "official family." The American Cabinet has, of course, no formal collective responsibility, but the psychology of departmentalism even militates against the establishment of what might be called mutual responsibility — a state of mind which stresses group concerns rather than separate and particular concerns. The subjective attitude hardest to come by among Cabinet members is this sense of corporate unity and common purpose, on which basis alone the potentialities of the institution can be realized.

The reaction of the Harding Cabinet, in the face of scandals which sent one member to the federal penitentiary and found another under extraordinarily severe pressure for malfeasance, is illustrative. The disclosures of Teapot Dome, coupled with the mismanagement and face-saving suicides which rocked the Department of Justice, were sufficient to have toppled any responsible European ministry. Yet, from the American Cabinet nothing but silence — "a distant, frigid, and unhelpful silence"[1] — was forthcoming. Only one member was directly involved, and he took the entire blame and the full brunt of the criticism. The rest of the group said simply that it had never been called to their attention and that it was none of their business.

"The question of the legality or the propriety of the oil leases [said Hughes] . . . were never brought before the Cabinet for its discussion."[2] Since Secretary of the Navy Denby and Secretary of the Interior Fall felt it was no one else's affair, this was good enough for their colleagues. Yet Hughes' biographer calls him "astonishingly tolerant of misconduct toward which he bore no responsibility," and the others (Hays and Mellon, for instance) behaved similarly.[3] No one thought of resigning or even of decrying the scandal publicly, and only the rankest opposition newspapers interpreted this as any reflection at all on the whole Cabinet.[4] These events and the attitudes of all concerned reflect a lack of responsibility, collective and mutual, which is characteristic of the Cabinet in action.

The American Cabinet does not fall together, but neither does it stand together; the lack of mutual responsibility is but the obverse side of the departmental attitude. Each Cabinet member maintains his aloofness from his fellows. As an epitome of the attitude, one might take Jesse Jones' blunt statement that "I made no other suggestions to other Cabinet members about their departments and asked none from them." [5] For this official, as for many others, a fellow member's worth was judged in direct proportion to the extent to which he minded his own business. David Houston likewise said, "I have made it a rule not to take the initiative in any matter falling under the jurisdiction of another department and to try to be of assistance only when my aid was sought." [6] Secretary Hughes' colleagues "could not get him interested in matters outside of his department, although by so doing he could help to promote the spirit of cooperation." [7]

When Henry Wallace once sought financial aid for the Department of Agriculture, the reply of his colleague, the Secretary of the Treasury, bespoke a common attitude — "Henry, that's your cross, you bear it." [8] On those occasions when the energies of a department head carry him across departmental lines, the serious charge of "interference" or "meddling" is usually leveled against him — as Cordell Hull frequently charged his cohorts.[9] Secretary of War Garrison replied to Secretary of the Navy Daniels' offer of interdepartmental cooperation: "I don't care a damn about the Navy and you don't care a damn about the Army. You run your machine and I'll run mine." [10] An observer of the Wilson Administration concluded that, "The members of the Cabinet do not seem to have the habit of frankness with one another. Each lives and works in a water-tight compartment." [11]

The particularistic, departmental attitude of the Cabinet member manifests itself in his behavior at the Cabinet meeting. Ideally, the Cabinet meeting is the point at which the various department heads come together to work as a team, to cooperate and to coordinate and by so doing to help the President with his government-wide concerns. The effect of departmentalism militates against all these assumptions about teamwork. The Cabinet meeting tends to become a diplomatic assembly in which the departmentalism of the ambassadors replaces nationalism as the psychological bar to unity and cooperation. There is too often a lack of any sustaining desire within the group to function as a group, and a lack of the will to carry on serious business at the Cabinet meeting.

As Louis Brownlow says, "Each feels his responsibility — as indeed it is — personally to the President and not to the President in Council, nor to the President and his Cabinet, *and above all not to his Cabinet colleagues.*" [12] Jesse Jones stated the canon of behavior perfectly when he said, "My principal reason for not having a great deal to say at Cabinet meetings was that there was no one at the table who could be of help to me except the President, and when I needed to consult him, I did not choose a Cabinet meeting to do so." [13] This attitude converts the meeting into a joint enterprise, in which "joint" denotes a common determination to suppress vital issues and "enterprise" consists in the great variety of devices for doing so.

By all odds, the most important pieces of domestic legislation in Woodrow Wilson's first term were the tariff and federal reserve bills. Since Wilson made it a practice not to bring domestic issues before the group, it was left to the member concerned to raise these two vital questions for discussion. Mr. McAdoo, the Secretary of the Treasury, did not choose to do so, and his behavior effectively cut off this whole area, so vital to the success of the administration, from Cabinet discussion. As one of his colleagues wrote, "The truth is that the two important domestic issues, the tariff and the currency, are under the Treasury and that McAdoo is a solitaire player. He is self-reliant and has dash, boldness, and courage, but he does not cultivate Cabinet teamwork and does not invite discussion or suggestion from the Cabinet as a whole." [14] Multiplied by the number of individuals and problems, the departmental feeling can keep those issues which depend on Cabinet-member initiative from ever coming to the attention of the Cabinet.

Attempts to raise touchy interdepartmental issues may meet with resentment from a colleague and may founder on that account. Early in the Roosevelt administration, Miss Perkins precipitated Cabinet discussion on a public works bill being prepared in the Labor Department. She drew support for her measure from several members, but strong opposition from Budget Director Douglas. Rather than express his views, however, Douglas presented, according to Miss Perkins, "a mild and polite version in terms which he considered suitable for the Cabinet." He informed the group that he was working on a better plan, yet he would not tell them anything about it until "the time came." Even when Henry Wallace stumbled onto the plan and raised it in the Cabinet meeting, Douglas would not say anything specific about it. Yet, he was pressing his views with the President in private.[15] In the same Cabinet, Harold Ickes once raised the subject of the post-war disposition of the Japanese-held islands, a subject which had been the source of an "old feud between Navy and Interior." From Secretary of the Navy Forrestal, Ickes received a facetious rebuke which terminated discussion: "the Navy's suggestion [is] that Mr. Ickes be made king of Polynesia, Micronesia and the Pacific Ocean Area." In private, Forrestal's comments were far more bitter.[16] Under conditions like these the group could not come to grips with, or settle, policy.

When Secretary of State Hull brought up in Cabinet the impasse between State and Interior over the sale of helium to Germany, the shoe was on the other foot for Mr. Ickes. He only stiffened his attitude in the face of adverse comment from several of the members. Roosevelt himself inquired "Well, Harold, what do you say? The army assures me that the gas will not be used for military purposes. Can't you let them have the helium?" To which Ickes replied simply, "Mr. President, I can't surrender my conscience to the Army." Ickes' general contention that it was no one else's business received some confirmation by Roosevelt's refusal to overrule his Secretary of the Interior.[17] A few experiences like this in any single Cabinet would soon convey the impression that it is not considered acceptable to criticize or interfere with one's fellow members. And more than this, they would cause the Cabinet member to turn away from the Cabinet as a coordinating body to dig other, more private channels. Some time later Ickes wrote to Roosevelt, "As a matter of fact, since the helium incident I have been reluctant to communicate in any way with the Department of State on account of the hostility that is all too apparent in that department toward me. . . . Frequently, I have sent to you communications that, in ordinary course, I would have sent directly to the Department of State." [18]

Without doubt, departmentalism is aggravated by the traditional method of transacting the Cabinet's business. Without doubt, an agenda can encourage unity. But with respect to the Eisenhower reform, the roots of departmentalism are sunk too deep for technique to change. One reason why Eisenhower meetings at their best exhibit characteristics of Roosevelt meetings at their worst is the persistence of departmentalism. But in the Eisenhower system, where Cabinet business is screened through a planning process and where the President's presence is a strong influence for harmony, the most impressive manifestations of this force will not be found in the meeting itself. Most important for our purposes here, they will be found in the natural reluctance of the department head to place controversial or sensitive items on the agenda in the first place. This problem manifests itself further in the nature of Cabinet discussions.

The Department of the Interior, whose power and water resources programs are among the most publicly and interdepartmentally debated ones of the Eisenhower period, places only four or five items a year on the Cabinet agenda, and these are virtually always informational items or policy presentations such as "Mission 66." Other members do not look upon the Cabinet as a forum for the discussion of knotty problems in their particular field — except to brief the group on some *fait accompli*. The Cabinet Secretary or the Assistant to the President has succeeded in persuading and cajoling some items out of the department head's grasp, but very few of the ten line departments have been reasonably good contributors to the agenda. Here, admittedly and predictably, is *the most vulnerable link* in the Eisenhower Cabinet reform. The problem of overcoming departmentalism constitutes the real nub of the Cabinet Secretary's work, and it is a deep-rooted political problem rather than a procedural one.

Beyond these considerations of willingness, and less purposeful than they, is one concerning the basic competence of the members to discuss matters outside of their own jurisdiction. Secretary of State Hughes delivered a scathing indictment of Secretary Albert Fall's inability to contribute in the field of foreign affairs: "He would discourse at length on foreign affairs, showing neither acumen, discretion, nor accurate knowledge. But he thought he was an authority. His flow of words without wisdom was very boring to me at least, and I think to others. I had little to do with him, but I did not suspect him of having anything worse than vanity and mental indigestion."[19] Frequently time out must be taken in meetings to explain things to members that lie outside their jurisdiction.[20] With his energies devoted to his own department, its problems and its sources of strength, a Secretary may not, with or without agenda, be equipped to participate in many general discussions. This is to some extent a dilemma of departmental management; it is also a psychological attitude which is firmly ingrained. It may also be simply a matter of personal ability, which can many times be traced back to the vagaries of the appointment process. The net result is that even if a member is interested in dealing with matters beyond his immediate bailiwick, he may not be capable of adding anything to the group conference.

In addition, it is by no means certain that all members will be interested in their fellows' problems — or at least in the problems which are raised in Cabinet meeting. When each man keeps his own counsel and carefully guards departmental information and interdepartmental issues from the group, the cumulative result may be widespread boredom during routine Cabinet reports. Here, with Miss Perkins talking, one can catch the withering effect of departmentalism on a Cabinet "at work." Harold Ickes writes,

As usual, only the President listened to her. Harry Hopkins wrote me a note something to the effect: "Elementary course in government from four to five by Professor Frances Perkins." Later he passed this to Jesse Jones who was sitting next to Perkins. I looked at Jim Farley on one occasion and saw him with his eyes closed. Bob Jackson was nodding from time to time and at intervals he and Morgenthau were joking about something. Hull sat with the air of an early Christian martyr, with his hands folded, looking at the edge of the table without seeing it or anything else. I think that he was totally oblivious to what was going on. As usual, I studiously avoided being caught by Perkins' basilisk eye. Henry Wallace was contemplating the ceiling.[21]

The logically complementary aspect to the uninformative Cabinet meeting is the business-like manner in which members line up to see the President privately as soon as the meeting is over. After Wilson's Cabinet meetings, individual members remained for "a series of engagements . . . in which (frequently) more important subjects were discussed than at the Cabinet meeting itself." [22] In the Harding Cabinet, Hughes would say, "I have nothing to say now but I should like to see you after the meeting." [23] Jesse Jones, sphinx-like during the Roosevelt Cabinet conference, used to stay behind after every session for what was called "prayer meeting" at "Amen corner." [24] For Henry Stimson, the chief value of the Cabinet council was its usefulness "as a way in which to get into the White House to have a word with the President in private after the meetings were over." [25] President Truman's Cabinet members could accomplish the same end at the regular Cabinet luncheons which preceded meetings. The reluctance to raise issues in Cabinet meetings, to expose programs, difficulties, or plans to a fellow member, leads inevitably to the post-Cabinet (or pre-Cabinet) traffic jam. This phenomenon is, in turn, one hallmark of the Cabinet's own shortcomings.

Perhaps the capstone of mutual irresponsibility is the Cabinet "leak." Members do not acquire a sense of unity sufficient to deter them from revealing to outsiders the contents of the meeting. If the Cabinet were more of a corporate entity, in spirit at least, all members would feel (as many do) a compulsion to keep the proceedings to themselves. The results of the leak are clear. Both the President and the individual officials refrain from bringing important matters before the group. This pulling-in of horns adds cumulatively to the other centrifugal influences and fosters a further retreat from the Cabinet meeting. The Wilson, Harding, and Roosevelt Cabinets (at least) were all beset by this difficulty, and it helped none of them.[26] (The unprecedented publication of Eisenhower Cabinet discussions in Robert Donovan's book may have a similarly harmful effect on the future deliberations of that group.) With the threat of public embarrassment suspended over their heads, the participants will view their conference all the more as a safe forum only for banalities and straightforward reports, instead of a forum for a controversial exchange of ideas, opinions, and projected plans. The Cabinet leak, like departmentalism itself, is both cause and effect. It discourages Cabinet unity and activity, but it flows, too, from the lack of both.

The effects of departmentalism are, of course, subject to modification. Through conscious presidential effort and preliminary staff work, they can be minimized in the Cabinet meeting and in the public press, as has been the case under Eisenhower. Cabinet Secretary Rabb has said that in the Eisenhower Cabinet "The question is not 'What will be best for my department' or 'for me' but now always 'What will be best for the whole Executive Branch — for the President — for the nation?' "[27] This must be taken as an exercise in political hyperbole and not as a statement of fact. Departmentalism cannot be put to death by executive fiat nor can the frequent professions of allegiance to "the team" be taken as its death certificate. Cabinet members may be more privy to the President's views and more conscious of the virtues of harmony, but they are still department-oriented individuals, subject to the same centrifugal pulls as their predecessors. Secretary of the Treasury Humphrey's damaging public criticism of the President's 1958 budget is proof enough. After the Secretary at his budget press conference had stated, "I think that there are a lot of places in this budget that can be cut," the following exchange took place:

> QUESTION: Could you tell us a little something about why this strong call for economy comes from you rather than from the President himself and the budget? Has this been a result of consultation? Is this your view or are you speaking for the administration or the President? Just what is the background of that?
> SECRETARY HUMPHREY: *I am speaking for the Treasury Department largely.* We are responsible for the federal finances. . . .[28]

If the more obvious symptoms of departmentalism are absent from the meeting, and if observers of the meeting can say that "the Cabinet isn't a clashing Cabinet and has an amazing lack of differences," it does not follow that there are none. Intra-Cabinet controversies involving Messrs. Weeks and Durkin, Mitchell and Weeks, Stassen and Humphrey, and Dulles and Stassen have reached the public press. Others may have been driven underground. Or they may have been transferred to an interdepartmental committee, like those on Water Resources or Transportation Policy. Though its effects may be modified and its surface manifestations altered, departmentalism cannot be eliminated. It will always constitute a serious limitation on the effectiveness of the Cabinet meeting.

In the light of departmentalism, one can understand more fully why the Cabinet exhibits such a low degree of institutionality. Cabinet members, like the President, and for similar reasons of self-interest, may find a flexible system more congenial. The very life of the Eisenhower system as far as the Cabinet members are concerned depends on the retention of its flexibility. Let one department head be *told* that a particular item under his jurisdiction *had* to go on the agenda against his will, and the whole framework would collapse like a house of cards. Given departmentalism, it is not difficult to see why Presidents may be anxious to cancel meetings, or why a basically neutral procedure may fall subject to crippling influences, or why the Cabinet meeting tends to become a series of banal reports. One can also find here forces that may erode the President's power over his Cabinet, forces against which his countervailing power is limited because their origins are non-presidential. The President cannot shape the Cabinet completely in his own image in spite of the basic power-responsibility relationship. And this is one reason why he will seek help elsewhere, from an inner cabinet or a kitchen cabinet, or from some other agency. Considering the impact of departmentalism, it may be as great a cause for wonderment that Presidents use the Cabinet as much as they do, as it is that they use it so seldom.

THE CABINET MEETING AND INTERDEPARTMENTAL COORDINATION

The possible Cabinet function most affected by departmentalism is interdepartmental coordination. Whether manifested by a benign lack of interest or by purposeful competition, departmentalism operates to reduce the potentialities of the Cabinet as a coordinating mechanism. Yet in view of the extent to which executive decision-making must now be conducted across departmental boundaries, it does not seem too much to say that the Chief Executive's primary managerial task is precisely this one of coordination. From the seminal recommendations of the President's Committee on Administrative Management in 1939 to the present day, the President's need for assistance in this area has been widely recognized.[29] This, indeed, is the *raison d'être* for the phenomenal proliferation of those staff organs with interdepartmental planning, operating, and advisory functions which now comprise the Executive Office of the President. The expansion of this Office — of, for instance, the Budget Bureau, the National Security Council, the Office of Defense Mobilization, the Council of Economic Advisers, the White House Office[30] —

must be considered in part as an inevitable response to the new dimensions of governmental activity, but also in part as an adverse reflection on the ability of the Cabinet in coping with the difficult problems of coordination involved. In view of the increased urgency of overall coordination, it seems wise to devote some special attention to the nature of the Cabinet's shortcomings and to its place in the total complex of presidential coordinating bodies.

Accepting the caveat that "the process of coordination and integration is not one that can be readily described, but must be in considerable degree something that grows," [31] we can at least take a brief look at its requirements, as they are or are not fulfilled by the Cabinet.

In the *first* place, it would seem that before effective coordination can take place there must be an understanding of the goals toward which coordination will be pointed. Ultimately these goals are set by the President, but he needs assistance in developing them. He needs help in the "positive origination" of policy goals, which has been described as "policy staff" assistance.[32] If a concrete problem exists, he needs to have policy alternatives identified for him and needs to have their consequences discussed in terms of the larger objectives involved. He can also use the identification of future problems, and here coordination partakes, as it must, of the planning function. In either case, he needs help in setting goals, determining what problems are involved, and understanding their dimensions.

This job requires staff work of the best kind and at the highest level. It may require interagency consultation, but the impromptu, *ad hoc* type of consultation that so often characterizes the Cabinet meeting is not sufficient. It requires more than the offhand judgment of people quite unprepared to treat policy problems, in terms of adequate information, interest, or time. It requires a staff which not only has the ability to look ahead but which will do so from the presidential rather than any particularist point of view. It requires not political advice but the kind of substantive policy advice where the Cabinet is weakest. Adequate coordination rests on a coherent and thoughtful conception of overall policy objectives, which cannot be developed at the normal Cabinet meeting.

A Secretariat of the Eisenhower type, it may be added, is no help either, since it was not designed to have policy planning functions. The Assistants for Cabinet Coordination might possibly look over the horizon at policy problems and screen ideas before they were considered for an agenda. They, however, have concentrated almost exclusively on post-Cabinet, follow-up work and have done nothing by way of policy staff activity.

A *second* requirement of adequate coordination, related to the first, is the maintenance of communication among the agencies which are found to be involved in a problem. It finds its most important application in the matter of clearance. Since the character of so many present problems is interdepartmental, it is vital that as policy is made there be a constant clearing of information and a consideration, by each agency involved, of the effects of proposed policy upon it. This becomes especially important as policy is formulated for presentation to the legislature. Clearance of this sort is a systematic matter, and must become routinized to some degree. It must be ensured by a staff mechanism at the presidential level or by the participation of each agency in some form of high-level, interdepartmental committee with the requisite machinery.

Normally, the Cabinet fulfills the clearance function only on the lucky chance that something might pop up during casual Cabinet conversations. Since many matters have been left at the mercy of individual whim during routine around-the-table reports, since most members have been reluctant to discuss matters of vital importance to their department, and since the dominant pattern is so frequently one of in-Cabinet silence and out-of-Cabinet solicitation, the Cabinet forum functions very intermittently in this regard. Under President Eisenhower there has been some noticeable improvement, especially in the policy-presentation type of meeting, but there is still no assurance of forcing clearance. The method by which items are received or extracted from the departments and placed on the agenda is still, under Eisenhower, a basically haphazard, random, and highly personalized one, yielding good results with some departments and poor results with others. Indeed, one may even speculate that the existence of an agenda could become a protective device for a department which, not wishing to clear a touchy policy in the meeting, could satisfy everyone concerned by freely offering to clear some relatively innocuous proposal with his fellows. The question here is not so much the increased number of policies that get cleared in Cabinet meeting as it is the number and character of those which do not. In the first instance, the Eisenhower system has been quite successful. In the second, success is more doubtful.

A *third* essential of coordination is the treatment of outright interdepartmental or interagency disagreement. To the extent that there is staff work going on, identifying problem areas and forcing interdepartmental clearance, some minor disagreement can be averted. And if it cannot, then at least the issues in the dispute can be clarified and the necessary information on which to decide will be available for the President. The adjudication of interdepartmental disagreement is a presidential function, but he may obtain assistance in doing some of it. For this, he needs someone (or some group) to help him who has only the presidential viewpoint, whose decisions will carry the weight of the President's authority, and who has no operating responsibilities. The Cabinet, seen as a collectivity of competing, operating agencies, tends to throw problems in the President's lap rather than solve them. As for the settlement by the President of top-level disagreement, a meeting which includes a greater or lesser number than the actual disputants is not the optimum place to air such matters.

The limitations of the Cabinet as a place for settling differences of opinion can best be illustrated by citing a case which arose in the Truman Cabinet. Involved was a disagreement between the Interior and State Departments on the one hand and the Navy Department on the other over the sale of surplus United States tankers to foreign countries.[33] Eventually, the disagreement came up in Cabinet meeting where "the Cabinet after discussion seemed to concur" with the position of the State Department. Secretary of State Marshall interpreted this vague consensus as definitive. The Navy Department, strengthened by what was its statutory right to be consulted on any such sale, simply ignored the Cabinet action. Thus, an appeal to the Cabinet for adjudication of interdepartmental differences "had been in vain."

The question was raised in Cabinet meeting a second time, and although the consensus of the group was again favorable to State, its action was still vague, informal, and without binding force on anyone. Its opinion was "expressed but not formalized"; it stipulated (in some fashion) "some things with respect to the issue." It was not until two weeks later that Navy Secretary Forrestal even showed an awareness of the Cabinet's action, and this only after more active intervention by the President through his Assistant John Steelman. The Navy Department continued to stand firm behind its own statutory responsibilities and continued to take a position based on its own departmental outlook rather than on that of the President or the Cabinet. After more than two precious months of negotiation, a decision was reached by the Maritime Commission, which had been caught between the State and Navy Departments, a decision which was a compromise between the two and to that extent not in accordance with the Cabinet consensus. In this case, departmentalism was reenforced by statute, but its dynamics, shedding light as they do on the essential powerlessness of the Cabinet within the political system, are very familiar.

A *final* consideration in adequate coordination is that which involves a supervisory follow-through after the decision has been made, to see whether it is being implemented by the departments concerned. Here, on this end, coordination partakes, as it must, of the control function. The President needs the kind of assistance in post-checking decisions that the Budget Bureau might provide through its financial and management controls. He needs help in preventing decisions from languishing or becoming "layered" within the department by people who do not share the President's view. Only by some such means can continuity in policy be achieved. Since the Cabinet has traditionally been without formal records or staff machinery, its members could never be sure what the decision was or whether, indeed, one was made (as the tanker case illustrates); much less could they be expected as a matter of course to carry it out. Nor has there been, traditionally, any way of securing compliance by use of the Cabinet.

Where a follow-up is lacking, overall Cabinet performance may become lax and slipshod. In a Cabinet meeting of November, 1940, Harold Ickes came up with a random suggestion that the government set up some propaganda machinery to combat pro-Nazi sentiment in the United States. He discovered much to his surprise that he had hit upon a subject of interest to other members of the group, so much so that the President appointed on the spot a committee of ten Cabinet and non-Cabinet individuals to investigate the subject. Lacking any machinery to keep it before the President and Cabinet, however, the project floundered aimlessly. The committee met, prepared a report, and sent it to the President. Two weeks later, at Cabinet meeting, someone inquired as to the progress being made. The President, who had not yet read the report, asked to be filled in also. He expressed interest and said he would read the report "again."

Repeatedly during the winter Ickes, who was chairman of the committee, raised the subject in Cabinet; each time he received "absolutely no response" from anyone. In a March meeting the subject popped up again and the President finally spoke up to reaffirm his interest. Nothing more was done until, in late April, Henry Stimson asked about the status of the propaganda division idea. The President decided to take suggestions for a Director of the project. Cabinet discussion ended with the appointment of Henry Wallace, whom Roosevelt told to go ahead with some plans. Still the enterprise was not begun, and finally, Roosevelt told Wallace to forget the whole thing. Ickes comments that he felt "like a squirrel in a cage" during the handling of this matter and that it was a very "discouraging experience."[34] Some staff machinery designed to service the Cabinet might have averted this careless way of following up an idea. On the other hand, if the President was deliberately worrying the issue in this manner, additional machinery would have been quite superfluous.

It is with respect to the machinery of follow-through that the Cabinet Secretariat under President Eisenhower has provided one of its most noteworthy innovations. About one-half hour after each Cabinet meeting, a member of the Secretariat meets with a group of Assistants for Cabinet Coordination. Each member of this group is a close assistant of a Cabinet official, or in Rabb's language an "undershirt." This group is given a selective oral "de-briefing" on the substance of the meeting. Each Assistant is responsible for seeing that decisions relevant to his department are carried out. The Secretariat prepares for each Cabinet member, moreover, a convenient and time-saving record summarizing the action taken by the Cabinet. Here again, Eisenhower's military experience contributed to this idea, for he complained that in commanding an army he would sometimes make decisions only to find them evaporate into thin air. It is a key feature of the Secretariat system that all on-the-spot decisions, facilitated by an agenda, be followed through systematically to conclusion.

In addition to his meeting with the Cabinet "undershirts," Secretary Rabb developed another device to discourage delay in carrying out decisions — that is, whenever decisions are made. The Secretary circulates to all members of the Cabinet, at least quarterly and always yearly, a document which contains a list of all decisions not yet acted upon. Sometimes this Action Status

Report is considered at Cabinet meeting in "operation needling." "Cabinet members would rather not be on that list," said Rabb, for behind the action of the Secretary lies the support of the President. In view of his follow-through design, Secretary Dulles' description of Secretary Rabb as the "backstop" of the Cabinet is appropriate.

Decisions made in the Eisenhower Cabinet meeting are still highly elusive things. To the extent that they are, it will be only a limited success to have perfected a system for follow-through. For the Secretariat, the task of translating Cabinet discussions into action decisions is as tricky as we might expect, even though the President is so predisposed to come to conclusions in the meeting. Usually, President Eisenhower is fairly abrupt in moving from one item of business to another, so that the participants are often uncertain of what the decision was — if, indeed, one was made. He is not prone to sum up the discussion and state a consensus — if, in fact, there was such a thing. Thus the records of Cabinet *decisions* frequently go back through the system in such fuzzy form as "noted without objection" or "approved in principle." On those decisions affecting them, department heads want to know *not* what the President or the Cabinet said generally, but *only* what the President said specifically. Where this is not crystal clear, they may return to the President directly or simply "layer" the decision in time-honored fashion.

The follow-through can and does prevent matters from dropping out of sight unintentionally, but the Secretariat, except when it enlists the aid of someone like Sherman Adams, is really powerless to dredge up those which have been intentionally lost. Its very survival depends on its success in maintaining smooth relations with the Cabinet members. Its policy must be one of calculated inertia in pressing for action in the face of departmental resistance. To the Spring of 1957, only five Action Status Reports had been compiled and these were simply as gentle reminders. In policing the staff system, as elsewhere, the Secretariat can wheedle and needle, but it cannot brandish or use a big stick.

The President needs to relieve himself of some of the burden of coordination for which he alone bears final responsibility. The Cabinet, due to certain inherent characteristics and to fundamental forces operating upon it, has a very limited capacity for providing this assistance. Some of these limitations can be minimized by the introduction of new machinery, if that machinery is congenial to the President and if he makes a strenuous effort to use it, but not one of them can be eliminated. Their persistence makes it perfectly plain that no President can now administer the executive branch of the government through the Cabinet alone. This fact helps to explain why so many other organs of coordination have been introduced and then retained in the Executive Office.

A detailed inquiry into the form, function, and success of extra-Cabinet coordinating mechanisms, present or past, is beyond the scope of this study. Some general observations can be made, however, which seem justified by the evidence. In the first place, it cannot be said that these organs were designed to take over wholesale a set of functions previously developed by the Cabinet. Their existence is testimony to the inability of the Cabinet to provide all the assistance needed by the President. The adjustments have been in the nature of piecemeal and experimental responses to felt needs. Only their general use as coordinating organs could reconcile such disparity as is found in Wilson's "War Cabinet," Roosevelt's National Emergency Council, the National Security Council under Truman and Eisenhower, and the performance of such personal presidential assistants as Col. House, Harry Hopkins, James Byrnes, Averell Harriman, or Sherman Adams. There has been no grand design to create a substitute for the Cabinet or to impose a new hierarchical level between President and Cabinet. It is fair to say that insofar as non-Cabinet agencies have appeared to stand between the President and the Cabinet member, they have to that extent been unsuccessful in fulfilling their purposes.

In the second place, although most of these instruments of coordination have been created, in part at least, to combat departmentalism, they have enjoyed a strictly limited success. With respect to Wilson's "War Cabinet" (comprised of the Secretaries of War, Navy, and Treasury plus the heads of half a dozen wartime agencies) "considerable friction developed" between the departments and the "mushroom agencies." Food Administrator Herbert Hoover wrote that "We used the words coordination and cooperation until they were worn out. . . . We surrounded ourselves with coordinators, and we spent hours in endless discussions with no court of appeal."[35] The National Emergency Council (comprised of the Cabinet plus a great many other agency or board heads) frequently out-Cabineted the Cabinet in this respect, despite the fact that its expressed purpose was to coordinate. One observer wrote, "The President tells them to coordinate but finds that administration and policy requires that final decisions be referred to himself. Too often one executive agency is speaking and acting entirely at cross purposes with another."[36]

Despite its highly institutionalized character, the National Security Council (comprised of a few Cabinet members and other top-level officials) cannot insulate itself from the impact of departmentalism in military and foreign-policy matters. Thus during the Louis Johnson-Dean Acheson period, departmental disputes went on at all levels and in the Council itself. The State and Defense Departments had disagreements over Formosa policy, Japanese policy, Spanish policy, trade with iron-curtain countries, occupation policy, departmental jurisdictions, and many others, about which Johnson complained bitterly.[37] Conflicts like these will be thrown into the President's lap and may be ultimately soluble, as these were, only by the "resignation" of one of the disputants.

Departmentalism may be aggravated rather than moderated

wherever extra-Cabinet coordinators are involved, since fresh nuances of power and prestige arise to complicate interpersonal relationships. Cabinet members are likely to be acutely conscious of their hierarchical status and do not relish even the appearance of being "layered" by someone else. This is especially true with respect to the single presidential assistant. Newton Baker's resentment of Col. House is clear in this letter to Josephus Daniels.

I never knew House very well, which, of course, is a part of the general good fortune which has attended me throughout life. All told, I probably had no more than three conferences with him, none of which, so far as I can remember, were about the War Department, so that I am relieved from any anxiety lest he should claim . . . that he selected Pershing, planned the strategy of the Meuse-Argonne offensive, wrote the Selective Service Act, and organized the services of supply. Did he design any of the battleships? . . . I am trying to collect a few instances at least which will authoritatively show that he did not do everything that was done throughout the whole period of eight years.[38]

Apropos of Donald Richberg, who was Director of NEC, Harold Ickes fretted in his diary that:

The National Emergency Council held a meeting at two o'clock and it was evident that Richberg has been getting in some fine work. He is steadily building up his own power and he acted today like the fair-haired boy of the Administration. He looked like the cat that swallowed the canary. He is gathering under his control all of the various interdepartmental committees, although why the Director of an Emergency Council should have anything to do with committees that attach to the permanent branches of the Government is more than I can understand.[39]

With respect to Harry Hopkins, Ickes wrote, "The Hopkins intimacy disturbs me. I do not like him and I do not like the influence he has with the President."[40] From July 1940 to July 1941, Ickes saw Hopkins only once, and deliberately so.[41] Concerning Byrnes as well as Hopkins, "When the President (Roosevelt) asked an aide to settle a dispute between departments, some department head was pretty likely to appeal against the decision to the President himself."[42] The point is not that such arrangements may not facilitate Cabinet member-President relationships. Sometimes they do.⁴³ But there are excellent reasons why they may not. While it is true, in sum, that the spread of non-Cabinet coordinators casts a reflection on the Cabinet, it is equally true that the Cabinet's hierarchical prestige casts its shadow across the path of all other coordinators.

Inherent in the establishment of extra-Cabinet instrumentalities is still another dilemma, that of coordinating the coordinators. This is not only true as between the Cabinet and other agencies,⁴⁴ but among the non-Cabinet agencies as well. Within the Executive Office, James Byrnes, as head of OWMR, was empowered to adjudicate all inter-agency disputes concerning domestic policy, yet he could not coordinate the Budget Bureau. Averell Harriman was special Assistant to the President for foreign affairs, yet he could not coordinate the National Security Council. Byrnes' admonition to Hopkins to "keep the hell out of my business" is evidence enough that neither of these could coordinate the other. Also, as soon as any one of them assumed operating authority they became competitors with Cabinet departments, thus sacrificing much of their coordinating potentiality. Hopkins as Secretary of Commerce and Harriman as Director of Mutual Security demonstrate this, as do OWMR in its later days and ODM in more recent times.⁴⁵ The NSC, for all of its considerable success, is limited by statute to operate on what has been called "the axis of arms and diplomacy," and thus it spawns problems of coordination as well as solves them.⁴⁶ It would seem that although the operations of these various organs shed light on the shortcomings of the Cabinet, they also illuminate the fact that these shortcomings are more widely shared.

Since the ambitiously designed Cabinet machinery under Eisenhower represents an attempt to have the Cabinet coordinate some of the coordinators, the limitations it has encountered are instructive. Most important, the Eisenhower Cabinet does not even try to coordinate the activities of the NSC, and any group which obeys such a wholesale self-denying ordinance immediately loses any claim to the role of overall coordinator. Almost no items come to the Cabinet agenda from the Departments of State or Defense. Occasionally, the Secretary of State or the Vice-President will report to the Cabinet on some crisis situation or on a trip, but even then it is simply a matter of briefing the members rather than inaugurating a policy discussion. Sometimes another agency involved in international affairs will explain its program to the Cabinet as a matter of information. The result is that the Eisenhower Cabinet probably spends less time and assigns less importance to the area of foreign relations in its discussions than any other Cabinet of the period under investigation.

On the domestic side, the executive office agencies have been tied into Cabinet discussions by absorbing them into the group. Nearly fifteen of the people who sit with the Cabinet come from the Executive Office. The Chairman of the Council of Economic Advisers, for instance, reports fairly regularly to the group and enters into its discussions. The situation is similar with others like the Budget Director and the Director of ODM. Indeed, these three executive office agencies contribute more to the Cabinet agenda than any three line departments. Some agencies, like CEA, for whom attendance at meetings represents an elevation in status, may be happy with this arrangement. Others, which have cherished in times past their direct line to the President, may feel weakened by their presence in the group. The Budget Director, for example, may have been comprised in the matter of the 1958 budget by sitting with the Cabinet and hence may have been less effective in presenting his case against the Secretary of the Treasury, with whom he obviously disagreed. Coordination by absorption may be a mixed blessing for some executive office units.

As for the major department heads under Eisenhower, it is clear that they do not view the Cabinet as *the* coordinating instrument. Some of them, of course, already work almost exclusively through the NSC. Others, on the domestic side, have resorted to similar devices — to interdepartmental committees, to the legislative clearance staff in the Budget Bureau, to a close personal assistant like Sherman Adams, or occasionally to the President alone. For many members, the very nature of a body which coordinates by absorption may be too all-inclusive, too unwieldy, too impersonal, and too occupied with the business of less important agencies to be an attractive coordinating mechanism. They may resort to the Cabinet after all other recourses are closed, and only then if the President refuses to hear their problem in any other setting. It may not be coincidental that a majority of Eisenhower's Cabinet business originates from *outside* the ten departments. The American political system permits only one coordinator of the coordinators — the President himself. On the level below him there will always be alternatives.

Everything that has been said suggests a final conclusion: the Cabinet and the coordinating agencies of the Executive Office of the President co-exist, and will continue to do so, in the same presidential sphere of operations. Neither one can coordinate the other, and neither is wholly free of the dilemmas of the other. This is especially true of departmentalism. The task of interdepartmental coordination cannot be accomplished by the Cabinet alone, but neither can it be accomplished in a realm which excludes the Cabinet. Cabinet and Executive Office overlap and intertwine in an interlocking network of memberships, structures, and functions. Their multiple relationships are not well fixed. They retain, within the limits set by the President's participation, a basic flexibility — a flexibility which ensures that there be both room for accommodation and incentives for competition. It is unlikely that the first will always prevail or that the second will ever be abolished.

THE CABINET MEETING: CONCLUSION

President Truman once described the Cabinet as "a body whose combined judgment the President uses to formulate the fundamental policies of the administration . . . a group which is designed to develop teamwork wisdom on all subjects that affect the political life of the country." [47] The historians of the

Cabinet concluded, similarly though earlier, that, "The rule may be laid down that the President ordinarily consults the Cabinet on matters of grave public importance." [48] The Cabinet has been described by observers and participants as "the board of directors of the nation," as "a combination of qualified experts that have stood behind every President," and as producers of "committee government." [49] Pictures have been painted of the family circle thrashing out the great issues of the day under conditions of closest intimacy. "In fact, it is assumed today simply as a matter of course that the Secretary of a new department will become as such an intimate adviser and associate of the President." [50] Since it is impossible to obtain conclusive data on Cabinet proceedings, dogmatic conclusions are not in order, but on the available evidence of the last forty-five years, at least, these versions of Cabinet activity do not square with the facts. It is, perhaps, significant that President Truman's comment was made in December 1945, at a time when he had been in office less than a year. With respect to all of its possible functions, the group's performance has been haphazard and its success has been sporadic. This is not to say that the Cabinet should be classified as an ornamental antique. It is not. But neither does it correspond to the over-idealized discussions of its activity which have acquired, from time to time, substantial currency.

Instead of exaggerating its importance or relegating it to the dust bin, it is of more purpose to examine its activity in order to distinguish its areas of greatest strength and those of greatest weakness. It is weakest in performing the function of interdepartmental coordination and in making direct contributions to decisions through a well-informed, well-organized discussion of policy alternatives. It is most useful as a presidential adviser, in the sense of a political sounding board equipped to provide clues as to likely public or group reactions, and as a forum in which some overall administrative coherence can be secured. Neither of the latter two functions requires a high degree of institutionalization. The first can be carried on in the face of departmentalism; the second operates to combat it. With regard to administrative coherence, the importance of the Cabinet meeting may well be measured by the extent to which it prevents the degree of Cabinet-level disunity from becoming any greater than it is.

What is perhaps the most striking part of the over-all picture is the number of factors which operate to *prevent* the Cabinet from fulfilling its potential functions. They are factors, however, which cannot be eliminated at the level of the Cabinet meeting. Insofar as the President's behavior, e.g., his differentiation among members, constitutes a limitation on the effectiveness of the meeting, that behavior is grounded in the American conception of executive leadership. The limiting behavior of the department heads, e.g., departmentalism, stems from the basic pluralism of the American political system. The low degree of institutionality characteristic of the Cabinet meeting is not an independent limiting factor, but a political derivative determined by the interaction of President and Cabinet members.

The problem of greater or lesser institutionalization must be put in perspective as one possible method for capitalizing on assets or minimizing liabilities, but *not* as a fundamental solution to Cabinet weakness. Thus, one can find changes such as the Eisenhower ones to be helpful under the existing circumstances; but they should not be looked upon as permanent cure-alls. This is so because the President-Cabinet nexus will always be an unstable accommodation rather than a fixed relationship. What seems necessary for a successful accommodation is a degree of institutionality sufficient to hold the group together, coupled with a degree of resiliency sufficient to convince the President that he can use it. Insofar as this kind of relationship can be maintained, the successes of the Cabinet meeting are likely to underwrite its continuance, while its limitations are likely to guarantee the coexistence of other avenues of presidential assistance.

CHAPTER FIVE

The Cabinet and Politics: I

FACE-TO-FACE contact between the President and his Cabinet is occasional and limited. Both parties make their greatest expenditure of time and energy in activities beyond the immediate President-Cabinet nexus. For the Chief Executive, there are the multiple tasks of leadership — formal and informal, legal or extra-legal. For the Cabinet member, there are a host of involvements arising out of his departmental, constituency, partisan, and legislative relationships. What is the effect of these extensive extra-Cabinet activities on the President-Cabinet relationship? Do they help to account for the group behavior we have observed in the Cabinet meeting? Will the individual member's other involvements affect his position as adviser and "chief lieutenant" to the President? The answer to these questions must be sought by moving beyond the immediate President-Cabinet nexus and into the political system as a whole.

The President, it is commonly said, is "many men." He plays at least four distinguishable yet overlapping and frequently conflicting roles — as Chief Representative of the Nation, Chief of his Party, Chief Legislator, and Chief Executive. His leadership, like all leadership, can be understood in terms of the interrelation of personal and situational phenomena. In playing his variety of roles, singly or in juxtaposition, the President will be required to demonstrate many different personal abilities, involving intelligence, skill, and temperament. He will be required, also, to function in different contexts, with regard for the limitations imposed upon him, the social constituencies to which he speaks, the degree of support he wishes to get, the goals he seeks to achieve. In performing his tasks, the President needs assistance that is definable in terms of personal traits and assistance that is related to particular situations. The Cabinet member is a source of both of these types. Most Presidents display an awareness of their needs during the appointment process. If they should not, however, the search for diverse kinds of assistance will be pressed upon them by the necessities of survival.

The Cabinet member has built-in features which recommend him to the President as an extra-Cabinet-meeting source of assistance, for he, too, must be "many men." He, too, is cast in a diversity of roles, which require a corresponding diversity of personal talents and capabilities. The locus of his activities within the political system is similar to that of the Chief Executive. The Cabinet member too, acts, as the representative spokesman for the interests of large segments of the population. He, too, must reach out into a constituency to win and consolidate group support. As a member of a political party more or less committed to certain actions in the realm of policy or patronage, he is rarely free from the obligations and pressures of that relationship. Every Cabinet official is a chief executive in his own right — the head of a great administrative establishment. He is, next to the President, a top-level executive of the national government. In the conduct of the business of his department and in advocating its policies he is thrown into constant contact with the legislature. His usefulness to the President must be judged not just by what he does in the Cabinet meeting, but by his performance elsewhere in the political system. The ultimate question is, of course, how well suited the variety of Cabinet-member relationships is to the variety of presidential needs.

For the purposes of examination, the extra-Cabinet relationships of the Cabinet member have been divided into categories of public prestige, party, Congress, and departmental administration. They are designed to correspond roughly to the four presidential leadership roles mentioned earlier. The inclusion of a section on departmental administration under the rubric of "politics" is largely a matter of convenience, but it does indicate that it is the politics of administration with which that section is mainly concerned, and that no support is given here to a dichotomous view of politics and administration.[1]

PRESIDENT, CABINET, AND PUBLIC PRESTIGE

a. The President as Chief Representative

As Chief Representative of the Nation the President plays the most general of all his leadership roles. It transcends his position as leader of a party or as a legislative leader, involving as it does more than the task of mobilizing electoral and congressional majorities. As Chief Representative, the President speaks for the entire nation whenever a single voice is required, be it a time of crisis or of national ceremony. The Presidency in its unity can symbolize the nation as a whole; and as a human being, the President personalizes that symbol. He cannot avoid the role of preeminence in the public mind, though some individuals will make much more of it than others. Whenever he speaks or acts he commands nationwide attention. He can fix national goals, alter national morale, and raise national standards. In representing the nation the President finds his broadest basis of support in the population. He represents the most fundamental and most widely shared ideals of the community. He becomes a political leader in the highest sense of the term.

If the President's function as Chief Representative be construed in its purest sense, the Cabinet can be of little help. It is no match for the President, in terms of public relations. At the Republican National Convention of 1956, the members of the Eisenhower Cabinet were scheduled to make an unprecedented appearance before that body and before the American public via television. They were going to take turns reading the party platform. But scarcely had the first man opened his mouth when all television coverage abruptly switched to the San Francisco airport in anticipation of the President's forthcoming arrival. And while the members of the Cabinet spoke to the convention on the crucial policies of the Eisenhower administration, millions of Americans followed the presidential plane Columbine as it flew around in circles over the airfield. By the time the viewer was returned to the convention hall, the Cabinet members had long since disappeared in the crowd. The lesson, which the communications media understood, is obvious. There is only one President, and the gap in prestige between him and his closest subordinate is unbridgeable in the public eye. Even though, as in this case, it is the President's intention to publicize his Cabinet, he can, almost by moving a muscle, defeat that purpose.

His role as Chief Representative, however, is not exhausted by a single act performed at a moment when only he commands attention. He can fulfill the role only on the basis of the confidence he inspires and the prestige he commands in the nation as a whole. Confidence and prestige are intangible assets, accumulated over a period of time and amassed by actions in many areas of activity. Here, perhaps, the Cabinet member can be of assistance. By virtue of his performance in certain areas, he may bring to the administration as a whole an increment of prestige which can be banked or traded upon by the President. The net result may increase the President's success as Chief Representative of the Nation.

b. Cabinet and Prestige: Possibilities and Limitations

Taken as a group, the Cabinet may add to or subtract from the public's estimation of the President. "I should not fear to predict the result of your administration," wrote James Buchanan to Franklin Pierce, "as soon as I learn who are members of your Cabinet."[2] The selection of the Cabinet is a symbolic act for the interested public, and they hasten to judge the extent to which the appointments as a whole will bring him overall public support. The Cabinet is the show window of the administration, and a favorable reception for the group will be an asset which the President can use to augment his own public prestige.

Group prestige is, however, a highly perishable commodity. It may give the President a lift in the early days of his administration, while the concept of "the team" is uppermost in the public mind. There is usually a Cabinet honeymoon period while a partly-sympathetic and partly-apprehensive public waits for the Secretaries to act in their respective fields. The first Cabinet meeting is usually publicized with pictures and front page coverage. Quickly, however, "the team" and the Cabinet meeting vanish from sight. Departmental policies are the subject of attention. Praise and blame are allocated individually. Some members are constantly in the public eye and others hardly at all. The Cabinet group which had looked so "balanced" in the newspapers becomes less balanced in action. An attempt to achieve nation-wide prestige and support through a "representative" appointment such as that of Martin Durkin as Secretary of Labor may backfire within a year. Although the Cabinet group is periodically resurrected for public display, it rarely receives consideration as a whole.

If the Cabinet as a group, therefore, provides only minimal assistance by way of accumulating public prestige and confidence for the President, can the individual member do any more? The answer is probably yes — subject, however, to some very severe limitations of the political system in which the President-Cabinet relationship is placed. The appointment of a nationally known figure with an established reputation of his own can undoubtedly be of assistance to the Chief Executive. By any very strict standard, however, only two men could qualify out of the one hundred and sixteen appointed between 1912 and 1958. William Jennings Bryan had been three times a candidate for the Presidency; Charles Evans Hughes had been Governor of New York, candidate for the Presidency, and a Justice of the United States Supreme Court.

Five more might qualify in a second rank: Herbert Hoover had directed international relief programs and had been wartime Food Administrator; Henry Stimson had had Cabinet experience prior to two of his three appointments; James Brynes had been an important wartime official and a Justice of the United States Supreme Court; George Marshall had been Chief of Staff in World War II; John Foster Dulles had performed many tasks of international importance after 1945. None of the other one hundred and nine would qualify as nationally prominent men at the time of their appointment. The vagaries of the appointment process yield few men who are known beyond a small segment of the population and many who are virtually unknown. A President is fortunate if he has, in his Cabinet, one person who brings with him enough independent distinction in the country to enhance the President's role as the national leader.

The position of first rank in the Cabinet, the Secretaryship of State, is the most natural place for a man of national prominence and six of the seven men held it.[3] More than likely they would have accepted nothing else, though Secretary of Defense may now qualify. No other Cabinet position provides the opportunity to play upon a nation-wide stage. The Secretary of State has the best chance to gather and wield prestige in the eyes of the general public. He is not associated *a priori* with any special interest group, thus helping to establish for him a broadly representative role. Hughes certainly raised the general level of prestige of the Harding and Coolidge administrations. Marshall was of assistance to Truman in a similar way, helping to inspire public confidence in the President. Truman writes, "At home he enjoyed the confidence and esteem of the average citizen, regardless of political preferences, as well as the admiration of congressional leaders. Marshall's entire personality inspired confidence."[4] Neither Hughes nor Marshall could be Chief Representative of the Nation, yet each could speak with authority and command the attention of the country. They combined the prestige of their office with their personal prestige to gain the esteem of a large proportion of the general public. Both men worked closely in every way with the men whom they served, thus enabling the Presidents concerned to utilize more easily the increment of prestige to support their own.

The fact that an established national figure is appointed to the most prestigeful position in the Cabinet is by no means a guarantee that he will become a presidential asset. Bryan resigned, Byrnes resigned, and Stimson disagreed fundamentally with Hoover on foreign policy — all of which demonstrate the limitations of such an appointment, however prominent the man may be. He is a subordinate of the President and must work out some kind of accommodation with him. Bryan and Byrnes could only manage this for a short time. Because of the great stress which he placed on loyalty to the Chief Executive, Stimson's relationship to Hoover lasted for four years; but since Stimson was frequently no more than a mouthpiece, his opportunity for accumulating prestige for Hoover was restricted.

Under other circumstances, and with a more satisfactory *rapport* with the President, a Cabinet member appointed to a less prestigeful post can do more to add to the President's reputation. Thus, Stimson was a far greater public asset in the Roosevelt administration as Secretary of War than he was in the Hoover Cabinet as Secretary of State. When he contemplated resignation, Harry Hopkins, who usually spoke for the President, protested, "I told him that from my point of view he was the most respected member of the Cabinet; that he had the confidence of the American people, the rank and file of the army and General Marshall. I told him further that I was sure he had the President's complete confidence."[5] Hopkins' words bespeak a value and a kind of relationship of Stimson to the President which were not duplicated under Hoover. The appointment of Herbert Hoover as Secretary of Commerce is another example, like Stimson's, of a non-Secretary of State bolstering the public estimation of an administration.

The only generalization one can make about the seven cases mentioned is a statistical one — they are all equally rare. The appointment of a national leader to the Cabinet is an unusual occurrence. Cabinet appointees do not come from a pool of men with recognized public standing. The more likely possibility would be the accumulation of public distinction while in office. Every Cabinet office transmits to its occupant its aura of national importance. During the Hearings on the proposed recognition of a Department of Welfare, Federal Security Administrator Oscar Ewing and others repeatedly stressed "the prestige which attaches to a Cabinet officer in the minds of the public." Ewing related that when he, the Veterans Administrator, and the Secretary of Labor decided to go on the radio to discuss a problem together, they were told that the public wanted to hear only the Secretary of Labor.[6] Some degree of opportunity for gaining public attention thus inheres in every Cabinet position, but in order to translate this potentiality into a reality, the individual must capitalize on the assets of his title by his performance and the publicity that it receives.

He faces great odds, however, in this task, for the chance that the general public will ever become much interested in him is slim. Secretary of War John Weeks complained that ". . . the average American knows scarcely more of the problems and accomplishments of his own War Department than he does of the geography and history of the Netherlands."[7] Secretary of Agriculture Charles Brannan says that when he first took office no one even knew his name; he was frequently called "Anderson" (his predecessor) until he had the fortune to have his farm policy labelled "The Brannan Plan."[8] Public opinion polls document a widespread popular apathy toward the Cabinet. In May, 1938, people were asked to give their opinion of each Cabinet member in terms of whether or not each was "doing a good job or a poor job." Even on this crude scale, those who had no opinion at all ranged from a high of 55 percent in the case of Secretary of War Harry Woodring, to a low of 31 percent in the case of Secretary of Labor Frances Perkins. In May, 1943, a poll revealed that 34 percent of the respondents had never even heard of Secretary of Agriculture Claude Wickard, and that 29 percent of his own farm constituency could offer no opinion as to whether he was doing a good or a poor job. The most publicized intra-Cabinet feud of the Roosevelt years, the Jones-Wallace dispute in 1943, was followed by only 36 percent of "the American people." In December, 1945, at the time of the Byrnes-Wallace difficulty, 21 percent of those questioned had never heard of Secretary of State Byrnes.[9] Four years after his appointment, and in spite of the fact that he was generally considered to be one of the ablest and most successful members of the Eisenhower Cabinet, Treasury Secretary George Humphrey was still not known by 72 percent of the American people.[10] Insights such as these into the areas of public ignorance do not lead to optimism about the building up of general public prestige while serving in the Cabinet.

The activities of Cabinet members simply do not get reported in the public press. A scrutiny of the *New York Times Index*[11] reveals this situation graphically. During the eight-year period of the Wilson administration, the Secretaries of Agriculture, Interior, Commerce, and Labor got their names in the *Times* on an average of no more than once a week. In all but one of the eight years, the records of the Attorney General and the Postmaster General were the same. During the entire eight-year period, the name of the Secretary of Commerce appeared on the front page of the *Times* a total of eighteen times, the Secretary of the Interior, thirty-three times, the Secretary of Labor, forty-nine times, the Postmaster General, fifty-five times, and the Attorney General, seventy-seven times. In only one year did one of these men (the Attorney General, during the Red scare of 1919) average more than once every two weeks. At one time or another each of them vanished from the front page for a period of eleven or more consecutive months. The Secretary of Agriculture, David Houston, was in the eye of the general public least of all. His name appeared in the *Times* as a whole on an average of once a month during his seven-year tenure; he made page one only eleven times and at one point his name did not appear on the front page for a period of almost three years.

During the eight-year Harding-Coolidge period, the Secretary of Agriculture was front-page news only twenty-six times, the Secretary of the Interior, twenty-seven times, the Postmaster General, thirty-nine times, the Secretary of Labor, forty-five times, the Secretary of the Army, seventy-four times — all averaging less than once a month over the entire period. Each of them disappeared from page one for a period of not less than ten consecutive months, and some for as long as twenty-one months. A similar story can be repeated for the Hoover Cabinet. For four years, six members of the Cabinet did not average even a weekly appearance in the *New York Times*. The Secretary of the Interior's name was on the front page seven times during the period, the Postmaster General, eleven times, the Secretary of Labor, twenty-four times, the Secretary of Agriculture, twenty-eight times, the Secretary of the Navy, thirty-one times, the Secretary of Commerce, thirty-seven times, and the Attorney General, thirty-eight times. None of them averaged as much as once a month. The length of their consecutive absences from page one varied from a low of five months for the Attorney General to a high of nineteen months for the head of the Post Office Department.

It is a fair generalization to say that what does interest the public more than anything else about a Cabinet member is his coming and his going rather than what he does while he is in office. Much of the front-page coverage of the officials we have mentioned has been concerned with their appointment, their resignation, and rumors of their resignation. Between the headline announcement of his appointment in March, 1913, and a headline story on May 17, 1917, more than four years later, David Houston was on page one of the *Times* on only five occasions, four of which concerned rumors that he would resign as Secretary of Agriculture. Hubert Work, Postmaster General and Secretary of the Interior in the Harding-Coolidge period, was on the front page thirteen times in his six-year Cabinet career, five of them concerning his appointment and his resignation. From January, 1929, to January, 1933, the name of Herbert Hoover's Secretary of the Interior, Ray Lyman Wilbur, appeared eleven times on page one. Eight of these concerned speculation over his appointment and his resignation (which never came). During one period of three years, the only additional headline story about Wilbur featured his being knocked down by a curtain during commencement exercises at Long Island University. From the general public's viewpoint most Cabinet members like these, pass from obscurity to obscurity — and live in obscurity in between.

These figures should not be taken to convey anything beyond the idea that the activities of many Cabinet members are not likely to be of sustained interest to the general public and are not likely to be highly publicized. There are, of course, many changes and nuances in public attention which these figures do not purport to explain, but viewed in the large, the picture is strikingly similar. Those Cabinet members whose names do not appear regularly in a paper such as the *New York Times* (for whatever reason) and whose activities are rarely front-page material can hardly be expected to add much to the general prestige of the Chief Representative of the United States.

In some cases, the appointment process produces men without the personal capacity to achieve national prominence. Just as frequently men of ability pay the price of obscurity because of their past experience. Unschooled in public life they never succeed in adapting themselves to it. Only two members of the original Eisenhower Cabinet (Dulles and Wilson) held anything resembling regular, formal press conferences, some held only four or five in four years, and one member (McKay) did not hold any. They displayed what Miss Perkins once described as her "lamentable lack of instinct for publicity." [12] David Houston was another such person. An academician by profession, he was inept at self-advertisement and disliked the public arena. Josephus Daniels, with his own journalistic insight, said correctly that Houston was one of the "best informed Cabinet members," but added that he never knew a man "with so much information who could in [his] . . . speeches and writings so perfectly make the most interesting subject as dry as dust. [He had no] style or even a suggestion of eloquence. Quite the contrary." [13] Hubert Work, a physician before joining the Cabinet, admitted somewhat ruefully, "There's nothing colorful about me. All I do is work." [14] In neither of these two cases was their lack of public standing any reflection at all on their capabilities or on their relationship with the President.

A more fundamental limitation on the accumulation of nationwide prestige is the overall context in which a Cabinet member works. Most Cabinet members do not become known to the public at large simply because they do not serve the public at large. They serve, for the most part, many specialized publics, or constituencies. They require their own power base in order to survive and to put through their particular program, and so they seek to develop particular constituencies smaller than the nation as a whole. As Secretary of Commerce Daniel Roper said, "The major concern of the Department, as I saw it, was to promote the legitimate interests of business, large and small." [15] In the hearings on his nomination to the Cabinet, Ezra Benson told the Senate Agriculture Committee: "My first interest, Senator, as I envision it, is the national welfare. Then closely related to that is the welfare of the farmers. Having been one of them, having been closely associated with them, I think you can count on me being aggressive and helping them." [16] Martin Durkin said that as Secretary of Labor, "I will . . . represent the wage earners of the United States; keeping in mind that I must serve all wage earners." When Senator Taft queried, "You will regard yourself as a representative of the public in performing your duties as Secretary of Labor, and not as the representative of any particular group?" Durkin said, "That is correct." [17] If by a "particular group" is meant the AFL, Durkin's answer was correct; if by "the public" is meant the whole nation, it is a fiction to which no Secretary of Labor consistently adheres. Durkin's resignation, after his attempt to help his constituency had failed, is proof enough that his conception of the public welfare had to be filtered through a particular public.

Cabinet members like the Secretaries of Commerce, Agriculture, and Labor direct their public efforts toward their own organized constituents. If they acquire prestige it is a relationship to the particular public they face. The Secretary of Agriculture speaks regularly at the conventions of the Farm Bureau, the National Grange, and the Farmers Union. The Secretary of Commerce addresses his public at meetings of the Chamber of Commerce, National Association of Manufacturers, or other business organizations. His public pronouncements are grist for the mills of the trade newspapers and of private house organs of all sorts. The public appeals of the Secretary of Labor are directed at an organized clientele rather than to any amorphous public at large. Secretary Schwellenbach addressed the CIO convention in 1947 in this way:

If we are to have a strong Department of Labor, we will need the support of those in the labor movement who are organized. The Department was created for you and for all of the unorganized workers of America. We need your support. I came here to ask for it. I want that support not merely when the bills are a couple of days away from passage. I want it throughout all the year.[18]

Cabinet Secretaries face non-economic publics, too. The Secretary of the Interior will travel more, speak more, and hence be better known in areas concerned with public power or reclamation than on the eastern seaboard. Or, a Cabinet member may find prestige among a segment of the population who holds a certain social philosophy. The Cabinet member's publics represent the diversity of American political life, but all are smaller than the nation as a whole.

Another factor which may have a decisive impact on the importance — and thus the prestige — of particular Cabinet positions is the conditions of the time. The Secretary of State always has greater possibilities for developing public importance than the Postmaster General, but in other instances, the general climate of opinion and the vital tasks of the time may determine the relative significance of the departmental portfolios. From his perspective as Secretary of War, Dwight Davis spoke of the 1920's as "those discouraging years of curtailment of activities, reductions, demotions, and disinterestedness on the part of the public." [19] Henry Stimson wrote, too, of the Secretary of War that, "In time of peace, he is ordinarily one of the least noticed of Cabinet officers." [20] In the 1920's, Herbert Hoover grounded his rise to the Presidency on his performance as Secretary of Commerce, but from 1932 to 1935, Daniel Roper found only indistinction in the same position. "The Department of Commerce," he said, "important under normal conditions, was at this time suffering from the fact that business was in the doghouse." [21] The Cabinet member's opportunity for gaining any kind of public attention is often governed by the central or peripheral nature of his departmental function during the period in which he serves.

Even the Secretary of State, who has so many of the institutional factors in his favor, will find his public standing influenced by another factor — his relationship to the President. It is the Chief Executive who often determines the context in which a department head works. If, like Wilson, he chooses to stress the activities of the Treasury Department, he can help make a public figure out of a nonentity like William McAdoo. "Nobody in the larger political world knew anything about William G. McAdoo before he came to Washington as a member of the President's Cabinet," [22] and yet eight years later, he came within a few votes of becoming the Democratic nominee for the Presidency. When the President chooses to minimize the importance of a particular department in his administration, there is little anyone can do about it. Though Henry Cantwell Wallace came to the Cabinet with a recognized standing among the farmers, it was hard for him to do anything to develop his reputation among them, or with a larger public, because of the Harding-Coolidge attitude on farm problems.[23] Daniel Roper's efforts to establish relationships with the business community were often met by Roosevelt's admonition to "sit tight and keep quiet."[24] If the President does not really want to trade on the prestige of a particular Cabinet member he will tend to stifle his activities.

c. Andrew Mellon and Cordell Hull: Case Studies

Despite all of these limiting factors, some Cabinet members — a few — do rise from obscurity to achieve a national stature during their incumbency. They undoubtedly add to the public confidence and public prestige which are the fundamental underpinnings of the President's success as Chief Representative of the Nation. It is unlikely that a Cabinet member could achieve national standing without its redounding to the net credit of the President. In the Cabinet history of the last forty years two examples stand out of men who had no national standing when they were appointed to the Cabinet, but who achieved national distinction of a magnitude that gave great assistance to the Chief Representative. The two are Andrew Mellon and Cordell Hull.

Andrew Mellon came to the Cabinet in 1920 under the most favorable circumstances. The Treasury Department promised to be as important as any other office in the post-war period. With the strains on the economy lessened, "normalcy" meant above all tax cuts, debt reduction, foreign funding, and reduced expenditures. With the business community holding a position of dominant interest in the country, it was readily agreed that "the times" required a businessman, and a good one, to handle the nation's finances.[25] Mellon filled these specifications. His skill in managing his hundreds of millions of dollars was his greatest endorsement, not a drawback. His status as the third richest man in the United States seemed to bother no one.[26] "The point is that he is the kind of a man for the job, and nearly everyone in

Washington knows it," was the unanimous opinion of the commentators.[27] Yet Mellon was virtually unknown in public life, except among those legislators from Pennsylvania who urged his appointment. As one observer said, "He is not a public man. . . . He is without any sort of public experience."[28] He was shy and unassuming. "I had no substantial reason to refuse, but I did not really want to come," he remarked.[29] The President who appointed him did not know him at all.

Mellon's opportunity to become a public figure was enhanced by his relationship of complete confidence with Presidents Harding and Coolidge. For both, he was the chief architect of financial policy. Harding freely admitted his ignorance in such matters, and Mellon's financial measures were a perfect expression of Coolidge's fundamental faith in economy. What is more, Mellon popularized this faith. The prosperity of the 1920's made him "the most powerful man individually in either the Harding or the Coolidge Administration."[30] He was lauded as no other Cabinet member in the twentieth century as "the greatest Secretary of the Treasury since Alexander Hamilton." Only a few Democrats attacked him. Liberal critics conceded that "Mr. Mellon's job has been decidely the most popular and undoubtedly the easiest of any public man in a generation."[31]

Especially did he dominate the Coolidge Administration, placing his *imprimatur* on the "Coolidge prosperity" as its representative before the business world.[32] "It was said in the political campaign (of 1924) that most businessmen, including those engaged in small business, voted as much for Mellon as they did for Coolidge."[33] Mellon's great prestige, it is true, was linked primarily to the business group, but so thoroughly did their articulated interest dominate the period and so impressive was their success that Mellon achieved prominence far beyond the confines of this single group. He shared the national spotlight with the Presidents whom he served. They could inspire more public confidence because of his presence. Their prestige was increased by his. He came as close to symbolizing an administration to the general public as any Cabinet member possibly can. "Indeed, so completely did Andrew Mellon dominate the White House in the days when the Coolidge administration was at its zenith that it would be fair to call the administration the reign of Coolidge and Mellon." [34]

Herbert Hoover recognized Mellon's indispensability by retaining him in the new Cabinet. It seems quite probable that Hoover reappointed Mellon primarily on this basis — that it was an appointment which he could not afford not to make — for Hoover himself acknowledges that they were of "two schools of thought" [35] on financial policies. Journalists noted "quite a transformation" in Mellon's stature after 1928.[36] "There is in this administration nothing remotely like the awe and admiration of Mr. Mellon that there was in the last." [37] Hoover was in much closer agreement with Ogden Mills, the Assistant Secretary of the Treasury, and the President admitted his relief when Mellon was not around and he could deal "directly" with Mills.[38] Mellon's independent prestige was undoubtedly a public asset to Mr. Hoover, but because of the tensions which were present, this prestige was less of a net asset than in the previous administrations. The collapse of prosperity, moreover, did not help Mellon's reputation, and it was probably a help to Hoover when the aging Secretary of the Treasury was finally nudged upstairs into the Ambassadorship to Great Britain.

Cordell Hull was only a moderately well-known Congressman from Tennessee when he was appointed Secretary of State, yet he was able to utilize all the potentialities of that position to acquire a national standing that was of great assistance to President Roosevelt. He came to the State Department in 1933 with three visible assets. His service in Congress had won him many friends, and had given him an understanding of the legislative process on which he could (and did) capitalize throughout his twelve years of office. He had achieved, furthermore, a reputation for integrity, dignity, and high-mindedness, which seemed to be confirmed by his very distinguished physical appearance. Thirdly, foreign affairs were becoming increasingly important, offering opportunities for any Secretary of State to become a prominent spokesman for the whole nation.

Hull had another asset, which he developed within the context of the times and which lay, perhaps, at the root of his success with the larger public. Hull was not a New Dealer. He was a conservative Democrat, whose cautious views on domestic questions were generally at variance with those of the President and his advisers. Hull felt that Roosevelt was going "too fast and too far" with some of his reforms, and considered others to be "too drastic."[39] "I was frankly glad not to be invited into the White House group where so often the 'liberal' game was played on an extreme basis. I was known not to be an extreme liberal or semi-radical, as were some of those who were close about the President."[40] In his position of partial aloofness from the Administration, Hull was able to insulate himself from the violent controversies of the time and to build up his prestige among the whole population. He was proud of the fact that, "I did not generally participate in domestic affairs unless they dovetailed into our international policies and problems" — which they did more often than Hull was willing to admit.[41] Politically, he tried to maintain a non-partisan attitude. "Foreign affairs had to be kept out of domestic politics. I pursued it religiously during my twelve years in office. . . . I was not to make a serious political speech in my stay in the State Department, with the exception of two last minute addresses in 1940."[42]

Hull's concept of his job was to draw a narrow sphere of operations around himself and to maintain his own prestige within that area. He was extremely conscious of those jurisdictional boundaries which presumably sealed off his legitimate functions from those of others. Above all, he resented "trespassing," and he did not extend himself beyond minimum limits, thus immunizing himself from as much criticism as possible.[43] His own approach to foreign policy was, moreover, filled with idealism. Even his advocacy of reciprocal trade could be phrased on such a moralistic plane as to alienate fewer people than might otherwise have been the case. "As an elder statesman and a figure of great dignity, Hull . . . established for himself a position that was almost sacrosanct." [44]

Roosevelt, of course, realized the widespread and broadly based character of Hull's prestige, and "respected his high standing with the American people." Samuel Rosenman wrote further,

> In fact, I think that Hull was the one man in public life who could give the President substantial concern by threatening, in a basic disagreement, to resign. . . . If at any time he had resigned as a result of a disagreement with the President — either personal or official — it would have hurt the President's prestige with the American people, and Roosevelt knew it.[45]

The same could be said of only a handful of Cabinet members in a hundred years.

Hull's demeanor brought him support at nearly all of the pressure points of American politics, solidifying liberal Democrats, persuading old-line conservative Democrats, and reaching out beyond that party to the public at large to win the allegiance and calm the fears of many who were otherwise in hearty disagreement with the administration. In every survey of popular opinion the Secretary of State led his Cabinet colleagues by enormous margins.[46] When polled in 1938 as to whether Cabinet members were doing a good or a poor job, 53 percent (the highest) said that Hull was doing a good job and 8 percent (the lowest) said he was doing a poor job. When asked to name one presidential adviser of whom they disapproved and one of whom they approved, Hull received the highest percentage of approval (22 percent) and the lowest percentage of disapproval (1 percent). Eighty-five percent of the people who answered a point-blank question as to whether Hull was doing a good or a poor job responded in the affirmative. The partisan breakdown of this response was: Democrats, 91 percent good and 9 percent poor; Republicans, 75 percent good and 25 percent poor. During the 1940 campaign, the Republican candidate blasted everyone in the Administration except the untouchable Secretary of State; Wendell Willkie even "made it clear" that he would ask Hull to remain in office if he were elected.[47] Willkie's estimate of the prestige of "The Saint in Blue Serge" was borne out by public opinion surveys. Forty-five percent of those polled agreed that Willkie should ask Hull to remain, only 18 percent said "no," and 37 percent were undecided. Before the 1944 election the same proposal was put by the pollsters. Fifty-six percent of the respondents approved, 16 percent disapproved, and 28 percent were undecided. Among Republican voters, the corresponding figures were: 52 percent yes, 22 percent no, and 26 percent undecided.[48]

Given their vast differences in opinion and in temperament, the President and this Cabinet member established a relationship of accommodation quite dissimilar to the dependent Mellon-Harding or the Mellon-Coolidge relationship. They were friendly and considerate of one another, but never intimate on a personal basis.[49] They could work out an agreement with a comparatively narrow range of operations for Mr. Hull, and extensive control over foreign affairs by Mr. Roosevelt. Although this system strained their relations almost to the breaking point on several occasions, they survived — to the benefit of all concerned. Hull's own rigid concept of his proper functions was a two-edged sword and could be turned against him. Thus, Hull was given no influence over the Democratic foreign-policy planks of 1936 and 1940, and he was excluded from top-level international conferences on the grounds that "military" and not "political" problems were involved.[50] It is probably true that "Mr. Hull was regarded by the President simply as a useful political and moral asset, to be allowed freedom of maneuver only in the relatively harmless sphere of his devotion to the trade agreements program."[51] In view of the fact that Roosevelt could trade on the public prestige of his Secretary of State and yet maintain a free hand in the conduct of foreign policy, the appointment of Cordell Hull in 1932 was, in spite of the difficulties, one of the master strokes in the history of Cabinet-making.

The idea of "public prestige," though elusive and difficult to measure, is felt and acknowledged as real by sensitive students of opinion and by working politicians. For the Cabinet member, it is most likely to be found where a nationally prominent figure is appointed to the Secretaryship of State, or where a lesser known person is appointed to a post under optimum conditions. Both Mellon and Hull were given important positions in the context of the times; both developed relatively broad and relatively independent constituencies on which to base their prestige (the business community and the social conservatives); and each achieved a relationship with his superior which permitted him to make positive contributions to the President's national standing.

Without detracting from the ultimate success of Mellon and Hull, it is evident that all may not be for the best even with the best of all possible Cabinet members. The problems that Hoover had with Mellon, and the problems that faced Roosevelt and Hull, are surface indications of deeper problems which underlie the Cabinet member-President relationship in a highly pluralized political system. In any political system characterized by a vast number of forces in constant and unpredictable motion, tensions are being created and dispelled continuously, turning assets into liabilities and back again. Given this situation, a source of prestige always has potentialities for trouble. If the Cabinet member is "given his head" like Hughes or Byrnes, there will be difficulty in terms of presidential control; if the President and his subordinate are in fundamental disagreement on policy as in the Hoover-Mellon or Hoover-Stimson cases, the Cabinet member's usefulness as an adviser will be impaired; if the President wishes to be, in effect, his own Cabinet official, as in the cases of Bryan and Hull, additional strains will be placed on their relationship.

More constant and more predictable than any other potential source of friction is the dispersion of power and prestige in

American politics. As Chief Representative of the Nation, the President needs to centralize enough power and prestige to perform his leadership functions. But he does not monopolize this power and parcel it out to his Cabinet members. "A picture of the President as a reservoir of authority from which the lower echelons of administration draw life and vigor is an idealized version of reality." [52] If a Cabinet member has a national standing or a standing among a particular public which is sufficient to make the President more effective than he otherwise would be, he has an increment of prestige which is independent of that which the President has. He can channel that prestige so as to help the President, but by the same token he can, consciously or not, withhold it from the President. Obviously, prestige is relative to given situations and cannot be carried around like a suitcase. Obviously, too, grand-scale warfare in which the Cabinet member refuses to help the President rarely occurs. But the point is this: to the extent that the Cabinet member does not owe his prestige to the President, he may have a sphere of activity relatively free from presidential control. Given the constant push and pull of President-Cabinet relations, the independent prestige of a Cabinet member with the public at large or with a smaller constituency may not always contribute to more effective presidential leadership.

PRESIDENT, CABINET, AND PARTY

a. The President as Party Chief and Chief Legislator

The President is the head of a political party, a position which carries with it an involvement in the legislative process. In a system of party government, the executive can dominate the legislature through the instrument of party. In a more pluralistic arrangement, such as that created by the separation plus the functional sharing of power, the situation is different. The source of the President's party position does not rest in the legislature, nor is his party position sufficient to give him all the influence he needs in that body. His connection with the legislature, unlike his party one, has a constitutional basis which involves activities with no necessary relation to his party connection. The President's role as Party Chief is connected to his role as Legislative Chief, but they are distinguishable. One is never absorbed by the other.

As soon as nationally organized parties began to contend for the Presidency, their nominees became the titular party leaders. At the head of the "ticket" of partisans throughout the country the presidential nominee personifies for the electorate the party in which he stands, and he carries the main burden of the campaign. His object is to weld together many groups and factions into a coalition sufficient to provide him with enough votes to win. It is useful to distinguish this party task as dealing with the *party-in-the-electorate*.[53] It is the party-in-the-electorate which is responsible for the President's election. Among this group the President's leadership role is clearly established. Even though he will not be called before them for four years, he must retain his leadership in order to be renominated and reelected. Depending on what he can make of it, his strength among the party-in-the-electorate may provide leverage for him during his term of office.

Once elected, the President faces another party relationship — his interaction with the members of his own party in the legislature or, to continue V. O. Key's terminology, the *party-in-the-government*. Since his relation to the legislature has a constitutional basis, he cannot escape dealing with it, but the leadership of his party in the legislature is wholly a product of custom. He may or may not choose to exercise strong leadership over his party-in-the-government. There is no settled custom one way or another, and there are traditions to support both courses of action. On the one hand, he may wish to try to maintain the party alliance with which he won the election as a positive instrument of government, to create legislative majorities out of his party supporters. He will try to persuade them to enact a national program with some similarity to that endorsed by the party (or one more to his own taste). On the other hand, the President may choose to defer to party leadership in the Congress and not try to guide their actions. He may even attempt to rise above parties to govern on a non-partisan basis, appealing for support wherever he can find it in the country at large and in the legislature. He may prefer to follow a literally constitutional view and fashion majorities from issue to issue without regard to party.[54]

It is only rarely that even the strongest President can retain and rely upon his party-in-the-government for solid or consistent support. He may not have a working majority in both Houses, and even when he does, it will be shifting and fragile, always on the verge of dissolving. In leading his party he faces the formidable task, also, of winning locally oriented legislators over to his national program. Moreover, he does not have any constitutional prerogatives to fall back on in seeking to weld partisan loyalties. The upshot of these difficulties is that the President's legislative relations will invariably be both partisan and nonpartisan or bipartisan, regardless of his own preferences. When he is partisan, he is acting as Party Chief; when he is nonpartisan, or bipartisan, he is acting as Chief Legislator. Cabinet members can be of assistance in each of these two distinguishable areas. As might be expected, too, a Cabinet member is of maximum assistance in each if he is of assistance in both.

b. Cabinet and Party: Possibilities and Limitations

The Cabinet as a group has no institutionalized relationship with the political party. A few traditions have grown up by which it is made susceptible to party influences, but in no sense do they make it a party organ. Cabinet members are usually taken from the same party as the President, and customarily one or more members are party managers dealing with such partisan matters as the distribution of patronage. Otherwise, the party impact on the Cabinet and the Cabinet's effect on the party are

THE CABINET AND POLITICS: I

not regularized.⁵⁵ The President's actions will be influential in settling the nature and extent of party-Cabinet relationships, if and when he tries to turn the Cabinet to some advantage in performing his functions as Party Chief.

The appointment of the Cabinet may symbolize some of the President's own notions about party leadership, and it may provoke some kind of response among the interested public. He could alienate large numbers of his party followers by its composition, and thus with one stroke undermine his party position. Ordinarily no President does this, however, and while each of his appointments does not please everyone, taken as a whole they do not threaten his leadership. On the other hand, his selection may do something by way of consolidating the party behind him. He may try to consolidate his party-in-the-electorate by bringing into the Cabinet representatives of those groups in the country which helped form his majority coalition — as when Roosevelt appointed independent Republican Harold Ickes and Eisenhower selected southerner Oveta Culp Hobby. He may choose to accentuate his own leadership within the party by selecting for representation only such individuals or factions as supported his original nomination — as Roosevelt did. He may, in an extreme case, wish to symbolize his independence of both his "parties" with a bipartisan selection — such as that of Martin Durkin.

The best known of all the types of Cabinet-party relationships is produced by the attempt to weld together the various factions within the party-in-the-government by bringing them into the President's advisory group. Such a move will be taken as a definite bid for party unity, looking toward harmonious relationships between its leader, the President, and the rest of the party. The President may seek out the leaders of the various factions or merely seek representatives of each. The most radical experiment of this sort on record was made by Lincoln, who invited and obtained for his Cabinet all of his major rivals for the Presidency. Warren Harding tried to get his two major opponents and failed, but he then selected representatives of various factions. Mark Sullivan commented that, "From the point of view of party and personal politics, Mr. Harding in his Cabinet selections has tied together so many groups and factions that any insurgent movement along the lines of the defections of the past eight or ten years in the near future is almost impossible."[56] Eisenhower solicited suggestions from his major rival, Senator Taft, and selected at least one and possibly two of them. One cannot say, however, that the future role which the President will assume vis-à-vis the party is forecast by his quest for harmony. He may be, in effect, abdicating his leadership of the party-in-the-government as Harding was; he may be able to harness the group under his own leadership as Lincoln was; or he may be feeling his way along in a new situation as Eisenhower was, caught between the desire to be above party and the fear of isolating himself from it.

The symbolic appeal for party unity may, in itself, be a helpful gesture in keeping the party intact. Probably the best it can do, as in the case of the Cabinet's group prestige, is to postpone party splits long enough to get the new administration off on the right foot. Its net effect upon the party will be distinctly minor. Depending upon the condition of the party and the President's own self-confidence, however, it is a move which many Presidents cannot afford not to make.

The Cabinet in action is what really counts — and in action the Cabinet's group character begins to break down. Individuals become important, but the group, with its very fragile underpinnings, quickly declines in importance. The familiar mutation from symbolic paper harmony to real operational disharmony often takes place. James Buchanan advised Franklin Pierce that, "He who attempts to conciliate opposing factions by placing ardent and embittered representatives of each in his Cabinet will discover that he has only infused into these factions new vigor and power for mischief."[57]

Lincoln's bold attempt to form a political coalition produced an "uncongenial and contentious group." Burton Hendrick concludes:

For the most part, Lincoln's councillors were forceful men, with their own programs, their own ambitions, their own vanities, jealousies, obstinacies, and defects of temper. Each had his own set of ideas and his personal following, and on few matters any two agreed. The criticism constantly made that the Cabinet was not a unit, that each of its members went his own way and lived by himself in a watertight compartment, was largely justified.[58]

Nearly every one of the Lincoln group considered himself superior in ability to Lincoln, and none of them joined the group with the idea of pulling as a team under Lincoln's guidance. Only a person with Lincoln's self-confidence would ever choose such a group, and only a person with his extraordinary political skill could have handled them as well as he did. In order to make the most effective use of a Cabinet composed of party factions, it would seem that top party leaders should be chosen. This is usually not possible. But when it is, as in Lincoln's case, the leaders are apt to be strong individual personalities who may use their Cabinet positions as bases and steppingstones from which to further their own ambitions.

If the President obtains, not the party leaders themselves, but representatives of party factions or men acceptable to factions, there is much less of a possibility that they will be of any help to him in leading the party-in-the-government. Certainly Harding's attempt at conciliation did not prevent Republican insurgency in the 1920's. Ezra Taft Benson was the first choice of Senator Taft and hence representative of the "Taft wing" of the Republican party in 1952, but he has not aided the President in his role as party leader. Indeed, from the day of his nomination, he has been under constant attack by some members of the midwestern, conservative Republican faction that was supposed to be conciliated by his selection. And, more than any other member of the Eisenhower Cabinet, he has been a political liability. It is impossible to play politics in the party-in-the-government in the United States without some power base. An ordinary representative of a faction is not likely to have much of a base of support for the President to lean on.

Indeed, few Cabinet members have much party support at all, and most of them ride into and through the Cabinet on the President's political coattail. Some manage to move off this coattail somewhat and obtain a party following of their own. If they do, the chances are good that they will be using this party position to promote their own ends as much as those of the President. A Cabinet which was originally a fairly harmonious group politically may spawn factions with the passage of time. In 1940, nearly half of the Roosevelt Cabinet had presidential fever. The political support of Hull, Hopkins, Farley, Jones, Wallace, and Vice-President Garner was not all used to buttress Roosevelt's position as Party Chief, and three of these men were opposed to his renomination.[59] The particular explanation in each case is not important. The net result does illustrate the centrifugal tendencies within the Cabinet — in party matters as in others — which militate against its use as an organ for promoting party unity.

It is a commonly held view that, as Pendleton Herring has written, "the chief significance" of the Cabinet is that it "offers an opportunity for consolidating political strength through a coalition of leaders whose adherence brings the strength of their political following to the administration."[60] One can agree with him that "the opportunities are wide for bolstering the presidential position by the inclusion of factional leaders in the Cabinet," but one must also be conscious of the limitations of such a view. Given the low degree of institutionalization and the weak pressures for colleagueship in the Cabinet, a group of factional leaders is as apt to splinter the Cabinet as to put it to work for the President. It is a constant temptation to endow the Cabinet with more of a corporate character than it realistically has. Any variant on the Herring theme, such as Professor E. E. Schattschneider's suggestion of a "party cabinet,"[61] is subject to the same limitations: a collegial party group at the Cabinet level is not a very likely possibility until some of the forces making for the dispersion and decentralization of the party system have been organized and centralized first. The extreme susceptibility of the Cabinet to disintegrative forces (of which the party is but one) only serves to highlight the extent to which the Cabinet is a secondary or dependent political institution.

Although the Cabinet group is of only small importance as a party unifier, individual department heads may possess talents and influence which are of assistance to the President politically. One customary role of the Cabinet member relates to solidifying the party-in-the-electorate. That role is the partisan speech-making which most Cabinet members carry on at the time of the President's re-election, or during the mid-term congressional elections. Departmentalism, however, may plague the President in this area as in others. In planning the 1948 presidential campaign, for instance, National Democratic Party Chairman (and Postmaster General) Hannegan had to go to extraordinary lengths to persuade members of the Truman Cabinet to mention the President's name in their public speeches. Referring to the exasperating attitude of his colleagues, he said, "The Cabinet doesn't seem to think that there's anybody named Truman. Its about time Cabinet officers recognized the fact that they hold their offices at the pleasure of the President, and the policies they talk about in their speeches are not theirs but the President's." After talking with them, he reported that, "Some of these people had the gall to say that the President has nothing to do with what they had to say." Hannegan did, finally, secure agreement from them that they would not make a speech without mentioning Truman's name. To ensure this result, the National Committee staff collected Truman quotations, distributed them to the Cabinet members, then checked their speeches to make certain some quotes were used, and, for a while, prepared a weekly summary of findings which was presented by Hannegan to his colleagues before Cabinet meeting.[62] Even this elaborate system must have yielded spotty results, because President Truman seems to have used Cabinet electioneering as a criterion for reshuffling his Cabinet in 1948. Certainly Cabinet members can help keep the President's policies before the public. And he can use all the help he can get in this regard. At a time when speakers are very much in demand, their very prestige as Cabinet members will make them desirable. But their effectiveness is very much an individual matter. Hughes made a "vigorous speechmaking campaign" in 1924 and became, because of his own prestige in the party and beyond it, "the right bower of Coolidge's campaign." [63] Franklin Roosevelt, on the other hand, complained that most of his Cabinet campaigners "get into matters they have no business touching on — like Ickes discussing oil and Roper interpreting the neutrality agreement." [64] Agriculture Secretary Benson traveled more miles (20,000), in more states (20), and made more speeches than any other member of the Cabinet in the 1958 midterm election, yet his party was overwhelmingly defeated in the farm belt area.

Herbert Hoover, who needed political assistance, leaned heavily on the oratorical abilities of Secretary of Agriculture Hyde and Secretary of War Hurley to explain and defend his administration.[65] But Hurley, for example, had no party strength of his own, which limited his role to that of presidential mouthpiece. Little more is required of a mouthpiece than "eloquence," which is about all Hoover officially remembers about Hyde. The task of consolidating the party-in-the-electorate requires more than platform oratory, and where it does require speech-making it is the President who carries the key to success. Hoover is a good case in point. The 1932 campaign was one involving his "personality and ideas," and his Cabinet, however skillful on the stump, could not do much.[66] Likewise, where the President wishes to appeal to the party-in-the-electorate to light fires under the party-in-the-government, he and he alone can make the appeal effectively. Few Cabinet members have sufficient party standing to be more than mouthpieces. Theodore Roosevelt complained that his Cabinet was a weak one simply because "there is no one of them, with the possible exception of Root (who is so busy that he can hardly ever speak) who can appeal before the country with the prestige of a great political leader to explain and champion my administration." [67] This weakness is not a mark of differentiation among Cabinets. It is a condition common in some degree to all of them.[68]

There are many limitations on the Cabinet group and on the individual Cabinet member in providing the President with help in his role as Party Chief. It is perhaps easier to understand the possibilities as well as the limitations by examining actual examples.

c. Harry Daugherty and William Jennings Bryan: Case Studies

Harry Daugherty makes an interesting case study of a party politician in the Cabinet. Daugherty was a party regular in every sense of the word. He disdained the "so-called progressives." "I believe," he said, "in playing the game by the rules. . . ." "I just play ball with the fellows on my team." [69] He was an unknown figure at the time of Harding's nomination, yet he was more responsible for it than any single person.[70] He demonstrated beyond doubt a great skill in "playing the game" of politics by engineering the nomination of a political dark horse for the Presidency. Daugherty had, as do most politicians at convention time, a little nucleus of power. He constructed it around the person of Harding, around a part of the Ohio delegation, and around those friends which he could win over with his personal influence. Relying on this small base of support, Daugherty worked out a strategy by which to manipulate the complex of forces to the advantage of Harding. Though the decision to nominate was made by legislative party leaders, Daugherty's staging of the event qualified him as an example par excellence of the political wire-puller.

Daugherty went on to manage Harding's successful election campaign. By the time he was nominated as Attorney General, he was generally conceded to be one of the three "outstanding figures in the Cabinet"⁷¹ — "outstanding" in this case having reference to his acknowledged political expertise. According to him (and this is what is most important), he accepted Harding's request on the same two bases upon which he had worked before. First, he responded to the appeal of personal friendship when Harding asked, "Are you going to continue to stand by me or desert me after all these years?" In the second place, Harding's plea that "I've never needed you in my life as I do today" was taken by Daugherty to mean (at least in part) that he was needed to do some of the skilled political maneuvering that he had done in the past.⁷² "The main reason I want to be in Washington," he told Mark Sullivan, "is to protect Harding from the crooks. I know how trustful Harding is and I know who the crooks are, and I want to protect Harding from them." ⁷³

He was placed in one of the posts most commonly given to party managers, the Attorney Generalship. He, rather than Postmaster General Hays, was given charge of the distribution of most of the patronage.⁷⁴ "His view of the world being highly personal," wrote one commentator, "his instinctive view of office is that it, too, is something personal, something to be used, always within the law, to aid friends and punish enemies." ⁷⁵ There is little doubt but what Daugherty had an important influence on the President and that, in Harding's eyes, he was a help. Certainly, he was personally loyal. The interesting and crucial fact is that a party politician of this magnitude, placed in the President's Cabinet and given political functions, could seem to have so much political influence and yet in reality have so little. Why?

In the first place, Daugherty's wire-pulling talents had no relation to his administrative ability. He was a poor executive, and even during Harding's lifetime indications of malpractices within the Justice Department began to stain his administration. The scandals which ultimately drove Daugherty from office under suspicion of criminal violations became progressively more damaging to the prestige of the administrations he served. In the second place, Daugherty's political influence was attached to

Harding and had no independent character of its own. Daugherty had never had an independent constituency which he delivered to Harding. He had always been a political broker, trading on Harding's assets. Divorced from Harding, he simply had no base of support from which to operate. After Harding's death, Daugherty brought the new administration nothing but what Coolidge called "ever increasing embarrassment."[76]

In the third place, and because of his dependence, Daugherty could not duplicate his success in dealing with the party-in-the-electorate when it came time to deal with the party-in-the-government. At the time when the problem of his status in the administration was coming to a head, his complete lack of support in Congress became evident. The party leadership, in the persons of Senators Lodge, Pepper, and Borah, made repeated pilgrimages to the White House to urge his dismissal.[77] Only one Republican Senator ever rose to his defense in this latter period and he, significantly, was a Senator from Ohio (Willis). After his resignation not a single Republican defense of him was heard; the public press was almost unanimously agreed that the Administration had lost a millstone; and the Cabinet, some of whose members had been urging Daugherty's dismissal, gained in prestige.[78] Coming from a man who had entered the Cabinet with all the apparent credentials of a party leader, Daugherty's comment that Coolidge had fired him for reasons of "party expediency" is particularly ironic.[79]

William Jennings Bryan is a second revealing example of the party politician in the Cabinet. Unlike Harry Daugherty, Bryan's party position was a net asset to the President, but like Daugherty, Bryan's successes and failures help to describe the metes and bounds of party figures in the Cabinet. The fundamental and decisive difference between Daugherty and Bryan as political figures was the degree of independent party support which Bryan had and which Harding's Attorney General did not have. Bryan was a party leader, not a wire-puller; he was three times the Democratic nominee for the Presidency and had dominated the Party since 1896. Six million voters had followed him through thick and thin with almost religious loyalty. He had strong constituencies among the party-in-the-electorate — economically among the farmers and laborers, sectionally in the West and South, religiously among many church groups. Because he was a champion of groups and of causes, rather than a successful broker of conflicting interests, Bryan had many enemies as well as friends. Within the Party, he was not popular with the organization men of the eastern and central regions.[80] His appointment as Secretary of State was not designed to bring nation-wide prestige to the Cabinet, but rather to cement Bryan's particular following to the administration, thus allowing the President to draw upon his influence. Accordingly, the selection pleased Bryan's friends and infuriated his enemies.

As Secretary of State, Bryan did not exercise the dominant influence over our foreign policy. Except where he attempted to carry out his own deeply held peace philosophy by negotiating a series of bilateral treaties (and in some Caribbean matters), the large principles of American foreign policy were Wilson's. "In general, Bryan was a first lieutenant carrying out his captain's policies, sometimes influencing them, but more often being influenced by them." [81] He and Wilson almost never differed on a matter of policy, however, and between the two there was genuine confidence and admiration. Bryan was willing to follow Wilson's lead and he felt that, on the whole, he had been consulted and that his views had been given weight by the President.[82]

Bryan was not ideally equipped for his executive functions. His approach to problems was political and moral rather than legal, and his successes, such as the peace treaties, drew their strength from this approach. Yet he was not a good administrator. His concentration on rewarding "deserving Democrats" resulted in some egregiously poor appointments, though his attention to patronage was often a help to Wilson. Because of his partisan activities, diplomats and foreign officials thought of him with scant respect, and Department morale was not high.[83] The drafting of diplomatic messages was done either by Wilson or, in more technical cases, by Counselor John Basset Moore. In fact, "John Basset Moore used to attend Cabinet meetings. . . . He attended meetings when Mr. Bryan was not there, *but even when he was*," for the purpose (evidently) of advising the President in matters in which Mr. Bryan was not competent.[84] At the time of the crucial negotiations with the British and Germans in 1915, American policy was clearly out of Bryan's hands. Colonel House refers to Bryan as being on "the outside" of things, and expressed fears that Bryan might decide to do something "on his own initiative." [85] Ray Stannard Baker concluded that: "We find Mr. Bryan with almost no hand in the discussion, befuddled by legalisms, dreaming of peace, and anxiously watching the voters of the Middle West." [86]

Regardless of his success as Secretary of State, it was the eye which Bryan had cocked toward domestic politics that proved of inestimable value to the Wilson administration. It was for this reason, after all, that he had been appointed — to see if his power with the party-in-the-electorate could not be applied to influence the party-in-the-government. This was accomplished. Bryan's only prior public office had been legislative, two years in the House of Representatives, and he understood the congressional mind. With regard to his peace treaties, "Bryan showed much greater skill in handling the Senate than his predecessors." [87] Many men in Congress were subject to Bryan's influence, and he threw it loyally behind the President even on those international issues such as the repeal of the Canal Tolls Exemption Act where "he seems to have been consulted little if at all by the President." [88] Here his influence was important in securing the repeal, particularly in the Senate. Bryan's usefulness to Wilson is most evident, however, on the tariff and the currency reform bills, which pieces of legislation comprised the heart of the New Freedom.

On the matter of currency reform Bryan compromised with

Wilson on some of his former views and then backed Wilson to the limit of his ability. The letter which he wrote in support of the administration bill swayed his supporters and "broke the back of the radical opposition in the House."[89] Afterwards, Representative Carter Glass, Chairman of the House Banking Committee and the legislative father of the bill, wrote to Bryan as follows:

> Looking back over the remarkable campaign for currency reform just ended in the House, one thing stands out, conspicuous in the retrospect, and that is that we are immensely indebted to you for effective aid in critical periods of the contest in committee and in caucus. . . . I desire to thank you for your great assistance to me and to the cause, and also to express my personal gratification at the manner in which you have disappointed your enemies and pleased your friends by standing firmly with the President for sound legislation in behalf of the American people. The country and your party are greatly obliged to you for the skill and discernment with which you have helped along the fight, and I am particularly grateful.[90]

The *New Republic* editorialized, "There is no exaggeration in saying that but for Mr. Bryan's presence in the Cabinet, the Democrats could never have passed the best piece of constructive legislation in their history — the Federal Reserve Act."[91] A Cabinet member of whom such things can be said on such a key controversy is an exceptionally strong bulwark to the President in his leadership of the party-in-the-government.

Bryan resigned when he and Wilson differed over a diplomatic note to the Germans. There is some evidence that Bryan felt that he was just a "figurehead," but there was no personal animosity involved. Wilson tried to dissuade Bryan from resigning and did not want to lose him. Significantly, Wilson felt that Bryan's loss would symbolize to the public a division of opinion within the Cabinet and, perhaps, because of Bryan's standing, hurt the administration. Most of the newspapers, in fact, condemned Bryan on this very score, that he was committing an act of "treason" against the administration by leaving.[92] The fact that no such reaction was ever heard after the Daugherty resignation reflects their contrasting importance as members of an administration team.

When Bryan launched his peace campaign and, later, his antipreparedness campaign, a handful of members of Congress continued to follow his lead, so strong was the hard core of his following.[93] But Bryan's political influence slowly declined as Wilson developed his own party standing. Indeed, by his progressive program he captured much of Bryan's constituency. Bryan was not even elected as a delegate to the Democratic National Convention from Nebraska in 1916, running sixth in a delegation of five. Still and all, he became the convention "hero" when he descended from the galleries to speak in support of Wilson. These later events place Bryan's Cabinet activities in some perspective and show the extent to which a political figure like Bryan was dependent upon the President. He was, in a word, far more influential attached to Wilson than he ever was when he left and fought against him. His final triumph came only when he supported Wilson.[94] Place this fact together with the liabilities of the Bryan appointment and the dimensions of his success are seen to be relatively moderate.

The Cabinet career of Bryan confirms some of the lessons of Daugherty's career with regard to Cabinet-member assistance to the Party Chief. First, an individual whose abilities are in party politics may not be particularly well qualified to handle the administrative side of his job. This is by no means an unexceptionable rule, but men who have partisan political qualifications frequently do not have a proportionate executive ability. The appointment process subjects either type of talent to a host of counterconsiderations. Where marked disparity in political and administrative ability is present, the President will undoubtedly be faced with difficulties which he may or may not be able to compensate for in assets.

Secondly, the greatest partisan political benefit which the President can derive from a Cabinet member is an independent core of support in the party. Admittedly, there are few Bryans in American politics, but in order to be helpful to the President a member must have a constituency of his own over which he has visible influence. Since influence in American politics is held in so many small and diverse packages, a politician whose strength is derived parasitically from the President is not likely to become a strong political figure. Yet by the same reasoning, as Bryan's case clearly shows, the President is not wholly dependent on any one area of support — at least not one within the grasp of a single individual. Bryan's service drew much of its strength from his total loyalty to Wilson, and his loss was by no means irreparable.[95]

The Daugherty and Bryan careers, each in their own way, help to furnish an answer to Teddy Roosevelt's complaint that he had no "great political leaders" in his Cabinet. The answer is that in America there are very few such people. Political power is fragmented and decentralized in the United States. The failure of Daugherty and the success of Bryan are largely the story of the possession of one area of influence out of the many that exist. Daugherty's lack of success despite his seeming potentialities, and Bryan's moderate success because of his exceptional qualifications, delineate, perhaps, the small area of Cabinet-member effectiveness in a political system that is so localized and so diversified. Political power is, as Riesman says, mercurial. It is easy to grasp for a moment in time and in tiny particles, but difficult to hold, to consolidate, and to use. It is especially so for a Cabinet member, but it is also true for the President. He never holds much power at any one time and is endlessly engaged in the process of making majorities out of minorities, of trying to consolidate enough power to get a decision and to support it. A Cabinet member can help in ways which can be crucial though modest and which may provide difficulties as well.

If it be permissible to read into the Daugherty-Bryan studies another generalization which is not so obviously there, it would be this: that the President's job in dealing with the party-in-the-government is more difficult than his control of the party-in-the-electorate. Once elected to the presidency he is safe for four years from the electoral battle, but not from his interactions with the legislature. History demonstrates that Presidents have been far more successful, in recent times, in securing their renomination than in securing legislative cooperation. Daugherty's exclusive relation to the party-in-the-electorate was one factor which made him far less important than Bryan, whose support in legislative matters was his point of real usefulness. The President's legislative relations involve him in a more complex role than that of leader of the party-in-the-electorate. And he must play his role in the context of an institutional arrangement which encourages antagonism. Above all, then, the President needs assistance in his legislative relations.

CHAPTER SIX

The Cabinet and Politics: II

PRESIDENT, CABINET, AND CONGRESS

a. The Cabinet Member in the Legislative-Executive Context

THE executive and legislative branches of the government interact within a constitutional framework, which provides for independent bases of power but a sharing of decision-making authority. The President is given the constitutional authority to send messages to Congress, to "recommend to their consideration such measures as he shall judge necessary and expedient," to call special sessions, to exercise a veto power over legislation, and to control certain aspects of our foreign relations. The Congress, on the other hand, has the legal authority to set up executive departments and agencies, to appropriate money for the executive branch, to confirm presidential appointments, to conduct investigations in the executive branch, and to share with the President the control and conduct of foreign relations. This is by no means a complete catalogue of the points of formal contact, but it is sufficient to show the basis of the President's role as Chief Legislator and the basis of congressional control over the executive branch.

Threaded through and around the formal legal structure are a whole set of informal, less visible relationships which help to shape the character of the President's legislative relations. The subtle threat of a veto, a well-timed distribution of patronage, personal confidence or hostility — all these may be decisive in the making of a legislative decision favorable to the Chief Legislator. Interpersonal contact between the President and legislative leaders or between members of the executive branch and Congressmen may be most effective in winning cooperation. Nor is the continual interplay of the legislature and the executive branch through interest groups recorded in formal documents. The President needs help in both formal and informal legislative activities, and since the Cabinet member is constantly involved in both, he has the opportunity to furnish it.

The Cabinet member's position in the context of executive-legislative relations is by no means a consistent one. He will find himself playing two roles at once when he faces Congress — he is a presidential adviser, but he is also a department head. In the first role, he is bound tightly by the power-responsibility relationship to the Chief Executive. According to the hierarchical or vertical conception of authority, he acts as the agent of the President helping him to carry out his ultimate responsibility. But as a department head, the lines of responsibility are not quite so distinct. His department is subject to *both* presidential direction and legislative control — to both vertical and horizontal lines of responsibility. This conception of the Cabinet member's activity is not an internally harmonious one, and opportunities to help the President may also be opportunities to harm.

When Attorney General-designate Herbert Brownell was asked by the congressional committee investigating his nomination to discuss the executive-legislative relationships of Cabinet members, he answered blithely that ". . . they would be making a tremendous mistake if they didn't work with the head of the executive division of the government, which I propose to do, and they would also be making a great mistake if they didn't work in close cooperation with the legislative branch of the government, which I propose to do."[1]

Brownell's reply, whether born of diplomacy or naïveté, reveals the dilemma, for the Cabinet member cannot always cooperate as closely with one as with the other. Where his ultimate responsibility is concerned, he cannot serve two masters. He confronts this dilemma because the separation of powers, as we have seen, contains within it the seeds of executive-legislative antagonism and at the same time prescribes no patent solution for it. The problem is as old as the republic, as the early behavior of Alexander Hamilton will attest. There is "an unresolved difference concerning the presidential versus the congressional theory of responsibility for administrative action." [2] The Cabinet member is caught and torn by this conflict. According to the orthodox, vertical conception of presidential responsibility, department heads are subject to the final control of the Chief Executive. The "congressional theory," however, takes off from the areas of legislative control over the department heads and proclaims his horizontal responsibility to that body.

Consider this statement by Representative Hay with respect to the Secretary of War: "His office is not a constitutional one. He derives no power from the Executive. He is the creature of the Congress of the United States and as such is amenable to it. He has no power which the Congress does not confer." [3] Or consider this one by Senator Thomas Walsh: "I regard the Secretary of the Navy and the Secretary of the Interior . . . as the agents and representatives of the Congress of the United States. They do what we tell them to do." [4] While Congress accepts the Cabinet member as a presidential adviser, they do not view him as the President's man in his extra-Cabinet relationships. Thus the Cabinet member functions in a twilight region of executive-legislative responsibility with all of the dilemmas of role conflict which that produces. When theoretical conflict is translated into the actual day-to-day functioning of the government, writes Herring, "there is a maze of cross-crossing relationships between the President, Congress and the departments." [5]

Theoretical ambiguities become reinforced by ambiguities in the realm of informal power relationships, and the upshot is that the President-Cabinet member, power-responsibility relationship will not suffice as an explanation of the extra-Cabinet activity of the Cabinet member. The legislative branch is found to be competing with the President for control over the department head's activities. The clientele publics from which the Cabinet member draws so much of his support may have easy access to the legislature and may work through it to establish a proprietary relationship with the department. The department head, for his part, knows that from the President alone he cannot get all of the power that he needs to operate his department as he wishes. He frequently responds favorably to legislative control in return for the power which he draws from it. It may be of mutual benefit to the Cabinet member and "the legislature," i.e., a committee or a Congressman, to develop horizontal relationships. In formally institutionalized ways, in informal contact, or in combinations of both, department head-legislative-interest group relations develop and become counterweights to presidential control.

Depending on the circumstances, the Cabinet member will probably have alternatives of action when he confronts Congress. He may play his role as presidential adviser and department head in such a way that they mutually reinforce one another — in which case he may not only help the President but himself as well. Or, at the other extreme, he may be able to divorce one role from the other. If he appears as the President's man, he may aid his superior and may or may not (probably not) improve his own departmental position. If he operates independently of the President, he may aid his own future and may or may not (probably not) help the President. Between these extremes lie the intermediary positions most often taken — positions which accommodate, with shifting emphasis, one role to the other. The context in which this accommodation goes on is filled with sources of difficulty, as well as help, for the Chief Legislator.

b. Cabinet and Congress: Possibilities and Limitations

The Cabinet has no formalized relationship to the Congress. Yet, as in the cases of public prestige and party, the composition of the Cabinet may have a useful early effect — in this instance, the forestalling of congressional criticism. Through his use of the appointment process, the President may signify his intention of cooperating closely with Congress. When President Truman, an ex-Senator, appointed four legislators or ex-legislators to his Cabinet after the preceding group had contained none, his action was a symbolic indication to Congress of the President's desire to establish cordial relations. But at best the effect is temporary: before Congress, as in other areas of politics, it is every man for himself. The Cabinet member must stand on his own feet, depending for success on his balancing ability and the outside supports which he can locate. One cannot imagine Secretary of State Dean Acheson protesting his immunity to a scalp-hunting Congress on the grounds that, after all, the Truman Cabinet had four ex-legislators in it. While over-all impressions may be helpful or detrimental, real assets and liabilities are counted in units of one.

1. *The Cabinet member and the liaison function.* Every President, if he is to be successful in his congressional relations, needs men around him who can act as his eyes, ears, and mouth in that part of the government. They must be men who understand Congress and can secure the confidence of its members as well as that of the President. Presidential aides wise in the ways of the legislature can be of great importance in the manifold tasks of "bridging the gap." Some Presidents have a formal liaison man to interpret congressional sentiment to the President and to urge his view upon the legislators. Major General Wilton Persons did this for President Eisenhower. A Cabinet member has too much to do ever to qualify for any such post; whatever liaison work he does is applied in non-institutionalized ways, but he is apt to be more effective, in crucial cases, than a formal liaison officer. He carries more prestige and more independent bargaining power. He is not so likely to have diluted his influence by over-exercising it in routine matters. He is not restricted by habits or expectations born of regularized performance.

In the Wilson Cabinet, Postmaster General Burleson performed as congressional liaison and as "the political manager of the Cabinet." [6] Burleson served seven terms in the House and had just been elected to an eighth when he was picked for the Cabinet by his fellow Texan, Colonel House. Wilson, rather cold and aloof in his personal political relations, needed the kind of knowledge and assistance Burleson gave him. During their very first discussion about postmasterships, Burleson taught Wilson a fundamental lesson in party and congressional relations that he never forgot. Wilson was disposed to ignore the non-progressive Democrats in distributing the patronage, but Burleson convinced him otherwise.[7] After the legislative successes of his first two years, Wilson wrote appreciatively to Burleson, "What you told me about the old standpatters is true. They at least will stand by the party and the administration. I can rely on them better than I can on some of my own crowd." [8]

Burleson was recognized by Cabinet members as the congressional liaison man and was used by Wilson as "his dependable adviser as to developments on Capitol Hill." [9] Wilson turned to Burleson for advice on some of the most ticklish questions of his congressional relations — for example, on whether or not to demand a showdown vote on a key House Resolution which he opposed. Burleson alone sat in with the President and members of Congress in drafting the Adamson Law. His advice was sought when Cabinet disputes threatened to cause political repercussions.[10] Burleson acted as the President's man, giving advice and active assistance in congressional matters even when he disagreed with Wilson.[11] His usefulness was summed up by the *Baltimore Sun* as follows: "Those who know the facts recognize that up to the time Mr. Wilson went to France, it was the Burleson influence in Congress that, more than any other, helped to get through the Wilson program of legislation, and that in every fight 'on the hill' he was a tremendously potent factor." [12]

Since the importance of the Burleson-type service is derived from its informal *ad hoc* character, it can be performed by almost anyone, provided only that he have access to the thoughts of both President and Congress and that both branches realize it. A Cabinet member has no special qualifications for the job except the prestige that accrues to his position. In many situations, a member of the "kitchen cabinet," like James Byrnes, will do the same thing. In the Wilson administration, liaison functions fell, largely by chance and default, to a Cabinet member, and his success charts another area of potential Cabinet-member usefulness. Burleson's influence was not based, like Bryan's, upon a party following or a bloc of support. It was based on personal ability, on his congressional experience, his skill at political negotiation, and his sensitivity to legislative attitudes. He did not work through the conventional channels of executive-legislative intercourse. His role was that of presidential adviser, not that of department head, and his success did not depend at all on his performance as Postmaster General. The post was strategic for the handling of patronage, but Burleson's advice went far beyond this realm to help Wilson in his task as Chief Legislator. Wilson had sought and found "one thoroughgoing politician" for his Cabinet — a political expert.

Burleson's own opinion was that, though "Wilson never appreciated politicians," "he used them and knew he needed them." [13] For the Burleson-type individual to be appointed, the President need not "appreciate" politicians, but for the Burleson-type individual to be useful, the President must "appreciate" the liaison function. Neither Harding nor Coolidge, for example, aspired to lead the Congress, and neither appreciated the liaison function to the extent of doing much about it. Though Harding appointed three ex-Senators to his Cabinet, he was content to watch the Senate drift leaderless. He appointed no former members of the House and remained for three years "a stranger to the innermost thoughts of the House." When he did act, his ignorance of legislative opinion was evidenced by a complete lack of timing.[14] Calvin Coolidge complained about the Harding Administration's lack of organization in Congress but did nothing to develop contacts during his term of office — at least not in the House.[15] His most famous attempts at congressional liaison — his breakfasts

— were of little use politically.[16] "With his own party in control of Congress," one correspondent wrote, "Mr. Coolidge has been utterly and incredulously unable to get through the things he wanted or to keep from going through the things he did not want." [17]

It is not possible to say whether influential Cabinet members could have been of much use to Harding or Coolidge in their difficulties with Congress. When the President pares the concept of Chief Legislator to a bare minimum, he cuts the potential role of a liaison man as well. But some contact work undoubtedly goes on, and Cabinet members chosen with an eye to this task might have tempered somewhat Harding's ineptness with the House of Representatives and such humiliating incidents in the Coolidge period as the Warren rejection. Granted that the attitude of Congress was hostile to presidential leadership, adequate liaison work might at least have prevented the prestige of the President from slipping backward. The root impulse, however, must come from the President himself. It is easy enough to repeat that "the President needs help" in his congressional relations, but there is little one can say or do when he affirms that he does not want it.

2. *The Cabinet member and legislative control.* One fixed element in the environment of a department head is that complex of relationships which we call legislative control. The nomination of a Cabinet official must be approved by the Senate, and sometimes a nominee is called to testify before a Senate committee even prior to his confirmation. Once approved, he readily perceives that the successes and failures of his official lifetime may depend upon the legislature. His department is powerless without the money which only Congress can give; its functions can be expanded or altered only if Congress passes a law. At any time his department may be subjected to a searching congressional investigation of its activities; or, it may be reorganized out from under him and some of its functions taken away.[18]

Formal contacts in areas of legislative control beget a host of informal ones. For every staged committee appearance there are hundreds of informal contacts between congressmen and department heads. Whether in public or in private, in bold or attritional moves, the Cabinet member is engaged in a constant struggle for the survival of his organization, his policies, and his control. His relationship with the legislature is unavoidable, and he will seek to make it as harmonious as possible. And at every point where legislative control is operative, the Cabinet member has a chance to help the President as well — to help him in ways that go beyond the liaison role as we have circumscribed it. His general success with the Congress can be an asset to the President by smoothing over ruffled feelings, by persuasively advocating the President's policy, and by gathering support for the President's program. Indeed, his "main job," said James Forrestal, "is to sell Congress . . . to merchandise an idea to the really controlling power. . . ." [19]

Cordell Hull established an outstandingly cordial relationship with Congress. His success here was reinforced by and interrelated with the prestige he had established elsewhere; nevertheless, his legislative relations had a separate basis — his experience in both houses of Congress. This prior service had made him extremely conscious of the value of harmonious relations. When his assistants threatened to attack certain Congressmen, Hull would stop them: "Don't forget, you may need some of these fellows some day." [28] He frequently sought informal meetings at lunch or elsewhere with selected members of Congress. "These visits were prompted both by my feeling of comradeship for my old associates and by a desire to achieve cooperation and teamwork between Congress and the State Department." [21] In a more formal way, he established close working relations with the Foreign Relations and Foreign Affairs Committees in working out postwar problems. And it is a commentary on his success that he was the first Cabinet member in history to be invited to address a joint session of the Congress — after the Moscow Conference in 1944. Hull's appearances before congressional committees were invariably occasions for mutual congratulation on the effectiveness of their relations — scenes duplicated only by one other member of the Roosevelt Cabinet (Jesse Jones). Their felicitations always centered upon Hull's prior experience in Congress.

Hull would be introduced as "an old friend" who "understands problems on the hill," and he would reciprocate in kind with references to his "old colleagues." This exchange is typical:

> MR. RABAUT: Being a former member of the House yourself, it is always with added pleasure that we have you before us, because we know that you, by your experience, know what it is to sit on this side of the table and you are truly sympathetic to our problems. . . .
>
> SECRETARY HULL: Mr. Chairman and members of the Committee, I always look forward with the most pleasant anticipation when I get notice that you gentlemen have assembled here for consideration of the State Department budget, because it gives me an opportunity to have an enjoyable visit with you again and to renew our many agreeable associations of the past.[22]

Committee hearings frequently ended on the same note, with the reassertion that Hull was still a Congressman at heart. Consider this:

> SECRETARY HULL: I have particularly enjoyed this visit here and I want to thank you for not asking me any harder questions than you have. But at any rate I want to say that my door is open to any of you people. I will tell you what I would tell any other persons. . . .
>
> MR. RABAUT: It is my experience that the Secretary himself has never joined the bureaucrats.
>
> SECRETARY HULL: It is too late in life for me to undertake to do that.[23]

Congress, it seems, constructed its own unshakable image of Mr. Hull. It is probable that many others echoed the sentiment of one Representative, who said,

> I would like to say, Mr. Secretary, that I feel that your position at the present time [1941] carries with it the greatest responsibility of any man in this country. I am not unmindful of the President of the United States. But your office is the contact and the focal point between this country and the other nations of the world. You are carrying a very heavy burden.[24]

The speaker continued, as was usually the case, by stating that he was ready to give Secretary Hull whatever he wanted in the way of appropriations. Hull was often encouraged to revise his estimates upward. President Roosevelt husbanded this "aces high" standing with Congress as a valuable resource, and refrained from doing anything that might weaken it. In turn, "his popularity often won the Administration a narrow victory on major fights." [25]

The Hull case is exceptional, but only the exceptional cases offer material for ready examination. The great majority of Cabinet members establish a viable, respectful, uneventful legislative relationship without peaks of cordiality or valleys of hostility.[26] Their contacts are pursued in many inscrutable ways — a close working arrangement with some key figure, a personal favor, an informal meeting. Harmony is a cumulative product of many small efforts and courtesies — mostly unrecorded. Yet, unless a Cabinet member develops the kind of positive influence in Congress which Hull did, his usefulness to the President is hard to document. Some individual efforts to secure good working relations are evident, but it is difficult to say whether these represent credits or debits as far as the President is concerned.

Some Cabinet members, for example, have made a special effort to find ways of improving their relations with Congress. Given the power of legislative committees, it is natural that much effort has centered here. Josephus Daniels, Wilson's Secretary of the Navy, always discussed his program and policies with influential committee members informally before he presented them formally. He attributes his marked success with Congress to this procedure.[27] Henry Stimson found that a series of confidential meetings would help appease "his ancient enemy 'congressional government'." [28] Wilson's Secretary of Commerce, an ex-Congressman, records his practice of attending all committee hearings pertaining to his department. He found this helpful, especially since "most of my Cabinet colleagues did not do so." [29] When the new Postmaster General, Frank Walker, appeared before a subcommittee of the House, he was greeted as follows:

> . . . this is one of the very few times in the experience of this committee that we have been honored by the presence of the Postmaster General himself at committee hearings. Personally, I want to express what I conceive to be the opinion of the minority, and I am sure that it is the opinion of the majority, that it is a very pleasant experience and a very hopeful indication when we are honored by the presence of the Postmaster General himself to give us the benefit of his wisdom and experience in the matters of this appropriations bill. I want to express my personal appreciation to Mr. Walker for showing us the courtesy of coming here to meet with us at this time.[30]

Can we say of Daniels or Redfield or Stimson or Walker that he became, because of his efforts, a positive asset to the Chief Legislator? Certainly their attention to Congress paid dividends in terms of easier personal relations. But this does not mean, nor is it likely to mean, that they brought additional increments of support to the President's program by this kind of action. They smoothed over their own departmental contacts, but their help to the President is calculable in negative terms. That is to say, a Cabinet member who performs in this way reduces the President's burden. He performs some of the chores of diplomacy which the President might be forced to undertake in other circumstances. He maintains legislative-executive relations in an equilibrium and prevents them from deteriorating to the point where they hurt the President. What the ordinary Cabinet member supplies is a kind of *preventive assistance.*

One reason why the ordinary Cabinet member cannot have enough of an impact on the Congress to provide a substantial, positive lift for the President is that the opportunities to do so are rare. Power is atomized in the Congress. Committees, committee chairmen, individual Congressmen (especially Senators) all control islands of influence in the legislative process. The Cabinet member does not confront the entity, "Congress." He appears before select groups, talks with interested individual legislators, and responds to particular pressures operating through Congress.

The best that he can ordinarily do is to help the President in small amounts — probably disproportionate to the time he consumes in doing it — one individual converted by patient lobbying, a committee persuaded to reduce an appropriation less than originally planned. The cumulative effect of his fragmentary efforts will be, by and large, preventive in character. Dean Acheson, who estimates that he spent one-sixth of his working time in Washington either meeting or preparing to meet with congressional groups, has emphasized this point:

In all these hours and days of meetings and consultations, as in all work, the moments of positive accomplishment, of forward movement, are disappointingly few. Much of the time is spent in what Secretary Stimson used to call "stopping rat holes." But that, too, is important work — as one finds out when it is neglected — even though it leaves the big tasks untouched.[31]

Preventive assistance, if it keeps relations on an even keel, is not to be deprecated. This is especially true because the decentralization of influence within Congress, coupled with the diversity of legislative-departmental contact points, offers many opportunities for the Cabinet member to become a drag upon (or even injurious to) the President. The mere avoidance of these harmful possibilities becomes, therefore, a success. Moreover, nothing is done to prejudice more positive success, when the opportunity presents itself. Again, in Acheson's words, "If these occasions of real accomplishment in cooperation are rare, they would be even more rare were it not for the far larger number of meetings . . . preventing grievances from going unaired, preserving *amour propre,* giving a sense of participation and an opportunity to exercise authority over detail."[32] Most of the assistance which the average Cabinet member brings to the President must be figured in small, but nonetheless important, increments.

What are the possibilities and kinds of tensions which develop in the Cabinet member-Congress relationship, and how do they affect the President? One rather common problem which arises is plain lack of understanding of Congress by the Cabinet member. Frequently men who come from non-political, administrative positions cannot adjust to performing in a political atmosphere. Congress is quick to react to anything which smacks of executive dictation or even of an overbearing attitude. When Charles Wilson testified before the Armed Services Committee on his nomination as Secretary of Defense, he repeatedly referred to Senators of long public service as "you" and "you men." During his questioning, he protested that ". . . I really feel you are giving me quite a pushing around." Having bragged a little bit about his business success, which did not settle very well with the Committee, he later confessed somewhat contritely, "When I appeared before you gentlemen before, I talked too much about my past in General Motors because I was just trying to give you a picture of the thing. I did not do it very well. . . . I am an amateur at this business of testifying before a committee like this." [33]

Three and a half years later, he was still offending senatorial sensitivities in such a way as to draw down criticism from his own party leaders for "an unwarranted slur upon Senators." [34] Said Senator Smathers, "I do not know when we have had anyone in the Government of the United States who has managed more often to insult not only those with whom he must work within his own Department, but members of Congress as well." [35] Amateurs who fail to develop a professional deference toward Congress can be a serious drag upon the President.

Lindley M. Garrison, Wilson's Secretary of War, is an example of a talented department head whose maladroitness with Congress was a heavy charge upon the President and led eventually to the Secretary's resignation from the Cabinet. Garrison's approach to his job was that of an energetic administrator. "I don't want merely to draw my breath and my salary here, and have the honor of being in the Cabinet." [36] He conceived of his role as presidential adviser in broad terms, and interested himself in general problems as well as those of his department. This attitude did not endear him to his colleagues, but he gained considerable public prestige for "the wisdom, prudence, and intelligent conception of his duty." [37] Joseph Tumulty, Wilson's public opinion expert, advised him that Garrison "has the ear of the country, and any (defense) program suggested by the President with which he would not agree would be looked upon with suspicion throughout the country." [38] Wilson gave Garrison his head in the War Department and tacitly acquiesced in his preparedness plans. These plans, however, quickly ran into strong opposition in Congress and especially from the influential Chairman of the House Military Affairs Committee (Rep. Hay). The situation called for political tact and negotiation, but Garrison's abilities lay elsewhere. Without prior political experience, he had been uninterested in establishing any *rapport* with the legislature. From the beginning "Congress was especially suspicious and critical of Garrison. He exhaled a kind of military impatience and authority, highly irritating on the hill." [39]

Faced with concrete hostility to his program, Garrison was adamant and refused to compromise. Convinced of his rightness, he pushed his own program in Congress in a "peremptory, abrupt, impolitic, and intolerant way." His terms were all or nothing, a threat to which no Congress is likely to accede. As relations deteriorated, Garrison demanded that Wilson back him up 100 percent in his position; Wilson refused and Garrison impulsively resigned. Wilson's letter to Garrison rebuked him for his unyielding attitude toward the House Committee on Military Affairs, and said that he, Wilson, welcomed "a frank interchange of views." "I do not share your opinion that the members of the House who are charged with the duty of dealing with military affairs are ignorant of them or of the military necessities of the nation." [40] The previous Secretary of War reflected a large body of public opinion when he called the resignation "a national calamity," [41] but Wilson's hand with Congress was undoubtedly strengthened on the crucial matter of preparedness. Though Wilson's own pleasure was to let Garrison handle the entire matter himself, the Secretary of War was incapable of doing so because of his poor congressional relations. Measured in loss of time and good will, Garrison definitely hindered Wilson in his legislative relations.

Garrison's failure, although it was precipitated by a programmatic difference of opinion, was primarily the product of his own temperamental deficiencies — his extreme "executive attitude." Given his unwillingness and inability to conduct normal negotiations with the legislature, his resignation almost automatically followed. Larger issues did not get woven into the conflict. However, the stormiest of Congress-Cabinet controversies arise when a department head personifies a policy or a point of view which is strenuously opposed by certain groups in Congress. In such cases, personality is a secondary matter, and the Cabinet member becomes the focal point of a larger struggle over policy. Although the main object of the legislature is to defeat that policy, its immediate target may be the Cabinet member in the policy-making position. The legislature calls upon its variety of control procedures to check the Cabinet member, and he becomes a bone of contention in a legislative-executive tug of war which is of little help to the President.

President Truman's proposals to elevate the Federal Security Administration to Cabinet status were blocked in Congress because the Administrator and Cabinet-officer-to-be, Oscar Ewing, was identified with a highly controversial policy. As Senator McClellan said to "Mr. Socialized Medicine,"

Of course it is in the minds of many that you are to become Secretary of it. . . . The apprehension is that by reason of the increased prestige of having Cabinet status and you being a Secretary in the Cabinet, you would naturally be able to bring to bear additional force and persuasion to your advocacy of the compulsory national health insurance program.[42]

Several years later, with a less controversial person about to be elevated to the Cabinet, the most strenuous opponents of the Department became its warmest advocates. Pressed for a reason for this reversal, one of them, Senator Dirksen, admitted, "If I was seeking a reason why Congress was rather reluctant to do anything about the plan in earlier years, I might say that it was because of the gentleman . . . Oscar Ewing, whose views have become a symbol, I believe, of compulsory medicine . . . a symbol of something the American people did not like." [43] Ewing's presence in this case proved to be a heavy charge on the President in his relations with Congress, which body succeeded in doing by one method what it probably could not have done by another — it prevented Ewing from becoming a member of the President's Cabinet.

Henry Wallace, in his years as Secretary of Commerce, was another controversial figure whose standing in the Congress was a source of difficulty for the Presidents he served. In eight years as Secretary of Agriculture and four years as Vice-President, he had accumulated very little support on the hill.[44] In a time of reaction away from the New Deal philosophy, Wallace was the personification of more liberal socio-economic measures and increased governmental intervention in the economic life of the country. Roosevelt's selection of Wallace was a political reward which followed on the heels of his rejection by the Democratic Convention for a second Vice-Presidential nomination. The fight over his confirmation was a bitter one in which Wallace was shorn of authority over a major part of the Department, the Reconstruction Finance Corporation.[45] It demonstrated how deep-seated the opposition and suspicions of Congress were to him and to his ideas. "I cannot understand," said Senator Taft, who led the opposition, "why any Senator who opposes Mr. Wallace's strange philosophy should vote to confirm him as Secretary of Commerce." [46] The final vote, 56–32, to acquiesce in his appointment to a debilitated Commerce Department was an unusually close one considering the huge margins by which Cabinet officials are ordinarily confirmed.

By no stretch of the imagination could the net effect of this appointment be considered to be a help to the President in his job as Chief Legislator, and Truman's stock in Congress did not sink when he ultimately fired Wallace. Might not a less controversial figure, less closely identified with extreme views, have been less troublesome to the President in his congressional relations? Would not a man who could have held the reins of the RFC and the Commerce Department have been better able to implement the President's program? Most Cabinet members get along with Congress simply because a sufficient number of people are not sufficiently interested to bother them. An individual who, like Ewing or Wallace, arouses interest because of his connection with a controversial policy may cause the President more trouble than he is worth.

In the final analysis, it is for no one but the President to decide whether a Cabinet member is an asset or a liability. If he is not very influential with Congress, his helpfulness in some other capacity may more than compensate for his weakness. Yet if he runs into trouble with Congress, he will be particularly dependent upon the President to back him up, and the President will have to expend some of his prestige and influence in doing so. This presents a dilemma for the President. The institutional and psychological antagonisms between the executive and legislative branches will yield him little enough power in Congress. And such is the effect of the democratic context that the more he uses his power the less he has. His ability to use it is limited by the necessity of holding it. Legislative influence becomes a presidential resource to be husbanded for use at crucial points. If he has to battle too hard to save a Cabinet member, he may use too much of his influence in doing so. He may, like Alice in Wonderland, have to run twice as fast to stay in the same place. Yet, if the Cabinet member is of sufficient value to him, the President will retain him in the face of criticism and will be willing to suffer whatever consequences may result, in terms of congressional problems.

President Truman acted in this fashion in his spirited defenses of an embattled Secretary of State, Dean Acheson. In large part, the congressional attacks upon Acheson were partisan ones, grounded in differences of opinion on foreign policy. Republicans of both Houses passed, in caucus, the resolution that: "We earnestly insist for the good of our country that Mr. Acheson be replaced as Secretary of State."[47] But few Democrats rose to vote him confidence, and only the President's rugged defense and his refusal to dismiss him could be heard in his behalf. Though Acheson made determined attempts to establish good relations with Congress, such as his informal question period in the Library of Congress, he did not succeed very markedly. His personality tended to annoy Congressmen and make them suspicious.[48] As Secretary of State, moreover, he was on the exposed flank of the Cabinet — fair game for all critics, without organized interest-group support, and peculiarly reliant on the President.[49] Thus Acheson's unprotected position, his poor relations with the legislature, and his policy differences went to make him a political liability. The President, however, "leaned on him for constant advice" and believed him to be "among the truly great Secretaries of State our nation has had." In view of the fact that, "There never was a day during the four years of Dean Acheson's Secretaryship that anyone could have said that he and I differed in policy," his retention was deemed to be worth almost any price.[50]

The result of congressional opposition to a Cabinet member is not always as happy for him. Secretary of the Navy Edwin Denby came under concentrated legislative fire in the wake of the Teapot Dome scandals. Denby had permitted the transferral of oil lands from his department to the domain of Secretary Fall. His "lamentable ignorance" of what had transpired was evident from his testimony before the investigating committee, and his "lack of competence" was freely admitted even by those who rose to defend him.[51] After sharp debate on the proprieties of the move, the Senate passed by a vote of 47–34 (35 Democrats, 10 Republicans, 2 Farmer-Laborites in favor) the resolution: "It is the sense of the United States Senate that the President of the United States immediately request the resignation of Edwin Denby as Secretary of the Navy." [52] Coolidge replied not primarily, as Truman had done, in defense of Denby's actions, but in defense of his executive power. He realized that he might be better off without Denby, but said, "I do not propose to sacrifice an innocent man for my own welfare." Denby wrote to Coolidge *apropos* of the situation in Congress, saying that he appreciated "how difficult your situation has become. I fear that my continuance in the Cabinet would increase your embarrassment." [53] Surely it would have, since Denby was of no particular value to Coolidge anyway. He resigned, thus relieving the President of a serious difficulty with Congress.

The congressional relations of people like Garrison, Ewing, Wallace, Acheson, and Denby created difficulties which might not have been so acute had other individuals held Cabinet office, and which place in relief the success of those members who can provide preventive assistance. The really fundamental and perplexing problems of Cabinet member-Congress interaction, however, arise from the basic conflict of executive-legislative responsibilities. Granted that Dean Acheson was not popular in Congress, would he have increased his value to the President by casting about for support in Congress? If he had permitted certain influential Congressmen to dictate United States foreign policy, he would have increased his support and his popularity. But he would also have forfeited the President's foreign policy responsibilities. More seriously, he would have severed his own vertical lines of responsibility to the President by acting not as an arm of the executive, but as an arm of the Congress. Buttressed by a cordial relationship with the Congress, he might then have proceeded to ignore the President. Acheson, who was retained in spite of legislative unfriendliness, would then have been fired for being too friendly. This hypothetical possibility is illustrative of the serious cross-pressures within the American political system. The line which separates those Cabinet member-Congress relations which benefit the President from those which are so intimate that they injure him is a very thin line indeed.

Depending on the strength of his horizontal ties with the legislature, the Cabinet member has varying degrees of operating freedom. He may be able to appeal to Congress for support from an adverse decision by the President. Beyond this, he might be able to function from day to day with considerable immunity from the exigencies of the executive branch. He can further secure this independence by trading on his prestige standing with "publics" outside the legislature — especially with those which have easy access to the legislature. At the best, such behavior is disruptive of the President's control through the formal administrative hierarchy; at the worst, it can transform a Cabinet adviser into a virtual enemy. If and when this pattern of activity occurs, the student of politics should recognize that its underpinnings lie in the "crisscrossing relationships" of the political system and not in happenstance or in human perversity.

PRESIDENT, CABINET, AND DEPARTMENTAL ADMINISTRATION

a. The President as Chief Executive

"The executive power shall be vested in a President of the United States," who shall "take care that the laws are faithfully executed," and who "shall nominate, and by and with the consent of the Senate shall appoint" thousands of public officials. Such are the broad, vague lines of the President's mandate to function as the nation's Chief Executive. By following them, and by assuming responsibility for the effective management of the executive branch of the government, he performs his role as *Chief Executive-Administrator*. In 1848, President James K. Polk entered a pair of comments in his diary which may stand as one high-water mark in the performance of this leadership role:

I have not had my full Cabinet together in council since the adjournment of Congress on the 14th of August last. I have conducted the government without their aid. Indeed, I have become so familiar with the duties and workings of the government, not only upon general principles, but in most of its minute details, that I find but little difficulty in doing this. I have made myself acquainted with the duties of my subordinate officers, and have probably given more attention to details than any of my predecessors.[54]

No president who performs his duty faithfully and conscientiously can have any leisure. If he entrusts the details and smaller matters to subordinates, constant errors will occur. I prefer to supervise the whole operations of the government myself than entrust the public business to subordinates, and this makes my duties very great.[55]

The first comment that comes to mind *apropos* of such a feverish expenditure of energy is this: Polk died a few months later, surviving his tenure of office by only one month. But the essential point to be made involves the extraordinary primitiveness of Polk's prescription for presidential administration of governmental activity. In the twentieth century, no President can treat his department heads as superfluous.

The trenchant statement of the President's Committee on Administrative Management that "the President needs help" is well enough known. Quite apart from the specific context in which it was written, the sentiment has always been a valid one. It was George Washington who first recognized "the impossibility that one man should be able to perform all the great business of the state," and who found the solution to his problem by "instituting the great departments." From that day to this, the executive departments of the national government have been, formally speaking, "the major organizational and crucial elements in the administrative structure of the executive branch below the presidency."[56] The department head becomes an "outpost of the President in an assigned field of administrative activities."[57] He helps to implement the broad policy views of the President within his department, provides a responsible line of communication between the department and the President, and functions in general as a link in the hierarchical chain of command running from top to bottom within the executive branch. In addition to his functions as a presidential lieutenant, the department head is a chief executive in his own right, "the administrative leader of the agency to which he is assigned." [58] He has an immense organization whose activities he must direct, coordinate, and keep on an even keel. He is positioned at the peak of one distinct pyramid of authority, concerned with the particular interests and problems of those groups of people subordinate to him. Administratively, then, the department head is cast in two interrelated yet distinguishable roles — one President-oriented, the other department-oriented. His formal responsibilities extend both upward toward the President and downward toward his own department.

In the frictionless world of organization-chart hierarchies, this double-jointed job presents no analytical problem. The department head takes his marching orders from the President and transmits them to his organization. He accepts political responsibility for day-to-day administration according to the standards established by his superior. Thus does he help the administrator-in-chief increase his own effectiveness. The political universe inhabited by the department head is, however, not so simply understood. Just as his possibilities of helping the Chief Legislator in Congress are complicated by the impingement of non-presidential forces upon him, so too are his possibilities of helping the Chief Executive-Administrator in the departments. There is, to begin with, the personality factor, the set of attitudes and abilities which the department head brings to his job. Furthermore, within his department he operates according to formal organizational prescription and under the influence of less formalized group interests, all of which set limits on his activity. As for the environment outside of his department, it is one of conflicting responsibilities and institutional rivalries, certain to involve him in problems of role conflict.

b. Cabinet and Departmental Administration: Possibilities and Limitations

Every administrator possesses certain personal attitudes and capacities which influence and condition the actions of his department, and hence the assistance he may give to the President. By way of illustration on the most general level, there is the possibility that the Secretary's social outlook will orient the activity of his department by determining the priorities within and the nature of the support without. Under the aegis of a strong union man, the Department of Labor from 1913 to 1920 reflected the views of William Wilson that "The Department of Labor was created in the interests of the wage earners of the United States . . . an executive department especially devoted to their welfare." In pursuance of this view, Wilson cultivated trade union relationships and placed special emphasis, within the Department, on the Conciliation Service and the settlement of labor disputes. But when James Davis took over the reins of the Department in 1920, he articulated a different philosophy. "The Department of Labor," he said, "will be a department of the United States Government, run for the general benefit and not for the particular interest of organized or unorganized labor." Davis predicted "a great change" in the methods of the Department, and he oriented its activities not toward the trade unions, but in such a way as to gain the confidence of the business community with which he was identified. Major emphasis was placed on immigration.

After Davis' tenure, the Department's orientation changed again. In discussing the post-1933 Labor Department changes, a close student has written: "One of the most significant was the difference in the orientation and beliefs of Miss Perkins from those of any previous Secretary of Labor." Deriving her viewpoint from a social welfare background, she looked upon the Department as a "poor people's department." She retained a skepticism about the trade unions which meant that although the Department's activities increased markedly, they never became union-oriented. Secretary Tobin reversed this attitude in attempting to identify the Department and its actions with organized labor.[59] The example could be multiplied by references to any of the other departments. So long as the President shares any given outlook with the Secretary, the possibilities for help are increased. But should they differ as, for example, Eisenhower and Durkin did concerning the Labor Department, the Secretary may appear as more of a hindrance.

In more specific terms, the department head's administrative competence is of primary importance in assessing his potential value to the President. "If a head of a department is competent, if he has first-rate executive ability," wrote Secretary Houston, "he can spare the President much time and worry." [60] Woodrow Wilson wrote in this vein to his Secretary of Commerce, William Redfield, "I have throughout my administration been able to think of the Department without any concern because I had such perfect confidence in you and was so sure that everything would be looked after as it should be." [61] The ability to conduct his organization in such a way as to keep from unnecessarily increasing the President's burden is a minimum requirement, similar to the ability of a department head to keep from exacerbating the President's political worries. Many Secretaries, especially those in relatively noncontroversial (depending on the circumstances) departments, can help in this way. It is once again a negative, preventive contribution, measurable by contrast to what the consequences might have been if the situation were otherwise. Nonetheless, this type of assistance is a substantial achievement not easily accomplished.

The kind of positive assistance that talented executives can bring to the President is well illustrated by the examples of William G. McAdoo and Herbert Hoover. Different in temperament, yet possessing a similar genius for the direction of large enterprises, they performed invaluable services for Presidents Wilson and Harding. Their usefulness had its roots in an energetic and efficient management of their respective departments, under which the capacities and functions of each were expanded. Both Treasury and Commerce were raised to peaks of prestige and performance under their leadership, yet each man conceived of his role in governmental as well as departmental terms. That is to say, he made of his department an agency of expert intelligence and specialized functions, and he worked to harness the thought and action of his organization in the formulation of national policy. "I stated [writes Hoover of his acceptance] that for the Department to be of real service, I must have a voice on all the important economic policies of the administration. I stated this would involve business, agriculture, labor, finance, and foreign affairs so far as they related to these problems." [62] Hoover's counsel became important in all of these areas and decisive in some.[63] When Calvin Coolidge offered to shift him to the Secretaryship of Agriculture, he declined with the observation that he could help the farmers more as Secretary of Commerce.[64] The same wide-ranging interest in national programs characterized McAdoo's tenure. During the war he held (among others) the following extra-Secretarial jobs: head of the Liberty Loans, Chairman of the Federal Reserve Board, Chairman of the Federal Farm Loan Board, Chairman of the War Finance Corporation, and Director General of the railroads. He played a contributory role in the decisions leading to each of these administrative establishments and was a pivotal figure in wartime domestic policy. His record stands in sharp contrast to the record of any of the Cabinet members during World War II.[65]

One cannot generalize about an ideal administrative personality. There is none. The promotional flair of McAdoo was different from the reflectiveness of Hoover. Each did have a prodigious energy, a quality of inventiveness, and a capacity for making decisions, but the only lesson to be learned is this — each fitted into a context where his administrative capabilities made him an asset to the President in his role as Chief Executive. Each is an example of what can be done by fitting the right man to the right job at the right time, but McAdoos and Hoovers are rarities. "The trouble is," writes Houston, in concluding the paragraph quoted earlier, "that the average head of a department is not highly competent and has not first-rate executive ability." [66] His conclusion is a common one.[67]

Given the fact that the members of the Cabinet do not come from any recognized pool of national leaders, administrative talent will have to be produced from men of widely divergent backgrounds. And it is by no means assured that such ability will be forthcoming, given the limitations inherent in the prior experience of most selectees. Paul Appleby has summarized the problem from the administrative point of view.

> By the time members of Congress come to Cabinet posts, they are likely to be set in a non-administrative pattern of individual performance. Business executives usually have come to dominate particular organizational situations rather than having developed a flexible general administrative ability that might enable them to adjust to the wholly strange political environment. Bankers and farmers, in so far as they are qualified for specific Cabinet posts, are qualified in technical familiarity with some aspects of the subject matter rather than as political leaders and administrators. Editors, lawyers, and educators tend to have a more general policy understanding, but are primarily individualists without actual administrative understanding.[68]

In each case, the rationale of Cabinet appointment may be defensible in some important respect which bears no necessary relationship to administrative competence.

Thus, when one looks back upon the appointment process with administrative considerations in view, the internal conflicts of that complex process are as evident as they were in the cases of Daugherty and Bryan. In practice, the political and administrative components of the Cabinet norm are not usually fulfilled in the same person. Deficiencies in the administrative personality of the Cabinet member are partly the product of countervailing forces inherent in the appointment process.

An administrative liability to the President may have landed in the Cabinet, and/or may be retained there, because of his political talents. Albert Burleson, the Postmaster General who did the bulk of Wilson's congressional liaison work, was under almost constant attack in the public press for his administrative activities. Referring to his management of the Post Office Department and the telephone and telegraph companies during the war, one paper called him "the heaviest burden that President

Wilson has had to carry." [69] Burleson admitted that he had made more enemies than any other Cabinet member, a situation which doubtless did not benefit Wilson, and this in spite of Burleson's usefulness in other areas. Indeed, given the tradition with respect to the Postmaster General, the possibility of a conflict in political and administrative talent is built into the job itself.[70]

The administrative inabilities of Cordell Hull present another example of a Cabinet member of overwhelming political influence who lacked comparable executive talent. He allowed the appointments of many of his subordinates to be made by others, thus hampering his own control of the Department by establishing lines of influence between his lieutenants and others, e.g., the embarrassing Welles-Roosevelt relationship. Moreover, Hull permitted the President to place his own men in the Department without even a formal relationship to the chain of command, i.e., Moley.[71] Hull's conception of his department's function, and his own function, was framed by a naïve and rigid jurisdictional point of view. His greatest administrative passion was to maintain the boundaries of the State Department absolutely inviolate from the inroads of Treasury, Agriculture, Interior, etc. His commentaries on his colleagues focus on this to such an extent that Hull seems to have had a kind of administrative paranoia.[72] It was this Balkan-like outlook which led Hull to feel that he could demarcate foreign affairs from domestic politics (e.g., reciprocal trade!). It led him to accept, though not without serious reservations, the jurisdictional line between military and diplomatic affairs which Roosevelt offered as his excuse for excluding Hull from much that went on in World War II.[73] Nothing could be further from the Hoover-McAdoo example than Hull's timid and cautious approach, under which the State Department slowly "atrophied" as an effective organizational contributor to policy making.[74] Some confirmation for the view that administrative and political talents are not a logical combination is found in the fact that in Hull's case his administrative views were related to his attempt to consolidate independent prestige. His lack of aggressiveness was in part designed to keep his public countenance free from unsightly blemishes.

As requisites to successful departmental administration, the two most important personal qualifications would seem to be administrative experience in a political environment and some acquaintance with the substantive policy problems of the department involved. These are the two elements most prominent in the individual application of the Cabinet norm. The vagaries of the appointment process are no more a guarantee of both these elements than they are of anything else. Indeed, the indeterminable interaction of the forces discussed earlier frequently results in the selection of an individual without either. "For the Navy Department [writes Mr. Dooley] you want a Southern Congressman from the cotton belt. A man that ever saw salt water outside of a pork barrel would be disqualified for the place. He must live so far from the sea that he don't know a capstan bar from a sheet anchor." [75]

This facetious description is sometimes more closely related to reality than we would like to think. Consider, for instance, pacifist Josephus Daniels, North Carolina newspaper editor and politician and devoted friend of Wilson's, who became Secretary of the Navy without any knowledge whatsoever of its substantive problems.[76] Or, consider Edwin Denby, ex-Congressman from Michigan, who was plucked out of the blue just before inauguration time to be Harding's Secretary of the Navy. His unwitting acquiescence in the transfer of the oil leases out of his department paved the way for the Teapot Dome scandals. Mark Sullivan's comment is typical, that "His record demonstrated him to be ludicrously unfit for his post. The man merited neither tears nor prosecution. He deserved to be laughed out of the Cabinet." [77] Or, consider Denby's successor, Chief Justice of the California Supreme Court, Curtis Wilbur, a man who knew nothing about the navy, whose policy statements were at times radically opposed to those of the President, and under whose administration the navy was allowed to languish in both organization and construction.[78] It is not to cast aspersions on any positive contributions which these men may have made to say that their qualifications, and in some cases their performances, were not well matched with the criteria of administrative experience and substantive knowledge.

A new Cabinet Secretary who is unacquainted with his department's organization and/or its policy problems is at an immediate disadvantage. "I was [wrote one] like a sea captain who finds himself standing on the deck of a ship that he has never seen before. I did not know the mechanism of my ship; I did not know my officers — even by sight — and I had no acquaintance with the crew."[79] A Secretary of the Interior said that "When I came to Washington, I didn't know we had charge of territories. I didn't know we had charge of anything exterior."[80] Another Secretary acknowledged, "I recognized that it was a hot seat, but actually I had no conception of its difficulties."[81] Cabinet members who find themselves in this situation may not be able to have as much of an impact on their departments as some with prior acquaintance.

Though previous experience within a department may be an optimum recommendation for the Cabinet from an administrative angle, it is often not possible to find individuals who are available. When the White House changes party hands, the likelihood of such a person's being appointed declines.[82] And where it is done, as in the recent case of Secretary of State John Foster Dulles, it may still not produce the administrative ideal. The Dulles example illustrates as well as any other the possibility of conflict even within the administrative aspect of the Cabinet norm. An expert in terms of substantive knowledge may turn out to be a very poor departmental administrator. Like Secretary Dulles, he may be so preoccupied with what he considers more important things that he is simply not department-oriented. He may live in the realm of his own ideas, "cut off from his own authority, his colleagues, and his duties."[83] If a Secretary does not establish internal lines of communication and does not keep his department apprised of over-all policy, the morale of the department will be low and it will be difficult to integrate that department's efforts into the larger goals of the President. In view of these many personal variables, there are a large number of possibilities for less than satisfactory departmental administration, and there is room for considerable uncertainty in Chief Administrator-department head relations.

We must, however, resist the temptation to over-personalize organizational activity and to exaggerate the influence which an individual Secretary can have on his department.[84] The most ambitious and talented department head confronts a formidable complex of situational limitations on his activity. The new appointee finds himself amid a framework of established relationships, of goals already fixed and of forces long since set in motion. He faces an impersonal bureaucratic structure with great resistance to change. Most of his organization is staffed with career personnel, relatively unaffected by changes in high-level policy. Power relationships among constituent elements of the department, or between departmental units and clusters of interest outside the department, tend to be in an equilibrium which reflects an optimum adjustment for all concerned. Their desire to survive may confront the Secretary with serious limitations. He has, of course, some formal controls with which to countervail departmental resistances, but these are frequently minimized by the very forces he is trying to combat.

One control, for instance, which is a prerequisite to successful departmental management is the power of appointment. Yet the Secretary frequently operates under considerable restriction — statutory or otherwise. Harold Ickes complained that, "Without the power to appoint subordinates there is no power of control at all. I think this power should lie with the Secretary because, at least in the public mind, he is charged with the responsibility. As it is now, he has the responsibility without any authority, and that makes for bad administration, bad morale, and misunderstanding." [85]

The appointments of the Under Secretary and Assistant Secretaries are subject to many non-Secretarial influences.[86] During party turnovers these positions are eminently suited for the payment of political rewards. Both President and Congressmen may press personal favorites upon the department head. In any case, the result may be unfortunate from the standpoint of internal administration, as, for example, Stimson's experience with Under Secretary Castle will attest.[87] Or, interested groups may lay claim to some of these positions. The desire of the AFL and the CIO for one Assistant Secretaryship of Labor apiece is a case in point. With regard to Bureau Chiefs, the Secretary operates under severe statutory handicaps.[88] Inability to remove these officials follows where the power of appointment is lacking.

The department head's formal managerial weapons may be further blunted by organizational inflexibilities. We have already noted the historical evolution of the so-called "holding company" type of department, which includes Interior, Defense, Commerce, and Health, Education and Welfare. Many constituent units of these departments have their own separate statutory bases, thereby helping to establish an authority with non-departmental roots. Since built-in unity is lacking, it can come to the "holding company" organization only by super-imposition from above, yet it is part of the organizational pattern that such authority is hard to come by. In an "integrated" type of organization the Secretary has substantive grants of authority over the constituent units, whereas in the more loosely structured department he has a vaguely defined responsibility to "direct and supervise" them.[89] In practice, however, such a mandate is "an almost meaningless generality." [90]

This limitation is most obvious in terms of authority to reorganize the relationships of the subordinate units. Frequently, he cannot transfer activities from one unit to another, make adjustments in his field organization, or alter the budget so as to make organizational changes possible. Congress may want to exercise minute supervision over all such organizational changes. When Chairman Carl Vinson of the House Armed Services Committee proposed that the Secretary of Defense should consult his Committee before making any organizational changes, Secretary Louis Johnson exclaimed, "Why, you would become the Secretary of Defense. That completely ties the hands of the Secretary." Said Vinson in reply, "We don't want Congress by-passed." [91]

What appear, from a bird's-eye view, to be limitations on the Secretary's managerial discretion appear from another perspective as the phenomenon of "bureau autonomy." Hoover described the Commerce Department as "a congeries of independent bureaus . . . all old establishments created prior to the Department itself. . . . Each was an inbred bureaucracy of its own. There was little department spirit or *esprit de corps*. Some of the bureaus even placed their own names on their letterheads, without mentioning the Department." [92] Franklin Lane described the Interior Department as "a rather disjointed department [in which] the bureaus have stood up as independent entities." [93] The independence of the Army Corps of Engineers is a classic instance of the pattern of relationships which may develop, and it has been admirably related in another place.[94] The important thing to be noted about bureau autonomy, for our purposes, is that its dynamics are by no means explainable in wholly organizational terms. An administrative organization like a bureau does not hang motionless in a political vacuum waiting to be directed according to statute and hierarchy. In order to gain and hold any degree of autonomy, its position must be shored up by sufficient political support. This usually derives from those groups in the political system to whose advantage it is to maintain such autonomy. In addition to bureau personnel, these groups will ordinarily include the clientele for whom the bureau provides services, and members of the legislature who have an interest, corporate or otherwise, in controlling the activities of an administrative agency.[95] The intimate *rapprochement* which the Corps of Engineers have established with local organizations and with influential Congressmen is a key to their continued administrative independence.

Considered in these broad situational terms, the problems raised by bureau autonomy may arise to some degree in every executive department. Even though a departmental executive may possess considerable authority, a bureau will possess its own independent base of support to which it may appeal. In fact, and this is the point, it must do so in order to get the power to operate. Regardless of statutory relationships with Congress (though these help), direct bureau-legislature relationships will be legion, including appropriations, investigations, appointments, etc. Every governmental bureau has one vested interest, one constant preoccupation — survival. And in the interests of survival, it must cultivate sympathetic attitudes and support on the part of those who can do it harm, which most often means the legislature. In the interests of control, the legislative unit whose relations with the agency are most frequent will encourage and attempt to enforce responsibility to it. This mutuality of interests may create a concentration of power which can undermine the authority of the Secretary over his department.

Interwoven with the bureau-legislature "sub-system," and operating on both parties to it, are the interested private groups. Regional labor groups interested in employment may work with both bureau admirals and pork-barreling Congressmen to keep the control of naval shipyard and supply contracts out of the hands of an economy-minded Secretary of the Navy. In the process of administration, policy is made by the operating bureaus. Each bureau develops its own clientele — people interested in the policy questions within the bureau's area of discretion. Thus, "a structure of interests friendly or hostile, vague and general, or compact and well defined encloses each significant center of administrative discretion." [96] If the bureau is to survive and develop a program, it must have support from these sources.

To the private groups, on the other hand, the bureaus "represent the institutionalized embodiment of policy, an enduring organization actually or potentially capable of mobilizing power behind policy." [97] Here again, mutual dependence dictates a close relationship, one which may not be logically consistent with the policies or desires of the Secretary. Little can be known about these informal power clusters by studying the formal intradepartmental hierarchy, yet they may be in direct competition with it. Where this is so, they impair the Secretary's ability to manage his department and to provide the President with good administration just as surely as any lack of adequate formal authority.

Time is still another complicating factor for every Cabinet official. If he wishes to help the President by rendering him good departmental administration, he must focus his energies downward into the department. But as he provides this kind of negative assistance, he has little time left for positive and constructive assistance. Men of large vision and extra-departmental enthusiasms like Secretary of the Interior Franklin Lane will often leave, like him, a testament of frustration in office: "Ability is not lacking, but it is pressed to the point of paralysis because of an infinitude of detail. . . . Every man is held to details, to the narrower view which comes too often to be the departmental view or some sort of parochial view . . . there was little opportunity to think of anything more than the immediate." [98] William Redfield, the man who received Wilson's letter of praise for efficient departmental administration, admitted that "I looked at my duties too much as a busines matter — too little as the creative counsellor." But, he explained in defense, "My nose is kept closely to the grindstone in my own Department." [99] The tendency to become sucked in and submerged by routine or detail or immediacy has been called "the most insidious hazard both to the executive and his organization." [100] He cannot lift up his head often enough to look at things from a government-wide, i.e. presidential, standpoint. If he is to be of help to the President, his time is a precious resource, easily exploited and difficult to conserve.

Department Secretaries live in a world which has many extra-presidential dimensions. We have seen the multiplicity of forces within the political system which impinge upon him — forces built into his department by its history, by forces of the appointment process, by forces emanating from Congress, and by forces generated by the publics which the department serves — forces of interest, of authority, and of partisanship. Up to this point in our discussion we have discussed what might be called a series of objective factors which affect departmental administration, with potentialities for lightening or increasing the President's burden. They are objective factors in the sense that the assumption is made that the overriding concern of the Secretary is to manage the internal affairs of his department in the interests of the President. The implicit image of the Cabinet member thus far has been something akin to that of a person whose administrative life history is one ceaseless struggle to surmount a veritable network of obstacles, personal and situational, in an effort to act as the agent and servant of his superior. Such may, indeed, be the case. The Secretary may be exclusively President-oriented, and instances where he fails to help the President may be written off as the result of forces which he cannot bring under control. But it is an equally likely possibility, in view of the department head's problems of success and survival, that he may deliberately assume postures and adopt positions that are department-oriented, and which may not accord with presidential desires.

Secretaries of Agriculture have frequently faced the problem of reconciling the views of the Farm Bureau with their loyalty to the Chief Executive.[101] Secretary of Labor James Mitchell has lived amid similar cross-pressures from his union constituency and from President Eisenhower on such matters as right-to-work laws and FEPC legislation, and he has taken positions on them which the President himself refused to take.[102] There is present, almost always, this dilemma of competing responsibilities, loyalties, and demands, bringing with it the potentiality of conflict. Conflict may, of course, be avoided, but its presence colors the Secretary's whole pattern of behavior. Every department head finds himself caught and torn between alternatives of action — President-oriented or department-oriented — in an environment where the rationale, the means, and the incentives for pursuing either are readily available.

His very position as head of one executive establishment among several carries with it certain attitudes and organizational necessities non-presidential in character. He inherits an immense bureaucratic structure with its own traditions, its own *raison d'être,* and its own operating methods. None of these depend on him, nor will he be able to alter them very significantly. He cannot help but become a part of this particular organization, supporting its vested interests, concerned for its *esprit de corps,* and speaking for it in all of its conflicts.

A Secretary of the Interior will predictably contest the location of the Forest Service (now in Agriculture) with the Secretary of Agriculture.[103] He will do it not because it is a personal or partisan matter, but because it is a long-established, organizational tenet within Interior that the Forest Service belongs there. Secretaries may "defend or [be] governed by bureaus they themselves do not control," which in turn may lead them to "take positions hostile to presidential needs and policy." [104]

The department head is not to be viewed as the unwilling captive of his organization or as someone who "fronts" for bureaus against his own subjective inclinations. No admiral of the navy ever defended bureau autonomy more stubbornly, more vigorously, and more willingly than did Secretary of the Navy Josephus Daniels.[105] If a Secretary is to accomplish any of his goals, he must cultivate the support of his own organization. He cannot, as the Hoover Commission seems to think, trade exclusively on the influence of the President in his operations.[106] Beyond his own organization, he must locate his support within the legislature and with interested private groups. Without non-presidential support of this kind, his department may be decimated — as the Secretary of Labor lost some of his bureaus by congressional action in a period when these units and the department in general had insufficient support from organized labor.[107]

Harold Ickes' attempt to change the name of his Department from "Interior" to "Conservation and Public Works" illustrates how impotent a Cabinet official can be when he operates on the assumption that presidential support is all that he needs to run his department. Relying on Roosevelt's assurances that he was interested, that he would request other executive departments (Agriculture, War, and Navy) not to oppose it, and that he would urge congressional leaders to take favorable action, Ickes introduced his measure. When the bill failed to pass even a congressional subcommittee, Ickes was shocked, and interpreted the result as an act of personal perfidy by the President. What happened, actually, was that other executive departments which felt their interests threatened by the change were able to muster congressional support in the person of the Chairman of the subcommittee, and external support from the farm organizations.[108] The President could not have made the difference in any event. More than this, it is not realistic to expect the President to give strong support to those pet projects of a Cabinet member which affect so many of his fellows. The Cabinet member is left on his own most of the time simply because the President, for most of his time, must remain relatively detached as between competing departments. And where Congress is concerned, if the President exerts his power too frequently he may, by virtue of a familiar political paradox, lose it.

In the interests of effective departmental administration, most Cabinet members will be led at one time or another to exploit the presence of the competing lines of authority, running vertically to the President and horizontally to the Congress. The spectacle of Secretary of War George Dern supporting the Corps of Engineers in their autonomous operations is explainable only by looking behind the vertical, hierarchical rationale. Dern did everything he could to resist integrated planning on water resources because he felt it would dilute the functions of one of his bureaus. He even went so far as to claim that the Corps was "an agency of the legislative branch," thereby protecting his department by renouncing his own control over it![109] Many Secretaries, like him, have nourished the notion of horizontal responsibility in order to preserve their organizations. The point is that conflict between President-oriented actions and department-oriented actions inheres in the American political system. It is as evident in the administrative realm as in the legislative. The Cabinet member is subject to strong non-presidential or extra-presidential influences, creating a gap between fact and theory in the formal power-responsibility relationship. The case study of Jesse Jones illustrates the general problem as it has been stressed in this chapter.

JESSE JONES: A CASE STUDY

Jesse Jones' behavior as a Cabinet officer must be set in the context of his previous experience in government. A Texas Democrat, he was appointed by President Hoover in 1932 as a Director of the Reconstruction Finance Corporation. One year later he became its Chairman, a position he held until 1939 when President Roosevelt designated him to be Federal Loan Administrator. In this post he was given general supervision over several loan agencies in addition to the RFC. In 1940, Jones was made Secretary of Commerce, and by a special, unanimous resolution of Congress he was allowed to remain as Federal Loan Administrator.[110] That agency was formally incorporated into the Department of Commerce in 1942. Three features of his RFC experience shed light on Jones' perception of his job and his pattern of behavior as Secretary of Commerce.

In the *first* place, the RFC was a creature of the Congress, a government corporation whose authority and functions were determined by the legislature. With the exception of the appointment of its Directors, it was relatively independent of the President. A statutory relationship thus bound Jones closely to the Congress during his entire thirteen years of government service. He assiduously cultivated and strengthened these ties at every opportunity in order "to make the RFC a dependable favorite of Congress."[111] At the forefront of his accomplishments Jones always spoke, not a bit modestly, of his smooth relationships with that body:

Throughout the entire period, we received in a manner probably unique in the history of federal agencies, the complete cooperation and confidence of each successive Congress. Not a single request that I made of Congress during those thirteen years was refused. On the other hand, Congress increased and broadened our power from year to year.[112]

Under congressional authorization, and subject only to the routine approval of the President, Jones lent between 1940 and 1945 "anything that we think we should . . . any amount, any length of time, any rate of interest."[113] The following remark by Senator Adams bespeaks the unusual willingness of Congress to grant discretionary authority to him: "Of course, the credit you are using comes from the Congress, and we have heard it said across this table and in the Senate and House that these vast credits were being extended largely because of the confidence the Congress has in Jesse Jones. Now that has been said time after time."[114] Senator Taft described the incorporation of the RFC into the Commerce Department, as "an extraordinary precedent, justified only by the character of the man."[115]

For Jones, congressional hearings were not inquisitions or ordeals about which to become apprehensive, they were informal, friendly, laudatory — almost clubby — interchanges.[116] Frequently he would sit on the witness table and chat in an off-the-cuff manner. Or, if there happened to be a vacant seat between committee members, he would take it and the "hearing" would begin. Indeed, so comfortable did this executive official feel among congressional committees that he designed, bought, and presented to the Senate Committee on Banking and Currency a new table for their hearing room — one is tempted to say their clubroom — in order that he might see them all better while testifying.[117] Jones pursued this cordial alliance in casual, day-to-day contacts. Once a week he would lunch on Capitol Hill with members of the legislature, in the office of Vice-President Garner, Speaker Rayburn, or Senate Secretary Biffle. On other occasions he would come to Garner's office for morning or afternoon coffee. "I guess it's *our* office," commented Garner, "Jones uses it as much as I do." [118]

A *second* crucial element in Jones' RFC experience was its nonpartisan character. Like most independent agencies, its plural executive was composed of members of both political parties. Jones himself had been a very active Democrat as Director of Finance for the Democratic National Committee in 1924, as a favorite son candidate for President in 1928, and as a faithfully heavy contributor to party causes. He had influential Democratic friends like fellow-Texan John Nance Garner and Senator Carter Glass. And though he retained these ties the RFC acquired a reputation for non-partisanship. Jones, moreover, was a conservative in politics, and as the Republican-Southern Democratic coalition took shape within Congress, his Democratic politics became less of a liability. He continually stressed the nonpartisan nature of his organization and won the support of Republicans as well as Democrats. The ranking Republican member of the House Banking and Currency Committee spoke of Jones as "a man whom I so much respect for his wisdom, his intelligence, and his patriotism that without giving it much consideration, I would accept almost any proposal he might make." [119] Or, consider this colloquy between the ranking Republican and the ranking Democrat on the Senate Appropriations Committee:

SEN. WHITE: . . . I have to confess that there is a disposition for me to favor anything that Mr. Jones recommends.
SEN. MCKELLAR: That is for me, too. I do not think that there is a finer man anywhere in the world.[120]

Jones' extraordinary standing with Congress was built partly on his success in keeping his organization in close touch with that body and yet outside party conflict.

A *third* factor, intertwined with the other two, was the close *entente* between Jones' organization and a powerful social constituency — the business community. During Jones' government service, agencies under his supervision authorized expenditures of fifty billion dollars to assist various enterprises in business, industry, and banking. He was in constant contact with representatives of this group, as consciously and as inevitably reaching out for their support as they did for his. His public speeches were aimed at this particular clientele, and the groups which gave him a forum were business groups — the Chamber of Commerce, the American Bankers Association, the National Wholesale Association Council, the Economic Development Committee, the Department of Commerce's Business Advisory Council. Jones himself was a businessman who had become by 1929 "the best known private citizen in Texas," due to his ownership of a newspaper, several hotels, a bank, several skyscrapers, and other assorted real estate.[121] He identified himself completely with business, and he considered the RFC to be "America's largest corporation and the world's biggest and most varied banking agency." [122]

Jones never passed up the opportunity, before Congress, to attribute the success of the RFC wholly to the fact that it was a "businesslike, non-political organization." Again and again he reiterated that "Our agency is a business agency composed entirely of business people." [123] He was tireless in his praise of his agencies as paragons of businesslike efficiency and economy, and he loved to make invidious comparisons between himself and the "do-gooders," "idealists," and "screwballs" in the government who did not possess the same virtues. His organizations were run as businesses, by businessmen, and for businessmen. Jones fastened himself to a powerful constituency which cut across party lines and which gave him leverage both in and out of Congress. Moreover, his appeals to Congress and to his business constituency were mutually reinforcing. Throughout the Roosevelt Administration the executive branch had not been especially hospitable to business, and its channels of access to government coursed mostly through the legislature. Members of Congress tended to be very sympathetic to Jones' emphasis on business and identified themselves with his efforts to help it, especially small business.[124]

As head of the RFC, Jones developed lines of responsibility and areas of support which had few presidential dimensions. On the basis of his personal and institutional resources, he had fashioned a substantial enclave of power and, hence, a considerable degree of political independence. As Secretary of Commerce, however, he was brought into a different, and theoretically more dependent, relationship to the President. He joined the "official family" at Cabinet meetings; his formal responsibility now ran directly up the hierarchy to the Chief Executive; and with a closer relationship came greater opportunities for him to help the President. Jones himself had no intention of allowing either of the two patterns of relationships — least of all the President-oriented one — to absorb the other. And as if to underscore the point, he refused to accept the Commerce post until Roosevelt agreed to let him retain all his RFC functions.[125]

However this may be, the key idea is that Jones' network of relations with Congress, with a social constituency, and with political partisans is the kind of network within which nearly every department Secretary must operate. It is the essence of his extra-Cabinet activity. The vividness, perhaps, but not the validity of this proposition depends upon Jones' peculiar RFC background and his perception of his new role. His situation, faced with alternative lines of responsibility to the President and to the Congress, is a normal one in the American political system. In his first appearance before the House Appropriations Committee, he spoke as any Secretary of Commerce would when he said, "If the Department of Commerce means anything, it means as I understand it, the representation of business in the councils of the administration, at the Cabinet table, and so forth."[126] The duality of roles, as presidential lieutenant and departmental executive, promotes ambiguity, conflict, and, as the Jones case illustrates, a pattern of behavior quite unknown to any hierarchical image of President-Cabinet relations.

In 1943, Congress was considering legislation to set up a single agency to coordinate the disposal of surplus government property. It provided for coordination by the President and, as a practical matter, by the Bureau of the Budget. With an eye to uniformity and control, the Budget Bureau desired that all agencies in the executive branch be tied into the program. This, of course, included the RFC and its various subsidiary corporations, which comprised one of the largest government purchasers and holders of property. In the Senate hearings, the Bureau expressed its wish that ". . . the disposal policies of these corporations should be subject to review under this bill, for assurance that they are tied in, that there is cohesion and coordination, and that they are not out in a competitive status."[127] Jones was willing to listen to the advice of a unifying agency but fought for the complete autonomy of the RFC in disposing of its property. In effect, he argued against the wishes of the Chief Executive, and did so without even consulting Roosevelt. Before the committee, Jones stated his own position and appealed for support to his favorite constituencies, Congress and business.

Arguing from the standpoint of business, he said,

I don't see any excuse for a new agency to handle and dispose of these properties. You have a perfectly good one. . . . I should think that you would use the RFC and give it such additional manpower as it needs, because it is a business agency and this is a business proposition. There would be no purpose in setting up a new one, but Congress can do it if it wants.

At the suggestion of the Committee, he was "willing" even to enlarge his own domain and leave out the Budget Bureau altogether in the area of real property.

SEN. FERGUSON: Could the RFC become the agency and dispose of all properties? Is that the logical place to place it, because it is a business organization?
SECRETARY JONES: I think that is where it belongs; that is all plants, equipment, machinery, machine tools, and so forth. *I have not discussed the matter with anyone in authority in the government.* Those are my views and they are very strong. . . . I do not understand why they (Budget Bureau) would be a natural agency to do this job.
FERGUSON: Who would be the natural agency in the government?
JONES: The RFC. . . . When I say the RFC, I mean also the Department of Commerce, because they are the business end of the government.[128]

The hearings closed on a familiar note: Jones' appeal to the Congress and reciprocated congressional sentiments of affection for him.

CHAIRMAN: (Senator Hill) You feel that your agency, having built these plants and secured this property, is the agency to make this disposition?
JONES: The RFC is your agency, an agency of the Congress.
CHAIRMAN: Mr. Jones, when you first appeared here this morning, I spoke about your many different titles. I am going to confer another title on you, and that is that you are a great diplomat, too. That was a fine way to put it. But as you say, it is Congress' agency that has secured this property. It is your feeling that it is the agency that Congress should use for the disposition of this property better than anybody else?
JONES: Yes, sir. . . . I do not intend to be immodest.
CHAIRMAN: We would not have you immodest. We do not want you to be.
SEN. FERGUSON: The entire country is going to be very fortunate if all the other agencies feel about Congress as you do I am sure.
CHAIRMAN: I want to say this, too, since the Senator has said what he has, that Mr. Jones' actions always square with his words. He is always most considerate of the Congress.[129]

One point at which Jones' double-barreled efforts to mitigate presidential control were effective was in the appropriations process. The major purpose of the executive budget is to provide for coordination of the expenditures of the executive branch in the name of economy and efficiency. The reverse side of the coin is the President's central control over programming through his control over expenditures. The Budget Bureau, as a staff arm of the President, prepares a document which expresses unity in policy as well as in finance. Reductions that it makes in agency requests represent the complex judgment of the President and his staff on matters of priority, cohesion, and purpose. Insofar as Cabinet members can make successful appeals to the Congress against this judgment, they can operate their departments with little dependence on the President and, virtually, if not literally, in defiance of him.

In drawing up the Department of Commerce budget for fiscal 1944, the decision was made to eliminate the field service of the Bureau of Foreign and Domestic Commerce. This was done because wartime restrictions on trade had reduced the usefulness of this service, and because that part of the job which needed to be done could, in the eyes of those dealing with the budget, be performed better by a wartime agency. To Jones, the reduction represented an attack upon his domain by people who were ignorant of his problems, and he lobbied strenuously before the appropriations committees in the House and Senate to restore the cut of $430,000 in the interests of his clientele.

In the House Subcommittee hearings, Jones began by stressing the efficiency and economy of his own agency while taking pot shots at others, both tactics designed to identify his aims with those of Congress.

We have a seasoned organization, which would work in cooperation with the RFC and its agencies. We have been in the government a long time. You don't hear much fuss about us. We get along pretty well and we think we know how to do the job better than some big shot that you would get in as temporary head, building up an organization which would be partly made up of volunteers and inexperienced people who do not know how to work together. . . . Of course, we do not spend any money which does not seem to be necessary. I believe in economy, but there are apparently not a great many people who do. There seem to be a good many in Congress who do, but not the boys on the spending line.[130]

With a little legislative arm-twisting, Jones freely stated his position on the budget cut.

MR. HARE: Mr. Secretary, . . . we all know of your wide business experience, and I wonder if you would give us the advantage of your judgment as to what extent and in what way these district offices would be able to contribute in giving assistance to small business activity?

JONES: If we had that money, we would expand the present organization instead of closing it. *But we have had advice from the Budget Bureau that this does not fit into the President's program. Of course, we are not trying to oppose the President, but we think the Budget is wrong.*[131]

Before the Senate Committee, Jones concluded his appeal for the restoration of the cut in terms of his particularistic clientele and without reference to any overall presidential program.

I think that the Department of Commerce has got to carry the ball for business. That is what it is set up to do. If we haven't got the right people to do the job, then others should be gotten to do it. But the Department is the representative of business at the Cabinet table and in the administration whatever the administration is. So I say that I think it is of importance that we not destroy or diminish this service by one iota, that it really ought to be expanded and encouraged.[132]

Of the $430,000, Congress restored $295,000, and only four of the thirty field offices were closed.[133]

Jones' consciousness of his high standing contributed to a psychological hypersensitivity to any attempt "to horn in on our RFC operations." He communicated this sensitivity to the Congress and they responded in kind. They were irritated when a wartime agency like the Office of Production Management or the Board of Economic Warfare infringed in any way on the discretionary authority of Jones over the money which they had appropriated.[134] Their solicitude, while a blessing to Jones, was a distinct burden to the President, for it allowed the Secretary of Commerce to prosecute, before friendly committees, an internecine warfare with other agencies of the executive branch, casting about for non-presidential support as he went. The most obvious of these adventures was that which resulted in the "acrimonious public debate" between Jones and Henry Wallace, who was head of the BEW, in June of 1943. This quarrel between subordinates obviously hurt and annoyed the President and hampered his direction of the war effort.

At least as early as December of 1942 Jones had been engaged in sidewise combat with the BEW before Congress. In an appearance before the Senate Banking and Currency Committee, Jones allowed himself, with little encouragement, to complain that he was really "working under" the BEW and was very dissatisfied with the arrangement. One of those informal gestures which seldom break into print provided Senator Tobey with an opening.

SEN. TOBEY: This matter of working with the BEW was enough to cause you to *raise your eyebrows,* as you did the first time it was mentioned here, is that right?
JONES: That is right, I suppose, but I don't quite know what you mean.[135]

Of course, Jones knew very well, and only had to be coaxed a little more to reveal that "we negotiate contracts and arrange financing and none of them (other agencies) except the BEW ever interferes with our negotiations. They leave it to us, feeling that we are the business organization with experience, preferring to have us negotiate the contracts; and because of our responsibility to Congress, we quite naturally prefer to do it."

TOBEY: But the BEW does interfere.
JONES: They do a great deal of the negotiating, yes. . . .
TOBEY: Would you want to answer this question, having in mind the talk here this morning about the BEW and its extraordinary powers? Would you feel that if the BEW were curbed . . . . it would be a wise procedure?
JONES: The Executive Order is made by the President.
TOBEY: Yes, I know.
JONES: I think I would not care to discuss that.
TOBEY: But here is a nation and we are all striving to serve it. . . . *Such a thing as I suggest might contravene the President . . . but whether the nation would be better served by having a better*

setup . . . would you feel that some other arrangement would be wiser than the present arrangement?

JONES: *Inasmuch as you press the question, I will say I think it could be improved.*[136]

Jones did not consider his relationship with Roosevelt in terms of subordination or hierarchy. He saw it, instead, as a marriage of convenience between co-equal potentates. "I never considered that I was working *for* him, but *with* him for the country." [137]

In the twelve years I worked with him, we never had an argument. We did not always see alike. If he asked me to do something which in my opinion we could not or should not — and that happened only a few times — we just did not do it. For me that was the only way to operate without having a break with the President.[138]

His biographer describes how Jones "layered" Roosevelt's proposals.

He granted such demands as he deemed wise or safe, but when Roosevelt wanted something that Jones considered wrong or clearly unwise, he listened, withheld argument, and then contrived an escape by inconspicuous inaction.[139]

Neither was there any feeling of intimacy between the two men.

In no sense did I feel his superiority over other men except that he was President and the greatest politician our country has ever known, and ruthless when it suited his purpose.[140]

Roosevelt, for his part, was willing to work on a relatively thin margin of loyalty, both personal and programmatic — which is undoubtedly one reason that their association lasted as long as it did. Ultimately, however, the personalities of the two men cannot explain the difficulties or the endurance of the relationship.

Roosevelt retained Jones in the Cabinet because his presence was helpful — not in spite of his independent strength, but because of it. The most persistent political problem facing any President is that of consolidating enough support for his policies. From this standpoint, Jones' influence with groups in and out of the government was an asset on which Roosevelt could trade. He saw Jones' conservatism as "a good thing for this administration," "a good antidote for the extreme liberals, a sort of balance as it were." [141] In 1940, Jones spoke over a nation-wide radio hookup to his business constituency, urging that the reelection of the President was in their best interests. Roosevelt realized, too, that Jones' strength in Congress, with its hard core in the influential Texas delegation,[142] was useful to him. It was a strength calculated by some as "ten votes in the Senate and forty in the House" on matters within Jones' area of competence.[143] He was able on one occasion, for instance, to persuade reluctant legislators to vote a huge export-import loan to South America.[144] Thus the total picture of the Jones-Roosevelt relationship was an admixture of help and hindrance. Neither assets nor liabilities were constants, and the ultimate judgment, of participant and observer alike, is one of subtle calculation.

As the 1944 Democratic Convention approached, Roosevelt's calculations "convinced" him that Jones' influence was being used to support a conservative revolt, and to persuade the Texas delegation to vote against a fourth-term nomination. Jones denies it, but whatever the case, the decisive thing is that Roosevelt believed it was true. Moreover, it was the kind of behavior which touched his most sensitive political nerve. Jonathan Daniels writes that in 1944 the President was speaking contemptuously of "Jesus H. Jones," and that he was planning then to remove him from the Cabinet.[145] Judge Roseman feels that the move was a mistake and that "Roosevelt would never have made it under ordinary circumstances, but the vindictiveness aroused by the reports of Jones' activity impaired his usually clear political insight." [146] The puzzle of the curt Roosevelt-to-Jones note after the election can best be explained in this way. It stressed Henry Wallace's "utmost devotion to the cause, travelling almost incessantly and working for the success of the ticket in a great many parts of the country." [147] As Joseph Harris says, "Roosevelt chose this means of letting it be known that Jones was dismissed because of his failure to support Roosevelt politically. On any other grounds, the dismissal of Jones would have caused a great furor." [148]

Jones did not go down without a fight in which he uncontestably demonstrated his independent power. Divorced of the prestige of office, he nonetheless could summon enough political support to keep his base of operations, the RFC, out of the hands of his successor. His letter blasting Henry Wallace and his testimony on the George Bill were in the nature of a valedictorian appeal to business and to the Congress. Congress responded with majorities of 400–2 and 74–12 in favor of removing the RFC from the Department of Commerce. Wallace, with that lack of perspective so common to a man who has been run over by a steamroller, but with the sure knowledge that he had been thoroughly flattened, said later that "Jesse Jones wielded greater power for a longer period that any human being in the history of the United States." [149]

A more sober and pertinent comment, perhaps, would be that the denouement, like the rest of the story, illustrates something of the fragmented, decentralized nature of power in the American political system. Norton Long has written that "To deny that political power is derived exclusively from superiors in the hierarchy is to assert that subordinates stand in a feudal relation in which to a degree they fend for themselves and acquire support peculiarly their own." [150] Jesse Jones built, inhabited, and manipulated a political fiefdom with a degree of independence which brought a heavy burden to his lord-President. But the feudal analogy is only partially correct, for within the democratic political process there are no laws of primogeniture and entail. Jones' fiefdom was, in the final accounting, a web of relationships peculiarly his own, held only for so long as he could hold it. It was not a transferable property. At the very end, he boasted facetiously about his two-headed job that, "I do not believe there is another man in the world that will do it except me." [151] It was an accurate assessment not alone of the man, but of the system.

Power in the American political system is both fragmented and, in David Riesman's description, "mercurial." It can quite easily and logically be won by the Cabinet member, but as the Jones case demonstrates, no particular constellation can be held, or held together, permanently. The Jones case also demonstrates that the winning, the holding, and the losing are not likely to make the tasks of the Chief Legislator-Chief Administrator any easier.

THE CABINET AND POLITICS: SOME CONCLUSIONS

The investigations which we have made into Cabinet-member activity in the areas of public prestige, party, Congress, and departmental administration lead to a few conclusions about the Cabinet and the political system in which it operates. One striking circumstance is the extent to which the Cabinet concept breaks down in the course of the members' activities outside the Cabinet meeting. In matters of prestige, partisan politics, and legislative relations alike, the Cabinet as a collectivity has only a symbolic value, a value which readily disappears when the need for action supersedes the need for a show window. In the day-to-day work of the Cabinet member, each man fends for himself without much consideration for Cabinet unity. His survival, his support, and his success do not depend on his fellow members. His performance is judged separately from theirs. This condition is but another result of the combination of the centrifugal tendencies in our political system with the low degree of institutionalization which characterizes the Cabinet.

The political help which the President receives comes not from the group but from individual Cabinet members, who can and do augment the President's effectiveness in his leadership roles. It would be a serious mistake not to emphasize the possibilities for crucial assistance by individuals. But probably most striking is the fact that the possibilities for such assistance are very frequently negated by the number of limitations which surround them. There are pervasive limitations of a personal or a situational nature, and there are limitations inherent in the political system — all of which make it neither easy for a Cabinet member to help the President nor axiomatic that he should do so. In the final reckoning, the President receives much less assistance of a positive, non-preventive type from his individual Cabinet members than one might expect. This fact serves to accent the high degree of success which is represented by preventive assistance. It also helps to underline the tremendous gap which separates the presidential level of responsibility from that of his subordinates. It demonstrates, too, the extent to which the two levels are subject to the pulls of different political forces.

The President-Cabinet power-responsibility relationship is, according to the analysis of this chapter, inadequate as a total explanation for the extra-Cabinet performance of the individual member. As a group the Cabinet draws its life breath from the President, but as individuals the Cabinet members are by no means so dependent on him. In many instances, we are presented with the paradox that in order for the Cabinet member to be of real help to the President in one of his leadership roles, the member must have non-presidential "public" prestige, party following, legislative support, or roots of influence in his department. And in any case, the problems of his own success and survival will encourage him to consolidate his own nexus of power and will compel him to operate with some degree of independence from the President. For his part, the President's influence over the Cabinet member becomes splintered and eroded as the member responds to political forces not presidential in origin or direction. From the beginnings of his involvement in the appointment process, the President's power is subject to the pervasive limitations of the pluralistic system in which he seeks to furnish political leadership.

One final conclusion takes the form of a restatement of the pluralism of American politics. In every area we have noted the diffusion, the decentralization, and the volatility of political power. The same kaleidoscopic variety which characterized the factors influential in the appointment process is evident in the political processes which engulf the Cabinet member. Each member interacts with a great variety of political units, interest groups, party groups, and legislative groups, and each has his own pattern of action and his own constellation of power. The feudal analogy is an apt one. It frequently makes more sense to describe the Cabinet member as part of a "feudal pattern of fiefs, baronies, and dukedoms than . . . an orderly and symmetrical pyramid of authority." [152]

Here, then, is an underlying explanation for Cabinet-meeting behavior. Departmentalism is a condition whose roots are grounded in the basic diversity of forces which play upon the individual member. By the same token, this pluralism generates centrifugal influences which help to keep the Cabinet in its relatively non-institutionalized state. The greatest problems for Cabinet and President, like the greatest problems in American politics, are those which center around the persistent dilemmas of unity and diversity.

CHAPTER SEVEN

The Cabinet and Reform

For people concerned with improving the operation of the American political system, the Cabinet is a perennial object of affection. They see it as a feeble, inactive institution which should be revitalized, reinvigorated, and engaged in more profitable pursuits. The end in view varies, as does the assessment of present conditions from which each reform proposal springs. Particular panaceas vary from the introduction of Cabinet government to the construction of a Cabinet building.[1] But the failure to analyze the Cabinet within the going political system has been a constant. The Cabinet has always been approached as an object to be manipulated, and not as a subject to be understood. Some brief Cabinet's-eye observations, then, may put various reform ideas in a better perspective. Without passing final judgments or making program recommendations, an inquiry can be made into how some of the proposals might affect the Cabinet and its fundamental relationship to the President.

Reform suggestions involving the Cabinet fall into two categories. One places a heavy emphasis on the improvement of legislative-executive relations. The other focuses on the improved organization of the Presidency. Within each category the scope of the plans scales from sweeping to moderate. Some students, doubting the adequacy of the American political system to meet new problems, seek basic reorganization. Others, less anxious about its adaptability, seek modifications within the existing structure.[2]

IMPROVING EXECUTIVE-LEGISLATIVE RELATIONS

One of the earliest and sharpest critics of the workings of the separation of powers and of executive-legislative relations was Woodrow Wilson, whose pre-presidential writings have been a fountainhead of reformist criticism. In classic terms, he attacked the "division of authority and concealment of responsibility" which he felt resulted from the "isolation" of the executive from the legislature.[3] Wilson condemned what he called a "disintegrated structure" of government, productive of irresponsibility, inefficiency, and disunity in the conduct of public affairs.

The seat of the trouble was the excessively fragmented and irresponsible power of Congress. "The only hope of wrecking the clumsy misrule of Congress," wrote Wilson, "lies in the establishment of responsible Cabinet Government."[4] The heart of Wilson's conception of Cabinet Government revolved around the notion of a "binding link" between the two branches of government — along the lines of the British system.

So long as we have representative government, so long will the Legislature remain the imperial and all-overshadowing power of the state; and so long as it does remain such a power it will be impossible to check its encroachments and curb its arrogance and at the same time preserve the independence of the Executive without joining these two great branches of government by some link, some bond of connection, which, whilst not consolidating them, will at least neutralize their antagonisms, and, possibly harmonize their interests. A Cabinet-committee would constitute such a bond.[5]

What we need is harmonious, consistent, responsible party government, instead of a wide dispersion of function and responsibility; and we can get it only by connecting the President as closely as may be with his party in Congress. The natural connecting link is the Cabinet.[6]

In order to constitute the Cabinet as a hyphen for an un-hyphenated system, Wilson proposed that the Constitution be amended to allow Cabinet members to have seats in the Congress, with "privileges of initiative in legislation and leadership in debate."[7] He further urged that the President be "authorized and directed to choose for his Cabinet the leaders of the ruling majority in Congress." [8] The principle of ministerial responsibility would then "necessarily" develop. A Cabinet member would resign when a proposal which he favored was defeated,

> and resignation upon defeat is the essence of responsible government. In arguing, therefore, for the admission of Cabinet officers into the legislature, we are logically brought to favor *responsible Cabinet Government* in the United States.[9]

> Moreover, the members of the Cabinet would always be united in their responsibility. They would stand or fall together in the event of the acceptance or rejection of any measure to which they had given their joint support.[10]

In these early views, which have been so influential, Wilson was never very clear as to what the Cabinet was or what he wanted it to be. His confusion prevented him from perceiving what is a paradox of his radical reformist position. *If Cabinet Government comes to the United States, the Cabinet will do little to bring it about.* The important thing about Cabinet Government is not the Cabinet, but the context in which it operates — the lack of an independent executive, the absence of a separation of powers, the existence of a responsible party system.[11] In the presence of the separation of powers and the checks and balances wielded by an independent Chief Executive, the Cabinet's characteristics and behavior are highly derivative. If one wishes to alter appreciably the nature of the Cabinet, he must treat underlying causes and not surface symptoms. It seems as if Wilson thought he could introduce something like Cabinet Government without affecting the principle of separation of powers or the basic check and balance system, and that he could do this by directly changing the role of the Cabinet.

He was led to take this position in large part because he underestimated the potentialities of the Presidency and hence tended to overestimate the relative importance of the Cabinet as a potentially autonomous force in American politics. Of the President's executive authority vis-à-vis the Cabinet, Wilson wrote that,

THE CABINET AND REFORM 253

The President is no greater than his prerogative of veto makes him; he is, in other words, powerful rather as a branch of the legislature than as titular head of the executive. Almost all distinctly executive functions are specifically bestowed upon the heads of the departments.[12]

Insofar as the President is an executive officer he is the servant of Congress; and the members of the Cabinet, being confined to executive functions, are altogether the servants of Congress.[13]

Wilson's view consistently depreciates the President's executive function as it relates to the Cabinet and Congress. The highly contingent power-responsibility relationship of Chief Executive and Cabinet was not as clear to him as it could have been. In discussing the Cabinet, for example, he said that "the characters and training of the Secretaries are of almost as much importance as [the President's] own gifts and antecedents,"[14] and that a weak President would be wise in "overshadowing himself with a Cabinet of notables."[15] In view of what he deemed the importance of the Cabinet, Wilson wrote that "The Presidency is thus inevitably put, as it were, into the hands of a sort of commission, of which the President is only the directing head."[16]

Only on the basis of a set of views like this could Wilson propose to "direct" the President to choose his advisers from a certain set group — perhaps not even members of his own party[17] — and yet claim that the Chief Executive would not be inconvenienced or his independence affected. It was only on some such exaggerated view of the Cabinet's collegial activity that Wilson could predict the "necessary" adoption of united responsibility. It was only on the basis of such a President-Cabinet conception that Wilson could argue for Cabinet Government in a context that would not permit Cabinet Government and/or could believe that he could modify the workings of the separation of powers to any great extent by focusing primarily on the Cabinet. Wilson's Cabinet Government was a halfway house which rested upon his own misconceptions of the strength of the presidential pull on the Cabinet and of the nature of the centrifugal forces in the political system which tend to debilitate it as an institution. It is likely that strong presidential influence plus the Cabinet's institutional impotence would have prevented any substantial change along the lines envisioned by Wilson. On the other hand, one can say that if Wilson's Cabinet Government had ever been put into effect it would have had the very results which Wilson did not sanction — namely, an alteration in the whole check and balance system by compromising the independence and power of the President.

Though Wilson's own enthusiasm for Cabinet Government waned in his later years, his diagnoses and prescriptions have turned many another reformer in the general direction of the British parliamentary model. Henry Hazlitt has followed one side of Wilson's position to its extreme by seeking to abolish the separation of powers, the independent executive and, hence, the American Cabinet.[18] William Y. Elliott and Thomas K. Finletter, both sympathetic to Wilson's charges of irresponsibility, disunity, and conflict in executive-legislative relations, have advocated a greater degree of party responsibility as a remedy.[19] Their basic innovation would be to enforce responsibility and prevent deadlock by giving the President a limited power to dissolve Congress and call a general election. They do not focus directly on the Cabinet and they do not, with Wilson, believe that any party responsibility can be achieved by simply collecting party leaders in the Cabinet. But in each proposal, the Cabinet has a supplementary role in improving relations between the two branches. Elliott suggests that Cabinet members sit and vote in Congress; Finletter's idea involves the formation of a Legislative-Executive Cabinet. These ideas are popular favorites and will be considered shortly.

A program purporting to be a moderate one and one which focuses more directly on the Cabinet is Edward S. Corwin's interesting plea for "A New Type of Cabinet."[20] Starting with the assumption that we face "an incipient total breakdown in democratic governmental process," he develops the need for better executive-legislative relations as the crucial problem area. "Any suggestion for improving and stabilizing relations between the President and Congress at once centers attention on the Cabinet," he writes. "This is not because the Cabinet as at present constituted is a success but for exactly the contrary reason. For the truth is that the Cabinet as it exists today is, like the vermiform appendix, a standing refutation of the axiom that it is usefulness that keeps alive."

Professor Corwin does not explain why anyone concerned with legislative-executive relations should "at once," as if by automatic reflex, focus upon the Cabinet. Nor does he tell us why he is so disturbed at the Cabinet's failure to play a vital role in legislative-executive affairs. One must surmise that both viewpoints rest on some prior vision as to what the Cabinet should be like — a vision which is based less upon the facts of our Cabinet's existence than upon contemplation of the British model. The analyst of the American Cabinet might be excused for wishing that Walter Bagehot's classic had never been written, for it has predisposed students of American government to view the President's Cabinet as fulfilling its most important function by bridging the legislative-executive gap. There is no reason why the Cabinet might not help in this regard, but to assume that it should hyphenate or buckle together the American system is to ignore its indigenous power-responsibility relationship to the President.

Corwin does not, however, rest his case on these allusions to something British. He develops his own version of the historic American Cabinet and sets the problem in terms of an appeal from the present to the past. Thus, his aim is that of "restoring the Cabinet to something like its original significance." "There was a time," he writes, "when the Cabinet was a vital factor of government." Between the end of Jefferson's presidential tenure and the beginning of Jackson's, Corwin says — not without enthusiasm — "it practically took over the Presidency." He does not tell us what features of this "original significance" he applauds, but the most recent and thorough historical treatment of the Cabinet in the Madison, Monroe, John Quincy Adams period gives no support to his picture of extreme Cabinet ascendancy.[21]

In any case, he is primarily concerned about the modern-day relationship between the President and a group of advisers who cannot give him "responsible counsel" in "politics." "As a board of advisers on matters of the first importance, the Cabinet is a sham; a screen for advisers without official status or accountability." What is needed are Cabinet members "whose daily political salt did not come from the presidential table, whose political fortunes were not identical with his, who could bring presidential whim under an independent scrutiny which is now lacking." Professor Corwin's fundamental concern is with the exclusively presidential orientation of his immediate advisers. He wants the President to take advice from men who are responsible to the legislature as well as (or instead of) the President. He proposes to establish an "organic" relationship between the Cabinet and the Congress. Henceforth, the Congress will institutionalize its leadership in a Joint Legislative Council, and the President will select his Cabinet from its membership. This would "guarantee" the subordination of advisers who were exclusively presidentially oriented to a group of "politically responsible advisers."

This proposal carries a label of moderation, yet nothing less than the entire President-Cabinet power-responsibility relationship would be altered by it. The President's power of appointment would be drastically curtailed. He would be forced to take advice from a set group of advisers not determined by himself, thus abandoning the element of flexibility so characteristic of the present arrangement. These advisers would even be members of the opposing political party if the Presidency and Congress are in the hands of different parties, producing a rigidity which contrasts with the inclinations of all the Presidents studied here. The "politically responsible advisers" would no longer be primarily responsible to the President. Indeed, Corwin freely acknowledges that the Cabinet should control as well as support the President. The President, he suggests, "might" choose to be

THE CABINET AND REFORM 257

less forceful about putting through his program, and "might" even want to resign if difficulty arose with his advisers.

One cannot know how Corwin's new Cabinet would work if inaugurated, but by the same token, one cannot rely on his assurances that nothing very drastic would happen. Surely an "organic" relationship between the Cabinet and Congress would only aggravate the problems of horizontal responsibility which already plague every President. Corwin's preoccupation with "presidential whim" has led him to underestimate the independent whim of other actors in the political system. He has underestimated the dispersive forces of American politics that provide both incentive and elbow room for independent activity — all of which might change his picture of the present and his vision of the future. As for the future, his "new kind of Cabinet" is feasible only insofar as the power and independence of the President are altered. As in the Wilson case, the Presidency is most likely to be the real loser in any serious attempt to change the nature of the Cabinet. Since Corwin is free from the misconceptions of Wilson, one must conclude that he wishes to reduce the relative power and independence of the President.

One of the persistent foci of legislative-executive reform, related to Corwin's approach but more moderate, is the suggestion that the two branches be further integrated in their policy-formulating activities by some joint consultative device.[22] Commonly, the suggestion is for the institution of a Joint Executive-Legislative Council, in which the representatives of the Executive branch are to be all or some of the Cabinet members. Joined with them will be the members of a Legislative Council (or Cabinet) selected by the legislature, and the group will be headed by the President. A proposal of this kind was included in the recommendations of the Joint Committee for the Organization of Congress, but was omitted in conference. The end in view is more adequate and regularized channels of communication between branches in advising the President.

The proposal rests, it would seem, on a fundamental overestimation of the collegial character of the Cabinet in action. How will a group with so low a degree of institutionality fit into an institutionalized structure like the Joint Council? If the Cabinet is to participate in any other organization, and there to speak for the executive viewpoint, it would seem that it should first have its own collective house in order. Presumably the Joint Cabinet would produce an organizational result; if so, that product would only be as coherent as its parts. If the Cabinet maintains its traditional lack of mutual responsibility, its departmental tendencies, and its lack of group cohesiveness in general, one is led to skepticism about its ability to play any role in a joint enterprise with consistency and efficiency.

Among the proponents of the Joint Council idea, George Galloway and Thomas Finletter, for example, there is also a tendency to view the problem of legislative-executive relations, and hence of advice to the President, as a purely institutional one.[23] Galloway prophesies without reservation, "The Joint Cabinet idea . . . would institutionalize the relations of Congress and the President and overcome the cleavage between legislators and administrators."[24] But if the lessons of this study are applicable, and if this Joint Council is to be an advisory organ for use by the President, its success or failure will be very much more a human, non-institutional matter than its proponents would seem to indicate.

Some Presidents would find it more congenial than others, but it seems most likely that all Presidents would view it as suspect. Given the departmental and horizontal influences which already impinge upon the Cabinet member, and operate to give him areas of independence from the President, the projection of the Cabinet into regularized, extra-presidential contact might serve to place a further burden on the President. Furthermore, legislative leaders made it clear during hearings on the proposal that their understanding and their hope were for a strengthened congressional hand in relations with the President.[25] "In the matter of liaison with Congress [it has been written] . . . it seems to us that formal machinery of the type of legislative-executive councils would be contrary to the logic of the American system. . . . It seems necessary, in short, for the President to choose his own methods of contact with Congress." [26]

Probably the most popular of all proposals which stress the Cabinet as the vehicle for improved legislative-executive liaison — and undoubtedly the one with the most ancient and honorable ancestry — is that which asks that Cabinet members be allowed to sit in the Congress. Like the Joint Council, it qualifies (so long as the power to vote is not attached [27]) as one of the more moderate reform ideas. Its history since 1833 has been chronicled elsewhere, and the arguments in favor of it as an improvement in legislative-executive communication have been set forth in several places by its latest proponent, Senator Estes Kefauver.[28] The idea has two parts, found singly or in combination: (1) that Cabinet members be allowed to participate in debate at their discretion; (2) that Cabinet members answer congressional questions via some regularized procedure such as the British question period.

One of the standard arguments offered in support of the Cabinet-in-Congress idea is that it will improve the quality of the Cabinet member. This is not necessarily so by any complete standard. One can say that if Cabinet participation in the legislature becomes sufficiently important,[29] the appointment process will be affected — in the sense that legislative experience or an aptitude for congressional co-operation will become more prominent as a criterion of availability. Better men in this area probably will be secured, but this by no means insures that the other criteria of Cabinet selection will be satisfied. It is no guarantee, either, that on balance the member will be any better fitted for his Cabinet job or for total group performance. Experience demonstrates that a person skilled in "political" techniques may be a poor administrator, or lack the very kind of substantive intelligence that Congress most needs. Unless the Cabinet-in-Congress proposal alters the distribution of power in American politics, the most likely result is that the appointment process with its multitude of variables, all rooted in the larger political system, will continue to operate with only minor changes in the relative emphasis among them.

A second consideration raised by this discussion is the possibility that this nominally moderate proposal might have effects which would profoundly reorient existing governmental relationships. Harold Laski has vigorously and persuasively championed precisely this line of argument. He contends that the Cabinet-in-Congress proposal would "wholly alter the balance of forces which history has evolved in the American system of government," [30] and would result in "a constitutional revolution of the first magnitude." [31] It would tend toward the accretion of power in the Cabinet until the Cabinet became the "main lever of executive authority," and the President was transformed "into a person more akin to the President of the French Republic than to that of the United States." [32] The Cabinet would become a unity, the leader of the Cabinet would become similar to the Prime Minister, and the United States would move from the presidential to the parliamentary system.

The logic is pure Wilsonian logic,[33] and it is to be rejected for the same reason. The Cabinet is not enough of an autonomous force, not enough of a central institution in the American political system, that the independent executive and the checks and balances so central to the system can be broken down by giving the individual Cabinet member a chance to establish a new relationship with the legislature. Any type of argument which follows the line that "as the twig is bent, the tree will grow" is fallacious to the extent that the Cabinet is *just* a twig and by no means the trunk of the tree. Like Wilson, Laski underestimates at one and the same time the force of the presidential pull on the Cabinet *and* the centrifugal forces which militate against group unity. In general, their fault is similar to that of some other reformers, the tendency to over-concentrate on formal institutional interaction in both diagnosis and prescription. In this

THE CABINET AND REFORM

case the result is a devaluation of the basic resiliency of the system, its ability to generate its own institutional antibodies, and its capacity to absorb some change without getting completely out of kilter in the process.

It is to be hoped that it will not appear to be too contradictory if, as a third point, the Laski argument is immediately exhumed as having considerable merit. The opinion is offered here that as to the final results which he so unhesitatingly predicted, Laski was wrong, but as to the matter of tendency he was right. Laski accurately perceived the direction if not the force of the proposal's impact: that it would affect the Presidency, and that from the presidential point of view it would affect it adversely. To the extent that Cabinet members have successful relations with Congress, Laski said, they would tend to become independent of the President, develop a status of their own, and "become rivals of the President himself for influence with Congress." The analysis of this study strongly supports this probability. The problem which the President already faces, of controlling his Cabinet in the face of diverse non-presidential pressures, would be exacerbated. Cabinet members might be encouraged to stake out Jesse Jones-like areas of influence and independence. In view of everything we have observed, the President's problem would be one of the increased atomism of the Cabinet members and not (as Laski predicted) a corporate threat to his position in American political life.

Proponents of the Cabinet-in-Congress idea find it "difficult to give much weight to this argument" because the President has the power to dismiss any member of the Cabinet at his discretion."[34] Dean Acheson expressed the opinion that the Kefauver question period would induce the President to use his removal power to produce Cabinet unity:

I think what would happen would probably be that the casualty list among executive officers would be very high, and that after that had occurred for a while, the survivors out of self-preservation, would work out some method of unifying their policy. They would create a strong Cabinet which would carry out the policies laid down by the President.³⁵

This emphasis is valuable as an antidote to the Laski position that the President would be defenseless in the face of adversity. However, the forces which make for individualistic Cabinet activity are deeply rooted in the pluralism of the American political system and are not amenable to change through such a superficial and intermittent action as the removal of a Cabinet officer. The treatment of Cabinet loyalty, moreover, is very much a matter of presidential personality.³⁶

Day-to-day President-Cabinet-Congress relationships are not as understandable in terms of ultimate constitutional authority (like the removal power) or crisis decisions, as they are in terms of a whole series of small and separate interactions. Change occurs by slow accretion or equally slow attrition, rather than by monolithic power rivalries. In this less apocalyptic and more confusing context, the President is not likely to get any more help from his Cabinet by having them seated in Congress than he is by procedures already established. To the extent that the proponents of Cabinet-in-Congress underestimate the horizontal forces which already pull on the Cabinet, they also underestimate the amount of co-operation and contact which already exists between the two — for example, in places like congressional committees.³⁷ In view of the possibilities for trouble, Presidents are not likely to look with enthusiasm on this proposal.³⁸

Considered from the standpoint of the President-Cabinet nexus, suggestions to facilitate executive-legislative relations via the Cabinet do not seem likely to improve the President's position or his influence vis-à-vis the Cabinet. Whatever the intentions or the misconceptions of their sponsors, one can conclude that the probable effect of these reforms will be a deleterious one for the President. The Wilson and Corwin proposals come, whether or not by design, as innocent looking trojan horses which threaten to conquer the presidential citadel from within. Other proposals, less noxious in their effect, would simply aggravate existing presidential difficulties without evident compensation.

IMPROVING THE ORGANIZATION OF THE PRESIDENCY

In recognition of the problem of staffing and co-ordinating the Presidency, many reorganization proposals have been brought forward. Some make the Cabinet the keystone around which any reform must fit. Marshall Dimock has written that ". . . the President's Cabinet should become the center of executive co-ordination. There are few faults of bureaucracy more serious than lack of coordination. . . . There is no alternative but to make the President's Cabinet the means to that end." [39] Bradley Nash's National Planning Association pamphlet, "Staffing the Presidency," repeatedly emphasizes that there must be "augmented use of the Cabinet as a vehicle for coordination." It is his view that "the Cabinet as a whole, assisted by [an office which he proposes to create] . . . could become the basic administrative vehicle of the government." [40] Some of those who do not state their views as bluntly as Dimock or Nash come almost willy-nilly to the Cabinet as having a key role in staff reorganization. Thus Edward Hobbs' book on presidential staff agencies concludes by advocating a substantial reform, which he labels "A Proposal to Strengthen the Cabinet." [41]

Two threads of consistency, found singly or in combination, seem to run through most of the recent reform discussion. The first revolves around the NSC-type device — organization around interdepartmental, subject-matter foci — and comes in several varieties. Before the war had ended, Arthur MacMahon speculated about the value of supra-departmental policy groupings, each with an operating head of its own. "One can envisage," he wrote, "a new type of departmental overseer, assigned to a broad domain of policy, equipped with a compact staff, and exercising his influence partly as high adviser and partly as negotiator, and also the source of coordinating suggestions, directives, and decisions." [42] These "chief policy co-ordinators" would then comprise an "inner and active Cabinet," reminiscent of the British War Cabinet device. The Cabinet would be "a double body" with an inner and an outer group, and the inner group would become the key co-ordinating organ for the President.

Clinton Rossiter foresees, not supra-departmental operating officials, but "a series of functional Cabinets and Cabinet-level committees," with the traditional Cabinet existing simply as a "dignified holding company for the half dozen sub-Cabinets." [43] Slightly different is Edward Hobbs' notion of interdepartmental subject matter committees in the Executive Office, composed of both administrative and legislative officials — "a Cabinet subcommittee system" which functions ultimately by "working through the Cabinet." His proposals take a highly institutionalized form. He finds the NSC to contain the essence of his advisory policy group (minus some legislative officials), and he urges that a number of others be established on a "relatively permanent basis," most appropriately by "statutory authorization." [44] Hobbs' proposals are in the nature of a blown-up version of ideas nurtured earlier by others. William Y. Elliott, in a study for the President's Committee, urged the creation of several broad, functional groupings of legislative and executive officials in the Executive Office as part of a Cabinet Secretariat. He felt that the entire apparatus might well increase the utility of the Cabinet, but did not conceive of these groupings as Cabinet sub-committees.[45]

More moderate still, but in a similar vein, were the proposals by John Gaus for six subject-matter, administrative assistants to be added to the White House Office to help co-ordinate the activities of the executive branch in interdepartmental fields.[46] Even less institutionalized is Nash's recommendation for ". . . the development of the requisite number of interdepartmental committees. . . . The objectives of these committees should vary from time to time in accordance with the judgment of the President. Committees should be dissolved when their usefulness has ceased." [47] These several proposals are not mutually ex-

THE CABINET AND REFORM

clusive, but they do indicate a number of possible variations on a similar theme.

A second line of thinking has its focus around the Byrnes-Harriman role and/or a presidential secretariat. That is to say, some advocate a secretariat to help co-ordinate, and some would propose that a staff chief of some sort head the secretariat and be recognized as the single focus of co-ordination short of the President. A secretariat of some kind is envisioned by nearly all of those who seek interdepartmental devices. It is considered the vehicle for tying together the variety of activities of the Executive Office and Cabinet, and is the most common of all proposed administrative reforms affecting the Cabinet.

The most highly rationalized and centralized proposals come from those who would follow the OWMR device. Thus, Herman Somers calls for a Chief of Presidential Staff to head both an elaborate Office of Program Co-ordination and a Cabinet Secretariat. The Office would be undergirded by a whole set of Cabinet committees serviced by the Secretariat. The Chief of Presidential Staff would utilize this apparatus to perform all the functions of coordination which relate to present problems.[48]

The general staff-chief of staff solution has won many adherents among students of the Presidency.[49] Such a man would head Elliott's Cabinet Secretariat and would superintend Hobbs' functional policy groups in co-ordinating for the President. The Hoover Commission took a small step in this direction when it advocated the establishment of "a staff secretary . . . to assist him in clearing information on the major problems on which staff work is being done within the President's Office, or by the Cabinet or interdepartmental committees."[50] Its cautious language reflects a desire to "facilitate teamwork" (i.e., co-ordinate) only in a minimum sense; it scrupulously refrains from discussing any of the staff secretary's interrelationships, in the desire to give him no authority over departments or Executive Office agencies. The proposal is a modest one and does not envision any secretariat attached to it.

Most of those who call for change do seek the development of a secretariat whose purpose would be to increase executive co-ordination by facilitating and systematizing interdepartmental contact. Some have advocated a Cabinet Secretariat similar to the one established in the Eisenhower administration; others prefer a general secretariat with broader functions roughly comparable to those split, under Eisenhower, between the Cabinet Secretary and the Staff Secretary. John Gaus' proposal includes one general secretary to provide "for the general ordering of business of the Cabinet, the preparation of agenda, and the following up in the departments concerned with the decisions arrived at."[51] Professor Elliott's Cabinet Secretariat would furnish more ambitiously "not only summaries of actual performances, but indications of lines of policy, probable effects, and difficulties experienced in operation."[52] The Nash study calls simply for "a management staff," "a central secretariat . . . to knit together programs and policies and to utilize the present Cabinet and the departments and agencies for operational purposes."[53] Like Nash, Don K. Price eschews the idea of a staff chief, but develops the idea of a secretariat designed to "develop and systematize the process of counseling with his department heads" and to "tighten up the relations between them."[54] Each of Rossiter's functional sub-Cabinets would have its own secretariat.[55]

With respect to the scope of the various proposals, the analysis of this study casts grave doubts on those that point toward apocalyptic results. The Cabinet is not likely to be abolished by administrative fiat, nor is it likely to slip silently out of sight. It is highly improbable that it will be superseded by some inner cabinet imposed on it from without.[56] Nor is it probable that the Cabinet will ever become the central agent of government-wide co-ordination. In short, it has at one and the same time a *raison d'être* which is not likely to disappear and limitations which are not likely to be overcome. At its worst, it is both useful and

THE CABINET AND REFORM

immovable; at its best, it suffers from some inherent incapacities. The proposals which avoid extremes and fall within this limiting framework reflect a sound sense for the instrumental nature of the Cabinet. They assume that if substantial change comes to the Cabinet, it will come as the by-product of some larger reform. This assumption yields a modest view of what can be accomplished by focusing on the Cabinet directly, and it also drives the serious reformer to broaden his analytical framework.

Too frequently, however, the part of the argument that does involve the Cabinet is underdeveloped. There are a plethora of unsupported assertions to the effect that the Cabinet "would" react in such and such a manner. Or, the Cabinet is left to settle its own estate and somehow find some position somewhere in the spate of new administrative creations. There is a shallowness of analysis which might be counteracted by recourse to the complexities of the political system. Not that it is possible to state categorically what the reactive effect of each proposal would be on the Cabinet. Some of the ideas have already been incorporated in the Eisenhower Secretariat, and even in that case authoritative predictions cannot be made. What is important is that the analysis show an awareness of the relationships treated in this study. Some general points, already discussed in connection with the Eisenhower reform, bear repetition.

One problem area which is certain to dog the footsteps of the reorganizer concerns departmentalism and the relationship of the department head to the President. Changes here will obviously affect the Cabinet and it is important for a student to make some assessment of the likely repercussions of his proposal. He must know what the sources of departmentalism are so that he can assess the likely effects of particular changes upon it. If its sources lie deep in the pluralism of American politics, then there are limits to what can be accomplished by institutional changes at the top level. Departmentalism cannot be driven away like evil spirits, however much the medicine man may condemn it. The reorganization of the Presidency cannot be discussed in a realm apart from the real political world of interest groups, political parties, and the United States Congress.

When the reorganizer does worry about the impact of departmentalism on the President-Cabinet member relationship, he ought to recognize the possible effects which his remedy might have on that relationship. If he accepts the primary role of the department head in implementing the President's responsibilities, he ought to beware of interposing any hierarchical level between the two. The Cabinet member's resentment at being layered is a practical impediment to any such change. Moreover, the student ought to be clear on what he wants and what consequences he is willing to accept, for it is a constant danger, in the use of interdepartmental committees and chiefs of staff, that whereas they were originated to modify the effects of departmentalism, they may linger to affect the basic relationship of the department head to the President. The distance between co-ordinators and officials with operating responsibilities may not be very far, and the reorganizer ought to take frequent measurements. If an interdepartmental committee acquires a corporate status of its own, or if the President should become hostaged to a single chief of staff, the department head's role could be decisively altered.

It cannot be emphasized too often that the governing factor in reorganizing the Presidency must be the President himself. He can hardly blink the need for co-ordination, but it is difficult to see how he can be forced to be assisted in any particular way by the general will of political scientists if he does not so wish. Assuming his preeminent leadership position, he is free to find help in co-ordination wherever and from whomever he wishes. The most elaborate scheme is no stronger than the base of presidential acquiescence on which it must rest. Thus one cannot "institutionalize the Harry Hopkins function" [57] and expect the Hopkins-Roosevelt relationship to spring forth. Nor could one create new National Security Council-type committees and expect them to function as well as NSC has, without an eye to presidential support.

Just as the Eisenhower Cabinet Secretariat has come under the impact of one President's temperament and working habits, so will other changes come. If it outlives the man under whose auspices it was developed, it will be because succeeding Presidents recognized its usefulness as a practical matter.[58] What the Eisenhower system does, it does well. Its success, however, should be credited more to the working habits of one man than to the inexorable logic of the reorganizer. In view of what this system does not do, it seems premature enough to pronounce judgment on the Cabinet Secretariat as *the* solution to all of President Eisenhower's co-ordinating problems. But in view of its dependence on him, it would be positively reckless to commend it in these terms to any other President.

The Cabinet and the Executive Office, and the terms of their co-existence, will have to be left sufficiently flexible to meet the variety of uses to which Chief Executives will choose to put them. Institutionalization is not a virtue in itself, and the institutionalization of co-ordinating methods will always face the dangers of excess. Thus a highly rationalized scheme for "encircling the President with policy groups"[59] runs the risk of suffocating him in the process. It would be unfortunate if those people who urge reform in order to increase the President's effectiveness should go about it in such a way as to place just one more set of limitations upon him. One may support reform in this area. One may applaud presidentially directed reforms such as the Eisenhower Secretariat. Yet one should remain reluctant to prescribe it or any other specific reform as the solution to the President's problems, lest a rigid prescription or an over-institutionalization of the means defeat the very ends of executive leadership.

In broadest compass, the recurrent theme of this study has been the interaction of those forces which make for unity and those forces which make for diversity within the American political system. On every level of analysis, we have investigated dilemmas involving the relative consolidation and fragmentation of political power. The Cabinet as an institution, the President-Cabinet nexus, and the political system as a whole have been examined in terms of such ideas as teamwork, mutual responsibility, cohesiveness, harmony, dependence, and co-operation on the one hand, and heterogeneity, centrifugal forces, particularism, departmentalism, independence, and competition on the other. The life and the environment of the Cabinet are shaped by a continual action and reaction between and among these conflicting tendencies. If one acknowledges this description of flux to be a realistic analysis, he will be less tempted to see in either unity or diversity an absolute goal either desirable or possible. He will see the crucial problems as matters of degree, of balance, and of accommodation.

In general, the tendency of Cabinet-oriented reform proposals has been to underemphasize the diversity and the fragmentation of political power in the American system of government. The most common tendency is to overestimate the unified character of the Cabinet and to assume either that it is or that it can be made a relatively autonomous force in American politics. Or, similarly, there is a tendency to underestimate the impact of diversity upon the Cabinet, and to assume that this diversity can be exorcised as an unnatural force in politics. Another common tendency is to overestimate the degree of President-Cabinet unity and to assume, therefore, that the President's difficulties with the group can be solved by an exercise of will on his part. Or, similarly, there is a tendency to underestimate the forces that pull the two apart and thus to assume that the President can bear the strain of a few more centrifugal forces without difficulty. There is, finally, a tendency to insist upon further Cabinet institutionalization as an improvement *per se* without due regard for the necessity of a basic flexibility.

The oversights of the reformers help, by contrast, to sharpen the general conclusion which emerges most clearly from this study, that which stresses *the relative difficulty of promoting unity in the face of the basic pluralism of the American political system*. Most especially, the normal operation of the system tends more to place limitations on the President than to empower him to overcome them. A corollary proposition would be that one ought to examine *more critically* those reform ideas which tend to dilute unity than those which tend to promote it. Thus, all suggestions involving the Cabinet have been scrutinized from a position which values strong presidential leadership and which views with suspicion any change which seems likely to weaken his present position relative to the Cabinet, to the legislature, or to the executive branch of the government.

NOTES

Introduction

1. Edward S. Corwin, *The President: Office and Powers* (New York, 1948), p. 516, n. 88. For a similar earlier comment, see John Fairlie, "The President's Cabinet," *American Political Science Review*, February 1913, p. 29.
2. Mary Hinsdale, *A History of the President's Cabinet* (Ann Arbor, 1911); Henry B. Learned, *The President's Cabinet* (New Haven, 1912). The best single study of a Cabinet is Burton J. Hendrick, *Lincoln's War Cabinet* (Boston, 1946).
3. Luther Gulick, *Administrative Reflections from World War II* (Birmingham, 1948), p. 76.
4. Clinton Rossiter, *The American Presidency* (New York, 1956), p. 148.
5. See Herman Miles Somers, *Presidential Agency: OWMR* (Cambridge, Mass., 1950), pp. 216, 223; Schuyler Wallace, *Federal Departmentalization — A Critique of Theories of Organization* (New York, 1941), p. 224; Bradley Nash, *Staffing the Presidency*, National Planning Association Pamphlet (Washington, 1952), p. ix; Edward H. Hobbs, *Behind the President* (Washington, 1954), pp. 214–216; Pendleton Herring, *Presidential Leadership* (New York, 1940), pp. 96, 100; Edward S. Corwin, "Wanted — A New Type of Cabinet," *New York Times Magazine*, October 10, 1948, p. 14.
6. John L. Steele, "The New-Model Cabinet," *Life*, October 8, 1956, pp. 89–104.
7. E. E. Evans Pritchard, *Social Anthropology* (Glencoe, 1951), p. 38.
8. Carleton S. Coon (ed.), *A Reader in General Anthropology* (New York, 1948), p. 640.
9. David Easton, *The Political System* (New York, 1953), p. 291.

Chapter One. The Cabinet in Perspective

1. Aristotle, *Politics*, Modern Library Edition (New York, 1943), p. 165.
2. Henry B. Learned, *The President's Cabinet* (New Haven, 1912), p. 15. See also Lord Hankey, *Diplomacy by Conference* (London, 1946), chap. ii.
3. Learned, *President's Cabinet*, p. 2.
4. Leo W. Simmons, *The Role of the Aged in Primitive Society* (New Haven, 1945), p. 106.

NOTES TO CHAPTER ONE

5. E. Adamson Hoebel, *Man in the Primitive World* (New York, 1949), p. 387.

6. Committee of the Royal Anthropological Institute, *Notes and Queries on Anthropology* (London, 1951), p. 139.

7. M. Fortes and E. E. Evans Pritchard, *African Political Systems* (New York, 1940), pp. 33–54, 71; Robert Lowie, *An Introduction to Cultural Anthropology* (New York, 1940), p. 297; Robert Lowie, *Primitive Society* (New York, 1920), pp. 381, 383; George P. Murdock, *Our Primitive Contemporaries* (New York, 1936), pp. 174, 285, 524–525, 569, and chaps. x–xii.

8. Learned, *President's Cabinet*, p. 81; Mary Hinsdale, *A History of the President's Cabinet* (Ann Arbor, 1911), p. 2.

9. L. M. Short, *The Development of National Administrative Organization in the United States* (Baltimore, 1923), pp. 53–54.

10. Learned, *President's Cabinet*, pp. 59–63. For the detailed administrative history of the period, see Short, chap. ii.

11. Max Farrand (ed.), *The Records of the Federal Convention of 1787* (New Haven, 1927), II, 537–543.

12. *Ibid.*, I, 97.

13. *Ibid.*, I, 23; II, 135; III, 606.

14. *Ibid.*, II, 329.

15. *Ibid.*, II, 342–344.

16. *Ibid.*, II, 367.

17. Alexander Hamilton, John Jay, and James Madison, *The Federalist*, Everyman's Edition (New York, 1911), No. 70, pp. 363–364.

18. *Ibid.*, No. 50, p. 264.

19. 1 Stat. 28, 68 (State Dept.); 1 Stat. 65 (Treasury Dept.); 1 Stat. 49 (War Dept.).

20. John Fitzpatrick (ed.), *Writings of George Washington* (Washington, 1940), XXX, 334. See also Leonard D. White, *The Federalists* (New York, 1948), pp. 18–20.

21. Hamilton in *The Federalist*, No. 70, p. 263.

22. White, *Federalists*, pp. 20–25.

23. See James Hart, *The American Presidency In Action 1789* (New York, 1948), chap. vii.

24. *Ibid.*, pp. 86–97.

25. *Ibid.*, p. 234.

26. *Ibid.*, pp. 214–234.

27. P. L. Ford (ed.), *Writings of Thomas Jefferson* (New York, 1892), I, 189–190.

28. White, *Federalists*, pp. 31–36.

29. Ford (ed.), *Writings of Thomas Jefferson*, I, 165; V, 320.

30. Hinsdale, p. 14; see also Homer Cummings and Carl MacFarland, *Federal Justice* (New York, 1937), pp. 25–26.

31. Ford (ed.), *Writings of Thomas Jefferson*, IX, 273.

32. *Ibid.*, VI, 250.
33. Learned, *President's Cabinet*, p. 136. The name did not reach the statute books until 1907.
34. Fitzpatrick (ed.), *Writings of George Washington*, XXXIV, 315.
35. Ford (ed.), *Writings of Thomas Jefferson*, IX, 273.
36. *Ibid.*, IX, 69–70.
37. Henry B. Learned, "Some Aspects of the Cabinet Meeting," in The Columbia Historical Society, *Records*, vol. XVIII (1915).
38. "Not only is this institution totally unknown to the constitution; it would be no extraordinary application of a certain method of constitutional interpretation to show that it is unconstitutional." Edward S. Corwin, *Court Over Constitution* (New York, 1950), p. 88.
39. H. H. Gerth and C. W. Mills (eds.), *From Max Weber: Essays in Sociology* (New York, 1946), pp. 78ff, 216ff, 295ff.
40. Denis Brogan, *Politics in America* (New York, 1954), p. 5.
41. This weakness, always present, becomes especially apparent whenever it is suggested that the Cabinet take on some additional function. See Peter Frelinghuysen, "Presidential Disability," in Sidney Hyman (ed.), "The Office of the American Presidency," *The Annals*, September 1956, pp. 150–151.
42. Learned, *President's Cabinet*, p. 187; 16 Stat. 162.
43. 24 Stat. 1.
44. House and Senate Committees on Government Operations, *Joint Hearings on Reorganization Plan No. 1 of 1953*, 83rd Cong., 1st Sess. (Washington, 1953), pp. 52–53. Unless otherwise indicated by the context, "the Cabinet" should be taken to mean its hard core personnel — the nine or ten department heads which have traditionally met as a group to assist the President. Usually, however, the observations which are made will hold equally well for some of the non-department heads attending the Cabinet meeting. The important problems raised by both similarities and differences are discussed in several places, especially in Chapters Three and Four, but it seems wise to adopt the more restrictive definition as the basis for discussion.
45. Learned, *President's Cabinet*, p. 218.
46. Senate Committee on Expenditures in the Executive Branch, *Hearings on Reorganization Plan No. 1*, 81st Cong., 1st Sess. (Washington, 1949), pp. 1ff.
47. Learned, *President's Cabinet*, chap. x; 9 Stat. 395 (1849).
48. William Wanlass, *The United States Department of Agriculture — A Study in Administration* (Baltimore, 1920), p. 20; 12 Stat. 387 (1862).
49. Learned, *President's Cabinet*, p. 367; 32 Stat. 825 (1903).
50. Short, p. 190.
51. John Lombardi, *Labor's Voice in the Cabinet* (New York, 1942), p. 18; 37 Stat. 736 (1913).
52. Cummings and MacFarland, pp. 486–500.

53. For the 1947 Act and discussion, see 61 Stat. 507; 93 Cong. Rec. 8295, 8315, 9398–9399. For the 1949 amendments and discussion, see 63 Stat. 585; Senate Committee on Armed Services, *Hearings on the National Security Act Amendments of 1949*, 81st Cong., 1st Sess. (Washington, March and April, 1949).

54. *New York Times*, March 15, 1953, p. 1, col. 2. For Eisenhower's March 1953 message and some discussion, see *Joint Hearings on Reorganization Plan No. 1 of 1953* (note 44, above), p. 2. The group basis for this change was largely in terms of prior activity by the AMA, using what David Truman calls the "defensive advantage." Efforts of the proponents to buttress their arguments with a group appeal seem particularly unrealistic, i.e., Congressman Dawson's remark: "Now we are caring for the farmers, we are caring for business, we are looking after the armed services, we are looking after the Department of Agriculture, and we are looking after the welfare of the horses and cows and so forth, but nowhere in our government do we have any setup with departmental status that looks after the rank and file of the people of this nation." House Committee on Expenditures in the Executive Departments, *Hearings on Reorganization Plan No. 27*, 81st Cong., 2nd Sess. (Washington, 1951), p. 6.

55. Dorothy G. Fowler, *The Cabinet Politician; The Postmaster-General, 1829–1909* (New York, 1943), p. 2. Jackson's decision was finally "ratified" by an act of 1872 in which the Post Office Department was recognized as an "executive department"; see 17 Stat. 283.

56. Wanlass, *U. S. Department of Agriculture*, p. 20; Lombardi, *Labor's Voice*, pp. 18ff.

57. In general, see David B. Truman, *The Governmental Process* (New York, 1951); Earl Latham, "The Group Basis of Politics: Notes for a Theory," *American Political Science Review*, June 1952, pp. 376–397. In particular, see Fortes and Evans Pritchard, *African Systems*, and their discussions of the Ankole, Ngwato, Bemba, and Zulu tribes; Lowie, *Introduction to Cultural Anthropology*, pp. 293ff; Lowie, *Primitive Society*, pp. 370–376; Murdock, *Primitive Contemporaries*, pp. 416, 491.

58. For example, Fortes and Evans Pritchard, p. 41.

59. *Ibid.*, discussion of the Zulu tribe; Simmons, *Role of the Aged*, p. 113; Lowie, *Primitive Society*, pp. 386ff.

60. Lombardi, *Labor's Voice*, p. 67.

61. J. M. Gaus and L. O. Wolcott, *Public Administration and the United States Department of Agriculture* (Chicago, 1940), pp. 7–8.

62. Jonathan Daniels, *Frontier on the Potomac* (New York, 1946), p. 29.

63. Frederick A. Ogg, "The American Cabinet," *Parliamentary Affairs*, Winter 1949, p. 36.

64. Henry L. Stoddard, *It Costs to be President* (New York, 1938), p. 476.

65. Theodore G. Joslin, *Hoover Off the Record* (Garden City, 1934), p. 163.

66. *Ibid.*, p. 3.

67. Walter Johnson (ed.), *Selected Letters of William Allen White* (New York, 1947), p. 329. For similar comments, see also James E. Pollard, *The Presidents and the Press* (New York, 1947), p. 760; Henry L. Stimson and McGeorge Bundy, *On Active Service in Peace and War* (New York, 1947), p. 283; James E. Watson, *As I Knew Them* (Indianapolis, 1936), p. 248; Allan Nevins, "President Hoover's Record," *Current History*, July 1932, p. 387; Walter Lippmann, "The Peculiar Weaknesses of Mr. Hoover," *Harpers*, June 1930, p. 6; Eugene Lyons, *Our Unknown Ex-President* (New York, 1948), *passim*.

68. William Hard, "Sidelights on the New Cabinet," *Review of Reviews*, April 1929, pp. 53–58; *Outlook*, March 13, 1929, pp. 415–416, and April 17, 1929, p. 619; *Literary Digest*, March 16, 1929, pp. 8–10.

69. *Literary Digest*, March 16, 1929, pp. 8–10; William Hard, "Sidelights on the New Cabinet," pp. 53–58.

70. Joseph B. Bishop, *Theodore Roosevelt and His Times* (New York, 1920), II, 66.

71. See George A. Curran, "Woodrow Wilson's Theory and Practice Regarding the Relations of President and Congress," unpubl. diss. (Fordham University), 1948, pp. 108, n. 1, 265; Joseph P. Tumulty, *Woodrow Wilson As I Knew Him* (New York, 1921), pp. 377–378.

72. Ray S. Baker, *Woodrow Wilson — Life and Letters* (New York, 1931), VII, 510–514; John M. Blum, "Tumulty and the Wilson Era," unpubl. diss. (Harvard University), 1950, pp. 261–262, 257–258. For general comment, see Arthur S. Link, *Wilson — The Road to the White House* (Princeton, 1947), p. 307; James Kerney, *The Political Education of Woodrow Wilson* (New York, 1926), p. 10; Johnson (ed.), *Selected Letters of White*, p. 195.

73. Frederick E. Schortemeier, *Life and Recent Speeches of Warren G. Harding* (Indianapolis, 1920), p. 34.

74. *New York Times*, July 14, 1920, p. 8, col. 1; October 8, 1920, p. 2, col. 3.

75. Schortemeier, *Life and Speeches of Harding*, p. 36.

76. *New Republic*, December 15, 1920, p. 62.

77. Robert J. Donovan, *Eisenhower: The Inside Story* (New York, 1956), pp. 65, 83.

78. Hinsdale, p. 149.

79. William Allen White, *Masks in a Pageant* (New York, 1930), pp. 422–423. See also Letter to George Harvey, printed in W. F. Johnson, *George Harvey — A Passionate Patriot* (Boston, 1929), p. 280; Merlo J. Pusey, *Charles Evans Hughes* (New York, 1951), II, 499.

80. For this view of Wilson, see Charles Willis Thompson, *Presidents*

NOTES TO CHAPTER ONE

I've Known and Two Near Presidents (Indianapolis, 1929), pp. 253–254; Stoddard, *It Costs to be President*, p. 481; Clinton W. Gilbert, *The Mirrors of Washington* (New York, 1921), p. 219; Gamaliel Bradford, *The Quick and the Dead* (Cambridge, Mass., 1931), p. 73. For this view of Hoover, see Irwin H. Hoover, *Forty-Two Years in the White House* (Cambridge, Mass., 1934), pp. 186, 232; Pollard, *Presidents and the Press*, p. 748; John Hays Hammond, *The Autobiography of John Hays Hammond* (New York, 1935), II, 712. For Wilson's own refutation, see Baker, IV, 183. For Hoover's, see W. S. Meyers and W. H. Newton, *The Hoover Administration: A Documented Narrative* (New York, 1936), p. 473. For statements to the contrary by Wilson's colleagues, see Edward N. Hurley, *The Bridge to France* (Philadelphia, 1927), p. 177; Herbert Hoover, *The Memoirs of Herbert Hoover* (New York, 1952), I, 408; Robert Lansing, *War Memoirs* (Indianapolis, 1935), pp. 139–140.

81. Harry S. Truman, *Years of Trial and Hope* (New York, 1956), I, 546.

82. Stimson and Bundy, pp. 196–205; H. Hoover, *Memoirs*, II, 220.

83. Hoover's temperamental sensitivity, his intellectual superiority, and his personal reserve all would tend to reduce critical advice. See John Spargo, "Hoover — The New Phase," *North American Review*, April 1931, p. 294; W. A. White, in Johnson (ed.), *Selected Letters of White*, p. 311; Joslin, p. 5; Will Irwin, "Portrait of a President," *Saturday Evening Post*, January 17, 1931, p. 90.

84. A good comment on the kind of advice Wilson would and would not take is that by Harold Nicolson concerning the Peace Conference: "Mr. Lamont, one of the most unassailable figures at the Peace Conference, stated that the President consulted freely. Yet Mr. Lamont was a financial and economic expert and the President did not, in such matters, aspire to personal knowledge. Mr. Lansing, on the other hand, who was juridically and politically minded, contends that he took no counsel at all." Harold Nicolson, *Peacemaking 1919* (London, 1933), p. 200.

For examples of advice-taking, see Curran, "Wilson's Theory and Practice," p. 61; David Houston, *Eight Years with Wilson's Cabinet* (New York, 1926), I, 18–20; Hurley, *Bridge to France*, p. 319; H. Hoover, *Memoirs*, I, 263–264; Baker, VI, 481, n. 2; VIII, 36–37; Stoddard, *It Costs to be President*, p. 496; Blum, "Tumulty," pp. 125, 145, 148.

85. Baker, IV, 132, 162.

86. Robert E. Sherwood, *Roosevelt and Hopkins* (New York, 1948), p. 446; Rexford G. Tugwell, "The Preparation of a President," *Western Political Quarterly*, June 1948, pp. 131–153.

87. Stimson and Bundy, pp. 367–376; Harold L. Ickes, *The Secret Diary of Harold L. Ickes* (New York, 1953–1954), II, 638–656, *passim;* III, 509ff.

88. Joslin, p. 20. In reading the book by two of his Cabinet members,

Ray Wilbur and Arthur Hyde, entitled *The Hoover Policies* (New York, 1937), one is struck by the fact that, as the picture is painted there, Hoover did instigate nearly all of these policies. Cabinet members are almost never mentioned save for their occasional participation in a conference of some sort called by Hoover.

89. H. Hoover, *Memoirs*, I, 155, 241–242.

90. Joslin, p. 21.

91. Stimson and Bundy, pp. 196–205.

92. As one good example of this technique, see the reports of Cabinet discussion of the non-recognition doctrine by Secretaries Hurley and Wilbur in William Starr Meyers, *The Foreign Policies of Herbert Hoover* (New York, 1940), pp. 164–168; see also p. 139, and Joslin, pp. 4, 247.

93. Charles Seymour (ed.), *The Intimate Papers of Colonel House* (Cambridge, Mass., 1926), I, 126–127.

94. Edward H. Brooks, "The National Defense Policy of the Wilson Administration, 1913–1917," unpubl. diss. (Stanford University), 1950, p. 193.

95. See Baker, VIII, 242; *New York Times*, November 2, 1913, Sec. vi, p. 2, col. 6; Lansing, *War Memoirs*, pp. 349–350.

96. A. W. Lane and L. H. Hall (eds.), *The Letters of Franklin K. Lane* (Boston, 1922), p. 119.

97. *New York Times*, June 17, 1917, Sec. vi, p. 1, col. 1; see also Link, *Wilson*, p. 95; H. Hoover, *Memoirs*, I, 467–468; Rixey Smith and Norman Beasley, *Carter Glass — A Biography* (New York, 1939), chap. ix; n. 72, supra. The "Lusitania Postscript" was perhaps the most famous instance of Wilson's changing his mind. For discussion of the Cabinet members involved, see Baker, V, 338–358 and Blum, "Tumulty," pp. 160–161.

98. Stimson and Bundy, pp. 346, 414; also, Raymond Moley, *After Seven Years* (New York, 1939), p. 11 and Ernest K. Lindley, *Halfway with Roosevelt* (New York, 1936), pp. 79–80.

99. Stimson and Bundy, pp. 416–439; Paul Appleby, "Roosevelt's Third Term Decision," *American Political Science Review*, September 1952, pp. 754ff. His tendency to avoid flat agreement and yet to be an extremely agreeable listener oftentimes resulted in frayed personal relationships and misunderstanding. One example was Ickes' request to reorganize and rename the Department of the Interior: Ickes, *Secret Diary*, I, 310–311, 343–344, 388. See also Moley, p. 390; Eleanor Roosevelt, *This I Remember* (New York, 1949), p. 2.

100. For some of the many examples of this method of decision-making, see Moley, pp. 48–49; Jesse Jones and Edward Angly, *Fifty Billion Dollars* (New York, 1951), p. 200; Cordell Hull, *The Memoirs of Cordell Hull* (New York, 1948), II, 1198; Samuel M. Rosenman, *Working with Roosevelt* (New York, 1952), p. 357. See also H. S. Truman, *Years of Trial*, I, 55–56; Lindley, pp. 49–50; Hull, II, 598.

101. John Gunther, *Roosevelt in Retrospect* (New York, 1950), p. 115.
102. Claude M. Fuess, *Calvin Coolidge — The Man from Vermont* (Boston, 1940), p. 468. See also C. Bascom Slemp, *The Mind of the President* (New York, 1926), p. 5.
103. William Allen White, *A Puritan in Babylon* (New York, 1938), pp. 390–391, 394; Calvin Coolidge, *The Autobiography of Calvin Coolidge* (New York, 1929), p. 187.
104. White, *Puritan*, p. 433; Watson, *As I Knew Them*, p. 248; H. Hoover, *Memoirs*, II, 55–56. See also Charles Dawes, *Notes As Vice-President* (Boston, 1935), p. 90. For an example, see George Wharton Pepper, *In the Senate* (Philadelphia, 1930), pp. 75–76.
105. Duff Gilfond, *The Rise of Saint Calvin* (New York, 1932), p. 241; White, *Puritan*, p. 344. For the frustration of one farm group, see Orville M. Kile, *The Farm Bureau Through Three Decades* (Baltimore, 1948), chaps. x–xi.
106. Fuess, p. 468; White, *Puritan*, pp. 392–393.
107. Coolidge, pp. 203–204. For the deleterious effects of this method of decision-making, see Chester I. Barnard, *The Nature of Leadership* (Cambridge, Mass., 1940), p. 12.
108. Rowland R. Hughes, "The President and His Job" (address before Brown University Alumni, Providence, Rhode Island, June 3, 1955), p. 7.
109. Merriman Smith, *Meet Mr. Eisenhower* (New York, 1954), pp. 18, 129.
110. Hughes, "The President and His Job," p. 7.
111. Anthony Leviero, "Eisenhower: A Six Months Audit," *New York Times Magazine*, July 19, 1953, p. 22.
112. Donovan, *Eisenhower: The Inside Story*, pp. 197–198.
113. Leviero, "Eisenhower," p. 21.
114. Hughes, "The President and His Job," p. 8. See also Donovan, *Eisenhower: The Inside Story*, p. 67; Leviero, "Eisenhower," pp. 21–22.
115. The best example of an extreme laissez-faire policy of delegation during the period was Harding's delegation of power to Secretary of State Hughes (the man Harding felt "ought to be President"), with respect to the Washington Conference of 1921–1922. See Pusey, *Hughes*, II, 47, 428, 430, 455–465; *Outlook*, August 15, 1923, p. 576; John C. Vinson, "The Senate and the Washington Conference 1921–1922," unpubl. diss. (Duke University), 1950, p. 370.
116. White, *Puritan*, p. 371.
117. Fuess, pp. 406, 413, 420; see also p. 415.
118. Robert H. Ferrell, *Peace in Their Time* (New Haven, 1952), pp. 142–143, and see chap. x. See also White, *Puritan*, pp. 371–373; *Colliers*, January 22, 1927, p. 30.
119. Fuess, p. 323. See also White, *Puritan*, pp. 249–250; Harold Nicolson, *Dwight Morrow* (New York, 1935), p. 270.
120. Coolidge, p. 187. Presidents Truman, Hoover, and Harding brought

comparatively wide-ranging, close advisers (Averell Harriman, Ray Lyman Wilbur, and Harry Daugherty) within the formal hierarchy.

121. William Hillman (ed.), *Mr. President* (New York, 1952), pp. 10, 18.

122. H. S. Truman, *Years of Trial*, I, 328, 546.

123. Hillman (ed.), *Mr. President*, p. 21.

124. H. S. Truman, *Years of Trial*, II, 67.

125. Richard H. Rovere, "Eisenhower: A Trial Balance," *Reporter*, April 21, 1955, p. 15.

126. Donovan, *Eisenhower: The Inside Story*, p. 69; see also p. 68, and M. Smith, *Meet Mr. President*, p. 120.

127. On the Wilson-Lansing relationship, see Houston, I, 141; Julius Pratt, "Robert Lansing," *The American Secretaries of State and Their Diplomacy*, ed. Samuel F. Bemis (New York, 1929), vol. X; Baker, VI, 323; Josephus Daniels, *The Wilson Era* (Chapel Hill, 1946), II, 526; *New York Times*, February 14, 1920, p. 1, cols. 6–8; Lansing, *War Memoirs*, p. 172.

128. Frances Perkins, *The Roosevelt I Knew* (New York, 1946), p. 137; Sherwood, pp. 862–867; Appleby, "Roosevelt's Third Term Decision," p. 763.

129. Gunther, *Roosevelt in Retrospect*, p. 53.

130. Stimson and Bundy, pp. 495–496, 558–559.

131. William Y. Elliott, "Executive-Congressional Relations," unpubl. MS. (Harvard University School of Public Administration), ca. 1950, p. 46; Harold L. Ickes, "My Twelve Years with FDR," *Saturday Evening Post*, July 17, 1948, p. 97. For the Navy, see James A. Farley, *Jim Farley's Story: The Roosevelt Years* (New York, 1948), pp. 242–243; Jones and Angly, p. 307. For the Army, see n. 130, *supra*.

132. Hull, I, 200, 790; Sherwood, p. 616.

133. Henry Morgenthau, "The Morgenthau Diaries," *Saturday Evening Post*, October 11, 1947, p. 21; Sherwood, p. 135.

134. Hull, I, 195. Compare, for example, Hull's relation to the "Destroyer Deal" with that of Stimson, *ibid.*, vol. I, chap. lx; Stimson and Bundy, pp. 357–358.

135. Ickes, *Secret Diary*, III, 513. Roosevelt presented William Woodin with a *fait accompli* after the decision to leave the gold standard; later, when he decided to embark on a large spending program during the recession of 1937, he did so without ever consulting Henry Morgenthau. See Moley, p. 159; Lindley, p. 275; Morgenthau, "Diaries," *Sat. Eve. Post*, October 4, 1947, pp. 48ff.

136. On Ickes and Johnson, see Moley, p. 190. On Ickes and Hopkins, see Sherwood, pp. 53–71; Ickes, *Secret Diary*, vol. I, *passim*; Ickes, "My Twelve Years," *Sat. Eve. Post*, June 19, 1948, p. 95. On the NDAC, see *ibid.*, July 17, 1948, pp. 98–100; on the CCC, see Perkins, *Roosevelt*, pp. 177–181. For FDR's own description of the value of friction as a stimulus,

see *ibid.*, pp. 359–360. See also, *ibid.*, p. 381; Stimson and Bundy, p. 516; Hull, I, 205–206. When the WPB controversy broke out into the open, FDR wrote: "Of course, I have been aware of some dissensions within the WPB. I had hoped it would disappear." Harold Stein (ed.), *Public Administration and Policy Development* (New York, 1952), p. 259.

137. Seymour (ed.), I, 100–101.
138. For examples, see Baker, VI, 138; Sherwood, pp. 322, 833.
139. *The Hoover Commission Report on Organization of the Executive Branch of the Government* (New York, 1949), pp. 3–5.
140. *Meyers v. United States*, 272 U.S. 52 (1926).
141. Ickes, *Secret Diary*, II, 629.
142. Elliott, "Relations," p. 45.
143. Stimson and Bundy, p. 332.
144. Ickes, *Secret Diary*, III, 55, 180.
145. *Ibid.*, p. 12. See also, Farley, pp. 80–81; Morgenthau, "Diaries," *Sat. Eve. Post*, October 11, 1947, p. 72.
146. In addition to Woodring, there were times when Roosevelt would like to have seen Roper, Jones, Edison, and Swanson (at least) leave the Cabinet, but he kept silent rather than precipitate a quarrel. There is a particularly graphic account of Swanson's virtual uselessness in Ickes' *Secret Diary*, II, 419. When Morgenthau told the President that he was considering resignation, Roosevelt replied, curiously enough, with a dissertation on British Cabinet solidarity! See Morgenthau, "Diaries," *Sat. Eve. Post*, October 4, 1947, p. 49.
147. White, *Puritan*, pp. 267–268.
148. *Ibid.*; *New York Times*, March 29, 1924, pp. 1ff.
149. Truman, *Years of Trial*, I, 10; for his sharper comment, see Jonathan Daniels, *The Man of Independence* (New York, 1950), p. 2.
150. See the frequent stress on loyalty in Daniel F. Parker, "The Political and Social Views of Harry S. Truman," unpubl. diss. (University of Pennsylvania), 1951, pp. 11, 14, 26–27, 64, 143ff., 185.
151. "The President of course must be prepared to support his Cabinet members when they need backing. This is especially true with regard to the Secretary of State." H. S. Truman, *Years of Trial*, I, 330.
152. *Ibid.*, I, 546.
153. *Ibid.*, 543ff. On Byrnes, see *ibid.*, 546ff. On Wallace, see *ibid.*, 566ff.; James M. Byrnes, *Speaking Frankly* (New York, 1947), p. 242. On Louis Johnson, see *New York Times*, September 13, 1950, p. 10, col. 3; *U. S. News and World Report*, June 22, 1951, p. 22; Senate Armed Services and Foreign Relations Committees, *Hearings on the Military Situation in the Far East*, 82nd Cong., 1st Sess. (Washington, 1951), pp. 2576ff., esp. pp. 2612, 2618, 2624–2625. On J. Howard McGrath, see *New York Times*, April 4, 1952, p. 1, col. 8; April 6, 1952, p. 1, col. 1; April 9, 1952, p. 18, col. 3.

Chapter Two. The Appointment Process

1. Samuel M. Lindsay, "The New Cabinet and Its Problems," *Review of Reviews*, April 1921, p. 382.
2. Finley Peter Dunne, *Mr. Dooley in the Hearts of His Countrymen* (Boston, 1899), pp. 143–48.
3. The Senate debate on the Warren controversy can be found in 67 Cong. Rec. 1ff., 69th Congress, Special Session. The controversy can also be followed in *New York Times* during March, 1925.
4. 67 Cong. Rec. 75, 83.
5. *Ibid.*, p. 234; see also pp. 256–257.
6. *Ibid.*, p. 274; see also p. 269.
7. See Sidney Hyman, *The American President* (New York, 1954), p. 225.
8. R. S. Baker and W. E. Dodd (eds.), *The Public Papers of Woodrow Wilson* (New York, 1925), p. 222.
9. *Ibid.*, p. 220.
10. Woodrow Wilson, *The President of the United States* (New York, 1916), pp. 57–59. This book was written, however, in 1908.
11. Josephus Daniels, *The Wilson Era* (Chapel Hill, 1946), II, 520–521.
12. *New York Times*, February 14, 1920, p. 1, cols. 6–8.
13. Clinton W. Gilbert, *The Mirrors of Washington* (New York, 1921), pp. 97–98.
14. Theodore G. Joslin, *Hoover Off the Record* (Garden City, 1934), p. 28. See also John Spargo, "Bainbridge Colby," in Samuel F. Bemis (ed.), *The American Secretaries of State and Their Diplomacy* (New York, 1929), X, 182.
15. For Hoover's twin emphasis on integrity and administration, see Joslin, *Hoover Off the Record*, p. 28, and Herbert Hoover, *The Memoirs of Herbert Hoover* (New York, 1952), II, 217–218.
16. Frederick E. Schortemeier, *Life and Recent Speeches of Warren G. Harding* (Indianapolis, 1920), p. 34. For more of his stress on parties, see *ibid.*, p. 35, and Harold F. Alderfer, "The Personality and Politics of Warren G. Harding," unpubl. diss. (Syracuse University), 1928, p. 217.
17. Alderfer, "Personality and Politics," p. 215, quoted from *Good Government*, April 1922, pp. 41–42.
18. Harry M. Daugherty, *The Inside Story of the Harding Tragedy* (New York, 1932), p. 209. On pp. 73–74 he mentions his "frequent discussions of the Cabinet" with Harding.
19. Arthur S. Link, *Wilson — The Road to the White House* (Princeton, 1947), p. 269; George Creel, *The War, the World, and Wilson* (New York, 1920), pp. 21–22; James Kerney, *The Political Education of Woodrow Wilson* (New York, 1926), pp. 283, 295; David Lawrence, *The True Story of Woodrow Wilson* (New York, 1924), p. 71; Ray S. Baker, *Woodrow Wilson — Life and Letters* (New York, 1931), III, 447.

20. Charles Seymour (ed.), *The Intimate Papers of Colonel House* (Cambridge, Mass., 1926), I, 111.

21. The man was A. Mitchell Palmer, who called the offer a "horrible incongruity" and declined. See Robert K. Murray, *Red Scare* (Minneapolis, 1955), p. 192; Baker, III, 455.

22. William G. McAdoo, *Crowded Years* (Boston, 1931), p. 186. By contrast, the Eisenhower Cabinet was selected and announced one month after the election.

23. Lela Stiles, *The Man Behind Roosevelt: The Story of Louis McHenry Howe* (New York, 1954), p. 231. This was said to Louis Howe, Jim Farley, Ed Flynn, and Frank Walker. For a similar statement, see Clinton Gilbert, "New Dealers Choice," *Colliers*, May 20, 1933.

24. Raymond Moley, *After Seven Years* (New York, 1939), p. 109. In each case that Farley mentions in his book, Roosevelt did not ask him for advice, but simply told him. See James A. Farley, *Jim Farley's Story: The Roosevelt Years* (New York, 1948), pp. 33–35. Immediately after the election, Farley made it quite clear that he knew absolutely nothing about Roosevelt's thoughts on the Cabinet: *New York Times*, November 10, 1932, p. 4, col. 2. See also, John Gunther, *Roosevelt in Retrospect* (New York, 1950), p. 52.

25. Howe's biographer presents no evidence that would substantiate Howe's influence and admits that he opposed Ickes: Stiles, *Man Behind Roosevelt*, p. 231. Howe's urging may have had some effect in the case of Hull, but his choice of Owen D. Young was rejected. See Moley, pp. 112–114.

26. Moley, pp. 109–110.

27. H. Hoover, *Memoirs*, II, 218. The four refusals were by Hughes, Lowden, Harlan Stone, and Henry Robinson.

28. McAdoo, *Crowded Years*, p. 183; Kerney, *Political Education*, p. 284ff. For a case study in senatorial confirmation of a Cabinet member whose views were suspect by many of the Senators, see Felix Nigro, "The Wallace Case," in Felix Nigro (ed.), *Readings in Public Administration* (New York, 1952), pp. 445–460.

29. In the Wilson administration, McAdoo and Lane hesitated because of finances. They both retired early for this reason, and Newton Baker was "penniless" when he left. See Frederick Palmer, *Newton D. Baker — America At War* (New York, 1931), II, 416.

30. A. W. Lane and L. H. Hall (eds.) *The Letters of Franklin K. Lane* (Boston, 1922), p. 108. Lane was "drafted" nonetheless, and accepted.

31. Jesse Jones and Edward Angly, *Fifty Billion Dollars* (New York, 1951), pp. 256–257. He accepted finally, only on the condition that he could be Federal Loan Administrator as well as Secretary of Commerce.

32. *Independent*, March 12, 1921, p. 269.

33. Henry L. Stimson and McGeorge Bundy, *On Active Service in Peace and War* (New York, 1947), p. 156.

34. Cordell Hull, *The Memoirs of Cordell Hull* (New York, 1948). I, 157.
35. 65 Cong. Rec. 1976, 68th Congress, 1st Session.
36. Senators Hiram Johnson, Bronson Cutting, Carter Glass, and William McAdoo declined. The one that Roosevelt did get was Claude Swanson, an elderly man for whom Cabinet office was a fitting end to his career, and whose appointment was also designed to make room for Governor Harry Byrd of Virginia in the Senate.
37. Harold L. Ickes, *Autobiography of a Curmudgeon* (New York, 1943), p. 269; Harold L. Ickes, "My Twelve Years with F.D.R.," *Saturday Evening Post*, June 5, 1948, p. 15. Both of these accounts tell the story of how Senators Johnson and Cutting declined, and Arthur Mullen put Ickes' name before FDR. Mullen told FDR "that I knew nothing at all about his [Ickes'] personal record and that I thought he should get that from the Illinois Democrats. He [Roosevelt] said that he hadn't time for an investigation. He had to appoint someone at once." Arthur J. Mullen, *Western Democrat* (New York, 1940), p. 303.
38. Joseph P. Tumulty, *Woodrow Wilson As I knew Him* (New York, 1921), p. 138.
39. Moley, p. 119.
40. *U. S. News and World Report*, October 30, 1953, p. 17.
41. Richard Strout, *Christian Science Monitor*, November 22, 1952, p. 4.
42. "Straight from the Shoulder" (Washington, D. C., Republican National Committee, November, 1955), p. 15.
43. Henry Ford II, "Business Is on the Spot," *Saturday Review of Literature*, January 24, 1953, p. 22.
44. *New York Times*, October 14, 1956. See also Merriman Smith, *Meet Mr. Eisenhower* (New York, 1954), p. 302.
45. Senate Committee on Armed Services, *Hearings on the Nomination of Charles E. Wilson*, 83rd Cong., 1st Sess. (Washington, 1953), Part I, p. 26.
46. Elting E. Morison (ed.), *The Letters of Theodore Roosevelt* (Cambridge, Mass., 1951), III, 158.
47. *Christian Science Monitor*, November 22, 1952, p. 1.
48. *Ibid.*, November 25, 1952, p. 1.
49. Lindsay, "New Cabinet," p. 384.
50. William H. Crawford, "The Cabinet," *Outlook*, May 11, 1921, p. 67.
51. Baker, III, 439.
52. *New York Times*, February 22, 1921, p. 1, col. 6.
53. Herbert Hoover, *Memoirs*, II, 218.
54. *New York Times*, September 24, 1952, p. 24, col. 6.
55. Daugherty, pp. 71–72.
56. Frances Perkins, *The Roosevelt I knew* (New York, 1946), p. 391.
57. Ickes, "My Twelve Years," *Sat. Eve. Post*, July 17, 1948, p. 88.
58. Herbert Hoover said of Mitchell, his Attorney General, that he

"was a Democrat by registration but a Republican in ideas." Hoover, *Memoirs*, II, 219. But the appointment was also cited as evidence of Hoover's attachment to the Cabinet norm. See Ray Lyman Wilbur and Arthur M. Hyde, *The Hoover Policies* (New York, 1937), p. 544.

59. Stimson and Bundy, pp. 335–336. See also *ibid.*, p. 324; Robert E. Sherwood, *Roosevelt and Hopkins* (New York, 1948), p. 163.

60. Jones and Angly, pp. 278–283.

61. Marie Chatham, "The Role of the National Party Chairman from Hanna to Farley," unpubl. diss. (University of Maryland), 1953, pp. 184–185.

62. Baker, III, 446.

63. This is true, I think, in the cases of McAdoo, Payne, John Weeks, Mellon, Woodin, and of Louis Johnson in 1948. Sinclair Weeks, chairman of the Republican Finance Committee, was made Secretary of Commerce in 1952. His fund-raising activities were important, but not crucial; his reputation as a business man and party leader in Massachusetts were more important.

64. *Roosevelt:* all but Ickes; *Wilson:* Daniels, Burleson, McAdoo, and W. B. Wilson; *Eisenhower:* Wilson, Brownell, Weeks, and Hobby; *Hoover:* Brown and Good; *Harding:* Daugherty.

65. Seymour (ed.), I, 100. Of Lane, Garrison, Wilson, MacReynolds, Redfield, and Houston, there is evidence only that Wilson had met Houston once before his election. See David Houston, *Eight Years with Wilson's Cabinet* (New York, 1926), I, 18. See also Link, *Wilson,* index; John Lombardi, *Labor's Voice in the Cabinet* (New York, 1942), p. 85; nn. 22, 38, *supra.*

66. Quoted in Leonard D. White, *The Jeffersonians: A Study in Administrative History* (New York, 1951), p. 83.

67. Harold L. Ickes, *The Secret Diary of Harold L. Ickes* (New York, 1953–1954), II, 457.

68. Senate Committee on Interior and Insular Affairs, *Hearings on the Nomination of Oscar C. Chapman,* 81st Cong., 2nd Sess. (Washington, 1950), p. 3.

69. Howard M. Gore served briefly in 1924–1925.

70. With respect to both sectional and urban-rural factors, Cabinet membership is a more accurate index of the distribution of power in the population than it is of most other census categories. See Richard B. Fisher, "The American Executive," unpubl. MS. (Stanford University), 1951, pp. 28–29, 38–39.

71. Harwood Childs, *Labor and Capital in National Politics* (Columbus, 1930), chap. viii, esp. p. 220.

72. *New York Times,* July 13, 1920, p. 2, col. 4.

73. *Ibid.,* October 31, 1924, p. 2, col. 3.

74. *The World's Work,* April 1930, pp. 94–95.

75. David MacEachron, "The Role of the United States Department of Labor," unpubl. diss. (Harvard University), 1953, p. 175.
76. Childs, *Labor and Capital*, pp. 209–210.
77. MacEachron, "Role of the Labor Department," p. 24.
78. H. Hoover, *Memoirs*, II, 215–221.
79. *American Mercury*, January 1932, pp. 53–62; *Literary Digest*, December 13, 1930.
80. *New York Times*, December 14, 1932, p. 11, col. 1; December 20, 1932, p. 9, col. 4; Perkins, *Roosevelt*, p. 151.
81. Perkins, *Roosevelt*, pp. 116–117.
82. Harry S. Truman, *Years of Trial and Hope* (New York, 1956), I, 110–111.
83. *New York Times*, February 2, 1913, Sec. v, p. 5.
84. Seymour (ed.), p. 98; Tumulty, pp. 174ff.
85. Mark Sullivan, *Our Times, The Twenties* (New York, 1936), VI 153.
86. Daughery, pp. 95–96. This letter was written February 9, 1921; Harding tendered the appointment on the 24th.
87. General Leonard Wood declined the War post, and Governor Frank Lowden, the Navy. See Samuel Hopkins Adams, *Incredible Era* (Boston, 1939), p. 197. Hoover offered Lowden a post, but he was not a serious rival. See H. Hoover, *Memoirs*, II, 218.
88. Farley, p. 33.
89. In fact, his appointment of Curtis D. Wilbur, an anti-Hiram Johnson man and Chief Justice of the California Supreme Court, was felt by many to be a direct slap at Johnson, a progressive leader. See the comments excerpted in the *Literary Digest*, March 29, 1924, p. 13. His failure to conciliate the progressives drew comment from them on the appointment of Harlan Stone as Attorney General. Alpheus T. Mason, *Harlan F. Stone: Pillar of the Law* (New York, 1956), p. 144.
90. Claudius O. Johnson, *Borah of Idaho* (New York, 1936), pp. 432–433.
91. Secretary of Agriculture Ezra Taft Benson was a nominee of Senator Taft. The Secretary of the Treasury, George Humphrey, was a desirable choice from Taft's viewpoint.
92. Henry Morgenthau, "The Morgenthau Diaries," *Saturday Evening Post*, October 25, 1947, p. 85; Ickes, *Secret Diary*, I, 147.
93. E. Allen Helms, "The President and Party Politics," *The Journal of Politics*, February 1949, p. 49.
94. *Wilson:* Burleson (Tex.), Daniels (N. C.), MacReynolds (Tenn.); *Roosevelt:* Hull (Tenn.), Roper (S. C.), Swanson (Va.); *Truman:* Byrnes (S. C.), Clark (Tex.), Vinson (Ky.).
95. *Christian Science Monitor*, April 10, 1953, p. 1.
96. Richard Strout, *Christian Science Monitor*, December 2, 1952, p. 1.
97. *U. S. News and World Report*, October 2, 1953, p. 46.

98. Robert Sherwood observes, for instance, that in spite of the fact that FDR preferred "peace and harmony," his Cabinet appointments turned out to be "peculiarly violent, quarrelsome, recalcitrant men." Sherwood, p. 9. Such a result is not paradoxical when the nature of the recruitment process is considered.

99. See Morgenthau, "Diaries," *Sat. Eve. Post,* October 25, 1947, p. 83, and H. S. Truman, *Years of Trial,* II, 43.

100. Whereas Wilson hardly knew his first Attorney General, W. R. MacReynolds, his next two selections for that office were both original and influential Wilson men, T. W. Gregory and A. M. Palmer. The same situation holds for his later Secretaries of Interior and War. He knew neither Lane nor Garrison, but both Payne and Baker were early Wilson supporters. For the decreasing importance of geography as a factor for Wilson, see Josephus Daniels, *Wilson Era,* II, 312.

101. Health, Education and Welfare Secretary Folsom had been Undersecretary of the Treasury; Treasury Secretary Anderson had been Deputy Secretary of Defense; Attorney General Rogers had been Deputy Attorney General; Interior Secretary Fred Seaton had been an administrative assistant to the President; Health, Education and Welfare Secretary Flemming had been Director of ODM; Secretary of Commerce Strauss had been Chairman of the AEC. The only one with whom Eisenhower was unacquainted was Labor Secretary Mitchell.

102. Ogden Mills had been Undersecretary of the Treasury and Patrick Hurley had been Assistant Secretary of War. Of the four, only Mills was a politically experienced man. Hurley had not even been a delegate to the Convention in 1928, and Labor Secretary Doak was opposed by the AFL. See George Milburn, "Mr. Hoover's Stalking Horse," *American Mercury,* July 1932, p. 258; *American Mercury,* January 1932, pp. 53–62.

103. The early appointments of Vinson, Schwellenbach, Byrnes, and Anderson reflect this legislative sensitivity, as compared to those of Marshall, Acheson, Forrestal, and Chapman.

104. Coolidge acted without the advice of his most intimate advisers, and against the will of the Michigan delegation in Congress, to appoint Charles Warren, resulting in "the most humiliating defeat of his career." Claude M. Fuess, *Calvin Coolidge — The Man from Vermont* (Boston, 1940), p. 364; *Literary Digest,* January 24, 1925, p. 6. Smarting from the opposition to Warren's corporation ties, Coolidge then "made up my mind to send them the name of a lawyer who wouldn't know a corporation if he saw one — John G. Sargent of Ludlow, Vermont. The senators had never heard of Sargent — so they confirmed him." Henry L. Stoddard, *It Costs to be President* (New York, 1938), p. 134. In choosing Frank Kellogg to succeed Hughes, he at least failed to consult his closest single adviser, Senator Butler, and the Minnesota delegation, strongly establishing the presumption that the choice was particularly unaffected by outside influence. *Literary Digest,* January 24, 1925, p. 6.

105. Mason, *Stone,* p. 144.
106. Ickes, *Autobiography of a Curmudgeon,* p. 270.
107. See the nomination hearings of the Eisenhower Cabinet for repeated expressions of this sentiment.
108. *World's Work,* July 1930, p. 75. Lamont was appointed March 2, 1929. *New York Times,* March 3, 1929.
109. *New York Times,* March 6, 1921, p. 9, col. 1. For the surprise of everyone else, see *ibid.,* February 23, 121, p. 1, col. 8.
110. For the general approach, see Harold Lasswell, Daniel Lerner, and C. Easton Rothwell, *The Comparative Study of Elites* (Palo Alto, 1952). For the Cabinet in particular, see Fisher, "American Executive"; for other studies of Cabinet personnel, see *New York Times,* March 5, 1933, p. 10, col. 2; H. D. Anderson, "Educational and Occupational Attainments of Our National Leaders," *Scientific Monthly,* 40:516 (1935).

Chapter Three. The Cabinet Meeting: I

1. Henry B. Learned, "Some Aspects of the Cabinet Meeting," The Columbia Historical Society, *Records,* 18:106, 109, 113, 122 (1915).
2. *Ibid.,* pp. 129–130; Burton J. Hendrick, *Lincoln's War Cabinet* (Boston, 1946), pp. 188–191; *New York Times,* March 13, 1913, p. 1, col. 2.
3. William C. Redfield, *With Congress and Cabinet* (New York, 1924), pp. 67–68. Cordell Hull, *The Memoirs of Cordell Hull* (New York, 1948), I, 204.
4. Calvin Coolidge, *The Autobiography of Calvin Coolidge* (New York, 1929), pp. 203–204; William Allen White, *A Puritan in Babylon* (New York, 1938), p. 251.
5. William Hillman (ed.), *Mr. President* (New York, 1952), p. 18.
6. Ray S. Baker, *Woodrow Wilson — Life and Letters* (New York, 1931), VII, 225; *New York Times,* October 3, 1914, p. 2, col. 1; David Lawrence, *The True Story of Woodrow Wilson* (New York, 1924), p. 224.
7. Coolidge, pp. 203–204.
8. *Outlook,* May 27, 1925, p. 133.
9. Learned, "Aspects of the Cabinet Meeting," pp. 111, 120, 134–136, 142.
10. William Allen White, *Woodrow Wilson* (Cambridge, Mass., 1924), p. 288; Josephus Daniels, *The Wilson Era* (Chapel Hill, 1946), II, 549–550.
11. Redfield, *With Congress,* p. 67.
12. The discussion of the Eisenhower Cabinet in Chapters Three and Four draws heavily for factual material on interviews with the individuals cited in the Acknowledgements, especially with Cabinet Secretary Maxwell Rabb and Assistant to the Cabinet Secretary Bradley H. Patterson.
13. Harold L. Ickes, "My Twelve Years with FDR," *Saturday Evening Post,* June 5, 1948, p. 16. Coolidge once held a half-hour, three-man Cabi-

net meeting; see Irwin H. Hoover, *Forty-Two Years in the White House* (Cambridge, Mass., 1934), p. 175.

14. Harold L. Ickes, *The Secret Diary of Harold L. Ickes* (New York, 1953–1954), I, 402. See also A. W. MacMahon and J. D. Millett, *Federal Administrators* (New York, 1939), p. 5.

15. Ickes, *Secret Diary*, II, 577; Ickes, "My Twelve Years," *Sat. Eve. Post*, June 5, 1948, p. 17.

16. See Hull, I, 196–200.

17. Daniels, *Wilson Era*, II, 628–629; see also pp. 615–632 *passim*. Even the reporters came to look upon Cabinet meetings as story-telling contests; see *New York Times*, December 11, 1918.

18. Ickes, *Secret Diary*, III, 627–628.

19. For some examples, see *ibid.*, II, 5ff., 199.

20. This conclusion is not refuted by any of the memoir material cited herein. For evidence of the same result in earlier Cabinets, see Hilary A. Herbert, "Grover Cleveland and His Cabinet at Work," *Century*, March 1913, p. 741; Festus P. Summers, *The Cabinet Diary of William L. Wilson 1896–1897* (Chapel Hill, 1957), pp. 49, 51, 58, 74, 213, and *passim*.

21. Robert J. Donovan, *Eisenhower: The Inside Story* (New York, 1956), p. 65.

22. *Ibid.*, pp. 172–174. For an example of the closest approximation possible under traditional procedure, see Walter Millis (ed.), *The Forrestal Diaries* (New York, 1951), pp. 94ff.

23. Donovan, *Eisenhower: The Inside Story*, chap. iv; John L. Steele, "The New-Model Cabinet," *Life*, October 8, 1956, pp. 94–100.

24. Richard E. Neustadt, "Presidency and Leislation: Planning the President's Program," *American Political Science Review*, December 1955, p. 990.

25. Sidney Hyman, "The Cabinet's Job as Eisenhower Sees It," *New York Times Magazine*, July 20, 1958, pp. 40–41.

26. Donovan, *Eisenhower: The Inside Story*, chap. viii.

27. *Ibid.*, pp. 139–140; p. 354.

28. *Ibid.*, chaps. xv, xvii. See also pp. 93, 168, 313–314.

29. On the harmonious behavior of the Eisenhower Cabinet, see *ibid.*, pp. 370–385. On the conflicts and lack of group effort in the Wilson Cabinet, one commentator wrote: "The members never having been trained together and having in reality been given little opportunity to pull together, not having been chosen to work out policies in helpful team play, their efforts to handle the coal strike met with such disaster as would inevitably, in any responsible government, have caused the fall of the ministry." *Nation*, January 3, 1920, p. 844. See also, James Kerney, "Government by Proxy," *Century*, February 1926; Robert K. Murray, *Red Scare* (Minneapolis, 1955), chaps. x, xii; Lawrence, *True Story of Wilson*, pp. 288ff; Daniels, *Wilson Era*, II, 524ff; *New York Times*, October 7, 1919, p. 1, col. 8; November 7, 1919, p. 2, col. 1; December 14, 1919, p. 1, col. 7.

30. See Maxwell Rabb, "The New Cabinet," Speech delivered in Jacksonville, Florida, February 14, 1957.
31. Coolidge, pp. 203–204.
32. On the bitter wrangle between Secretary of Commerce Hoover and Secretary of Agriculture Wallace, see Russell Lord, *The Wallaces of Iowa* (Boston, 1947), pp. 169, 200–201, 211–258; Herbert Hoover, *The Memoirs of Herbert Hoover* (New York, 1952), II, 109, 174. On the "widely divergent viewpoints" of Hoover and Mellon, see White, *Puritan*, pp. 251, 396; H. Hoover, *Memoirs*, II, 56.
33. Coolidge, pp. 203–204.
34. Millis (ed.), *Forrestal Diaries*, pp. 87, 92.
35. *New York Times*, November 5, 1920, p. 1, col. 5.
36. Clinton W. Gilbert, *The Mirrors of Washington* (New York, 1921), p. 19.
37. Joe M. Chapple, *Life and Times of Warren G. Harding — Our Afterwar President* (Boston, 1924), p. 138.
38. Mark Sullivan, *Our Times, The Twenties* (New York, 1936), VI, 240–241. Harding relied a great deal, too, in the earlier period on Secretary of War John W. Weeks; see *Current Opinion*, August 1931, pp. 176–178. The *New York Times* reports a great many conferences on a great many subjects between Harding and this official.
39. This story has been taken from Harry M. Daugherty, *The Inside Story of the Harding Tragedy* (New York, 1932), pp. 135–149, and H. Hoover, *Memoirs*, II, 47–48.
40. On this shift, see Coolidge, p. 167; Gilbert, *Mirrors*, pp. 70–71; Harold F. Alderfer, "The Personality and Politics of Warren G. Harding," unpubl. diss. (Syracuse University), 1928; David Hinshaw, *Herbert Hoover: American Quaker* (New York, 1950), p. 136. After the Railroad Strike Hoover's influence was predominant in labor policy. See Edwin Emerson, *Hoover and His Times* (New York, 1932), pp. 487–492; Ray L. Wilbur and Arthur M. Hyde, *The Hoover Policies* (New York, 1937), p. 125. On the similarity of view between Hughes and Hoover, see H. Hoover, *Memoirs*, II, 58; Merlo J. Pusey, *Charles Evans Hughes* (New York, 1951), II, 427–428. Cabinet meetings, according to Hughes, were "brief and not very helpful, talk running to generalities and politics." Pusey, *Hughes*, II, 427–428.
41. *Ibid.*, p. 565.
42. See Chapter Five, *infra*.
43. Lord, *Wallaces*, pp. 249–251; see also White, *Puritan*, p. 344.
44. Henry L. Stoddard, *It Costs to be President* (New York, 1938), p. 92.
45. White, *Puritan*, p. 396.
46. Richard H. Rovere, "Eisenhower: A Trial Balance," *Reporter*, April 21, 1955, pp. 19–20.
47. Hoover's opinion of Mills was that he was "one of the best and

most reliable intellects of our generation. His economic sense was uncanny." H. Hoover, *Memoirs*, II, 219. On Mills' role, see Perry Osborn, "Ogden Mills," *Proceedings of New York Bar Association*, March 15, 1938, p. 11 — "President Hoover's closest confidant and adviser"; I. Hoover, *Forty-Two Years*, p. 247 — "Never did I know a President so dependent upon a Cabinet officer."

48. David Houston, *Eight Years with Wilson's Cabinet* (New York, 1926), I, 89.

49. Baker, VII, 182–183. On June 1, 1918, he sent a letter to the Secretaries of Treasury, Agriculture, Commerce, Labor, and Interior, part of which follows: "In performing my obvious duty of presiding over the war activities of the government and trying to get them properly correlated, so that they may cooperate and function in the most effective way, I find myself hampered by the fact that I have nowhere a complete picture (either in my mind or on paper) of the special war activities which the several departments have undertaken or which have been allotted to them from time to time through myself or through other departments."

50. During the important meeting of Tuesday, March 20, 1917, Houston reports that "Lansing said little or nothing, as usual." Houston, *Eight Years*, I, 243. See also Daniels, *Wilson Era*, II, 549–550.

51. Baker, V, 333; *New York Times*, June 1, 1915, p. 2, col. 2.

52. Oswald G. Villard, *Prophets True and False* (New York, 1928), p. 121; see also p. 162.

53. Baker, V, 338; *New York Times*, June 1, 1915, p. 2, col. 3.

54. Baker, V, 341. As a sharp contrast to this type of presidential behavior, one might take the letter which Grover Cleveland sent to Great Britain stating United States policy with respect to the Venezuelan boundary dispute in July, 1895. Herbert, "Grover Cleveland."

55. Baker, V, 351; Houston, I, 136–139.

56. Houston, I, 139.

57. *Ibid.*, 139–145, 147–148.

58. *Ibid.*, 219.

59. Baker, VI, 455.

60. Houston, I, 229–230.

61. Baker, VI, 456.

62. A. W. Lane and L. H. Hall (eds.), *The Letters of Franklin K. Lane* (Boston, 1922), p. 241.

63. Houston, I, 235–236; Lane and Hall, p. 240.

64. Lane and Hall, pp. 239–240; Daniels, *Wilson Era*, II, 12, 19–20, 620; *New York Times*, June 9, 1915, p. 6, col. 2.

65. Lane and Hall, p. 238.

66. Baker, VI, 487–488, 502–507; Houston, I, 241–244; Charles Seymour (ed.), *The Intimate Papers of Colonel House* (Cambridge, Mass., 1926), II, 461.

67. Seymour (ed.), II, 461.

68. *Ibid.*, 467; Lane and Hall, p. 243; *New York Times*, March 24, 1917, p. 1, col. 8. For a completely different procedure in preparing a war message, cf. Polk's Cabinet consultation in Allan Nevins (ed.), *Polk: The Diary of a President 1845–1849* (New York, 1929), pp. 81–86.
69. Baker, VI, 505ff.
70. *New York Times*, August 26, 1918, Sec. vii, pp. 3–4; Lawrence, *True Story of Wilson*, p. 224; Stoddard, *It Costs to be President*, p. 482.
71. Lane and Hall, p. 267; see also p. 266.
72. *Ibid.*, p. 293.
73. Ibid., pp. 293–297; Houston, I, 308–320; Baker, VIII, 500.
74. Edward N. Hurley, *The Bridge to France* (Philadelphia, 1927), pp. 322–324.
75. Ickes, *Secret Diary*, I, 308; see also pp. 315, 402.
76. Jesse Jones and Edward Angly, *Fifty Billion Dollars* (New York, 1951), pp. 303–304.
77. Henry L. Stimson and McGeorge Bundy, *On Active Service in Peace and War* (New York, 1947), p. 561.
78. Frances Perkins, *The Roosevelt I knew* (New York, 1946), p. 377; Forrestal — Senate Committee on Armed Services, *Hearings on the Unification of the Armed Services*, 80th Cong., 1st Sess. (Washington, March and April, 1947), pp. 40–41; Truman — Jonathan Daniels, *The Man of Independence* (New York, 1950), p. 259. Perhaps Farley is an exception; see James A. Farley, *Jim Farley's Story: The Roosevelt Years* (New York, 1948), pp. 39, 200, 215.
79. W. Leon Godshall (ed.), *Principles and Functions of Government in the United States* (New York, 1948), p. 365; Ickes, *Secret Diary*, I, 273–274, 371–374, 524–531; II, 31; Ickes, "My Twelve Years," *Sat. Eve. Post*, July 3, 1948, p. 30; Daniel C. Roper, *Fifty Years of Public Life* (Durham, 1941), p. 295; Farley, p. 54.
80. Hull, I, 674–675.
81. Robert E. Sherwood, *Roosevelt and Hopkins* (New York, 1948), pp. 433–434.
82. Farley, p. 45; Hull, I, chap. xxii; Ickes, *Secret Diary*, II, 273ff.
83. Hull, I, 203.
84. *Ibid.*, I, 203; II, 1057–1058; Stimson and Bundy, p. 390; Perkins, *Roosevelt*, p. 377; House and Senate Joint Committee for the Investigation of the Pearl Harbor Attack, *Hearings on the Pearl Harbor Attack*, 79th Cong., 2nd Sess. (Washington, 1946), Part II, p. 5432.
85. Farley, pp. 103–107; Henry Morgenthau, "The Morgenthau Diaries," *Saturday Evening Post*, October 4, 1947, p. 21; Ickes, *Secret Diary*, II, 240ff. See also Ickes, *Secret Dairy*, II, 468ff, for another example.
86. *Saturday Evening Post*, September 30, 1933, p. 32. For examples of Ickes' empathy, see his *Secret Diary*, I, 147, 157.
87. Perkins, *Roosevelt*, p. 385; see also Roper, *Fifty Years*, pp. 290ff.
88. *Christian Science Monitor*, March 4, 1953, p. 1.

89. For examples of the Truman Cabinet as a political sounding board, see Millis (ed.), *Forrestal Diaries*, pp. 90, 250ff. Of one Cabinet meeting Forrestal writes: "The President announced that he was going to veto the labor bill [the Taft-Hartley Bill]. Anderson and I both registered dissent with the decision, and in particular expressed regret that there had been no Cabinet discussion of this matter such as had occurred on the price controls, on the portal-to-portal pay and on the tax bill, all of which discussions had been productive of a unanimity of view and which enabled members of the Cabinet to support with vigor the President's position." *Ibid.*, p. 280.

Chapter Four. The Cabinet Meeting: II

1. Charles Merz, "At the Bottom of the Oil Story," *Century*, May 1924, p. 89.

2. *Ibid.* Attorney Daugherty said the same thing: Harry M. Daugherty, *The Inside Story of the Harding Tragedy* (New York, 1932), pp. 194, 200. See Coolidge's conversation with John Hays Hammond in Hammond's *The Autobiography of John Hays Hammond* (New York, 1935), II, 695–696.

3. Merlo J. Pusey, *Charles Evans Hughes* (New York, 1951), II, 568. In spite of the fact that they both had financial dealings with Mr. Sinclair, neither Will Hays nor Andrew Mellon mentioned it or offered it during their testimony in the Albert Fall investigation. Both said they had not been asked about these dealings and felt it was not their responsibility. See Samuel H. Adams, *Incredible Era* (Boston, 1939), pp. 409–410; Harvey O'Connor, *Mellon's Millions: The Biography of a Fortune* (New York, 1933), pp. 268–269.

4. "Not one of them has opened his lips as to these oil scandals from beginning to end — not one word of regret that their party is so befouled that it reeks with filth, that it is in a quagmire of corruption and crookedness of which they have been the political beneficiaries." *Nation*, March 21, 1928, p. 310.

5. Jesse Jones and Edward Angly, *Fifty Billion Dollars* (New York, 1951), p. 303.

6. David Houston, *Eight Years with Wilson's Cabinet* (New York, 1926), I, 40–41.

7. Everett Colby, "Charles Evans Hughes," *Scribners*, May 1928, pp. 564–565. See also Pusey, *Hughes*, II, 427.

8. Henry Morgenthau, "The Morgenthau Diaries," *Saturday Evening Post*, September 27, 1947, p. 82.

9. Cordell Hull, *The Memoirs of Cordell Hull* (New York, 1948), I, 204, 207–209, 902; II, 1156–1157.

10. Josephus Daniels, *The Wilson Era* (Chapel Hill, 1946), I, 451. Daniels said of Garrison: "He simply could not cooperate and did not try." *Ibid.*, 447.

11. From the diary of Walter H. Page, September 1916, as quoted in

Arthur S. Link, *Wilson: The New Freedom* (Princeton, 1956), p. 76.

12. Louis Brownlow, *The President and the Presidency* (Chicago, 1949), p. 100.

13. Jones and Angly, p. 303.

14. Houston, I, 68. Of the Cleveland Cabinet, one of its members wrote, similarly: "It has been a long time since anything of special interest took place at Cabinet meetings. The State and Treasury Departments furnish most of the subjects of conference, and Olney is far more reticent about State matters, and more in the habit of consulting with the President alone than of bringing them before the Cabinet." Festus P. Summers, *The Cabinet Diary of William L. Wilson 1896–1897* (Chapel Hill, 1957), p. 69.

15. Frances Perkins, *The Roosevelt I Knew* (New York, 1946), pp. 198, 268–273.

16. Walter Millis (ed.), *The Forrestal Diaries* (New York, 1951), pp. 21, 232. One member of the Wilson Cabinet who took a broad view of the advisory functions of the Cabinet officer was Lindley Garrison. "It was his theory of government that a cabinet officer should be broad and versatile, as intimately interested in the problems affecting other departments and Administration policy as in the management of his own department. . . ." David Lawrence, *The True Story of Woodrow Wilson* (New York, 1924), pp. 151–152. Carried into the Cabinet meeting, such an attitude yielded only the resentment of his colleagues. Said Josephus Daniels: "He loved to argue and discuss hypothetical cases, and often he wearied the President in Cabinet meetings by his legalistic arguments. Upon almost every subject that came before the Cabinet he liked to be heard, and often he would take up two thirds of the time of the discussion at a meeting of the Cabinet." Daniels, *Wilson Era*, I, 447–448. For comments on Garrison's resignation indicating that it resulted from a relatively minor disagreement on War Department policy, see *New York Times*, February 11, 1916, p. 2, col. 7.

17. Hull, I, 598. Harold L. Ickes, "My Twelve Years with FDR," *Saturday Evening Post*, June 5, 1948, pp. 81–82; Saul K. Padover, "Ickes: Memoir of a Man without Fear," *Reporter*, March 4, 1952, p. 36; Ickes, *The Secret Diary of Harold L. Ickes* (New York, 1953–1954), II, 396.

18. Ickes, *Secret Diary*, III, 566; see also pp. 543–568, *passim*.

19. Pusey, *Hughes*, II, 427.

20. Millis (ed.), *Forrestal Diaries*, pp. 190, 305; Ickes, *Secret Diary*, III, 409ff.

21. Ickes, *Secret Diary*, III, 190. See also John Gunther, *Roosevelt in Retrospect* (New York, 1950), pp. 132–133; James A. Farley, *Jim Farley's Story: The Roosevelt Years* (New York, 1948), pp. 54, 360; Morgenthau, "Diaries," *Sat. Eve. Post*, October 18, 1947, p. 16, October 25, 1947, p. 85; Jones and Angly, p. 539.

22. Lawrence, *True Story*, pp. 90–91; William C. Redfield, *With Congress and Cabinet* (New York, 1924), p. 67.

23. Pusey, *Hughes*, II, 427.

NOTES TO CHAPTER FOUR

24. Jones and Angly, pp. 278, 303–304. See also Perkins, *Roosevelt,* p. 393; Robert E. Sherwood, *Roosevelt and Hopkins* (New York, 1948), p. 357; Harry S. Truman, *Years of Trial and Hope* (New York, 1956), I, 55.

25. Henry L. Stimson and McGeorge Bundy, *On Active Service in Peace and War* (New York, 1947), p. 561.

26. Pusey, *Hughes,* II, 427; *Independent,* March 28, 1925, p. 342; Ray S. Baker, *Woodrow Wilson — Life and Letters* (New York, 1931), IV, 298; Houston, I, 217; Perkins, *Roosevelt,* pp. 134–135; Farley, p. 135; Hull, I, 204; Ickes, "My Twelve Years," *Sat. Eve. Post,* June 5, 1948, pp. 16, 78, 81.

27. Maxwell Rabb, "The New Cabinet," Speech delivered in Jacksonville, Florida, February 14, 1957, p. 9.

28. From the transcript of the Secretary's press conference, January 16, 1957, as reprinted in the House Committee on Appropriations' *Hearings on The Budget for 1958,* 85th Cong., 1st Sess. (Washington, 1957), pp. 5, 7.

29. *Report of the President's Committee on Administrative Management with Special Studies* (Washington, 1937); Bradley Nash, *Staffing the Presidency* (Washington, 1952), p. 32. See also "The Executive Office of the President: A Symposium," *Public Administration Review,* Winter 1941.

30. For a good description of these agencies, see E. H. Hobbs, *Behind the President* (Washington, 1954).

31. Paul Appleby and Arnold Brecht, "Organization for Overhead Management," *Public Administration Review,* Winter 1942, p. 64.

32. Arthur Maas, "In Accord with the Program of the President," *Public Policy,* 4:77–93 (1953).

33. Louis W. Koenig, "The Sale of the Tankers," in Harold Stein (ed.), *Public Administration and Policy Development* (New York, 1952), pp. 446–532.

34. Ickes, *Secret Diary,* III, 368–505, *passim.*

35. Herbert Hoover, *The Memoirs of Herbert Hoover* (New York, 1952), I, 263–264. On the War Cabinet, see also Edward N. Hurley, *The Bridge to France* (Philadelphia, 1927), pp. 319–320; Baker, VIII, 36–37; Henry L. Stoddard, *It Costs to be President* (New York, 1938), p. 496.

36. William Y. Elliott, *The Need for Constitutional Reform* (New York, 1935), p. 215. On the NEC, see also Donald Richberg, *My Hero* (New York, 1954), pp. 177–178; Richard E. Neustadt, "Presidency and Legislation: The Growth of Central Clearance," *American Political Science Review,* September 1954, pp. 648–652; Ickes, *Secret Diary,* I, *passim.*

37. Senate Armed Services and Foreign Relations Committees, *Hearings on the Military Situation in the Far East,* 82nd Cong., 1st Sess. (Washington, 1951), Part IV, pp. 2586–2687 *passim.*

38. Baker, VI, 540.

39. Ickes, *Secret Diary,* I, 242–243; see also pp. 221, 264–265.

40. *Ibid.,* III, 371, 471; see also pp. 429–480, *passim.*

41. *Ibid.,* III, 577.

THE CABINET AND POLITICS: I

42. Don K. Price, "Staffing the Presidency," *American Political Science Review*, December 1946, p. 1164.

43. Charles Seymour (ed.), *The Intimate Papers of Colonel House* (Cambridge, Mass., 1926), I, 137–150; Daniels, *Wilson Era*, II, 535; Stimson and Bundy, pp. 333–334.

44. For a good example, involving Wilson's "War Cabinet" and the Cabinet, see Baker, VIII, 311.

45. H. M. Somers, *Presidential Agency: OWMR* (Cambridge, Mass., 1950), pp. 65, 84; Arthur W. MacMahon, *Administration in Foreign Affairs* (Birmingham, 1953), pp. 54–55.

46. MacMahon, *Administration*, pp. 44ff.

47. Louis W. Koenig (ed.), *The Truman Administration* (New York, 1956), p. 360.

48. Mary Hinsdale, *A History of the President's Cabinet* (Ann Arbor, 1911), p. 326.

49. Farley, p. 39; Henry B. Learned, *The President's Cabinet* (New Haven, 1912), pp. 4–7.

50. Learned, *President's Cabinet*, p. 6.

Chapter Five. The Cabinet and Politics: I

1. See Dwight Waldo, *The Administrative State* (New York, 1948), p. 128.

2. *Golden Book Magazine*, March 1929, p. 56.

3. Hoover was in the same Cabinet as Hughes, and took the Secretaryship of Commerce. Stimson was given the Secretaryship of War in the Roosevelt Cabinet, but had previously been Secretary of State in the Hoover Cabinet.

4. Harry S. Truman, *Years of Trial and Hope* (New York, 1956), II, 115; see also pp. 90, 112; Robert Payne, *The Marshall Story* (New York, 1951), p. 292. On Coolidge-Hughes, see Chapter Four, *supra*.

5. Robert E. Sherwood, *Roosevelt and Hopkins* (New York, 1948), p. 835.

6. House Committee on Expenditures in the Executive Departments, *Hearings on H. R. 782*, 81st Cong. 1st Sess. (Washington, 1949), p. 17.

7. Charles G. Washburn, *The Life of John W. Weeks* (Boston, 1928), p. 314.

8. Charles Brannan, in speech delivered at Amherst College, April 1953.

9. All of the foregoing poll results are to be found in Hadley Cantril (ed.), *Public Opinion: 1935–1946* (Princeton, 1951), pp. 81–84.

10. *American Institute of Public Opinion Release*, April 6, 1956. On Secretary Ezra Taft Benson, see *ibid.*, October 9, 1953.

11. All of the figures that follow have been compiled from the pertinent volumes of the *New York Times Index*.

12. Richard L. Strout, "Press Conferences Then and Now," *Christian

Science Monitor, December 29, 1956, p. 16; Frances Perkins, *The Roosevelt I knew* (New York, 1946), p. 221.

13. Josephus Daniels, *The Wilson Era* (Chapel Hill, 1946), II, 317–318. For Houston's political inexperience, see *Current Opinion*, May 1914, pp. 346–347; for Houston's own reaction to "politics," see David Houston, *Eight Years with Wilson's Cabinet* (New York, 1926), I, p. 192.

14. Henry F. Pringle, "Hubert Work, M.D.," *Outlook*, September 5, 1928, p. 723.

15. Daniel C. Roper, *Fifty Years of Public Life* (Durham, 1941), p. 283.

16. Senate Committee on Agriculture, *Hearings on the Nomination of Ezra T. Benson*, 83rd Cong., 1st Sess. (Washington, 1953), p. 26.

17. Senate Committee on Labor and Public Welfare, *Hearings on the Nomination of Martin P. Durkin*, 83rd Cong., 1st Sess. (Washington, 1953), p. 4. The "closed" hearing on the nomination of Douglas McKay as Secretary of the Interior was attended by several representatives of interested groups, among them J. Bryon Wilson, Secretary of the Wyoming Wool Growers Association. His interests are in grazing land policy. *Congressional Quarterly*, January 16, 1953, p. 101.

18. Quoted in David MacEachron, "The Role of the United States Department of Labor," unpubl. diss. (Harvard University), 1953, pp. 116–117.

19. Washburn, *Life of Weeks*, p. 274.

20. H. L. Stimson and McGeorge Bundy, *On Active Service in Peace and War* (New York, 1947), p. 408. Of course some individuals in this kind of position have moved outside of their department to cultivate a public. Secretary of War John Weeks became an important spokesman to and for the business community. *Current Opinion*, August 1921, pp. 176–178.

21. Roper, *Fifty Years*, p. 288.

22. James C. Hemphill, "William G. McAdoo," *North American*, July 1917, p. 80.

23. It is no wonder that in the three and one half years between his confirmation and his death, and in spite of worsening agricultural conditions, Wallace's name appeared on page one of the *New York Times* less than twice a year.

24. J. A. Farley, *Jim Farley's Story: The Roosevelt Years* (New York, 1948), p. 101; see also E. K. Lindley, *Halfway with Roosevelt* (New York, 1936), p. 414; H. L. Ickes, *The Secret Diary of Harold L. Ickes* (New York, 1953–1954), II, 24, 213, 224.

25. See Mark Sullivan, "The Men of the Cabinet," *World's Work*, 44:81–94 (May 1921). Clarence W. Barron of the *Wall Street Journal* said of the Harding Cabinet, "All that could be desired or asked for . . . I have not a criticism to make of anyone of the ten." *Literary Digest*, 68:8 (March 12, 1921).

26. Richard Barry, "Mr. Mellon," *Outlook*, July 20, 1921, p. 473. "For

many years he relied on his own judgments solely in arriving at decisions involving many millions. For twenty-five years his was a one-man bank, without a board of directors among whom to apportion responsibility." When Harding exhibited some hesitance about Mellon's money as a recommendation, Harry Daugherty assured him, "A man who can quietly make the millions this modest little man has gathered is little short of a magician. If there is one think he knows it is money." H. M. Daugherty, *The Inside Story of the Harding Tragedy* (New York, 1932), p. 74. On Mellon's wealth, see Phillip H. Love, *Andrew W. Mellon: The Man and His Work* (Baltimore, 1929).

27. Barry, "Mr. Mellon," p. 473.
28. Edward G. Lowry, *Washington Close-ups* (Boston, 1921), p. 158.
29. *Literary Digest*, February 20, 1932, p. 12.
30. Silas Bent, "Andrew Mellon," *Scribners*, January 1928, p. 32; H. O'Connor, *Mellon's Millions: The Biography of a Fortune* (New York, 1933), pp. 129–130.
31. Frank R. Kent, "Andrew Mellon," *The Nation*, March 17, 1926, pp. 281–282. See also the same author and title, *New Republic*, March 24, 1926, pp. 135–138.
32. W. A. White, *A Puritan in Babylon* (New York, 1938), p. 377.
33. R. V. Oulahan, *New York Times*, March 1, 1925, Sec. viii, p. 1, col. 1.
34. White, *Puritan*, p. 251. It was to Mellon that Coolidge would send all those who would come to him with misgivings about the market situation; see *ibid.*, p. 336.
35. H. Hoover, *The Memoirs of Herbert Hoover* (New York, 1952), II, 30–31.
36. *Outlook*, April 17, 1929, p. 619.
37. *New Republic*, March 27, 1929, p. 172.
38. H. Hoover, *Memoirs*, II, 68; *Outlook*, December 23, 1931, p. 522.
39. C. Hull, *The Memoirs of Cordell Hull* (New York, 1948), I, 196.
40. *Ibid.*, I, 199.
41. *Ibid.*
42. *Ibid.*, I, 174.
43. *Ibid.*, I, 204–209.
44. R. E. Sherwood, *Roosevelt and Hopkins* (New York, 1948), p. 483.
45. S. M. Rosenman, *Working with Roosevelt* (New York, 1952), pp. 205–206.
46. These poll results are all to be found in Cantril, pp. 81–83.
47. Sherwood, p. 185.
48. Cantril (ed.), pp. 82–83.
49. Hull, I, 191, 195.
50. *Ibid.*, I, 485–486, 862 (on the foreign-policy planks); II, 1109–1111, 1367 (for the wartime conferences).
51. W. Y. Elliott, "Executive-Congressional Relations," unpubl. MS

(Harvard University School of Public Administration), ca. 1950, p. 45.

52. Norton Long, "Power and Administration," *Public Administration Review,* Autumn 1949, p. 258.

53. V. O. Key, *Politics, Parties, and Pressure Groups* (New York, 1952), pp. 181–182.

54. For a discussion of these possibilities, see Arthur N. Holcombe, *Our More Perfect Union* (Cambridge, Mass., 1950), chap. viii.

55. Shortly after the beginning of the Eisenhower Administration Wesley Roberts, Republican National Chairman, met with the Cabinet in order to "discuss party political matters, with accent on appointments and the necessity of getting clearance from the appropriate politician." Roscoe Drummond, "Eisenhower Cabinet Works as a Team," *Christian Science Monitor,* March 16, 1953, p. 1.

56. *Literary Digest,* March 12, 1921, p. 7.

57. *Golden Book Magazine,* March 1929, p. 56.

58. Burton J. Hendrick, *Lincoln's War Cabinet* (Boston, 1946), p. 369.

59. Sherwood, p. 170.

60. Pendleton Herring, *Presidential Leadership* (New York, 1940), p. 92; David B. Truman, *The Governmental Process* (New York, 1951), p. 405.

61. E. E. Schattschneider, *The Struggle for Party Government* (College Park, Md., 1948), p. 41.

62. Jack Redding, *Inside the Democratic Party* (Indianapolis, 1958), pp. 47–49.

63. M. J. Pusey, *Charles Evans Hughes* (New York, 1951), II, 569.

64. Farley, p. 57. In the 1934 congressional campaign Roosevelt did not want Cabinet members other than the Postmaster General making speeches outside of their home states. Ickes, *Secret Diary,* I, 220.

65. On Hyde, see H. Hoover, *Memoirs,* II, 220; on Hurley, see George Milburn, "Mr. Hoover's Stalking Horse," *American Mercury,* July 1932, pp. 258ff; Parker La Moore, *"Pat" Hurley: The Story of an American* (New York, 1932).

66. Stimson and Bundy, p. 285.

67. E. E. Morrison (ed.), *The Letters of Theodore Roosevelt* (Cambridge, Mass., 1951–1954), III, 158–159.

68. For instance, McAdoo said that "the weak point of the Wilson Cabinet . . . was . . . in the matter of political prestige. Most of its members were unknown to the country and were without political experience or political following. From the beginning, I saw that the Cabinet would be unable to give the President the effective support which he needed to meet the strenuous opposition that was certain to confront the Administration." W. G. McAdoo, *Crowded Years* (Boston, 1931), p. 192.

69. Daugherty, pp. 78, 209.

70. " 'Credit' for the nomination of the Ohio Senator must be apportioned among those responsible for these events, but the major share should

go to *Harry Daugherty,* who had groomed Harding for years, had sold him to organization leaders and the delegates, and had made the necessary deals." Wesley M. Bagby, "The 'Smoke Filled Room' and the Nomination of Warren G. Harding," *Mississippi Valley Historical Review,* March 1955, p. 673.

71. Clinton W. Gilbert, *Behind the Mirrors* (New York, 1922), p. 134.
72. Daugherty, p. 81. Daugherty called his acceptance, "in a moment of mental aberration," "the tragic blunder of my life." *Ibid.,* p. 91.
73. M. Sullivan, *Our Times, The Twenties* (New York, 1936), VI, 229.
74. Marie Chatham, "The Role of the National Party Chairman," unpubl. diss. (University of Maryland), 1953, p. 188.
75. Gilbert, *Behind the Mirrors,* p. 138.
76. *New York Times,* March 29, 1924, pp. 1–2.
77. Daugherty, pp. 282ff; *New York Times,* February 19, 1924, p. 1, col. 7; February 21, 1924, p. 1, col. 8; February 24, 1924, p. 1, col. 8.
78. *New York Times,* March 29, 1924, p. 2, col. 6 (on public reaction); Pusey, *Hughes,* II, 566 (for Hughes-Hoover efforts to oust Daugherty).
79. *New York Times,* March 29, 1924, pp. 1–2.
80. On these matters, see Charles E. Merriam, *Four American Party Leaders* (New York, 1926), chap. iv.
81. Merle E. Curti, "Bryan and World Peace," *Smith College Studies in History,* July 1931, pp. 165–166.
82. J. M. Blum, "Tumulty and the Wilson Era," unpubl. diss. (Harvard University), 1950, p. 359.
83. Curti, p. 167; see also Lowry, p. 47, on Bryan as an administrator; on the reactions of one high-level diplomat to Bryan's Secretaryship, see Burton Hendrick, *Life and Letters of Walter Hines Page* (New York, 1923), I, 194, 225, 235–236.
84. Franklin K. Lane, as quoted in *New York Times,* June 10, 1915, p. 2, col. 8; see also C. W. Gilbert, *The Mirrors of Washington* (New York, 1921), pp. 213ff.
85. R. S. Baker, *Woodrow Wilson — Life and Letters* (New York, 1931), V, 288.
86. *Ibid.,* V, 261.
87. Curti, pp. 151, 159.
88. *Ibid.;* Baker, IV, 414.
89. Baker, IV, p. 174.
90. W. J. Bryan and M. B. Bryan, *Memoirs of William Jennings Bryan* (Chicago, 1925), pp. 374–375.
91. *New Republic,* March 13, 1915, p. 139.
92. For these points, see Curti, pp. 219–220.
93. *Ibid.,* p. 235.
94. Arthur S. Link, *Woodrow Wilson and the Progressive Era: 1910–1917* (New York, 1954), p. 234 and chap. ix.
95. The *New York Times* editorialized, for instance, that the Cabinet's

prestige had risen with Bryan's resignation, that it was "trimmer, smarter, more shipshape; less ragged looking, less untidy, with the loose ends gone." *New York Times*, June 25, 1915, p. 10, col. 2.

Chapter Six. The Cabinet and Politics: II

1. Senate Judiciary Committee, *Hearings on the Nomination of Herbert Brownell*, 83rd Cong., 1st Sess. (Washington, 1953), p. 12.
2. Pendleton Herring, "Executive-Legislative Responsibilities," *American Political Science Review*, December 1944, p. 1157.
3. *House Report 508*, 62nd Cong., 2nd Sess. (Washington, 1912), III, 5.
4. 65 Cong. Rec., 1607 (1924).
5. Herring, "Executive-Legislative Responsibilities," p. 1159.
6. A. W. Lane and L. H. Hall, *The Letters of Franklin K. Lane* (Boston, 1922), p. 82.
7. R. S. Baker, *Woodrow Wilson — Life and Letters* (New York, 1931), IV, 44ff.
8. *Ibid.*, 49.
9. *Ibid.*, VI, 171–172; Josephus Daniels, *The Wilson Era* (Chapel Hill, 1946), I, 115; Lane and Hall, p. 82; *New York Times*, April 18, 1915, Sec. ii, p. 11, col. 1.
10. For these various examples, see *New York Times*, April 18, 1915, Sec. ii, p. 11, col. 1; September 1, 1916, p. 1, col. 8.
11. Baker, VIII, 187.
12. Quoted in *New York Times*, January 30, 1921, p. 10, col. 1.
13. Baker, IV, 44. See also p. 49.
14. George Rothwell Brown, *The Leadership of Congress* (Indianapolis, 1922), pp. 243ff. See also Samuel Hopkins Adams, *Incredible Era* (Boston, 1939), p. 257.
15. Wilfred E. Binkley, *The President and Congress* (New York, 1947), p. 225. See also W. F. Johnson, *George Harvey — A Passionate Patriot* (Boston, 1929).
16. Irwin H. Hoover, *Forty-Two Years in the White House* (Cambridge, Mass., 1934), p. 128; William Allen White, *A Puritan in Babylon* (New York, 1938), p. 273.
17. Frank R. Kent, "Assailing the President," *Forum*, January, 1927, p. 19.
18. The department head, writes Secretary Redfield, "must frequently struggle and struggle hard to keep in existence the organism which he is supposed to make affective . . . hardly a session of Congress passes without an effort to alter the structure of some department. . . . One was never sure of ending the year with the same organization with which it was begun." William C. Redfield, *With Congress and Cabinet* (New York, 1951), pp. 142–144.
19. Walter Millis (ed.), *The Forrestal Diaries* (New York, 1951), p.

475. For examples of Forrestal's own efforts, see Millis, pp. 227–228, 237–238, 246–247, 271, 292–293.

20. Cordell Hull, *The Memoirs of Cordell Hull* (New York, 1948), I, 215.

21. *Ibid.*, p. 178. For the best example of Hull's cooperation with Congress, see the description of his work regarding postwar organization. *Ibid.*, II, Chapter 121.

22. House Subcommittee of Committee on Appropriations, *Hearings on Department of State Appropriations Bill for 1942*, 77th Cong., 1st Sess. (Washington, 1941), p. 1.

23. House Subcommittee of Committee on Appropriations, *Hearings on Department of State Appropriations Bill for 1945*, 78th Cong., 2nd Sess. (Washington, 1944), p. 15. As an alternative kind of benediction, the same committee chairman would, on other occasions, invoke God's blessing on the Secretary of State. House Subcommittee of Committee on Appropriations, *Hearings on Department of State Appropriations Bill for 1943*, 77th Cong., 2nd Sess. (Washington, 1942), p. 7.

24. House Subcommittee of Committee on Appropriations, *Hearings on Department of State Appropriations Bill for 1942*, 77th Cong., 1st Sess. (Washington, 1941), p. 9.

25. Henry Morgenthau, "The Morgenthau Diaries," *Saturday Evening Post*, October 11, 1947, p. 79; Samuel Rosenman, *Working with Roosevelt* (New York, 1952), p. 205.

26. For an example of a "valley of hostility" before congressional committee, see Don Lohbeck, *Patrick J. Hurley* (Chicago, 1956), p. 93.

27. Josephus Daniels, *Wilson Era*, I, 337.

28. Henry L. Stimson and McGeorge Bundy, *On Active Service in Peace and War* (New York, 1947), p. 500.

29. Redfield, *With Congress*, p. 50.

30. House Subcommittee of Committee on Appropriations, *Hearings on Post Office Department Appropriations Bill for 1943*, 77th Cong., 2nd Sess. (Washington, 1941), p. 2.

31. Dean Acheson, *A Citizen Looks at Congress* (New York, 1956), pp. 65, 69.

32. *Ibid.*, p. 75.

33. Senate Committee on Armed Services, *Hearings on the Nomination of Charles E. Wilson*, 83rd Cong., 1st Sess. (Washington, 1953), pp. 113, 145.

34. 102 Cong. Rec. 9742 (1956). This was by Senator Styles Bridges.

35. *Ibid.*, p. 9741.

36. Arthur W. Page, "Garrison of the War Department," *Worlds Work*, July, 1913, p. 301.

37. *New York Times*, August 29, 1915, II, 14:2; David Lawrence, *The True Story of Woodrow Wilson* (New York, 1924), pp. 151–152.

38. John M. Blum, *Joe Tumulty and the Wilson Era* (Boston, 1951), p. 101.

39. Edward H. Brooks, "The National Defense Policy of the Wilson Administration, 1913–1917," unpublished dissertation (Stanford University), 1950, p. 31. Brooks contrasts Garrison's failure in Congress with Secretary of the Navy Daniels' success. *Ibid.*, pp. 94–95.

40. For this exchange of notes, see Joseph P. Tumulty, *Woodrow Wilson As I Knew Him* (New York, 1921), pp. 243–244.

41. *New York Times*, February 12, 1916, p. 2, col. 1.

42. House Committee on Expenditures in the Executive Departments, *Hearings on Reorganization Plan No. 1*, 81st Cong., 2nd Sess. (Washington, 1949), p. 18. See also, House Committee on Expenditures in the Executive Branch, *Hearings on H. R. 782*, 81st Cong., 1st Sess. (Washington, 1949), pp. 34, 50, 92; *Hearings on Reorganization Plan No. 1*, p. 126; Senate Committee on Expenditures in the Executive Departments, *Hearings on Reorganization Plan No. 27*, 81st Cong., 2nd Sess. (Washington, 1950), pp. 116–117.

43. 99 Cong. Rec., Daily Summary, March 30, 1953, p. 2551.

44. *Ibid.*, p. 510; Jonathan Daniels, *The Man of Independence* (New York, 1950), p. 292.

45. For the running account, see Joseph P. Harris, *The Advice and Consent of the Senate* (Berkeley, 1953), pp. 145–149.

46. 91 Cong. Rec. 1242 (1945). See also the debate concerning Wallace's alleged hostility to business and the argument that he could not, therefore, serve his clientele adequately, however he might be fitted for the job otherwise. *Ibid.*, pp. 1231–1252.

47. *New York Times*, December 16, 1950.

48. *Ibid.*, January 22, 1950, Sec. vi, p. 7ff; Elmer Davis, "The Crusade Against Acheson," *Harpers*, March, 1951, pp. 23–29. Senator Ralph Flanders demonstrated something of the highly personal nature of congressional reactions when he suggested that Acheson's "formal" mustache was symbolic of the Secretary's "poppa knows best" attitude toward Congressmen. "Even if he were correct, which we are by no means sure he is, we still wouldn't like it," he complained in reference to Acheson's attitude. *Christian Science Monitor*, June 5, 1951, p. 1.

49. See Chapter One, Note 151.

50. Harry S. Truman, *Memoirs*, II, 429–430.

51. 65 Cong. Rec. 1719, 1985 (1924).

52. *New York Times*, February 12, 1924, p. 1, col. 6.

53. *New York Times*, February 12, 1924, p. 1, col. 6; February 19, 1924, p. 2, col. 1.

54. Allan Nevins (ed.), *Polk: The Diary of a President 1845–1849* (New York, 1929), p. 345.

55. *Ibid.*, pp. 360–361.

56. John H. Millett and H. Struve Hensel, *Departmental Management*,

Task Force Report prepared by the Commission on Organization of the Executive Branch of the Government (Washington, 1949), p. 1.

57. *Ibid.*, p. 38.

58. *Ibid.*, p. 40.

59. For this Labor Department material, see David MacEachron, "The Role of the United States Department of Labor," unpublished dissertation (Harvard University), 1955, pp. 29–60.

60. David Houston, *Eight Years with Wilson's Cabinet* (New York, 1926), I, 89.

61. Redfield, *With Congress*, p. 292.

62. Herbert Hoover, *The Memoirs of Herbert Hoover* (New York, 1952), II, 36.

63. Especially in labor and agriculture; see Clinton W. Gilbert, *The Mirrors of Washington* (New York, 1921), p. 141; Edward G. Lowry, *Washington Closeups* (Boston, 1921), p. 212; Karl Schriftgiesser, *This Was Normalcy* (Boston, 1948), pp. 117–118, n. 2; David Hinshaw, *Herbert Hoover: American Quaker* (New York, 1950), Part 3, Chapter 1; James E. Pollard, *The Presidents and the Press* (New York, 1947), pp. 737–738; *New Republic*, November 8, 1922, p. 274.

64. *New York Times*, January 17, 1925, 1:3, H. Hoover, *Memoirs*, p. 111.

65. On McAdoo, see: Walter Lippmann, *Men of Destiny* (New York, 1927), pp. 112–119; Arthur S. Link, *Wilson — The Road to the White House* (Princeton, 1947), p. 330; *New York Times*, November 23, 1918, p. 10, col. 1; *Current Opinion*, January, 1919, pp. 20–21; Ray S. Baker, *Woodrow Wilson — Life and Letters* (New York, 1931), VI, 159; William G. McAdoo, *Crowded Years* (Boston, 1931), pp. 404ff.

66. See above, note 60.

67. Millett and Hensel, *Departmental Management*, p. 29.

68. Paul Appleby, "Organizing Around the Head of a Large Federal Department," *Public Administration Review*, Vol. 6, no. 3, p. 209.

69. *New York Times*, April 20, 1919, Sec. iii, p. 1, col. 6. See also *New York Times*, December 14, 1914, p. 10, col. 1; April 30, 1919, p. 10, col. 1; October 17, 1919, p. 16, col. 1; *New Republic*, every issue from March 29, 1919 to May 24, 1919.

70. See C. Herman Pritchett, "The Postmaster General and Departmental Management," *Public Administration Review*, Spring, 1946, pp. 130ff.

71. Hull, *Memoirs*, I, 202, 509–510; II, 1149, 1227–1230; Robert E. Sherwood, *Roosevelt and Hopkins* (New York, 1948), p. 135; Raymond Moley, *After Seven Years* (New York, 1939), pp. 110–111, 115.

72. See Hull, *Memoirs*, I, 204, 207–209, 902; II, 1156–1157.

73. *Ibid.*, pp. 1109–1110.

74. Sherwood, p. 135.

75. Finley Peter Dunne, *Mr. Dooley in the Hearts of His Countrymen* (Boston, 1899), pp. 146–147.

76. Josephus Daniels, *Wilson Era*, I, 122; II, 590; Brooks, *Wilson Administration*, p. 268; Elliott Roosevelt (ed.), *FDR: His Personal Letters* (New York, 1948), II, 233, 238, 243–245; *New York Times*, May 5, 1916, p. 10, col. 2; Burton J. Hendrick, "The Case of Josephus Daniels," *Worlds Work*, July, 1916, pp. 281ff.

77. Mark Sullivan, *Our Times, The Twenties* (New York, 1936), p. 342; see also pp. 295–296; Adams, *Incredible Era*, p. 344; *Current Opinion*, April, 1921, pp. 471–473.

78. Henry F. Pringle, "Wilbur — Benevolent Bungler," *Outlook*, January 25, 1928, pp. 123ff.

79. McAdoo, *Crowded Years*, pp. 187–188. Secretary of War George Dern defended himself against those critics who felt he should have inaugurated changes upon assuming office by saying, "I came in here a stranger and I had to see what was happening." *Literary Digest*, March 10, 1934, p. 9.

80. Interview with Douglas McKay, March, 1956.

81. William M. Blair, "The Benson Formula for Serenity," *New York Times Magazine*, April 11, 1954, p. 12.

82. This is often true even though the White House does not change party hands. Millett and Hensel, *Departmental Management*, p. 30.

83. William Harlan Hale, "The Loneliest Man in Washington," *Reporter*, October 18, 1956, pp. 11–16.

84. "Characteristically, a new Secretary simply exerts by the slant of his judgment a mild and moderate influence on a course or program already largely set." Appleby, *Big Democracy* (New York, 1945), p. 106.

85. Harold L. Ickes, *The Secret Diary of Harold L. Ickes* (New York, 1953–54), II, 251.

86. *Report of the President's Committee on Administrative Management with Special Studies* (Washington, 1937), p. 265.

87. Stimson and Bundy, p. 192.

88. Millett and Hensel, *Departmental Management*, pp. 10–11.

89. *Ibid.*, pp. 21–28, 35–37.

90. *Ibid.*, p. 36.

91. *Congressional Quarterly*, Vol. 5, 1949, p. 479; see also, David B. Truman, *The Governmental Process* (New York, 1951), p. 415.

92. H. Hoover, *Memoirs*, II, 42.

93. Lane and Hall, p. 148. Lane almost refused to take the Secretaryship for this reason, p. 130.

94. Arthur Maas, *Muddy Waters* (Cambridge, 1951). See also Herbert Hoover's testimony in Senate Committee on Expenditures in the Executive Departments, *Hearings on the Reorganization Act of 1949*, 81st Cong., 1st Sess. (Washington, 1949), p. 72.

95. J. Lieper Freeman, *The Political Process: Executive Bureau-Legislative Committee Relations* (Garden City, 1955).

96. Norton Long, "Power and Administration," p. 258. *Public Administration Review*, Autumn, 1949, p. 258.
97. *Ibid.*, p. 259.
98. *New York Times*, March 1, 1920, p. 1, col. 5.
99. Redfield, *With Congress*, p. 90; William C. Redfield, "What One Department Has Done," *Harper's Weekly*, March 18, 1916, p. 273.
100. Marshall E. Dimock, *The Executive in Action* (New York, 1945), p. 19.
101. David B. Truman, *The Governmental Process* (New York, 1958), pp. 406–407.
102. *New York Times*, March 4, 1954, p. 12; December 9, 1954, p. 20.
103. For one Secretary's never-ending struggle, see the index to Ickes, *Secret Diary* 1, 11. For the effort of his Republican predecessor, see *Ibid.*, 111, 69.
104. Appleby, "Organizing Around the Head of a Large Federal Department," p. 208; for an example, see Stimson and Bundy, p. 507.
105. Paul Y. Hammond, "The Secretaryships of War and the Navy," MS, Harvard University, 1953, Chapter Four, esp. pp. 147ff.
106. Millett and Hensel, *Departmental Management*, p. 35.
107. MacEachron, "Role of the Labor Department," pp. 88, 90, 92–93, 101.
108. Ickes, *Secret Diary*, I, 384–606 *passim*.
109. Maas, *Muddy Waters*, p. 74; see pp. 73–83.
110. House Joint Resolution 602, approved September 13, 1940.
111. Bascom Timmons, *Jesse H. Jones* (New York, 1956), p. 259.
112. Jesse Jones and Edward Angly, *Fifty Billion Dollars* (New York, 1951), p. vii.
113. *New York Times*, January 25, 1945, p. 14.
114. Senate Banking and Currency Committee, *Hearings on H. R. 5667*, 77th Cong., 1st Sess. (Washington, 1941), p. 14.
115. 86 Cong. Rec. 11862 (1940).
116. When they did subject him to a normally (for others) warm interrogation, Jones was quick to show a hair shirt and to take personal offense. For example, see House Subcommittee of the Committee on Foreign and Domestic Commerce, *Hearings on Petroleum Investigation*, 77th Cong., 2nd Sess. (Washington, 1942), pp. 105–107.
117. Timmons, *Jesse H. Jones*, pp. 263–265.
118. *Ibid.*, p. 264.
119. 83 Cong. Rec. 1988 (1938).
120. Senate Subcommittee of Committee on Appropriations, *Hearings on Department of Commerce Appropriation Bill for 1943*, 77th Cong., 2nd Sess. (Washington, 1942), p. 64. See also, Jones and Angly, *Fifty Billion Dollars*, p. 545.
121. Timmons, *Jesse H. Jones*, p. 153.

122. Jones and Angly, *Fifty Billion Dollars*, p. 3.
123. Senate Committee on Expenditure in the Executive Branch, *Hearings on Amendment of Budget and Accounting Act of 1921*, 78th Cong., 1st Sess. (Washington, 1943), p. 104.
124. House Subcommittee of Committee on Appropriations, *Hearings on Department of Commerce Appropriation Bill for 1944*, 78th Cong., 1st Sess. (Washington, 1943), p. 11.
125. Jones and Angly, *op. cit.*, pp. 257, 536; Timmons, *op. cit.*, p. 250; *New York Times*, January 25, 1945, p. 14.
126. House Subcommittee of Committee on Appropriations, *Hearings on Department of Commerce Appropriation Bill for 1942*, 77th Cong., 1st Sess. (Washington, 1941), p. 9.
127. Senate Committee on Expenditures in the Executive Branch, *Hearings on Amendment of Budget and Accounting Act of 1921*, 78th Cong., 1st Sess. (Washington, 1943), pp. 29–31.
128. *Ibid.*, pp. 113–114.
129. *Ibid.*, pp. 118–119.
130. House Subcommittee of Committee on Appropriations, *Hearings on Department of Commerce Appropriation Bill for 1944*, 78th Cong., 1st Sess. (Washington, 1943), p. 8.
131. *Ibid.*, p. 10.
132. Senate Subcommittee of Committee on Appropriations, *Hearings on Department of Commerce Appropriations Bill for 1944*, 78th Cong., 1st Sess. (Washington, 1943), p. 63.
133. House Subcommittee on Committee on Appropriations, *Hearings on Department of Commerce Appropriations Bill for 1945*, 78th Cong., 2nd Sess. (Washington, 1944), p. 107. Jones argued again in 1944 for the restoration of the original amount, using the same rationale. *Ibid.*, pp. 2, 6, 9, 13–14.
134. Senate Committee on Banking and Currency, *Hearings on Increasing the Borrowing Authority of the RFC*, 77th Cong., 1st Sess. (Washington, 1941), pp. 12–14, 20.
135. Senate Committee on Banking and Currency, *Hearings on Increasing the Borrowing Authority of the RFC*, 77th Cong., 2nd Sess. (Washington, 1942), p. 6.
136. *Ibid.*, p. 8. See also, *ibid.*, pp. 10, 41.
137. Timmons, *Jesse H. Jones*, p. 249.
138. Jones and Angly, *Fifty Billion Dollars*, p. 262.
139. Timmons, *Jesse H. Jones*, p. 394. See also Jones and Angly, *Fifty Billion Dollars*, p. 257.
140. Jones and Angly, *Fifty Billion Dollars*, p. 290. See also p. 283.
141. Jones and Angly, *Fifty Billion Dollars*, pp. 262–263; Timmons, *Jesse H. Jones*, p. 252.
142. It is not without importance to note that between January 2, 1932 and the date of the United States' entrance into the war, the RFC author-

ized loans of almost $180,000,000 in Texas. *Report of the RFC,* Third Quarter, 1941 (Washington, 1942).
143. John Gunther, *Roosevelt in Retrospect* (New York, 1950), p. 128.
144. Timmons, *Jesse H. Jones,* pp. 266–267.
145. Daniels, *Man of Independence,* p. 243.
146. Rosenman, *Working With Roosevelt,* pp. 84–85.
147. Jones and Angly, *Fifty Billion Dollars,* p. 218.
148. Harris, *The Advice and Consent of the Senate,* p. 147.
149. Timmons, *Jesse H. Jones,* p. 330.
150. Long, "Power and Administration," p. 258.
151. *New York Times,* January 25, 1945, p. 15.
152. Herring, "Executive-Legislative Responsibilities," p. 1160.

Chapter Seven. The Cabinet and Reform

1. For this architectural interpretation of politics, see David Lawrence, "A Cabinet Building," *U. S. News and World Report,* February 1, 1946, pp. 30–31.
2. Thomas K. Finletter, *Can Representative Government Do the Job?* (New York, 1945), p. 9; Elliott and others, *United States Foreign Policy* (New York, 1952), p. 257; Arthur N. Holcombe, *Our More Perfect Union* (Cambridge, Mass., 1950), p. 422.
3. Woodrow Wilson, *Congressional Government* (Cambridge, 1913), p. 282.
4. R. S. Baker and W. E. Dodd (eds.), *The Public Papers of Woodrow Wilson* (New York, 1952), pp. 128–129.
5. *Ibid.,* p. 127.
6. *Ibid.,* p. 222.
7. *Ibid.,* pp. 112–113.
8. *Ibid.*
9. *Ibid.,* p. 26.
10. *Ibid.,* p. 116.
11. Walter Bagehot, *The English Constitution* (New York, 1889), p. 84.
12. Wilson, *Congressional Government,* p. 260.
13. *Ibid.,* p. 266.
14. *Ibid.,* p. 257.
15. *Ibid.,* p. 259.
16. Baker and Dodd (eds.), *Wilson Papers,* p. 218.
17. *Ibid.,* p. 139.
18. Henry Hazlitt, *A New Constitution Now* (New York, 1942).
19. Elliott and others, *U. S. Foreign Policy,* pp. 256ff; William Y. Elliott, *The Need for Constitutional Reform* (New York, 1935), chap. 9; Finletter, *Representative Government,* Part 3.
20. Edward S. Corwin, "Wanted: A New Type of Cabinet," *New York Times Magazine,* October 10, 1948, p. 14ff. All of the succeeding quotations from Corwin are from this article.

NOTES TO CHAPTER SEVEN

21. Leonard D. White, *The Jeffersonians: A Study in Administrative History 1801–1829* (New York, 1951), pp. 36–37, 40–41, 77, 81–82, 88.

22. Charles Hyneman, *Bureaucracy in a Democracy* (New York, 1950), chap. 25; Roland Young, *This Is Congress* (New York, 1943), pp. 247ff; George Galloway, *The Legislative Process* (New York, 1953), pp. 445ff; House and Senate Joint Committee on the Organization of Congress, *Hearings on the Organization of Congress*, 79th Cong., 1st Sess. (Washington, 1945), pp. 242–243.

23. Finletter, *Representative Government*, p. 9; Galloway, *Legislative Process*, p. 446.

24. Galloway, *Legislative Process*, pp. 454–455.

25. House and Senate Joint Committee on the Organization of Congress, *Hearings on the Organization of Congress*, 79th Cong., 1st Sess. (Washington, 1945), p. 124. See also Holcombe, *Our More Perfect Union*, p. 233.

26. Elliott and others, *U. S. Foreign Policy*, p. 185.

27. The proposal that Cabinet members vote in the legislature is a more sweeping proposal and usually accompanies reform programs which lean in the direction of the British system. Cf. Wilson, *Congressional Government*; Elliott, *Constitutional Reform*.

28. Estes Kefauver, "The Need for Better Executive-Legislative Teamwork in the National Government," *American Political Science Review*, 1944, pp. 317–325; Finletter, *Representative Government*, Appendix B; Harold J. Laski, *The American Presidency* (New York, 1940), pp. 96ff.

29. The procedural problems are discussed in Galloway, *Legislative Process*, pp. 445ff.

30. Laski, *American Presidency*, p. 110.

31. *Ibid.*

32. *Ibid.*, p. 107.

33. See Charles Seymour (ed.), *The Intimate Papers of Colonel House* (Cambridge, Mass., 1926), III, 47, for Wilson's later discussion of this contention, in which he agreed with Laski.

34. Finletter, *Representative Government*, p. 174.

35. House and Senate Joint Committee on the Organization of Congress, *Hearings on the Organization of Congress*, 79th Cong., 1st Sess. (Washington, 1945), p. 503.

36. For an example of this sort of disloyalty where no removal power was used, see Stephen K. Bailey, *Congress Makes a Law* (New York, 1950), pp. 162–163.

37. Bertram Gross, *The Legislative Struggle* (New York, 1953), pp. 128–129.

38. Senator Kefauver says that most of the Cabinet members to whom he spoke were in favor of the proposal, but that some were not. House and Senate Joint Committee on the Organization of Congress, *Hearings on the Organization of Congress*, 79th Cong., 1st Sess. (Washington, 1945), p. 85.

THE CABINET AND REFORM

For specific mixed reactions from Cabinet members, see David Houston, *Eight Years with Wilson's Cabinet* (New York, 1926), p. 56; William C. Redfield, *With Congress and Cabinet* (New York, 1951), pp. 48–50.

39. Marshall E. Dimock, *The Executive in Action* (New York, 1945), p. 242.

40. Bradley Nash, *Staffing the Presidency*, National Planning Association Pamphlet (Washington, 1952), p. 41.

41. Edward H. Hobbs, *Behind the President* (Washington, 1954), p. 216.

42. Arthur W. MacMahon, "The Future Organizational Pattern of the Executive Branch," *American Political Science Review*, December, 1944, p. 1186.

43. Clinton Rossiter, *The American Presidency* (New York, 1956), pp. 148–150.

44. Hobbs, *Behind the President*, pp. 223, 225.

45. William Yandell Elliott, "The President's Role in Administrative Management," unpublished manuscript, Harvard University Graduate School of Public Administration, ca. 1940.

46. John Gaus, Leonard White, Marshall Dimock, *The Frontiers of Public Administration* (Chicago, 1936), chap. 5.

47. Nash, *Staffing the Presidency*, pp. ix–x.

48. Herman Miles Somers, *Presidential Agency: OWMR* (Cambridge, Mass., 1950), pp. 219ff.

49. See Hobbs, *Behind the President*, p. 219.

50. *Hoover Commission Report on Organization of the Executive Branch of Government* (New York, 1949), pp. 17–18.

51. Gaus, White, and Dimock, *Public Administration*, pp. 83–84.

52. Elliott, "The President's Role in Administrative Management."

53. Nash, *Staffing the Presidency*, p. 38.

54. Don K. Price, "Staffing the Presidency," *American Political Science Review*, December, 1946, p. 1165.

55. Rossiter, *American Presidency*, p. 149.

56. The difference between superimposition and evolution from within is the difference between the reform proposals of George A. Graham, "The Presidency and the Executive Office of the President," *Journal of Politics*, November, 1950, and MacMahon, "The Future Organizational Pattern of the Executive Branch," pp. 1179ff.

57. Robert E. Sherwood, *Roosevelt and Hopkins* (New York, 1948), p. 159.

58. See Richard E. Neustadt, "Presidency and Legislation: Planning the President's Program," *American Political Science Review*, December, 1955, p. 1019.

59. Hobbs, *Behind the President*, chap. 9.

Index

NOTE. Material in the notes has not been indexed, except in cases where notes contain additional substantive material which the reader would not normally expect to find there. A large number of the notes not indexed contain extensive bibliographical references which might, in the absence of a bibliography, be consulted by the interested reader.

Acheson, Dean G. (Secretary of State, 1949–1953): 288; and H. Truman, 43, 49, 213, 214; and NSC, 150; and Congress, 200, 208, 213–214, 215, 304n48; and Cabinet reform, 261–262

Adams, Sen. Alva, 234

Adams, John Quincy, 256

Adams, Sherman, 96, 103, 148, 149, 154

Administration. *See* Departmental administration; Coordination, interdepartmental

Advice: presidential attitudes toward, 35–37; sounding board type of, 89, 112–113, 124–125, 128, 130, 155–156; specialized policy, type of, 89, 112–113, 142–143, 155; Cabinet and, 100, 104–107, 116–117. *See also* individual Presidents; President

Agriculture Department: 223, 232, 233; origins of, 24, 27; and F. Roosevelt, 62; policy, Cabinet discussion of, 107. *See also* individual Secretaries of Agriculture

American Bankers Association, 237

American Farm Bureau Federation, 73, 169, 231, 280n105

American Federation of Labor, 24, 74, 168, 227

American Livestock Association, 73

American Medical Association, 23, 276n54

Anderson, Clinton P. (Secretary of Agriculture, 1945–1948), 61, 288, 294

Anderson, Robert B. (Secretary of the Treasury, 1957–), 288

Appleby, Paul, 142, 222

Appointment, of Cabinet: general discussion of, 51–53, 259-260; President's influence on, 15, 53–58, 81–87; public attitudes toward, 51–53, 63–65, 82, 160–161, 166–167; predictions about, 52, 85–86; and the political system, 53, 84–87; finances as factor in, 59, 70, 284n29; incentives and drawbacks, 59-62; socio-economic factors in, 59, 62–63; 72–75, 80–81, 86, 284n29, 286n70, 289n110, 298–299n26; unplanned nature of, 61–62; ideal qualifications for, 63–67, 75, 82; political experience as qualification for, 64, 75–76, 79–80, 83–84, 193–194, 202, 205, 222–223, 288 notes 102–104, 298n13; administrative experience as qualification for, 64, 75, 76–77, 83–84, 193, 222–223, 224–226, 288 notes 101–103; availability as criterion for, 67–77; balance as criterion for, 67–68, 77–81; party factors in, 68–70, 78, 79, 80, 81, 83; loyalty as factor in, 70–71; geography as factor in, 71–72, 78–79, 286n70, 288n100; personal acquaintance as factor in, 71, 77, 83–84, 288 notes 100–102; interest groups as factor in, 72–75; key states as factor in, 79; in-term appointment, 82–84, 288 notes 100, 101, 102, 104

314 INDEX

Appointment, of other officials, 226–227
Aristotle, 9
Assistant to the President; Cabinet activity of, 94, 137, 145
Assistants for Cabinet Coordination, 143, 147
Attorney General: role of, 14, 16, 17, 20, 24, 25, 55; and party, 70; public prestige of, 165–166. See also individual Attorneys General
Attorney General's Office, 23

Bagby, Wesley, 301
Bagehot, Walter, 255
Baker, Newton D. (Secretary of War, 1916–1921): 288, 284n29; and W. McAdoo, 77; and Col. House, 151
Baker, Ray Stannard, 122, 191
Barran, Clarence W., 298
Barry, Richard, 171-172, 298–299
Benson, Ezra Taft (Secretary of Agriculture, 1953–   ): 85, 183, 297n10; Cabinet activity of, 168, 183; speechmaking activity of, 186
Biffle, Leslie, 236
Borah, Sen. William, 189, 287n90
Board of Economic Warfare, 242–244
Brain trust, 37
Brannan, Charles F. (Secretary of Agriculture, 1948–1953), 164
Brecht, Arnold, 142
Brown, Walter F. (Postmaster General, 1929–1933), 70, 286
Brownell, Herbert (Attorney General, 1953–1957), 70, 197, 286
Brownlow, Louis, 134
Brogan, Denis, 19
Brooks, Edward, 210, 304n39
Bryan, William Jennings (Secretary of State, 1913–1915): 60, 77, 202, 222; appointment of, 75–76; Cabinet activity of, 120, 121; resignation of, 121, 163, 192–193, 301–302n95; prestige of, 161; and party, 189–195; and departmental administration, 190–191, 193, 301 n83; and foreign policy, 190–191; and W. Wilson, 190–193; and Congress, 191–192
Buchanan, James, 160
Bullitt, William, 45
Bureau of Foreign and Domestic Commerce, 241–242
Bureau of Labor, 22
Bureau of the Budget: 5; Cabinet relations of, 20, 94, 99, 106, 135, 153; and coordination, 99, 141, 146, 152, 153; and Cabinet members, 239–240, 240–242
Bureaus, executive, 227–230, 232–234
Burleson, Albert S. (Postmaster General, 1913–1921): 286, 287; appointment of, 70, 201; and Congress, 201–202; and party, 201; and W. Wilson, 201–202, 222–223; departmental activity of, 222–223
Business groups, Cabinet relationships of, 63, 72, 127–128, 168, 169, 170, 171, 172, 237–238, 238–239, 242, 244–245, 298n20, 304n46
Butler, Sen. William, 288
Byrd, Gov. Harry, 285
Byrnes, James F. (Secretary of State, 1945–1947; Director, Office of War Mobilization and Reconverion): as Secretary of State; 177, 287, 288, and H. Truman, 43, 45, 49, 282n153; resignation of, 49, 163; prestige of, 162, 165; as Director of OWMR; 202, 265; and F. Roosevelt, 149; and Cabinet members, 151; and Budget Bureau, 152; and H. Hopkins, 152

Cabinet (American): need for study of, 3, 273n1; comment on, 3, 154, 155; origins of, 4, 9–20, 273n2; institutional characteristics of, 4, 5, 16–20, 92–98, 113; institutional weakness of, 16–17, 19–20, 29–33, 113, 130, 139–140, 156, 184–185, 247, 249, 257–258, 275n41; comparison with British Cabinet, 9–11; first use of term, 14, 17, 18,

275n33; membership in, 20–21, 86, 93–94, 99–100, 275n44, 289n 110; growth of, 21–28; public attitudes toward, 5, 62, 152, 159–161, 290n17, 300n68; and other executive agencies, 145, 149–154, 243–244, 268–269; reform of, 3, 250–271
Cabinet, idea of in other societies, 9–10. *See also* Great Britain, Cabinet; Primitive societies
Cabinet committees, 140, 146, 263–265, 268. *See also* National Security Council
Cabinet government. *See* Great Britain, Cabinet
Cabinet meeting: origins of, 17, 18; frequency of, 17, 92–93, 98–99; voting in, 18–19, 94, 118; potential functions of, 88–92; flexibility of, 92–114 *passim*, 154; personnel, 93–94, 99–100; procedures in, 94–97, 101–112, 142, 143, 145, 146–147, 290n20, 290n22; minutes of, 94–95, 96; limitations on effectiveness of, 98–103, 107–113, 114–119, 120–124 *passim*, 131–141, 142–149, 155; examples of activity in, 101–102, 104–105, 105–106, 108, 115–117, 120–124, 125–128, 131–141 *passim*, 145, 146–147, 138, 279n92, 290n22; effectiveness of, 104–107, 109–110, 112–113, 122–123, 126–127, 130, 155–156; attitude of members toward, 108–109, 131–141 *passim;* disclosure of information from, 139; follow through of action taken in, 145–149; public attitude toward, 161
Cabinet members: and Congress, 16, 173, 183, 189, 191–192, 197–216, 231–234, 236–246, 250–263, 302n 18, 303n26, 304n48, 310n36; conflict among, 18, 77–78, 112–113, 115–116, 131–136 *passim*, 140, 144, 145, 150, 151, 183, 242–244, 288n98, 290n29, 291n32, 295n16; roles and role conflicts of, 25, 56, 158–159, 197–199, 200, 217–218, 231–234, 238–239, 247–248; effects of socio-economic views of, 25, 77–78, 100, 111, 115–116, 117–118, 140, 169, 171–173, 174, 177, 189–190, 211–212, 219, 220, 244–245; attitudes toward each other, 27–28, 131–141, 247; public attitudes toward, 151–152, 159–178, 186; assistance to President by, 159–171, 180–187 *passim*, 194, 208–216, 224–234, 244–245, 246–249; and interest groups, 168–169, 231–233, 237, 238–239, 242, 244–245; political ambitions of, 183, 184; and political parties, 185–195, 227, 236–237, 300n64; departmental activity of, 217–234, 238–244; and other executive agencies 239–240, 240–242. *See also* individual Secretaries
Cabinet norm, 63–67, 75, 82
Cabinet rank. *See* Cabinet, membership in
Cabinet Secretary, activities of, 94, 96–97, 103, 104–110, 136–137, 147–149. *See also* Secretariat
Castle, William R., 227
Civilian Conservation Corps, 46, 103
Chamber of Commerce, 169, 237
Chapman, Oscar (Secretary of the Interior, 1948–1953), 288
Checks and balances. *See* Separation of powers
Christian Science Monitor, 64
Chief Justice, U. S. Supreme Court, 12, 17, 43
Chiefs of Staff, 37
Civil Service Commission, 94
Clark, Thomas C. (Attorney General, 1945–1949), 287
Clearance, legislative, 106, 143–144, 153. *See also* Coordination, interdepartmental
Cleveland, Grover, 290n20, 292n54, 295n14
Coherence, administrative, 91–92, 98, 99, 100, 104–107, 109–111, 117, 125, 128–130, 155–156, 294 n89
Colby, Bainbridge (Secretary of State, 1920–1921), 56

Collective responsibility, lack of, 13, 14, 27–28, 94, 115, 132
Commerce Department: 24, 227, 246; organization of, 26, 228; and F. Roosevelt, 62, 170, 171; under H. Hoover, 220–221, 291n40; under J. Jones, 234–247; Business Advisory Council of, 237. *See also* individual Secretaries
Commissioner of Agriculture, 22
Commissioner of Labor, 22–23
Committees, congressional, and Cabinet members, 168, 197, 204–210 *passim*, 228, 235, 236, 238–244, 262, 307n116
Confirmation, of Cabinet nominations. *See* Senate
Congress: and Cabinet members, 15, 16, 197–216, 233–246, 250–263; and Cabinet, 199–200, 302n18, 303n26, 304n48; creation of executive departments by, 22–26. *See also* Committees, Congressional
Congress of Industrial Organizations, 169, 227
Congressmen, appointment to Cabinet of, 60–61, 79–80, 83
Constitutional Convention, debates in relating to Cabinet, 11–13
Constitution: provisions of, relating to Cabinet, 13, 14, 15, 19, 275n38; and American political institutions, 19; provisions of, relating to President, 196, 216
Coolidge, Calvin: 221; decision-making techniques of, 40–41, 117–118, 280n107; and presidential leadership, 44, 202–203; techniques of delegation of, 42–43; attitude toward Cabinet, 43, 48, 111; attitude toward Cabinet loyalty, 48, 49; Cabinet selection methods of, 73, 78, 79, 80, 83, 288n104; Cabinet practices of, 92, 93, 95, 117–118, 289–290n13; and individual Cabinet members, 42, 48, 117–118, 162, 172–173, 176, 186, 189, 215, 224, 299n34; and Teapot Dome, 294n2

Coon, Carleton, 4
Coordination, interdepartmental: 27–29, 90–91, 99, 104–107, 141–154, 155, 263–269, 292n49. *See also* Departmentalism
Coordinator for Cabinet Affairs, 103, 105
Compensatory Cabinet theory, 30–33
Corps of Army Engineers, 228, 229, 233–234
Corwin, Edward S: and Cabinet reform, 254–257, 262; also quoted, 3, 275
Council of Economic Advisers, 141, 153
Cox, James, 73
Cummings, Homer S. (Attorney General, 1933–1939), 70
Custom, as basis for Cabinet, 16–20, 28, 92–101
Cutting, Sen. Bronson, 285

Daniels, Jonathan, 30, 245
Daniels, Josephus (Secretary of the Navy, 1913–1921): 101, 151, 286, 287, 304; and Congress, 206; appointment of, 224; departmental activity of, 232; also quoted, 168
Daugherty, Harry M. (Attorney General, 1921–1924): 30, 70, 71, 222, 281, 286; and C. Coolidge, 48, 189; removal of, 48, 189; and W. Harding, 115, 187–189, 300–301n70; Cabinet activity of, 116; appointment of, 187–188, 301n72; and political party, 187–189, 194; departmental activity of, 188, 193; and Congress, 189; also quoted, 57, 299
Davies, Joseph, 45
Davis, Dwight F. (Secretary of War, 1925–1929), 170
Dawson, Rep. William, 276
Davis, James J. (Secretary of Labor, 1921–1930): departmental activity of, 219; appointment of, 74
Defense Department: 227; origins of, 23, 26, 276n53; and interest groups, 24–25, 26; organization

of, 26; and Eisenhower, 153. See also individual Secretaries
Decision-making, presidential techniques of, 37–42. See also Advice; individual Presidents
Delegation of authority, presidential techniques for, 42–47
Democratic National Committee, 69, 70, 185
Democratic Party Chairman, 69, 70, 185
Denby, Edwin (Secretary of the Navy, 1921–1924): 30; appointment of, 85, 224; Cabinet activity of, 132, 214, 224; and Congress, 214–215; and C. Coolidge, 215; resignation of, 215
Departmental administration, problems of: appointment, 226–227; reorganization, 227–228, 302n18; bureau autonomy, 228–230; time, 230; presidential relations, 231–234
Departmentalism, 131–141, 140, 156, 185, 238–244, 247–249, 261, 267–268, 295n14, 295n21
Departments. See Executive Departments
Dern, George H. (Secretary of War, 1933–1936): Cabinet activity of, 79; departmental activity of, 233–234, 306n79
Dewey, Thomas, 79
Dimock, Marshall, 230, 263
Dirksen, Sen. Everett, 212
Doak, William N. (Secretary of Labor, 1930–1933), 74, 79
Dodge, Joseph, 21–22
Domestic policy: Cabinet discussions of, 112–113, 115–117, 125–126, 135, 294n89. See also individual Departments, policy of
Donaldson, Jesse M. (Postmaster General, 1947–1953), 70
Donovan, Robert, 44, 108, 139
Donovan, William, 45
Dooley, Mister (Peter Finley Dunne), 52, 76, 84, 224
Douglas, Lewis, 135
Dulles, John Foster (Secretary of State, 1953–): 148; Cabinet activity of, 140; prestige of, 162; press conferences of, 167; departmental activity of, 225–226
Dunne, Peter Finley. See Dooley, Mister
Durkin, Martin P. (Secretary of Labor, 1953): 220; appointment of, 69, 74–75, 80–81, 161; and S. Weeks, 78, 111, 140; resignation of, 80–81; and labor groups, 168

Easton, David, 7
Economic Development Committee, 237
Edison, Charles (Secretary of the Navy, 1940), 282
Eisenhower, Dwight D.: 156, 159, 160; Cabinet practices of, 3, 35, 92, 94, 96–97, 103–113, 118, 130, 136–137, 139–141, 143–144, 147–149, 152–154, 156; and presidential leadership, 35, 159–160; attitude toward Cabinet of, 35; decision-making techniques of, 41–42, 110–113, 147, 148; techniques of delegation of, 44, 110; Cabinet selection methods of, 63, 66, 71, 78–83 passim, 181, 182, 288n100; and individual Cabinet members, 118, 220, 231
Elliott, William Y.: and Cabinet reform, 254, 264, 265, 266; also quoted, 258–59
Evans-Pritchard, E. E., 4
Ewing, Oscar: 215; and Congress, 211–212, 213; also quoted, 164
Executive agencies: and the Cabinet, 93–94, 145, 149–154, 243–244, 268–269; and Cabinet members, 239–240, 240–242
Executive departments: in pre-constitutional period, 11; in Constitution, 12, 13, 14; and Cabinet membership, 20–21; origins of, 22–26; differences among, 22–26, 227; relation of President to, 14, 217–218; Secretary's personal influence on, 219–226, 306n79, 306

n84; administrative problems in, 226–231, 233
Executive Office of the President: 141, 148, 152, 153, 269; relations with Cabinet, 154
Executive-legislative relations. *See* Legislative-executive relations

Fair Employment Practices Commission, 231
Fall, Albert B. (Secretary of the Interior, 1921–1923): 30, 294; appointment of, 60; Cabinet activity of, 116, 132, 137
Farley, James A. (Postmaster General, 1933–1940): 47, 69; and Cabinet selection, 58, 284n24; Cabinet activity of, 100, 127–128, 138; and F. Roosevelt, 184; also quoted, 155
Farm groups: Cabinet relationships of, 72, 73, 168, 169, 170–171, 280n105
Federal Loan Administrator, 234
Federal Loan Agency, 94
Federal Security Administrator, 164, 211
Federal Security Agency, 20–21, 23, 94
Federal Works Agency, 94
Ferguson, Sen. Homer, 240
Finletter, Thomas K., 254, 258
Flanders, Sen. Ralph, 304n48
Flemming, Arthur (Secretary of Health, Education and Welfare, 1958–   ), 288
Folsom, Marion B. (Secretary of Health, Education and Welfare, 1955–1958), 288
Ford, Henry II, 63
Forest Service, 232
Foreign policy: Cabinet discussions of, 108, 109, 120–124, 126–127, 135–136, 145, 152–153, 279n92, 292n54, 293n68
Forrestal, James V. (Secretary of the Navy, 1944–1947; Secretary of Defense, 1947–1949): 125, 288; Cabinet activity of, 125–145; and H. Ickes, 135; and Congress, 204, 302–303n19; also quoted, 294
Fowler, Dorothy, 23–24

Galloway, George, 258
Garner, John N., 184, 236
Garrison, Lindley M. (Secretary of War, 1913–1916): 215, 286, 288, 304; appointment of, 61–62; and W. J. Bryan, 77; and J. Daniels, 133, 294n10, 295n16; and Congress, 209–211; and W. Wilson, 210–211; resignation of, 210, 295n 10; Cabinet activity of, 295n10
Gaus, John, 264, 266
General Post Office, 22, 23
Geography: as factor in Cabinet appointment, 71-72, 78–79, 286n70, 288n100
Glass, Carter (Secretary of the Treasury, 1919–1920; Representative; Senator): 61, 192, 236, 285
Good, James W. (Secretary of War, 1929), 286
Gore, Howard M. (Secretary of Agriculture, 1924–1925), 286
Graham, George A., 311
Gray, Robert K. (Cabinet Secretary), 96
Great Britain: Cabinet, 9, 10, 11, 13, 251–254, 255, 259, 260, 264, 273n2 (Ch. 1), 310n27, 282n146
Green, William, 74
Gregory, Thomas W. (Attorney General, 1914–1919), 101, 288
Gulick, Luther, 3

Hamilton, Alexander: 198; and Congress, 16; also quoted, 13
Hannegan, Robert E. (Postmaster General, 1945–1947), 69, 185
Hard, William, 32
Harding, Warren: 22; and presidential leadership, 30–31, 33, 34, 35, 182, 183, 202; attitude toward Cabinet, 30–31, 34–35, 65, 66; Cabinet selection methods of, 30–31, 57, 65, 66, 67, 71, 73, 76–80 *passim*, 181–182, 298n25; attitude toward advice, 36, 277n79; Cabi-

INDEX

net practices of, 92, 93, 114–117, 138, 139, 291n40; decision-making techniques of, 114–117; and Teapot Dome, 132; and individual Cabinet members, 114–117, 162, 172, 176, 187–189, 280n115, 291 n38, 291n40, 300–301n70; techniques of delegation of, 280n115, 280–281n120
Hare, Rep. Butler, 242
Harriman, W. Averell (Secretary of Commerce, 1946–1948; Mutual Security Administrator), 45, 149, 152, 265, 281
Harris, Joseph, 246
Hart, James, 16
Hauge, Gabriel, 103
Hay, Rep. James, 198, 210
Hays, Will H. (Postmaster General, 1921–1922), 69, 132, 187, 294n3
Hazlitt, Henry, 254
Health, Education and Welfare Department: 277; origins of, 20–21, 23, 276n54; and interest groups, 23, 24–25, 26, 276n54; organization of, 26, 27; policy, Cabinet discussion of, 105. *See also* individual Secretaries
Hendrick, Burton, 183, 273
Hensel, H. Struve, 217, 218
Herring, E. Pendleton, 3, 152, 184, 198
Hill, Sen. Lister, 240
Hinsdale, Mary, 155
Hobbs, Edward, 263, 264, 265
Hobby, Oveta Culp (Secretary of Health, Education and Welfare, 1953–1955): 286; appointment of, 79, 181; Cabinet activity of, 20–21, 105
Hoebel, E. Adamson, 10
Hoffman, Rep. Clare, 21
Hoover Commission, 46–47, 232, 265
Hoover, Herbert C. (Secretary of Commerce, 1921–1928; President): 234, 297; *as President* and presidential leadership, 31–32, 186, 277n67; Cabinet selection methods of, 32–33, 57, 59, 66, 71–83 *passim;* attitude toward advice, 36–37, 278n83; and individual Cabinet members, 36, 71, 119, 163, 173, 177, 186, 291–292n47; decision-making techniques of, 37–38, 278–279n88, 279n92; attitude toward Cabinet, 57, 66; Cabinet practices of, 93, 95, 279n92; techniques of delegation of, 280–281n120; *as Secretary of Commerce,* appointment of, 30, 60, 76–77, 221; Cabinet activity of, 114; and W. Harding, 117, 291n40; and C. Coolidge, 118; prestige of, 161, 163, 170; departmental activity of, 220–221, 228; and A. Mellon, 291n32; an H. C. Wallace, 77, 291n32; and C. E. Hughes, 291n40; also quoted, 150
Hopkins, Harry L. (Secretary of Commerce, 1939–1940; Presidential assistant): 45, 149; and F. Roosevelt, 46–47, 71, 184, 268; Cabinet relations of, 94, 138, 151, 152, 297n43; also quoted, 163
House, Col. Edward: 123, 149; and W. Wilson, 46–47, 71, 76; Cabinet relations of, 58, 151, 201, 297n43; also quoted, 38, 191
House of Representatives: 15, 16; former members of, in Cabinet, 79–80. *See also* Committees, congressional
Houston, David F. (Secretary of Agriculture, 1913–1920; Secretary of the Treasury, 1920–1921): and public prestige, 165–166, 167–168, 298n13; Cabinet activity of, 121–123, 133, 134; appointment of, 286n64; also quoted, 220, 221
Howe, Louis M., 58, 284n23, 284n25
Hughes, Charles Evans (Secretary of State, 1921–1925): 177, 284, 297; appointment of, 30; Cabinet activity of, 116, 132, 133, 138; and W. Harding, 117, 162, 280n 115; and C. Coolidge, 42, 117, 162, 186; and A. Fall, 137; public prestige of, 161, 162; and H. Hoover, 291n40

Hull, Cordell (Secretary of State, 1933–1944): 287; and F. Roosevelt, 45–46, 174, 175–177, 184, 281n134; appointment of, 60, 78, 85, 173; Cabinet activity of, 100, 126, 133, 135, 138, 174–176; public prestige of, 171, 173–177, 223–224; and Congress, 173, 204–206, 303n21, 303n23; and political party, 174, 176; departmental activity of, 174, 223–224

Hurley, Patrick J. (Secretary of War, 1929–1933): 45; and political party, 186, 288n102; appointment of, 288n102; and Congress, 303 n26

Humphrey, George M. (Secretary of the Treasury, 1953–1957): Cabinet activity of, 118, 140; and D. Eisenhower, 118; and public prestige, 165; appointment of, 287n91

Hyde, Arthur M. (Secretary of Agriculture, 1929–1933): speechmaking activities of, 186

Hyman, Sidney, 55, 107

Ickes, Harold L. (Secretary of the Interior): 47, 129, 279, 286; and F. Roosevelt, 37, 46, 184, 233; resignation of, 49; appointment of, 61, 68, 85, 181, 285n37; Cabinet activity of, 128, 135–136, 146–147, 186; and J. Forrestal, 135; and Hull, 135–136; and H. Hopkins, 77, 151; and D. Richberg, 151; departmental activity of, 233, 226–227, 307n103; also quoted, 71, 98, 125

"Inner cabinet," 117, 118–119, 141, 311n56

Institution: definition of, 4; study of, 4; Cabinet's characteristics as, 4, 5, 16–20, 92–98, 113; Cabinet's problems as, 16–17, 19–20, 97–113, 130, 139–141, 155–156, 184–185, 247, 249, 257–258, 269, 275n41

Interest groups: 276n57; and executive departments, 23–27, 168–169, 226, 227, 228–233, 276n54;

and Cabinet members, 72–75, 199, 237–238, 231–232, 238–239, 242, 244–245, 298n17, 298n20

In-term Cabinet appointment, 82–84, 288n100–102, 288n104

Interior Department: 223, 227, 232, 279n99; origins of, 22, 24; clientele of, 24, 71; organization of, 26, 228; policy, Cabinet discussion of, 105, 135–136, 145; under Ickes, 233. See also individual Secretaries

Jackson, Robert H. (Attorney General, 1940–1941), 138

Jackson, Andrew: 255; Cabinet practices of, 119

Jefferson, Thomas: 255; Cabinet practices of, 18; also quoted, 16

Johnson, Sen. Edwin, 71–72

Johnson, Sen. Hiram, 285

Johnson, Louis A. (Secretary of Defense, 1949–1950): 236; and Acheson, 150; resignation of, 150, 282n153; and Congress, 228

Jones, Jesse H. (Secretary of Commerce, 1940–1945): 261; appointment of, 60, 234, 238; and public opinion poll, 165; Cabinet activity of, 133, 134, 138; and F. Roosevelt, 84, 184, 238–246, 282; and Congress, 235–246, 307n116; and political parties, 236–237; and business groups, 237–238, 308–309n142; departmental activity of, 238–244; and H. A. Wallace, 77–78, 165, 242–244; resignation of, 245–246; also quoted, 125

Joint Legislative Council, 256, 257

Joslin, Theodore, 37, 38

Judd, Rep. Walter, 21

Justice Department: origins of, 20, 22, 23; under H. Daugherty, 132, 188. See also individual Attorneys General

Kefauver, Sen. Estes, 259, 261, 310

Kellogg, Frank B. (Secretary of State, 1925–1929): appointment of, 42, 288n104

INDEX

Kellogg-Briand Pact, 42
Kent, Frank, 172
Key, V. O., 179
"Kitchen cabinet," 5, 118–119, 141, 202
Knox, Frank (Secretary of the Navy, 1940–1944): appointment of, 68–69
Knox, Sen. Philander, 77

Labor Department: origins of, 22, 27; and labor groups, 24, 27, 169, 233; organization of, 26; and W. Harding, 62; policy, Cabinet discussion of, 135; under W. B. Wilson, 219; under J. Davis, 219; under F. Perkins, 219; under M. Tobin, 219. See also individual Secretaries
Labor groups, 72, 73–75, 168–169, 219, 227
Lamont, Robert P. (Secretary of Commerce, 1929–1932): 278, appointment of, 85
Landon, Alf, 80
Lane, Franklin K. (Secretary of the Interior, 1913–1920): and W. Wilson, 58; appointment of, 59, 284n29–30, 286, 288; Cabinet activity of, 122–124; departmental activity of, 230; also quoted, 39, 122, 123, 124
Lansing, Robert (Secretary of State, 1915–1920): and W. Wilson, 44, 56, 84; appointment of, 56; Cabinet activity of, 120, 122, 290n29, 292n50
Laski, Harold: and Cabinet reform, 260–261, 262
Learned, Henry B., 9, 155
Legislative-Executive Cabinet, 254, 257–258
Legislative-executive relations, 197–216, 235–246, 250–263. See also Committees; Congress; Congressmen
Lewis, John L., 74
Liaison, legislative-executive, 200–203, 258–259

Lincoln, Abraham: Cabinet practices of, 29, 92, 126, 181, 182, 183
Lindsay, Samuel, 51, 82
Lodge, Sen. Henry Cabot, 189
Long, Norton, 178, 229, 230
Lowden, Frank, 284, 287n87
Lowry, Edward, 172
Loyalty of Cabinet member: presidential attitudes toward, 47–49, 282n146; Cabinet member attitudes toward, 163, 244. See also Removal power
Luce, Rep. Robert, 236

MacEachron, David, 73, 219
MacMahon, Arthur, 263–264, 311n56
MacReynolds, J. C. (Attorney General, 1913–1914), 286, 287, 288
Madison, James, 14, 256
Maritime Commission, 145
Marshall, George C. (Secretary of State, 1947–1949): 163, 288; and H. Truman, 43, 162; Cabinet activity of, 145; public prestige of, 162
Marshall, Thomas, 93
Mason, George, 12
Mellon, Andrew W. (Secretary of the Treasury, 1921–1922): 286; appointment of, 30, 77, 171–172, 298–299n26; and W. Harding, 117, 172, 176; and C. Coolidge, 117, 172–173, 176, 299n34; public prestige of, 171-173; and business groups, 171–172; Cabinet activity of, 132, 172–173, 294n3; and H. Hoover, 173, 177, 291n32
Meyers v. United States, 47
McAdoo, William G. (Secretary of the Treasury, 1913–1919): 77, 286; public prestige of, 170; Cabinet activity of, 122, 123, 134, 225; departmental activity of, 220–221, 225; appointment of, 284n29; also quoted, 300
McClellan, Sen. John, 211
McKay, Douglas (Secretary of the Interior, 1953–1956): 63, 298; appointment of, 85; Cabinet activity

of, 106; lack of press conferences of, 167; departmental activity, 225
McKellar, Sen. Kenneth, 237
McKinley, William, 52
McGrath, J. Howard (Attorney General, 1949–1952): 70; resignation of, 282n153
Millett, John, 217, 218
Mills, Ogden L. (Secretary of the Treasury, 1932–1933): and H. Hoover, 119, 173, 291–292n47; appointment of, 288n102
Mitchell, James P. (Secretary of Labor, 1953–): and S. Weeks, 140; and Eisenhower, 231, 288; and labor groups, 231
Mitchell, William D. (Attorney General, 1929–1933): appointment of, 68, 285–286n58
Moley, Raymond: and C. Hull, 45, 223; and Cabinet selection, 58
Monroe, James, 71, 256
Moore, John Basset, 191
Morgenthau, Henry (Secretary of the Treasury, 1934–1945): 47; and F. Roosevelt, 45, 71, 281, 282n146; Cabinet activity of, 45, 127, 138
Morgenthau Plan, 40
Morris, Gouverneur, 12, 13
Mullen, Arthur, 285
Mutual Security Administrator, 94, 99
Mutual Security Agency, 152

Nash, Bradley, 263, 264, 266, 273
Nation, 290n29, 294
National Association of Manufacturers, 169
National Defense Advisory Commission, 46
National Grange, 73, 169
National Housing Agency, 94
National Emergency Council, 149, 150, 151
National Farmers' Union, 73, 169
National Security Council: 100; and coordination, 141, 150, 152, 153, 263, 264, 268–269

National Security Resources Board, 94
National Wholesale Association Council, 237
Navy Department: 22, 233; origins of, 18, 23; and Defense Department, 25, 276n53; policy, discussion of in Cabinet, 135, 145; under E. Denby, 224–225; under C. Wilbur, 224–225; and F. Roosevelt, 281n131. *See also* individual Secretaries
Neustadt, Richard E., 107
New, Harry S. (Postmaster General, 1923), 70
New York Times: publicity of Cabinet members in, 165–167; Cabinet speculation in, 85
New Republic, 192
Nicholson, Harold, 278

Office of Defense Mobilization (now, Office of Civilian and Defense Mobilization), 99, 141, 152, 153
Office of War Mobilization and Reconversion, 152, 265
Ogg, Frederick A., 30
Olney, Richard, 295
Ouhlahan, R. V., 172

Page, Walter H., 133
Palmer, A. Mitchell (Attorney General, 1919–1921), 284, 288
Patterson, Bradley H., 104, 105, 289
Payne, John B. (Secretary of the Interior, 1920–1921), 286, 288
Penrose, Sen. Boies, 77
Pepper, Sen. George W., 189
Perkins, Frances (Secretary of Labor, 1933–1945): 125; appointment of, 74–75; Cabinet activity of, 125, 126, 127, 135, 138; and public prestige, 164, 167; departmental activity of, 219; also quoted, 44
Permanent Representative to the United Nations, 94
Persons, Maj. Gen. Wilton, 200
Pierce, Franklin, 160
Pinckney, Charles, 12, 14

Policy discussions in Cabinet. *See* Domestic policy; Foreign policy; under individual Departments, policy

Political parties: and Cabinet appointment, 18, 68–70, 75, 78–83 *passim*, 181–182; and the Cabinet (general), 159–160, 180–183, 184–185, 227, 300n55, 300n64; and Cabinet members, 176, 182–184, 186–195, 201, 236–237; proposed changes in Cabinet relations of, 55–56, 251–254

Political system, American: pluralism of, 6–7, 28–29, 53, 84–87, 131, 161, 177–178, 194, 215–216, 246–249, 252–254, 255, 257, 260–261, 262, 266–267, 269–271

Polk, James K.: and presidential leadership, 216–217; Cabinet practices of, 216, 293n68

Post Office Department: origins of, 22, 23, 26, 276n55; under Burleson, 200–201, 222–223. *See also* individual Postmasters General

Postmaster General: role of, 69–70, 99–100, 223, 300n64; appointment of, 23–24, 85; and public prestige, 165–167

President: need for assistance of, 14, 88–92, 141–143, 149, 158, 160, 180, 194–195, 196–197, 200, 207, 208, 217–218, 220, 221, 247–248, 268–269, 292n49, 300n68; relations with the Cabinet, 5–7, 12, 13, 29–58, 81–87, 115, 141, 156, 233, 246–249, 251–269 *passim*, 269–271; relations with individual Cabinet members, 16, 114–119, 155, 156, 170, 177–178, 184, 185, 197–199, 238–246. *See also* individual Presidents, relations with individual Cabinet members

Presidential leadership: importance of, 29–33, 115, 119, 154, 156, 269–271; presidential attitudes toward, 34–35; variety of roles, 157–158; as Chief Representative, 159–160, 171, 178; as Party Chief, 178–187, 194–195; as Chief Legislator, 178–180, 194–195, 196–197, 202–203, 213, 247; as Chief Executive, 216–218, 221, 247

Presidential succession, 20

President's Committee on Administrative Management, 141, 217

Press conferences of Cabinet members, 140, 167

Public attitudes: toward Cabinet, 5, 62, 152, 159–161, 290n17, 300n68; toward Cabinet appointment, 51–53, 63–65, 82, 160–161, 166–167; toward Cabinet members, 151–152, 159–178, 186

Public prestige: and Cabinet, 159–161; and individual Cabinet members, 164–171

Price, Don K., 266

Primitive societies, 10, 19, 24–25, 247n7, 276n57

Public opinion polls, 164–165, 175–176

Public relations and Cabinet. *See* Public attitudes; Public prestige

Pusey, Merlo J., 291

Question period, 214, 259–263, 310–311n38

Rabaut, Rep. Louis, 205
Rabb, Maxwell (Cabinet Secretary), 96, 104–110, 139, 147, 148, 289
Randolph, Edmund, 17
Rayburn, Sam, 236
Reconstruction Finance Corporation, 212, 234–240, 242, 246, 308–309n142
Redfield, William C. (Secretary of Commerce, 1913–1919): 286; Cabinet activity of, 122; and Congress, 206; departmental activity of, 220, 230; also quoted, 302
Reed, Sen. James, 60
Removal power, 15, 47–49, 244–245, 261–262, 310n36. *See also* under individual Presidents, attitudes toward loyalty
Resignation of Cabinet members, 49, 80–81, 83–84, 121, 150, 163, 166–

167, 192–193, 210, 282n153, 284n29, 295n10, 301–302n95
Republican National Committee, 69, 70
Republican National Convention, 159–160
Republican National Party Chairman, 69, 70, 300n55
Richberg, Donald, 151
Riesman, David, 25–26, 194
Roberts, Wesley, 300
Robinson, Henry, 284
Rogers, William P. (Attorney General, 1957–   ), 288
Roles and role conflict. *See* Cabinet member, President
Roosevelt, Franklin D.: attitude toward advice, 37; decision-making techniques of, 39–40, 279n99; techniques of delegation of, 44–47, 281–282n136; and individual Cabinet members, 37, 45–46, 47–48, 71, 163, 174–177, 184, 206, 223, 233, 238–246, 281n134, 281n135, 282n146; attitudes on loyalty, 47–48, 71, 244–246, 282n146; attitude toward Cabinet; 58, 66; Cabinet selection methods of, 58, 61, 63, 68, 69, 71, 74, 78, 79, 80, 83, 181, 245, 285n37, 288n98; Cabinet practices of, 92, 93, 94, 95, 99, 101–102, 110, 111, 112, 119, 125–130, 135–136, 138, 139, 146–147
Roosevelt, Theodore, 34, 64, 186
Roosevelt, Theodore, Jr., 116
Roper, Daniel C. (Secretary of Commerce, 1933–1939): 282, 287; Cabinet activity of, 127–128, 186; and business groups, 168, 171; and public prestige, 170, 171
Rosenman, Samuel, 175, 245
Rossiter, Clinton, 3, 264
Rovere, Richard, 44, 118
Royal Anthropological Institute, study by, 10

Sargent, John G. (Attorney General, 1925–1929), 288n104

Seaton, Fred (Secretary of the Interior, 1956–   ), 288
Secretary of Agriculture: role of, 25, 73, 168, 169, 231; qualifications for, 72, 73, 79; under C. Coolidge; and public prestige, 165–166. *See also* individual Secretaries
Secretary of Commerce: 152, 234; qualifications for, 72; under F. Roosevelt, 72, 127–128, 170; role of, 25, 168–169, 238; under W. Harding, 163; under C. Coolidge, 163; and public prestige 165–166. *See also* individual Secretaries
Secretary of Defense, 162. *See also* individual Secretaries
Secretary of Health, Education and Welfare, 95. *See also* individual Secretaries
Secretary of the Interior: 225; under F. Roosevelt, 46; qualifications for, 71–72, 79; and public prestige, 165–166; and clientele, 169. *See also* individual Secretaries
Secretary of Labor: 95, 164; role of, 25, 168–169, 219–220; qualifications for, 72, 73–75; under H. Hoover, 72; and public prestige, 165–166. *See also* individual Secretaries
Secretary of the Navy: 150, 224–225; and public prestige, 166. *See also* individual Secretaries
Secretary of State: 62, 95, 170; and the President, 24; role of, 25, 214; under F. Roosevelt, 45; prestige of, 60, 85–86, 162, 176; qualifications for, 75; Cabinet activity of, 108; under W. Wilson, 120, 123; under D. Eisenhower, 153; under H. Hoover, 163. *See also* individual Secretaries
Secretary of the Treasury: 83, 150; under F. Roosevelt, 45; qualifications for, 75; under W. Wilson, 134; under D. Eisenhower, 153. *See also* individual Secretaries
Secretary of War: 150; and public prestige, 166, 170; under F. Roo-

sevelt, 163. *See also* individual Secretaries
Secretariat, Cabinet: under Eisenhower, 96–97, 103–113, 136–137, 140–141, 143, 147–149, 266, 267, 269; proposals for, 264, 265–266
Senate, U. S., and confirmation of Cabinet members, 14, 54–55, 59, 76, 212, 246, 284n28, 288n104, 298n17; former members of, in Cabinet, 79–80. *See also* individual Senators
Separation of powers, 12, 14–16, 178, 196
Schattschneider, E. E., 184
Schwellenbach, Lewis B. (Secretary of Labor, 1945–1948): 288; appointment of, 75, 79; and labor groups, 169
Sherman, Roger, 12
Sherwood, Robert, 288
Simons, Leo, 10
Snyder, John (Secretary of the Treasury, 1946–1953), 71
Smathers, Sen. George, 209
Socio-economic views, of Cabinet members. *See* Cabinet members
Somers, Herman, 3, 265
Spargo, John, 278
Special Assistant to President for Disarmament, 94
Special Assistant to President for National Security Affairs, 94
Stassen, Harold, 140
State Department: origins of, 14, 25–26; and interest groups, 24; and F. Roosevelt, 45, 176–177; and D. Eisenhower, 153; under C. Hull, 173–174, 223–224; under W. J. Bryan, 190–191; under J. F. Dulles, 225. *See also* individual Secretaries
State of Union Message, 107, 126
Stearns, Frank, 43
Steelman, John, 145
Stimson, Henry L. (Secretary of State, 1929–1933; Secretary of War, 1940–1945): 227, 297; *as Secretary of State*, and H. Hoover, 36, 163, 177; appointment of, 60; *as Secretary of War*, and F. Roosevelt, 37, 45, 163, 281n134; appointment of, 68–69; Cabinet activity of, 126, 127, 138, 147; public prestige of, 161–162, 163, 206; also quoted, 125, 170
Stoddard, Henry, 30, 288
Stone, Harlan (Attorney General, 1924–1925): 284; appointment of, 85, 287n89
Strauss, Lewis L. (Secretary of Commerce, 1958–), 288
Sullivan, Mark, 115, 182, 188, 224
Summerfield, Arthur (Postmaster General), 69
Supreme Court, U. S., 10, 15, 47, 161, 162
Swanson, Claude A. (Secretary of the Navy, 1933–1940): 287; Cabinet activity of, 282n146; appointment of, 285n36

Taft, Sen. Robert, 78, 168, 182, 183, 212, 235
Taft, William Howard, 47
Teapot Dome, 132, 224, 294n2–4
Timmons, Bascom, 139
Tobey, Sen. Charles, 243
Tobin, Dan, 74
Tobin, Maurice, 219
Treasury Department: 16, 139, 223; origins of, 14, 25–26; and W. Wilson, 62, 170; policy, Cabinet discussion of, 134; under A. Mellon, 172–173; under W. McAdoo, 220; and F. Roosevelt, 281n135
Tumulty, Joseph, 57; 61–62
Turner, Frederick Jackson, 27
Truman, David, 276
Truman, Harry S.: 125, 155; attitude toward advice of, 36; attitude toward Cabinet, 43, 44, 154; techniques of delegation of, 43–44, 280–281n120; and individual Cabinet members, 43, 45, 49, 71, 162, 185, 213, 282n15; attitudes toward loyalty, 48–49, 282n151; Cabinet selection methods of, 71,

79, 80, 83, 185–186, 200; Cabinet practices of, 92, 94, 95, 111–112, 130, 138, 145, 185–186, 294n89, 290n22; as party leader, 185

U. S. Agricultural Society, 24

Veterans Administrator, 164
Vice-President, in Cabinet meeting, 17, 93, 125, 127, 153
Vinson, Rep. Carl, 228
Vinson, Fred M. (Secretary of the Treasury, 1945–1946), 287, 288

Walker, Frank C. (Postmaster General, 1940–1945): 69; and Congress, 206–207
Wallace, Henry A. (Secretary of Agriculture, 1933–1940; Secretary of Commerce, 1945–1946): 45, 133, 147; resignation of, 49; appointments of, 68, 69, 212, 245; Cabinet activity of, 127, 135, 138; and public opinion polls, 165; and F. Roosevelt, 184; and Congress, 212–213, 215; 284n28; and J. Jones, 77–78, 165, 242–246; also quoted, 45
Wallace, Henry C. (Secretary of Agriculture, 1921–1924): and H. Hoover, 77, 291n32; and C. Coolidge, 117–118; and public prestige, 170–171, 298n23
Wallace, Schuyler, 3
Walsh, Sen. Thomas, 198
War Cabinet, of Woodrow Wilson, 124, 149, 150
War Department: 233; origins of, 14, 25–26; under H. Woodring, 47–48
War Production Board, 46, 282
Warren, Charles: rejection of as Attorney General, 54–55, 59, 83, 288n104
Washington, George: 68, 88, 92, 94, 217; Cabinet practices of, 14, 15, 17–19
Weber, Max, 19
Weeks, John W. (Secretary of War, 1921–1925): 164, 286; and W. Harding, 291n38

Weeks, Sinclair (Secretary of Commerce, 1953–1958): 286; and M. Durkin, 78, 111, 140; appointment of, 286n63
Welles, Sumner: 223; and C. Hull, 45; in Cabinet meeting, 127
Wheeler, Sen. Burton, 85
Whigs: Cabinet theory of, 35
White House Office, 141, 264
White, Sen. Wallace, 236
White, William Allen, 32, 173
Wickard, Claude B. (Secretary of Agriculture, 1940–1945): public opinion poll on, 165
Wilbur, Curtis D. (Secretary of the Navy, 1924–1929): departmental activity of, 224; appointment of, 287n89
Wilbur, Ray L. (Secretary of the Interior, 1929–1933): and H. Hoover, 71, 281; and public prestige, 167
Willis, Sen. Frank, 189
Willkie, Wendall, 74, 175
Wilson, Charles E. (Secretary of Defense, 1953–1957): 286; appointment of, 63; press conferences of, 167; and Congress, 209
Wilson, J. Bryan, 298
Wilson, William B. (Secretary of Labor, 1913–1921): 286; appointment of, 72–73; departmental activity of, 219
Wilson, William L., 295
Wilson, Woodrow: and Presidential leadership, 34, 35, 200–202, 292 n49; attitude toward advice, 36, 37, 278n84; decision-making techniques of, 38–39, 279n97; Cabinet practices of, 44, 92, 93, 95, 101, 119–124, 134, 138, 139; and individual Cabinet members, 44, 56, 190–193, 200–202, 209–211, 220–221, 222–223, 286n64, 288 n100; attitudes toward Cabinet, 55–57, 65; attitude toward loyalty, 56–57, 71; Cabinet selection methods of, 56–57, 57–58, 61–62, 65, 70, 71, 75–76, 78, 79, 80, 83, 202, 286n64, 288n100, 286n65;

and Cabinet reform, 251–254, 257, 260, 262
Wood, Gen. Leonard, 287n87
Woodin, William H. (Secretary of the Treasury, 1933–1934): 286; and F. Roosevelt, 281
Woodring, Harry H. (Secretary of War, 1936–1940): 84; and F. Roosevelt, 47–48, and public opinion poll, 164
Work, Hubert (Secretary of the Interior, 1923–1928): 70; and public prestige, 166–167, 168

Young, Owen D., 284

AUGSBURG COLLEGE & SEMINARY
George Sverdrup Library
MINNEAPOLIS 4, MINNESOTA